DEMYSTIFYING GOD

Redefining Black Theology in the Age of iGod

SHAHIDI COLLECTION VOL 2

Shahidi Islam

Book Ordering Information
Cover design provided by: https://www.fiverr.com/patrick_2013
Email: enquiries@divineblackpeople.com
https://divineblackpeople.com

Attention African American Theologians!!!

In an Age of American Empire What Real Hope is There for Black People?

On Cultural Islam is Shahidi Islam's third instalment in his Shahidi Collection series.
With the world becoming more plutocratic our freedom is becoming less and less certain. To learn how to resist shop now.

On Cultural Islam

This book is dedicated to the Gods and
Goddesses of God-Collective,
Who dwell beyond time, space, and infinity

Table of Contents

Preface to Shahidi Edition   vi

Introduction   viii

The Universal Order of Things   1

The Deification of Blackness   84

Shaitan's Way of Getting Us Back   139

Vampyrism and the 10 percent   193

The Eclipse of Black Sexuality   253

Spooks and Holy Ghost   334

Conclusion   421

Glossary   427

Bibliography   459

Preface to Shahidi Edition

For those who remember this book when it was still underground I must explain the need for this rewrite. See, I no longer go under the name Tony Saunders, which name is my slave name. My righteous name is now my government name properly and formally, and that is Shahidi Islam. For this reason I am re-releasing some of my former works under my new name so as to certify them. I have lots of other writings in circulation that go under the name Tony Saunders, some of which I am quite ashamed of. If you have found or read one of them please feel free to discard it. If it is not a book or writing under the name Shahidi Islam it is not something I am endorsing. Besides, Tony Saunders is a popular name and there are a few other authors by that name who have their own following. To separate myself from them and to permanently remove the embarrassment of my former works I have chosen to release this Shahidi Collection featuring a correct explication of my doctrine as it stands. Again, if it is not a work found either with the author name Shahidi Islam or endorsed by Shahidi Islam then I do not endorse what is written therein, even if it is one of my own former writings, as some of them have ideas I no longer endorse or agree with. To wipe the slate clean and to endorse ideas that I do agree with look out for upcoming books and articles from Shahidi Islam, this Shahidi Collection is itself one of them. As this book is in the Shahidi Collection not only am I endorsing it, but it is a part of my very philosophy and outlook on life. Therefore, I believe in what is written in these pages and believe the Black community would benefit substantially by paying close attention to what is being said.

As the second book in my Shahidi Collection *Demystifying God: Redefining Black Theology in the Age of iGod* was originally written to anticipate a fundamental shift transpiring in our time unlike anything we have seen from ages past. Simply put, we are heading into a new age, a postsecular age based on the intense gathering of knowledge and information by ordinary people through searching on Google, joining groups on Facebook, buying books through Amazon, and using advanced AI. All this information has allowed for a deep internalisation of God to occur, thus leading the world to what I have called the age of iGod. That said, this book also seeks to introduce the reader to a new perspective: the godbody perspective. This is a perspective that I will be applying to Black theology so as to allow Black theology to progress into this bright and beautiful future that lies ahead. See, Black theology currently has three permutations: the humanist, the liberationist/womanist, and the prosperity. While these have served the Black community well, to a degree, it is only godbodyism that will have the academic structure and design suited for this postsecular age we are heading into. Considering that the world is currently still under the spectre of White supremacy, it seems that the decisive time to set the pace for this coming age is now.

Introduction

> "8. Why does the devil keep us apart from his social equality? Because he does not want us to know how filthy he is in all his affairs. He is afraid that if we were to find out about him that we would run him from amongst us. Social means to advocate a society or group of men for one common cause. Equality means to be equal in all things" (Lost Found Muslim Lesson No. 1).

I decided to write this, the second book in my Shahidi Collection, mainly to highlight, firstly, the ways in which the godbody movement, as a thearchic movement, creates a new form of thearchy: one that I have called the Black Thearchy; and, secondly, as a refinement of those practices and ideas that already exist within the godbody movement so as to make us a more excellent movement. It must therefore be acknowledged as we proceed further into this discourse that the thearchic movement being presented and re-presented is anarcho-Islamism. It is Islamist not in the sense of being terroristic (most godbodies are anti-terrorism and supra-religious) but in the sense of being based on revolutionary Islam.

Nevertheless, the actual basis of the Black Thearchy is six categorical systems that are instituted for our continuance:

Black divinity, Black revolutionism, Black eroticism, Black astralism, Black demodernisation, and Black syndicalism. While all these also make up the godbody ideology that I teach – and are generally accepted within the godbody movement as a whole – they have never been spelled-out or outlined in this way before. What I hope to do with this undertaking is a complete renewal of the movement and the lessons of the movement as handed down to me by my mentor and enlightener God Born Supreme Allah so as to show where the movement can lead and to explicate why the teleology of the godbody movement is actually a positive and not a self-destructive one. I also try to refine and systematise those qualities of the movement that are exceptionally useful and build upon them. Finally, I take the two institutions that I have personally contributed: Black astralism and light exhibitionism, and articulate how they make effective add-ons to the original godbody programme I bore witness to in the 1990s.

This book is intended to provide those in the Black community with a means of understanding the changes being anticipated as we enter the age of iGod: "The Universal Order of Things" analyses godbody theory and the universal laws of existence, applying supreme mathematics to a godbody sociology so as to identify the relevant means of understanding natural theology within the godbody movement; all ultimately leading to the practicing of a Black demodernisation for the Black community. Next "The Deification of Blackness" considers the ancient Egyptian conception of godhood, and provides a social aetiology of Black divinity using both ancient Egyptian and godbody conceptions, reconsidering their theological usages for the purpose of empowering Black people. Following that "Shaitan's Way of Getting Us Back" takes a look at the White devil theory using social aetiology to examine the reasons why the godbody use it, and what the circumstances are that make it an actual probability; it also provides an in-depth look into Black revolutionism against this White devilishment and certain working class means of practicing it. Then "Vampyrism and the 10 Percent" explores a little deeper into Black bourgeois realities particularly with regards to the psychology of those who live it; thereby providing a social kinetics of the Black bourgeoisie, and how Black syndicalism organised correctly can alleviate some of the psychological pathologies (dysfunctions) inherent within the Black bourgeois. Next, within "The Eclipse of Black Sexuality" is provided a godbody analysis of Black women, the sexualisation of Black women, and the power of Black erotica to free Black women; it also provides an evolution of the godbody sociology of Black women through social kinetics. Finally, "Spooks and Holy Ghost" provides a godbody sociology of the Holy Ghost movement in the Black community and reveals the psychological devolutions that it has caused for the purpose of creating for the Black community a kind of Black astralism through which to understand astral phenomena.

Yet, while *Demystifying God* is a sociology and a psychology it is also, finally, a theology: a Black Godbody Theology that synthesises Black Liberation Theology with Black Prosperity Theology thereby becoming an evolution of both. It cannot be denied that the godbody has a theology as we have a theory of God, the devil, and of righteousness. Therefore, as instructed by my mentor and enlightener I have written this book to do justice to the genius of godbody theory. It is in that way that this particular book differs from the other books in this Shahidi Collection. Though they do present information about the godbody movement and were written primarily from a godbody basis they are far more focused on constructing complicated systems for Black people to see themselves and society with.

Demystifying God focuses on presenting the depths of godbody structures, institutions, and ideas using social mechanics, supreme mathematics, and *observant participation* (Wacquant 2008) as its primary sources: in particular lessons given me about the godbody movement from my experiences in both Brooklyn, New York and London, England, and the guidance I was given from my mentor in the godbody movement, who is currently doing time in prison for a crime he did not commit. It also includes lessons from the *Five Percenter* newspaper, and a vast assortment of other writings from revolutionaries, sociologists, psychologists, and African American theologians as its secondary sources.

As an African American theology the godbody theology is differentiated from the classical model of African American theology in an interesting way. If we take as an example the four degrees of faith (Skousen 2017): from no faith, to little faith, to great faith, to complete faith, we can see that classical African American theology features most of these four levels: the humanists have no faith, the liberationists/womanists have great faith, and the prosperous have complete faith. Well, we godbodies complete the cipher by having little faith, believing God to exist mainly in natural phenomena like a Universal Intelligence, the Universal Laws, the Asiatic Black man, and all Original people.

Basically, it is the aim and purpose of this book to represent the godbody movement by, firstly, seeking to introduce the godbody theology as an African American theology nuanced from Cone's in that it is not a survival theology but a thrival theology. It is a thrival theology that arose out of the ghetto experience so as to give the Black people of the ghetto the hope of a better future, one which we ourselves create. In this, Black Godbody Theology is a ghetto theology that promotes Black improvement and empowerment; as even James Cone himself also said, "Unless theology can become 'ghetto theology,' a theology that speaks to black people, the gospel message has no promise of life for the black man – it is a lifeless message" (Cone 2021: 37).

Secondly, this book seeks to introduce the godbody sociology as a form of critical social science that uses historical documentation, social mechanics, and supreme mathematics to critique and overcome White supremacy – a White supremacy based on the blindness of White people to the realities of their former and present discourse of White superiority. Even as James Cone further continued, "If white intellectuals, religionists, and assorted liberals can convince themselves that the white condition is analogous to the black condition, then there is no reason to respond to the demands of the black community." Moreover, "to make [that even] worse, they invariably miss the whole point of black power. They should know by now that, in view of white brutality against blacks and church participation in it, no white person who is halfway sensitive to black self-determination should have the audacity to speak for blacks" (Cone 2020a: 108, 66).

Finally, it is my intention for the current approach to be used to inform the course of the godbody movement in its rise to popularity, and to create an avenue for the acceptance of this theological perspective within the current discussions of African American theology. Within this context I pay homage to those who came before me in the classical schools: Anthony B. Pinn, William R. Jones, James H. Cone, Albert B. Cleage, Delores S. Williams, Kelly B. Douglas, Creflo A. Dollar, and Thomas D. Jakes Sr. Still, it must also be said at this point that although I am a fellow of the Society for the Study of Theology, all the ideas and outlooks presented in this book are purely my own and nobody else's.

The Supreme Mathematics

Potentials

k = knowledge (1)

w = wisdom (2)

u = understanding (3)

f = freedom – I choose not to add culture as freedom is the most obvious elevation from understanding and culture is implied in the whole mathematics (4)

p = power – (I use the term power neither in the Marxian sense, as in to dominate nor in the Foucauldian sense, as in to discipline or surveille; but instead use it in the Adlerian sense as in empowerment) I choose not to add refinement as power is the next elevation from freedom and progresses till it reaches equality (5)

e = equality (6)

G = God – where God is equivalent to the omnipresent, and not to a state of pure perfection (7)

B = build – when adding on (8)

D = destroy – when subtracting (8)

$\forall$ = born (9)

$^{\circ}$ = cipher (0)

Symbols

D = dialectical moment where *pa* > *na* becomes *na* > *pa*, or vice versa.

Lm = the limitation

∃ = when there is

+ = together with

∈ = the sum includes

> = greater than

≥ = greater than or equal to

< = lesser then

≤ = lesser than or equal to

→ = leads on to

↔ = if and only if

↗ = on the increase

↘ = on the decrease

∝ = proportional to

Values

∞ = infinity

o = zero

λ = wavelength

A = amplitude

d = displacement

t = time expended

v = rate of velocity

δ = astral forces ($> x^1$)

α = social forces ($> x^{10}$)

β = global forces ($> x^{20}$)

θ = environmental forces ($> x^{30}$)

ϕ = terrestrial forces ($> x^{40}$)

ϑ = solar forces ($> x^{50}$)

∂ = globular forces ($> x^{60}$)

φ = galactic forces ($> x^{70}$)

ψ = super-clusteral forces ($> x^{80}$)

ε = cosmic forces ($> x^{90}$)

Pa = positive action of an individual

pa = positive action of a social body

Na = negative action of an individual

na = negative action of a social body

x = social potential of a social body

n = level of social potentiality

g = a social movement

$opp.\,g$ = an oppressing social movement

$emp.\,g$ = an empowering social movement

(pa) = all the positive actions of a social body

(na) = all the negative actions of a social body

(v) = all the social velocity

(g) = the whole social movement

S = decelerative force caused by reaction of social body x_1

R = accelerative force caused by resistance of social body x_2

S = syndicalism

The Godbody System

The Universal Laws of Existence

1. The law of interaction (whose corollary is the pleasure principle),

2. The law of intersubjectivity (whose corollary is the vibratory law),

3. The law of self-organisation (whose corollary is identity law),

4. The law of opposition (whose corollary is the feedback law),

5. The law of repetition (whose corollary is the inertia law),

6. The law of self-similarity (whose corollary is the correspondence law),

7. The law of conservation (whose corollary is the reciprocity law),

8. The law of evolution (whose corollary is the power law),

9. The law of devolution (whose corollary is the entropy law),

10. The law of self-destruction (whose corollary is the phase-transition law),

11. The law of interconnectivity (whose corollary is the synchronicity law), and

12. The law of interrelation (whose corollary is the eternalist law).

The 10 Principles

1. No God but Allah

2. No power imbalances

3. No non-authors

4. No non-fighters

5. No Divine fights alone

6. No problems handled in the Square should ever leave the Square

7. No marriage or marriages

8. No denying another Divine

9. No underwear ever

10. No harassment or rape of any kind ever

What We Teach

1. That black people are the original people of the planet earth.

2. That black people are the fathers and mothers of civilization.

3. That the science of Supreme Mathematics is the key to understanding man's relationship to the universe.

4. Islam is a natural way of life, not a religion.

5. That education should be fashioned to enable us to be self sufficient as a people.

6. That each one should teach one according to their knowledge.

7. That the black man is god and his proper name is ALLAH. Arm, Leg, Leg, Arm, Head.

8. That our children are our link to the future and they must be nurtured, respected, loved, protected and educated.

9. That the unified black family is the vital building block of the nation.

The Hedgehog Concept (The Build Allah Square)

1. Eat, Train, Read, Write, and Share

The Core Concepts

1. Black divinity, Black revolutionism, Black eroticism, Black astralism, Black demodernisation, and Black syndicalism

The Physical Concepts

1. biophysics, quantum physics, molecular physics, geophysics, astrophysics, and digital physics

The Discursive Concepts

1. body, embody, and disembody

2. structure, infrastructure, and superstructure

3. subtle, subaltern, and subterranean

4. text, pretext, subtext, and context

5. discourse, discursive, pre-discursive, narrative, and performative

6. reality, surreality, sub-reality, hyper-reality, virtual-reality, and unreality

7. erase, absent, present, represent, reproduce, re-enact, legitimate, and counter

8. position, supposition, disposition, composition, superposition, opposition, exposition, and imposition

9. silence, distort, fabricate, exaggerate, implicate, explicate, delineate, propagate, and voice

The Chronological Concepts

1. historicism and historicity

2. linear-chronological and event-sequential

3. historical, ahistorical, prehistorical, and transhistorical

The Pneumatological Concepts

1. demonise and transfigure

2. divine, vampyre, and devil

3. elemental, natural, and universal

4. foresight, insight, and hindsight

5. *Sebi*, *Nebi*, and *Obi*

6. astral, astral body, astral force, astral plane, and supersensory

7. *Hakim*, *Alim*, *Karim*, and Allah

8. Horu construct, Hethor construct, Ausar conscious, and Auset conscious

9. existent, pre-existent, co-existent, de-existent, and re-existent

10. resurrected, incorporated, *phantomised*, internalised, and exorcised

11. empathic, psychopathic, sociopathic, *monopathic*, *duopathic*, *polypathic*, and *panopathic*

12. empath, dark empath, supernova empath, true empath, quiet empath, psychic empath, super empath, sigma empath, and Heyoka empath

The Psychological Concepts

1. conscious and unconscious

2. libido and superego

3. inhibition, prohibition, and exhibitionism

4. object, selfobject, objectify

5. subject, subjective, and intersubjective

6. trauma, complex, and therapy

7. power, empower, internalise, incorporate, and concretise

8. spectre, drive, constraint, ideal, and somatic

The Ideological Concepts

1. seduction, perverse seduction, and seductionism

2. sexualise, racialise, and criminalise

3. White superiority, White supremacy, and White privilege

4. acculturate, assimilate, integrate, and institutionalise

5. gaze, oppress, problematise, and deviate

6. shackling, unshackling, deshackling, and reshackling

7. typical, atypical, prototypical, and archetypal

8. institution, destitution, restitution, constitution, deconstitution, and reconstitution

9. sexual, asexual, heterosexual, homosexual, transsexual, intersexual, and hypersexual

10. modern, premodern, postmodern, late modern (liquid modern), anti-modern, and demodernise

11. colony, market-colony, industrial-colony, military-colony, penal-colony, settler-colony, spatial-colony, cultural-colony, corporeal-colony, mental-colony, epistemic-colony, counter-colony, neo-colony, and the Great United States Empire (GUSE)

The Sociological Concepts

1. embodied displacement (exile, migration, trans-migration, or tourism) and disembodied displacement (phantasy, fantasy, wish, dream, vision, imagination, or astral journey)

2. aetiology, teleology, and eschatology

3. locality, globality, and communality

4. ordination, subordination, and superordination

5. gnosis, prognosis, diagnosis, and epignosis

6. inertia, action, interaction (force), and act-species

7. interior, exterior, anterior, posterior, and ulterior

8. mechanic, elastic, static, dynamic, and kinetic

9. politics, geopolitics, biopolitics, necropolitics, transpolitics, hyper-politics, body-politics, racial-politics, and sexual-politics

The Sociological Axioms

1. The Axioms of Social Mechanics

a) $x > 1$

b) $v < 670,616,629$ mph

c) $v = \frac{d}{t}$

2. The Axioms of Social Force

a) $v\left(\frac{x^n}{x^n}\right) = \alpha$

b) $x_1 + R = Lm$ and $x_2 + S = Lm$

c) $\alpha > x^{10}$

3. The Axioms of Social Movements

a) $x_1 > x_2 \leftrightarrow x_2 \alpha \searrow o$

b) $g \propto \alpha$

c) $g_1(pa) \rightarrow g_2(na)$ and $g_1(na) \rightarrow g_2(pa)$

d) $d = (2\pi) \times \left(\frac{2\lambda+2A}{2}\right)$

4. The Axioms of Social Dynamics

a) $x_1 + x_2 \rightarrow na$

b) $x_1 + x_2 \rightarrow pa \leftrightarrow Lm \searrow$

c) $pa > Lm \rightarrow D \leftrightarrow pa \searrow$

5. The Axioms of Social Statics

a) $g(Lm) \leftrightarrow \alpha \searrow o$

b) $\exists \alpha \searrow o \rightarrow x^u \geq g$

6. The Axioms of Social Kinetics

a) $Lm > g$

b) $\exists(\alpha > Lm) \rightarrow g \nearrow$

c) $\exists Lm \rightarrow \alpha \searrow +g \searrow$

The Universal Order of Things

"11. Will you sit at home and wait for that mystery God to bring you food? Emphatically No! Me and my people who have been lost from home 379 years, have tried this so-called mystery God for bread, clothing, and a home, and received nothing but hard times, hunger, nakedness, and out of doors, also beatings and killings by the ones who advocated that kind of God. And, no relief came to us until the Son of Man came to our aid, by the name of our Prophet W. D. Fard" (Lost Found Muslim Lesson No. 2)."

Steven R. Covey (2004) presented a story about people lost in a forest to explain the distinction between managers and leaders. One group is effective at chopping down trees another group is most useful climbing the trees to map out where they are, which direction they should go in, and how close they are to reaching their destination. The choppers need the climbers or they will not be able to see beyond the tree in front of them. The climbers need the choppers or they will not be able to progress through the harsh terrain of the forest. Well, I see experts, scientists, physicists, and biologists as the choppers. They have been clearing a path for humanity to learn the intricacies of the universe. However, they have been chopping down random trees with no specific purpose but to chop down the tree that is in front of them. What I am going to attempt to do is provide a destination for them. I do not profess to be an expert or to know the intricacies of each specific tree or how they chopped them down. What I am trying to do is give a kind of order and direction to many of the scientific truths that have been discovered. The experts can and should take the assumptions that I will be presenting briefly and use them as a guide to where they can go and what trees to chop down next.

As a result of the many scientific discoveries of the last century it is clear that a plan to organise and redirect the great achievements of modernity will meet its detractors. Nevertheless my apprenticeship under various mentors including Art Katz and my godbody enlightener, God Born Supreme Allah, has meant that I am in duty bound to articulate in a stricter sense the outcome of their philosophies. That is not to say that I am just regurgitating what these two have taught me with no contribution of my own. Truly, any reader of my works, who has also read Katz will see how indebted I am to him for many of my positions and conclusions. Notwithstanding, I am all the more indebted to the Nation of Gods and Earths and to my enlightener within the Nation of Gods and Earths, without whom I would have simply been in the darkness.

The Nation of Gods and Earths was founded by a Black man whose honorable name was Clarence 13X but who we call Allah out of respect for the revelation he received of Black people's divine nature and calling. According to Born King Allah, "Allah's world was manifested through his word[:] a Nation was born from his mind and now is the time. It is apparent that Allah borned a Nation of Gods and Earths. From the beginning that never began dated October 10, 1964 the world saw for the first time they who are the Five Percent. They were the young who saw God when they met Allah in Harlem NYC the root of our civilization. Word quickly spread throughout the city that Allah in the flesh was walking and talking to the youth" (The Five

Percenter Vol 20.9; 2015: 3). Allah, as the Father of the Nation, birthed our movement, showed us our potential, and redirected our destiny.

Further, the traditions of the godbody movement he founded are currently based on the 120 lessons, which, again, are really just the Supreme Wisdom lessons of the Honorable Elijah Muhammad. In that sense they have been read and mastered by several heroes and heroines within the Black community: Minister Louis Farrakhan, Minister Malcolm X, Imam Warith Deen Muhammad, Dr. Khalid Muhammad, Dr. Sebi Alfredo Bowman, Dr. Malachi Z. York, Muhammad Ali, Jay Electronica, Busta Rhymes, Erikah Badu, Ice Cube, Rakim Allah, Nas, Mobb Deep, the Wu-Tang Clan, and Brand Nubian. Even so, while the United States government has attacked and attempted to discredit many of these Black leaders, all of them are still well beloved by the Black community in general. Again, if someone of the calibre of Frantz Fanon could be indebted to both Jean-Paul Sartre and the Negritude movement, surely I myself can be indebted to both Art Katz and the godbody movement.

I

Now the revelation of Allah, according to godbody theory, is found in none other than the sciences, both natural and social, as to a godbody the social sciences are, indeed, natural sciences. But what then is Allah's most essential self-disclosure? To be sure, though this section will attempt to prove that such can in fact be found in the pleasure principle, nevertheless, Allah as a whole is so much more than that. The pleasure principle may be the refined aspect of Allah even as the Black man is the human embodiment of Allah; still, as Fakim Allah also said, the 120 lessons show us "how to be successful, by employing rules, regulations and laws. Rules are for you. Laws apply to your cipher, once you establish them, those in your cipher must live up to your laws. Regulations apply to those who come amongst your cipher to regulate their behavior while they are there" (The Five Percenter Vol 22.10; 2017: 4). Hereby, we can see the basis of how the revelation of Allah can be found in the universal laws of existence, which are themselves based on the interaction of various driving forces on numerous types of bodies, each being of various shapes and sizes. The reason for this is that Allah himself is in fact that very force of interaction (*Allahu qudra al-taf'il*).

To qualify this statement, Newtonian gravitation may in fact have been misclassified. Newton (1999) accepted that both gravity and magnetism were centripetal forces, that is, forces which draw bodies towards a mathematical centre. However, he believed magnetic force only applied to metallic bodies like lodestones, while gravity applied to astronomical bodies like moons, planets, stars, and galaxies. To Newton there were two kinds of forces: inherent force and impressed force (Newton 1999). Newton believed inherent forces to be the inertial forces within a body that would drive it towards passivity, resistance to change, and centrifugal (cyclical/repetitious) behaviour. Impressed forces, on the other hand, he believed to be the interactive forces outside of a body that causes all progressive changes, accelerations, and has the potential to produce escape velocity (Newton 1999). Again, all this was purely in the mathematical sense (all Newton's theories were themselves to be taken as purely mathematical and never originally intended to be taken as physical truths, more than a means to understanding physical truths).

Newton spoke of space in both the absolute and the relative senses of the word, saying: relatively a body in motion in space could be in motion on several different levels – the sun motions through the houses of the twelve constellations, the earth motions around the sun, the ship motions around the earth, the captain motions around the ship, and such reductions could be continued indefinitely to bodily systems, cell-complexes, cells,

DNA double-helix spirals, complex molecules, simple molecules, atoms, electrons, quarks, et cetera. – as at each level there is motion. In that sense, the law of interaction could also be called the law of self-motivation. Hereby, the law of interaction also gives place to the concept of force itself, which, according to Newton, can either be centripetal, drawing a body toward a mathematical centre; or centrifugal, drawing a body to revolve or orbit around a mathematical centre. Again, an even deeper inference could also be drawn here: impressed forces are the centripetal forces external to a body that cause them to accelerate up to, but never beyond, their own speed, while inherent forces are the centrifugal forces internal to a body that always keep them in motion at a constant rate.

The law of interaction also states that one can communicate (*kalim*) with any and everything in the universe through influential activities, thus interactivity itself is the pre-eminent form of communication. Thereby also explaining the reason that the Vedas, Tawrat, Injil, Zabur, and Furqan all existed before the beginning (*qadim*) within the mind of Allah and will never have an ending (*baqi*) within the heart of Allah. Moreover, nothing in the universe is off-limits, everything is capable of being guided or manipulated by the influential or motivational communications made via these interactive forces. Hereby, through controlling what you interact with you can potentially control (or at least influence) what you receive from the universe.

That said, the universal law of interaction operates not only as a law of physics: it operates on a chemical, geological, biological, psychological, ideological, ethnological, anthropological, socio-logical, cosmological, and ethical level too. Moreover, looking further and deeper into this law we will also find that there is currently a debate existing in biology over the main sets of chemical combinations that originally came together to produce life within our universe. How does the inanimate, inert, and inorganic become organic? The question of how we produce life

5

from the lifeless. Within science, and particularly biology, there are three assumptions as to this question of life within the universe: (i) Is based on abiogenesis, the assumption that life can come from the lifeless, stating that the probability of producing life from the lifeless is so low that it must have taken exceptional circumstances for life to actually be produced, circumstances scientists fight desperately to find and replicate. (ii) Is based on biogenesis, the assumption that only a living being can produce another living being or produce the circumstances under which living beings can come about, and further stating that an intelligent designer had to have programmed or at least influenced the circumstances under which life came about. (iii) Is also based on biogenesis but it is a little more complicated. It states that the universe is itself an organism and that everything in the universe is also organic to greater or lesser degrees.

Accordingly, before going further in depth into the organic universe theory, it must be said as a preliminary that there is a difference between organic and conscious. We will briefly touch on some of the general inconsistencies in the current definition of life given by biology, nevertheless most organic beings in the universe may be unconscious but also still alive. How this works is, take a planet in our star-system: it unconsciously, or to use the more physical term, inertly, revolves around the sun. It does not have an exact path nor does it ever return to the same place twice. It does not make an exact cycle or ellipse, nor is the sun in the exact centre of the planet's revolution. The earth, itself, is a creature of habit. It knows it likes the distances it is from the sun and follows the path of least resistance. Turbulence can affect its motion but ultimately it is a cybernetic entity (or being) whose motion is based on the velocity of the forces interacting with it, i.e. its motion is unconscious.

Now it may be a bit confusing to think of the whole universe as a living being, yet many biological scientists have come to understand that the earth itself is a living being. It is effectively an ecosystem of ecosystems; just like the cells in our body are living beings that combine to form the ecosystems within our own bodies. Even so, obviously, with the animals and plants of nature, each combine among themselves to form the ecosystems of our own planet. Essentially, if you view the universe as just the open space that is between the various moons, planets, stars, and galaxies then the universe is not a living entity, as most of the open space between the moons, planets, stars, and galaxies is open – even if not actually empty – space. Nevertheless, if you take the universe to be the bodies and forces that interact within that open space then the universe can, indeed, be proven to be organic. But open space predominates in the universe. Our own bodies are predominantly open space. There is space between the cells in our body, space between the DNA strands, space between the molecules, space between the atoms in our body, and space between the subatomic waves in our body.

In this sense, there is an infinitude of ecosystems in the universe. Most superclusters have a large amount of galaxies within them all revolving around a central point. Within those galaxies are a large amount of globular clusters. Within those globular clusters are a large amount of star systems. Within those star systems are a large amount of planets. Within those planets are a large amount of ecosystems (even within dead planets). Within those ecosystems are a large amount of lifeforms. Within those lifeforms are a large amount of cell-complexes. Within those cell-complexes are a large amount of cells. Within those cells are a large amount of DNA double-helix spirals. Within those DNA spirals are a large amount of molecules. Within those molecules are a large amount of atoms. Within those atoms are a large amount of electrons. Within those electrons are a large amount of quarks. And the process of reduction could theoretically be continued *ad infinitum*.

These are all ecosystems within ecosystems, teeming with life. For years quantum physicists have themselves noticed planned, reasoned, and counterintuitive behaviour in the world of atoms, protons, electrons, and quarks. Quantum behaviour defies the idea of a lifeless atom, and if the atom is in fact alive then the lowly molecule (a group of atoms) can be said to be alive too, and such expansions could themselves also continue on *ad infinitum*.

In sum, according to biology there are seven verifiable signs of organic life: movement, respiration, sensitivity, growth, reproduction, excretion, and nutrition. While agreeing with most of these signs there is here provided a new way to interpret them. Within this system the seven signs of organism would be: automotion (self-motivation), self-organisation, self-destruction, evolution, devolution, intersubjectivity, and self-similarity. With this broader view of life everything in the universe, including the universe itself, could technically be said to be alive. Yet this new system is not too dissimilar from the currently accepted biological definition: automotion is really just movement by another name, devolution can be seen as a kind of respiration, sensitivity can be seen as a form of intersubjective feeling, evolution is itself just a variation of growth, self-destruction a variation of excretion, and self-organisation a variation of nutrition. Or at least they can each be rewritten as such. Not so with reproduction, though some living organisms are sterile. Yet many so-called inorganic entities possess self-similarity. In fact, some inorganic entities, such as computer programmes, are able to experience all the signs here provided for organism. In that sense, everything in the universe could in fact be respected as a living organism, even those entities perceived to be dead.

Moreover, to help us to fully comprehend the depths of the universal law of interaction, and how the pleasure principle can become its corollary, we must always remember that by the first law of thermodynamics mass and energy can be neither created nor destroyed. Again, mass is itself actually inertia and energy is itself actually activity. When most people think of energy they are usually thinking of electrical energy, but electrical energy is only one form of energy. Energy comes from the Greek word *ergos*, which means work. Therefore, the word energy is better translated as activity. Herein is found a fundamental truth in the universe: it is inertia and activity that are themselves not created or destroyed. Though to a degree we may understand this on a physical level we have not taken the time to consider its philosophical implications. If you subscribe to a form of carbon chauvinism then philosophically there is little that can be gleaned from this idea, yet if you have a more broad view then the implications are far reaching.

Firstly, inertia and activity (that is interaction) are eternal – they have no beginning and no ending – therefore the universe can theoretically also be said to have no beginning and have no ending (thereby negating the theory of a Big Bang: a subject that will be further explored briefly). Secondly, the eternal nature of inertia and activity (mass and energy) means that life is not as narrow as carbon-based or silicon-based entities. Life is rest and work, stasis and movement. Any self-motivating body is thereby a lifeform and all lifeforms themselves go through continual cycles of inertia and activity. Thirdly, there is a science governing everything in the universe that can itself be discovered and learned. Everything in the universe thereby has its own intelligence, its own inner workings, its own functions and purpose, its own capacity and abilities, and its own inner beauty and intricacies. These intelligences are called within physics, forces, and within psychoanalysis, drives, but they are effectively what influences and motivates all the behaviours and activities that transpire in the universe.

While these intelligences can be discovered through science, they are also themselves intelligent (in their own way) having full, even if unconscious, knowledge of what they are doing. There is even also a Grand Intelligence or Science that interconnects all things and is the primary cause of *all* the interactions that transpire within the universe. Aristotle called him the First Cause, the Brahmins called him *Brahm*; and the original monotheists all called him the Allah. Nevertheless, this idea of a Grand Intelligence that is both a concept and a person – basically an Intelligent Being – is itself the height of theocentrism.

Yet one could easily ask at this point: what is it that all these intelligences strive for? The answer provided in Freudian theory is, "they strive for happiness, they want to become happy and remain so. This striving has two goals, one negative and one positive: on the one hand it aims at an absence of pain and unpleasurable experiences, on the other at strong feelings of pleasure" (Freud 2002: 14). This is why these intelligences of the universe always drive interactive bodies to travel the path of least resistance. Moreover, all these interactive bodies gain their own lives by this means: as Freud continued, "it is … the programme of the pleasure principle that determines the purpose of life" (Freud 2002: 14). Hereby, showing that the true meaning of life is, and has always been, to strive after pleasure. The meaning of life could never be something so abstract as to seek after meaning or to find meaning; or even to find Reason, which both amount to the same thing. These are very anthropocentric views of life, but life itself is not limited to humanity. Given its full appreciation we can see that these ideas are merely views we have developed to sublimate the true meaning of life, which is to find pleasure and remove pain.

Nevertheless, a godbody may very likely quote from the 120 lessons at this point, saying, "What is the meaning of civilization? One having knowledge, wisdom, understanding, culture, refinement, and is not a savage in the pursuit of happiness" (Lost Found Muslim Lesson No. 2). However, that does not say that one should never pursue happiness, all it is saying is that the pursuit of happiness is the most primal and basic drive we have. Furthermore, the desire for happiness is the most primal impulse at all stages of evolution, making the pleasure principle the most fundamental and elemental principle in the universe, it is the *raison de vivre*: to find pleasure and remove pain. Indeed, Einstein once said "this is a friendly universe," and as a friendly universe its inner genius, its higher intelligence, is to influence us towards seeking pleasure and removing pain.

However, many philosophers and metaphysicians of the New Thought persuasion have mystified these ideas into a concept of positive thinking, claiming that by thinking positively we can attract positivity into our lives. That said, the law of interaction works in a relatively different way. The law of interaction states that attraction and repulsion affects all things on all levels based on libidinal communication. We must therefore come to appreciate that being a driving or motivating force the libidinal/anti-libidinal force is based on waves of both attraction and repulsion. In other words, the force of activity and interactivity is primarily a libidinal force, hence, Allah's essential manifestation must be al-Ashiq (the Libidinal One). This name is also befitting for Allah as it alludes to his greatness in causing all happiness, pleasure, and goodness to occur.

In further explaining our striving for pleasure Freud went on to use an example given to him by his friend Romain Rolland: "This was a particular feeling of which he himself was never free, which he had found confirmed by many others and which he assumed was shared by millions, a feeling that he was inclined to call a sense of 'eternity', a feeling of something limitless, unbounded – as it were 'oceanic'. This feeling was a purely subjective fact, not an article of faith; no assurance of personal immortality attached to it, but it was the source of the religious energy that was seized upon by the various churches and religious systems" (Freud 2002: 3). Freud noted that this "oceanic feeling" Rolland felt could very well be the pleasure principle in action, thereby making the pleasure principle the basis of all activity. But if all entities in the universe are thus driven by the pleasure principle then it also becomes the basis of all interaction.

In trying to understand further the relation of the pleasure principle to the first and most powerful universal law we need to remember that the desire for happiness inherent in all self-motivating entities drives humanity just the same. Freud mentioned one of the most common ways people use to satisfy this striving is through the removal of pain. Yet while this way of seeking happiness may alleviate most unpleasurable feelings it cannot grant us the ecstatic feelings of excessive happiness we gain from what Freud called Eros and what we call sexual love, "This kind of mental attitude comes naturally enough to us all; [indeed,] one manifestation of love, sexual love, has afforded us the most potent experience of overwhelming pleasure and thereby set a pattern for our quest for happiness" (Freud 2002: 19). Sexual pleasure is, thereby, the highest form of human pleasure available to us. Basically, it could even be said at this point that the actual motivator of *all* self-motivating beings is the sexual desire inspired by the pleasure principle. The pleasure principle itself, if considered more deeply, being nothing more than, "the tendency to seek the pleasure that comes from the gratification of instinctual impulses" (Galatariotou 2005: 15).

Moreover, as Hill also went on to say, "The pages of history are filled with records of great leaders whose achievements may be traced directly to the influence of women who aroused the creative faculties of their minds through the stimulation of sex desire" (Hill 2004: 214). This kind of sex desire Freud also called the libido; as he made abundantly clear further on, "The name 'libido' can once more be applied to manifestations of the power of Eros" (Freud 2002: 57). Here the libido was effectively being treated by Freud as that overwhelmingly orgasmic, ecstatic, and erotic light that fills all things in the universe. It thereby becomes that living force that adds beauty and love to all things.

Yet Freud also distinguished something quite different coupled with the Eros, "Beside Eros ... there [is] a death drive, and the interaction and counteraction of these two could explain

[all] the phenomena of life" (Freud 2002: 55). Basically, as Eros is the force that permeates the entire universe, a kind of "oceanic feeling" that encompasses all life, whereby the universe becomes an ocean of libidinal energy, even so, there is a death drive that also works in concert with it almost like its opposite. Here we can say that this death drive exists as an anti-libidinal, repulsive force that works with the libido against its quest to attract and connect all bodies through erotic and empathic love.

"In sadism, which has long been recognized as a partial drive of sexuality, one would be faced with a particularly strong alloy of the striving for love and the drive for destruction, just as its counterpart, masochism, would be a combination of inward-directed destruction and sexuality, through which the otherwise imperceptible striving became conspicuous and palpable" (Freud 2002: 56). While there may be a better definition of masochism found in calling it the gaining of massive pleasure through some form of pain or suffering; masochism and sadism are effectively the key to understanding the libido and anti-libido in their relation to the pleasure principle. Furthermore, the force between one body and another is always either libidinal or anti-libidinal, attractive or repulsive; and both, being subject to the pleasure principle, are in a technical sense able to give us pure pleasure.

This pleasure then dissects further to become various other instinctual drives, though the most powerful will still be the sexual drive, being the basis for all the other drives. Furthermore, in his own research on the subject Hill (2004: 207) also stated, "Destroy the sex glands, whether in man or beast, and you have removed the major source of action. For proof of this, observe what happens to any animal after it has been castrated. A bull becomes docile as a cow after it has been altered sexually. Sex alteration takes out of the male, whether man or beast, all the *fight* that was in him. Sex alteration of the female has the same effect."

Still, as Freud also continued, "The sex drive ... is probably more highly developed in human beings than in most of the higher animals. It is at any rate more constant, having almost completely overcome the periodicity to which it is subject in animals. It puts huge amounts of energy at the disposal of cultural activity; this is a consequence of one particularly marked characteristic – its ability to shift its aim without any great loss of intensity" (Freud 2002: 90). This shifting of the aim of the sexual drive Freud called sublimation. It basically says that all acts of spiritual, political, cultural, scientific, athletic, artistic, and military accomplishment are a result of sublimating sexual desire such that it cannot be affected by the external world (Freud 2002).

Indeed, according to Hill, "The desire for sexual expression is by far the strongest and most impelling of all the human emotions. For this very reason this desire, when harnessed and transmuted into action other than that of physical expression, may raise one to the status of a genius" (Hill 2004: 217). Or as Freud continued, "Sublimation of the [sexual] drives is a particularly striking feature of cultural development, which makes it possible for the higher mental activities – scientific, artistic and ideological – to play such a significant role in civilized life" (Freud 2002: 34). In this sense the drives, and particularly the sexual drives, as they seek expression, are the forces that motivate all our creative activities, and by us harnessing the sexual drives we thereby gain access to untapped resources of genius.

Nevertheless, my personal definition of the sexual drive is a little different from Freud's definition. To Freud the libido is pure sensuality or Eros; I, on the other hand, say the libido is a little more refined. Sensuality and Eros are unrefined sexual energy; libido, however, is refined sexual energy. Indeed, as sensuality is the currency of the pleasure principle so libido is a higher value currency. Thereby, my definition of the libido and the libidinal is further nuanced from the current definition: it goes on to include three of the four classical Greek definitions of love: the empathic, the erotic, and the agapic – the last Greek word that I have not included in libido is the *philic*.

From all this we can see that the first universal law produces the internal drive that motivates everything in the universe on an essential level. It thereby manifests Allah not only as the true meaning of life, but also as the force of life, the source of life, and even the very substance of life. From this place it could therefore be assumed that Allah's essential nature is actually Passionate (*Hamin*) or Erotic (*Shahwani*). ... Though, it is true that such may not be false: yet to say his essence is Sexual, Sensual, or Erotic is too hot, too emotive, and too affective. Then again, if we were to say that Allah's essential nature was actually Agapic (Rahman) or Empathic (Rahim); it is true that such also may not be false either. Truly, Allah's essence is Compassionate, Empathic, and Benevolent, yet such a vision and perception of Allah is incomplete too. It is too cold, too thoughtful, and too nice. Such is like the brain and the heart. The two work together to fully integrate love into what I call the libido, and it is in this sense that I perceive Allah's essential nature to in fact be Libidinal (or Ashiq).

This is also a central aspect of Black demodernisation: that the essence of Allah being the agapic, empathic, and erotic force permeating the universe, inspiring and motivating all things, coincides with godbody theory, and thereby the age of iGod. True indeed, to most godbodies there is one Allah, and we identify him as knowledge, science, or intelligence. Still to us Allah manifests himself and discloses himself not only through the sciences, he is in fact *the Grand Science*; but godbody theory also adds-on to knowledge so that it eventually evolves into understanding. Herein lies the genius of godbody theory, we all say, believe, and appreciate that understanding is the greatest – thereby the most important – nevertheless, we take that a step further by acknowledging that the highest form of understanding is love. Even so, all Black demodernisation does is take that a step further still, saying that the most refined form of love is libido (*ishq*). Furthermore, to us, as understanding is the greatest, the greatest aspect and property of Universal Intelligence is thereby libido. Effectively, the greatest attribute, that is, the most essential aspect, of Universal Intelligence, who we call Allah, is therefore libido.

II

The universal laws of existence are effectively the laws of Allah. These are laws that Allah himself is even bound to, if we take Allah to be the universe; and which he is not bound to, if we take Allah to be the driving force of every interaction. What then do we say to all this? The best we can come up with is to quote from the Quran, where it says: "Now surely they are in doubt as to the meeting with their Lord. Lo! He surely encompasses all things" (Quran 41: 54). So, what really does this Scripture mean? That Allah encompasses all things but inanimate mud? Or that Allah encompasses all things but subatomic waves? Or that Allah encompasses all things but plastic bags? Or even that Allah encompasses all things but evil people? Indeed, Allah encompasses all people, including the reader – making both selfishness and selflessness equally fallacious, as Allah can manifest himself in all people and all things.

Herein Islam has developed the perfect word to understand Allah: *tawhid* (oneness). However, my personal definition of this word is as theocentric-monism. Monism simply states that there is no duality or plurality in the universe. All things can be shown to be interactive, intersubjective, interdependent, interconnected, and interrelated. Creation and Creator, objective and subjective, physical and astral, material and ideal, cosmic and electromagnetic are all one. There is basically an intersubjective interconnection of everything in the universe to everything else in the universe. This is also the second most powerful universal

16

law: the law of intersubjectivity (whose corollary is that it is a vibratory law).

The depth of this second universal law of existence is perceived through the understanding that everything that happens in the universe is a result of electromagnetic waves attracting, repelling, and interacting with various bodies at differing charges, magnitudes, amplitudes, wavelengths, and frequencies (or said another way, at differing forces, sizes, heights, lengths, and rates of vibration). As all attractions and repulsions are electromagnetic, all the interactions that occur in the universe are thereby vibrational, being based themselves on electromagnetic waves. Again, everything we can see in the universe is made up of electrons, so everything we can see in the universe generates electricity or electrical energy. Electricity itself, however, is not eternal like the concept of energy (or interaction) but has an extremely short lifespan.

Still, there is an interesting phenom within the subatomic structure, if we choose to acknowledge and appreciate the wave structure of all atoms: based on the understanding that all atoms are just clouds of probability with numerous electron waves orbiting around a compound group of positively charged electrical waves at speeds of incalculable rotations per attosecond (one quintillionth of a second), an atom actually defies the speed limit of the universe (670,616,629 mph). Further, remember that all common (that is, negatively charged) forms of all electrical energy are produced by electron waves, while proton waves also produce electrical energy though not that commonly used or accessed. However, these electrically charged waves only remain within the cloud of probability due to the effects of electromagnetism. What the vibratory law says is that this electromagnetism is effectively the second most powerful force in existence. Basically, it is electromagnetism that interacts with most forms of mass and energy in the universe; that is, possibly except for what are called dark matter and dark energy.

17

Electromagnetism is thereby that external drive that motivates all visible activity in the universe. (Still, that is not to say that electromagnetism is itself the feeling of pleasure – but that it is itself, however, *the pleasure principle*, that is, the drive that pushes us towards attaining that pleasure, whether through attraction or repulsion). In that sense, electromagnetism could be said to be that essential drive that interconnects the universe at every single level: and although coming dangerously close to the theories of New Thought, neither the New Thought movement nor most of the teachings they espouse are here being promoted. The theories that are being promoted are that: (i) Everything in the universe is electromagnetic. (ii) Electromagnetism is everywhere and in all places. (iii) Electromagnetism comes in many different shapes and sizes and interacts with all objects in the universe. (iv) Thought is a form of electromagnetism that exists in all physical bodies. (v) Light is another form of electromagnetism that comes about at a specific wavelength. (vi) Though electromagnetism can cause bodies to move at various speeds it can never cause them to move faster than its own speed.

All these ideas also help to solve the debate between the idealists and the materialists as they show that all subjective thoughts possess a physical substance, electricity, and as we know, all electricity comes from electrons. Not all thoughts are like human thoughts, though they may be based on language (*kalam*) and image (*khayal*). For example, ants think, not through neurons but through antennae. These antennae transmit electrical signals to other ants. They are not thinking with human languages or producing human ideas or sensation but they are thinking. Even so, all electromagnetic waves speak and transmit signals and feedback in non-human languages. The electromagnetism that generates radiowaves and the electromagnetism that generates photonic images are two, but they are also language (*kalam*) and image (*khayal*). Again, the language may not be like those of human thoughts

18

(communication through word and image) but it is communicating with itself and other entities around it in a non-human/non-verbal language (*kalam*).

As for the image side of thought: it is well known that all electromagnetic energies come in the form of subatomic waves we call photons. For those that are unaware all the images that are captured by a photograph are captured within these electromagnetic waves/photons. Thus, as our human thoughts are a form of electrical energy that contains images and languages, so electromagnetism is a form of electrical energy that contains images and languages. Herein we can see how electromagnetism solves the idealism/materialism debate. All physical things have electrons and all electrons produce non-human ideas and sensations. So, if everything in the universe is electric, then the ability to make mass and energy passive or active must also be based on an intersubjective interconnection.

As the following ideas will enter a little into the paranormal I will now warn the reader that what I say next exists predominantly in the realm of the pseudoscientific. There are believed to be seven notable supernatural/supersensory abilities contained within the pineal gland: precognition, *retrocognition*, clairvoyance, clairaudience, *clairalience*, *clairgustance*, and clair-sentience. Precognition, *retrocognition*, and clairvoyance are foresight, hindsight, and insight respectively. These first three supersensory abilities are forms of remote seeing and astral vision, or what I call *omnivision*; then there is clairaudience, which is astral hearing; *clairalience*, which is astral smelling; and *clairgustance*, which is astral tasting. (Clairaudience is commonly called mediumship but is actually more than that, it is to hear into the astral plane. Clairsentience is also commonly called remote influencing or astral feeling but is actually more than that, as it is actually an empathic intersubjectivity that goes beyond the standard definition of perception).

Now there are fifteen empathic intersubjectivities one can attain through clairsentience; and there are gradations from a low to a mid to a high level empath that one can reach. At the same time, there are also three groups or categories that these abilities can come through: in the first category they come through being an elemental empath, thus having a deep understanding of *lithopathy, hydropathy, pyropathy, pneumopathy,* and *cryopathy.* In the second category they come through being a natural empath, thus having a deep understanding of *climateopathy, genopathy, agripathy,* zoopathy, and telepathy. In the third category they come through being a universal empath, thus having a deep understanding of *electropathy, technopathy, cosmopathy, chronopathy,* and *biopathy.* If someone is low, mid, or high level in any one of these empathic intersubjectivities they are a *monopath*; if someone is low, mid, or high in any two of these empathic intersubjectivities they are a *duopath*; if someone is low, mid, or high in any three or more of these empathic intersubjectivities they are a *polypath*; and if someone is low, mid, or high in all 15 of these empathic intersubjectivities they are a *panopath*: omnipresence itself being nothing more than total *panopathic* intersubjectivity.

Accordingly, we could be said to all have been natural born *panopaths*, but as time goes by we devolve into *polypaths, duopaths, monopaths,* dark empaths, sociopaths, or psychopaths. Still, as all this paranormality may sound a bit far-fetched and hokey I will simply say that humanity may not, now or ever, be able to communicate with other entities via our thoughts or via the law of intersubjectivity/clairsentience, and that supersensoriality may actually be a fantasy. For example, someone might argue that I myself could be defined as a mid-level *polypath* as there have been numerous times that I have displayed mid-level Heyoka empathy through mid-*climateopathy*, mid-telepathy, mid-*cosmopathy*, and mid-*chronopathy*. Also that *all* electrical energies do communicate, interact, and provide feedback (thus in a technical sense also proving that everything in the universe is alive). Still, I myself can present no solid or substantial evidence that either humanity or Black humanity will ever reach an undeniable phase where *we as humanity* will be able to communicate via our subjective or intersubjective thoughts.

Nevertheless, the first law of thermodynamics and seventh universal law of existence further teach us that mass and energy are both just passive and active versions of each other. Mass is energy with built up inertia, and energy is mass with built up momentum; and as all bodies have both mass and energy within them, all bodies have velocity, which is another way of saying speed. Again, as Allah is that interactive Force that drives all things in the universe to motion, change, and rest; mass and energy (stasis and movement) must both be *qadim* (beginningless) and *baqi* (endless) attributes that only he possesses. Furthermore, though only an outside drive is actually able to accelerate a physical body, all that drives accelerations will only ever be based on its own constant velocity. Therefore it proves itself to be a form of energy that possesses zero inertial mass, i.e. whose velocity never accelerates or decelerates.

Now, electromagnetism itself possesses zero inertial mass, but also technically has a kind of mass even if not inertial mass, even as there is gravitational mass even though gravity also has zero inertial mass. Effectively, as electromagnetism can only ever have one velocity, the speed of electromagnetism, even so it can never slow down or speed up, thereby technically making it infinitely passive (inertial). At the same time, any body that is moving close to the speed of electromagnetism will instantly begin to itself develop infinite inertial mass so as to keep it from ever actually reaching, let alone exceeding, the speed of electromagnetism (the universal speed limit).

A good example of all this would be a twig moving on the waves of a river. The waves of the river push the twig and carry the twig just like the waves of electromagnetism can push and carry a body, but the twig can never accelerate beyond the speed of the waves of the river. In like manner a body can never accelerate beyond the speed of electromagnetism; and though a body's force of interaction may vary according to the level of inertia that it has within, that force of interaction will never be greater than the speed of electromagnetism. Another way to understand this vibratory element to the law of intersubjectivity is by saying: if a body moves at an accelerated speed of displacement it will continue to do so indefinitely until acted upon by an inertial force. Therefore it is the interaction between inertia and electromagnetism that will determine a body's vibration.

Still, we have so far drawn no closer to understanding Allah. We have gotten a novel look at the universe and seen that it could be said to be alive, intersubjective, and electromagnetic but we have gotten no clearer a vision of Allah. Yet, if we take the idea that all the forces of the universe are just subatomic waves at different charges, magnitudes, amplitudes, wavelengths, and frequencies then we can see how the vibratory law becomes the corollary of the law of intersubjectivity. Allah's grosser body therefore manifests itself as the entire universe, while his subtler body can be seen to be electromagnetic waves. However, as stated, Allah is far more than electromagnetism; and the universe; and the *Tawhid*. Allah is actually the Force that causes all actions: the drive to get pleasure and remove pain.

Accordingly, we can see how at all levels any impressed force is actually electromagnetic: whether that force is a cosmic force, superclusteral force, galactic force, globular force, solar force, terrestrial force, environmental force, global force, social force, or astral force; reducing down further into a bonding force, radioactive force, strong force, or even a natural force. Every impressed force is thereby electromagnetic which is why for the most part all bodies in the universe usually only ever move up to but never passed the speed of electromagnetism. What then differentiates this vibratory law from the law of interaction is that while the law of interaction says you can communicate with any and everything in the universe through the pleasure principle; the vibratory law says that it will usually be through electromagnetic waves that these communications can or will transpire.

Skipping passed the third law, we shall now consider the fourth universal law and fourth most powerful law of the universe which is the law of opposition, one of the most misunderstood laws from a scientific perspective. Most people either say opposites attract or they say like attracts like. Technically both are wrong and right at the same time. To explain this further the example to be used will be the most recognisable form of attraction: a metal bar and a refrigerator magnet, now obviously the refrigerator magnet is of opposite charge to the metal bar so technically the physicists are right. However, the metal bar is not opposite to the refrigerator magnet in the way that say an eggshell or a piece of paper are. It is not opposite the way a pool of water or a reindeer's tongue is. Actually, the refrigerator magnet and the metal bar are more alike than unalike.

When Newton said every action has an *equal* and opposite reaction that equal side was the alike and the opposite side was the unalike, and as this is a reaction it is an immediate response to a universal phenomenon (universal in this definition applies to anything that happens anywhere in the universe including society and the human mind). But not all metals are attracted to a refrigerator magnet: tin and nickel have their own magnetic forces. There is more than one magnetic force, each one with its own group of metals that it attracts. So even here the refrigerator magnet is even more alike to the metals that it attracts than has been appreciated.

If we return again to the analogy of the wave it could be said that the law of opposition corresponds to the amplitudes, that is, the height and depth of energy waves that a body vibrates. The height of the wave is positive, the depth of the wave is negative, and is therefore its opponent. Conversely, according to James Clerk Maxwell an electromagnetic wave is actually two waves, both an electrical wave and a magnetic wave, both moving at opposite poles. Now although this law is less powerful than the first three, the law of opposition is still very immediate. The universe must produce an opposite reaction to an action – though they will be mostly alike except in one or a small few points. Call this opposition Murphy's Law, the Darkside, or the everyday struggle, shit a Charismatic may even call it Satan (Hebraic for opponent and adversary), it is still a universal law, and therefore will never disappear in some idyllic utopia.

Most of the New Thought specialists who love to teach on the law of attraction have been misinformed. If there is a law of attraction as they claim there is then it would really be more likely to be based on the reciprocity law. They have mistakenly called it a law of attraction as that has a stronger sense of inevitability to it than reciprocity. The law of opposition works in a completely different way though, the most obvious example of which can be found in the polarity of a wave. One pole of the wave is at equal and opposite sides from its height to its median point to its depth from its median point. The height and depth of the wave are called the amplitude and both ends are polar opposites to each other. Another way the law works is in simple mathematics: 10 at one pole becomes -10 at another until it returns again from that pole back to 10.

One more way this law works is based on the law of conservation: the action of a body accelerating produces an energy increase, but the reaction is that mass decreases. This is also an instant, equal, and opposite reaction. Again, if we consider the vibratory law: when a helium atom loses an electron it becomes a positive helium ion (remember all these are waves). The action (the loss of an electron) produces an equal and opposite reaction (the becoming of a positive helium ion). It is inescapable and instant. As a final example, a Gandhi (non-violent hero) must produce a Hitler (genocidal villain) – and just in case I am now asked the question: a Martin Luther King Jr. must produce a Eugene "Bull" Conner, even if on the surface he debates with a Malcolm X. The universe must produce an *equal* and opposite reaction. This is the law of opposition. Both sides are thereby the two poles of a current; no matter what the body, there must be an equal and opposite side as its opposition.

Nevertheless, the corollary of the law of opposition is that it is also a feedback law. Let me explain what I mean by this: the law of opposition is instant, just like a man punching a wall. The feedback or response will be that their hand will hurt as the force from the hand to the wall must be returned to the hand. This is, on the one hand (forgive the pun), is the power of negative feedback. However, if one was to keep on punching the solid wall at the same point and with consistency, eventually the wall will break – unless they know karate in which case their punch would be an amalgamation of the force built up from the repetition of weeks of practice punches. This is therefore the power of persistent repetition. Walls can break if one is willing to endure. If one will never give in despite the feedback then one can achieve any intention. Herein the law of repetition can be summed up in one word: persistence. The barrier to that persistence is the law of opposition. One can effectively break past any barrier so long as they refuse to give up.

Simple belief on its own is fruitless without persistent action, or, as the apostle James said: "faith without works is dead" (James 2: 26). Many nowadays love to say your thoughts create your universe, but thoughts alone can create nothing. We all receive feedback in our lives, both positive and negative, regardless of the thoughts we think. It is only the repetition of the right activities, over and over again, that ultimately creates for a person their universe. It is not enough to daydream about having a nice garden, one needs to work their garden, plant the right seeds, and, most importantly, continue to water and tend to them, only then will they actually have a nice garden. Same is true with their body, their brain, and their relationships. Effectively, as the old aphorism says, "The grass is not greener on the other side, it is greener where you water it."

A person can thereby create their own universe only through right and persistent action. Thoughts alone can create neither a universe nor attract a universe. All they can really do is define one. Hereby, perception is everything. If a person thinks they have received (or attracted) positive feedback from the universe, then they will believe that thought whether the evidence backs it up or not. Their own thoughts will provide all the evidence they need to back up what perceptions they have. Circumstances are only the product of our thoughts in that our thoughts produce our actions and our actions determine our circumstances. Thereby, all the mysticisms of New Thought pseudoscience is effectively done away with. True science teaches us that it is from our work that we receive all our feedback, positive and negative. But the main reason why the law of repetition is not here considered more powerful than the law of opposition is that though the law of opposition may sometimes appear to be weaker by comparison, it is also instantaneous, which in itself can sometimes prove to be more than enough, especially when the feedback is negative.

All bringing us to the fifth most powerful universal law: the law of repetition. Using again the analogy of electromagnetic waves, this law represents both the wavelength and frequency of all the waves generated by a body. To be sure, the first five universal laws could be considered interrelated – the first is to do with activity and passivity, the second is to do with the electromagnetic force that causes most activities, the third is to do with the magnitude or the overall size of the waves they produce, the fourth is to do with the amplitudes, that is, the heights and the depths of these waves, and the fifth is to do with the wavelengths and frequencies of these electromagnetic waves. At the same time, please try to remember that all of this is only an analogy. That said, the law of repetition itself goes by many different names, including the law of cyclical motion, the law of habitual consistency, the law of corporeal stasis, or the law of behavioural persistence; Einstein even called it the law of compound interest. In fact, when asked what he thought the most powerful law in the universe was Einstein replied that it was the law of compound interest, thus showing how powerful he thought it actually was; though the first four laws are actually far more powerful.

Einstein is obviously far more famous for saying that the definition of insanity is to do the same thing over and over and expect a different result. However, such a definition only applies to the short term. If someone was to lift a barbell ten times a day for three weeks and expect a different result they *would be* deluding themselves. But if they were to lift a barbell ten times a day for three years then to not expect a different result would in fact be the insanity. Indeed, not only would lifting the barbell become easier and even habitual, but the body size and strength of the lifter would have dramatically improved. The mental and physical composition of the person lifting the barbell would ultimately change too.

Newton also said concerning this law, if a body moves in the same direction at a constant speed it will continue to do so indefinitely until acted upon by an outside force. For this reason, the corollary for this law is that it is also an inertia law. The force that motivates a body may be an accelerating force, a decelerating force, or a non-linear force, either way it is resistant to the inertia, and without it the body will simply continue to do what it does well – and only do well what it continually does. Moreover, the only reason why solid matter is solid is itself due to their inertia, while fluid things are light due to their vibrational interactivity. The law of interaction (the pleasure principle) also maintains that an activity will not be continually performed by a living organism unless it enjoys doing it, it gets happiness from it, or it expects a future happiness as a result of doing it. Basically, all living things travel the path of least resistance in all the decisions they make.

Conversely, this corollary for the law of repetition, that it is also an inertia law, means that one cannot deny habit. Habit must continue until an outside influence affects it; and this inertia law affects everything. There is a problematic, however. For any progress to occur at this stage, it will take new impressed forces to motivate it. The pleasure principle generates those impressed forces that affect acceleration, the inertia law generates those inherent forces that bring one back to their habit. Basically, the inertia law causes all things in the universe to repeat their function, and only their function, unconsciously and habitually, until such a time as the pleasure principle inspires new impressed forces to interact with them. Every single thing in the universe has a teleology (destiny) and everything in the universe has organism. At the same time, the organism of an inanimate object is found specifically in the inert chemicals and atoms that vibrate within it, even as cells make up the body structure of inanimate trees. Even so the universe and everything in it, even the inanimate, can be said to be alive and have life.

As for the sixth universal law and sixth most powerful physical law that would be the law of self-similarity: whereby all patterns, shapes, and capacities will remain the same proportionately even as a body begins to grow or shrink. The Britannica further said on the subject, "A self-similar object is one whose component parts resemble the whole. This reiteration of details or patterns occurs at progressively smaller scales and can, in the case of purely abstract entities, continue indefinitely, so that each part of each part, when magnified, will look basically like a fixed part of the whole object. In effect, a self-similar object remains invariant under changes of scale—i.e., it has scaling symmetry" (Britannica 2022: Fractal). Or said another way, whether you zoom in or zoom out the pattern or potential will be the same at each scale.

Furthermore, with regard to dynamical systems any issues that are unresolved early will remerge bigger, stronger, and more tenacious as the body grows and become smaller, weaker, and less problematic as the body shrinks or divides into smaller sectors; that is, unless they resolves them altogether. Moreover, the strengths that a body has will be stronger yet as they grow and will reduce as they shrink, each in proportion to its scale. This also relates the law of self-similarity to the laws of evolution and devolution as both are self-similar. Basically, any results will be the same but on a much bigger or smaller scale depending on whether it is evolution or devolution producing the self-similarity. Again, whether a body is astral, social, global, environmental, et cetera., it will always be logarithmic and exponential due primarily to the law of self-similarity, and if a body is self-similar it will also be fractal.

Notwithstanding, the corollary to the law of self-similarity is that it is also a correspondence law. Within the hermitic tradition there is an interesting saying to express the deeper levels of this law: as above so below. Effectively, what applies at a really large scale, will apply also at the really small scale. Moreover, the larger the magnitude of vibration the greater the vibratory benefit they will receive. Again, if they have large magnitude actions they will be the same type as what they were when they were at smaller magnitudes, this is because exponential growth does not substantially change a body – it only exposes its strengths as well as its flaws.

III

Before we go any deeper into the question of Allah we shall now look at four more universal laws and see how they relate to what we have considered so far. The seventh most powerful universal law is the law of conservation, which is based on the principle that mass and energy (inertia and activity) both relate to each other through the speed of electromagnetism. Herein mass changes into energy and energy into mass through $E = MC^2$ or energy = mass × the speed of electromagnetism^2. Whenever mass and energy are at rest-mass and rest-energy they are both thereby interrelated. Hence, it is the law of conservation that essentially brings balance to all the interactivities in the universe. It also plays its part in revealing that the world of mass and the world of energy are interrelated to each other, that is, that each state is relative to the other. Obviously, as stated earlier, electromagnetism only ever moves at a constant speed and no physical body in the universe will ever be able to move faster than the speed of its electromagnetic force. The reason these bodies are unable to ever move faster than the speed of electromagnetism is due to the fact that all impressed forces are nothing more than different manifestations of this same electromagnetic force.

It is thereby that the corollary of this law is that it is also a reciprocity law, meaning if something big is given out something big will be given back again. Positive and negative may work with regard to the law of opposition but not so with regard to the reciprocity law. In that sense, the reciprocity law is fair and just, but not by the standards of human morality and immorality. Indeed, the reciprocity law is completely amoral, in that whatever is put out will be returned back, like for like *in measure*. This is true justice: the actions someone puts out, whether big or small, will return to them. The vibration is determined not through some moral code, which can change and develop over time, but by the strength or size of their actions. Moreover, as energy is just a fancy way of saying work, the energy they put out will come back to them like for like in measure. Now that is not to say that like *attracts* like but that due to the law of conservation saying that mass and energy must always remain conserved, the amount of mass or energy expended *by* any closed system will always be equal to the amount of mass or energy expended *on* that closed system.

Consequently, what this also means on a physical level is that corn can only produce corn, wheat can only produce wheat, we will only get back what we put in, and the measure put out will be returned to us again. For this reason it is also called karma, justice, and *maat*. Yet while this reciprocity law is a very powerful law, it is not as powerful as the first six universal laws, though still more powerful than all the rest of the universal laws. Moreover, due to the interrelatedness and interconnectedness of the universe what someone gets back in measure must be what they put out in measure; and there is no way to escape it. Or said another way: "with what measure [you] mete, it shall be measured to [you] again" (Matthew 7: 2). To clarify a little further: the realities that a person has measured out in their life, will always be in proportion to the measure of the activities that person measured out to reality. For example, if the reader were to vibrate at DNA size measures then the return in their lives will also be at DNA size measures; but if the reader were to vibrate at bull elephant size measures then the return in their lives will be at bull elephant size measures.

With that said someone may now ask the question: if, based on the reciprocity law, we only get back into our lives what we originally put out into the universe, and corn is only able to produce corn, then why do good (read positive) things happen to so many unjust and corrupt people? Why do bad (read negative) things happen to so many upstanding and honourable people? And why does New Thought teach that you only get back what you think about the most? The answer to these is threefold: firstly, good and bad things happen to all people alike, regardless of what they think about the most; secondly, the reciprocity law does not judge between good and bad like humanity does, the reciprocity law works purely based on measurements; and thirdly, the unjust and their successors may simply be yet to suffer the consequences of all their former actions and corruptions.

The universe always pays back its debts in reciprocity. Or said another way, the universe never gives anybody what they wish for or what they fear, it gives them only what they earn either by way of service or villainy like for like *in measure*. Take as another example the Roman Empire: while to all observers it looked unbeatable, eventually even Imperial Rome fell, as did Europe, into centuries of Dark Ages (not because of their belief in the Messiah – true, Islam also believed in the Messiah and they went through economic and intellectual prosperity during Europe's Dark Ages). This was the result of reciprocity returning to Rome all the actions of their blatant persecution of the messianic movement, putting many to death and subjecting them to torture, imprisonment, exile, and loss of property for not renouncing their devotion to the Messiah and his dominion.

It is well understood that Rome's fall was not at the hands of another empire but at the hands of what were considered to them barbarians. But how could barbarians have overcome the eternal city? It cannot be denied that the only reason for this was that the measure of Rome's past deeds came back again to them. There may obviously be many other things in the physical that correlate to the fall of Rome but there is only one metaphysical cause that I can think of. This is interesting as the United States is also an empire just like Rome which also has an equivalent force fighting against them in the person of the Jihadists (Nye 2004). Herein if it was to fall it may not be due to any physical factor they may seek to place the blame on. America's rise to power and maintenance of power has centrally been based on corruption, bullying, and exploitation (chattel and wage slavery). The universe is unlikely to let them get away with that regardless of how many hidden gems there are in their system or people.

Moving on now to the eighth most powerful universal law, that is, the law of evolution which works in two ways: the first way is that it says any muscle that is used gets stronger while any muscle that is unused must get weaker. However, a muscle that is used today may be unused tomorrow and muscle that is unused today may be used tomorrow. Conversely, not only are the muscles themselves worked out by use but even muscles connected to those muscles get worked out and grow stronger. For example, doing pull-ups works out more than just your shoulders, it also works out your triceps, your back, and your latissimus dorsi.

The truth is, the great always increase in value the more they exercise their strengths. Focus and determination builds power, and when power is hereditary it brings about evolution. As individuals become more refined in their area of expertise the skills they acquire become specialised and harder to imitate. Strengths cause differentiation and differentiation causes one to stand out. No entity should be ashamed of their strengths but should relish their strengths and use them to their own advantage. Indeed, a person or being's strengths may represent a somewhat unfair advantage, but all things, everything in the universe, has its own unfair advantage. Thereby the strong will always grow stronger.

As future generations further strengthen their stronger muscles or improve on their skills and methods within the art they have mastered, they will begin to supersede all previous generations with regard to their area of mastery. In these situations, and they are by no means inevitable, former strengths begin to become hereditary and further improvements begin to maximise potential, it is thereby that the corollary to this law of evolution is that it is also a power law. That said, an entity has to have knowledge of self otherwise it will not know or appreciate what its strengths are and therefore will be unable to differentiate itself or improve on it strengths, and thereby it will remain nothing more than a virtually invisible and insignificant untapped potential.

The second way is that it says the strong muscles of the strong do not grow iteratively, but instead grow exponentially stronger than all other muscles. Or, as Perry Marshall put it, "Everything that really matters … isn't linear, it's exponential" (Marshall 2013: 13). An example of how this works in nature is any animal with sharp hearing usually has weak eyesight and any animal with strong eyesight is usually far weaker at hearing than these animals. How this works in other dynamical bodies is through what Marshall (2013) called the King Effect, whereby the best 1-3 players in a particular field usually outperform their nearest competitor in the same field by a very wide margin. The example Marshall gave to prove this was in the earnings of the 1997-98 Chicago Bulls team. Michael Jordan, the highest paid, earned $33,140,000, which was over six times higher than the second highest paid player, Toni Kukoc, at $4,560,000. In most parts of the universe the best are so far above their competition that there is literally no competition.

The King Effect of the power law is based on what many mathematicians and economists call the 80/20 principle as 80 percent of the results usually come from only 20 percent of the resources (in this case even people can be resources). Although in actuality it may turn out to be a little more or less lopsided than 80/20, the point is that there is an imbalance with only 1-3 coming out on top. Herein it can also be related to the ninth most powerful universal law – the entropy law – while still remaining stronger. Either way, both laws are subject to the law of opposition, the law of repetition, and the law of self-similarity. This is in spite of the fact that they are definitely not equal opponents, as growth and evolution are formidably more powerful than weakness and devolution. Nevertheless, unused and weakened muscles are far more numerable in the universe than those that are used and thereby powerful. Thus making the entropy law seem somewhat equal, though the muscles that are used so exponentially outperform the rest that the law of evolution is still the more powerful law, and as a universal law the law of evolution applies to everything in the universe.

Conversely, the law of evolution factor only develops as a result of the law of repetition. Effectively, what the law of repetition says is that what is done over and over becomes habitual. It also says that what is done over and over gets mastered. As one gets better at an activity it becomes one of their strengths. As this strength become more refined and the activity becomes easier and easier it soon takes 20 percent of the effort to produce 80 percent of the results. Thus, the law of evolution is actually a development of the work put in due to cyclical and repetitive effect of the law of repetition; and the law of repetition only begins to take effect so long as one is continually inspired by the law of interaction. Basically, the law of evolution can be seen as the empirical expositor of these words from the Messiah: "unto every one that hath shall be given, and he shall have abundance: but from him that hath not shall be taken away even that which he hath" (Matthew 25: 29).

Accordingly, the law of evolution thus exposes the extreme overabundance of universal cases of imbalances and inequalities. This idea and universal fact may be a little difficult for our modernised minds to accept, especially with our current indoctrination into the theory that "all men are created equally". True indeed, that philosophical premise sounds beautiful and is very comforting – even though, interestingly enough, the very author of those words penned such a profound insight while himself holding substantial amounts of Black people in slavery, refusing to even acknowledge their very humanity.

The truth is, imbalance and inequalities are extremely rife throughout the universe and all entities have their own unfair advantages in some form or other. Such is true on a cosmic level as well as a social, Gladwell even had this to say, "Success [in itself] is the result of what sociologists like to call 'accumulative advantage.'" (Gladwell 2008: 30). Again, this is where the value of knowledge of self becomes most vital. Through taking a caring and *honest* self appraisal, considering our own strengths and weaknesses, without shame, denial, or victim syndrome; and developing a genuine pride, and even obsession, with our own strengths, and a brutal rejection of areas that we honestly do not value, we can cultivate and strengthen our unfair advantages into personal superpowers.

Indeed, most chaos theorist appreciate how even a very small initial advantage (especially if coupled with a concept like the law of evolution, or the law of repetition, or the law of interaction) *will always* develop into a massive and outsized result. Overtime that small initial advantage, just like the mustard seed spoken of by the Messiah, will grow to become full blown even to the point of domination. That location will literally become *their* location. On top of that, the longer and more regularly they work to improve and refine their craft (what programmers call optimisation) the more the King Effect will start to take over, even to the point that they enter the top 1-3 of all time, it not, at least of their own time.

But refinement of craft and building upon initial advantages are of utmost importance; and the most significant way to do that is to learn from, and be guided by one of the then currently reigning top 1-3 and modelling all their methodologies and techniques. Through *this* very methodology of modelling the best they will very easily gain quick wins, which will be extremely important for improving their talent and skills. Moreover, this is itself the basis of all the revolutionary changes and developments that transpire, and have transpired, throughout history.

Four events thereby prove to be particularly of necessity in the cultivation of personal strengths: (i) an initial unfair advantage based on a correct knowledge and appreciation of personal skills and abilities; (ii) a philosophical base or precursor to encourage the learning and development of those skills and abilities; (iii) the perseverance of the people to respect themselves, their personal abilities, and the developed philosophical foundation after the full force of failure and opposition have begun to get painful; and

(iv) a solid and even dogmatic culture that helps and allows them to maintain and improve on their unfair advantage, and even pass it on to future generations.

Conversely, our own knowledge of self and of our personal strengths and weaknesses will also allow us to remember and appreciate any positive feedback we may receive in a particular field or area, whether that feedback comes from a person or the results themselves. This positive feedback will likely be what inspires and motivates us to pursue the area of choice we decide on for our culture. If we then learn to immerse ourselves in the dopamine rush of that positive feedback it will inspire us further, especially during the dark days, which will inevitably come, when it no longer feels as good, and when the feedback is no longer so positive. Ultimately, that early positive feedback will produce in us all the momentum we need from that point on, until or unless we allow any negative feedback to distract us or ruin our love for the results. It is positive feedback that creates in us the exponential growth based on the power law.

Consequently, the actual way the science of the universe works is not based too much on equations, even though equations obviously do exist in the universe far more abundant are logarithms and algorithms. The rare existences of genuine equations in the universe has distorted our eyes and minds so as to seek the science of life and of existence (the Big TOE) in an equation rather than a logarithm or an algorithm. Herein is where the failure lies, not in the non-discovery of quantum gravity (gravity itself may not even be possible at quantum level, that is, if it exists at all). Still, such a notion can only be appreciated when we stop looking at the universe from the perspective of linearity and equations and start to look at it as non-linear, exponential, and algorithmic.

What we can see in all this is that the universe is actually extremely unbalanced, acausal, inequitable, non-linear, and non-egalitarian. Though the universe actually is just, it is not equal and has never been. In fact, there is a rarity of workable, realistic, and therefore honest, equations in theoretical physics. Most of physics, since the time of Newton to now, has been about trying to get the phenomena to fit the equations, and rarely vice versa. Every astrophysicist and cosmologist knows, and has heard of, the three body problem, and knows that the classical, linear, Newtonian system should, and does, only work when applied to two bodies; add a third and it should all fall apart (now think that our own star system has several planets, moons, rocks, asteroids, comets, and a massive star at its centre).

We probably should just have historically ignored Newton until something better came along (I say that for exaggerated effect). The truth is, it was the best science we had at the time for understanding our universe during a time period when spooks, mysteries, and superstitions ruled the day. A linear, egalitarian, causal – i.e. based on the principle of cause and effect – system and God were far more calming, understandable, and predictable. Then chaos theory and quantum theory destroyed all that. The clock maker God was replaced with a dice loading God. In a non-linear, exponential, logarithmic world causality is only one factor in a whole range of cosmic realities. Though chaos theory may sometimes use the somewhat causal nature of the universe, and of everything in it, for the purpose of creating predictability, they still appreciate that the universe's predictable aspects are based largely on factoring in the non-linear, self-similar, libidinal, inter-relational, interconnected, and intersubjective nature of the system. Herein, the law of evolution, just like the law of devolution, reveals itself as exponential as both growth and shrinkage are technically power laws: the law of evolution a higher order power law and the law of devolution an inverse power law.

All moving us on to the law of devolution, the ninth most powerful universal law. This law may not be absolute, nor more powerful than the law of self-organisation, which appears to contradict it, but it is based on a concept within computer science calls optimisation. What optimisation means is that all bodies that seek improvement need to and must focus their time and energy on developing their strengths and abandoning their weaknesses. It also means they will all eventually reach a point when these weaknesses will devolve even further till they are either removed or detached from the body as a whole. This is why its corollary is that it is also an entropy law, which is itself based on the second law of thermodynamics: that all unimproved bodies *will* eventually decay or fall apart over a period of time. During this time symptoms of their atrophying and decadence will become evident to alert all the entities it sustains or interacts with of its impending demise. Then, finally, it will reach a point that most chaos theorists call the "tipping point," when it will be fully removed and abandoned.

To be sure, entropy is the motor of the devolution, and the preparation for it; after the limit of devolution has been reached there is only pure chaos. For example, all throughout the process of boiling water the water heats up, yet it remains still for as long as it can, even when it is hot. The point of devolution is when the water bubbles, which is chaotic. The time of the water's bubbling ends (or the turbulence ends) when either the water has completely evaporated (called self-destruction) or when the heat stops being added (called self-organisation). Either way the water has been optimised by the method of enduring the heat, even if the only way was to completely take on another form, or through bodily destruction. Another example of the law of devolution would be in making a cup of tea. The teabag and the hot water will at one time both be separate. Then, as they are stirred together they eventually form a new entity. This change is self-organised and it is almost irreversible. However, the stirring process that produced the change used the law of devolution.

Not only so, but even the gases in the universe can be explained by the entropy law. Though the law of self-organisation may be far more powerful, the entropy law shows us that heat usually flows in one direction. As bodies become gases entropy increases, and can only ever decrease through self-organisation. Still, as astronomical bodies turn to gases in the universe the overall quantity of gas in the universe increases: all going a long way in explaining cosmic background radiation (CBR). Obviously, the oldest radiation in our universe has been traced back to the so-called Big Bang (around about 13.797 billion earth years ago): or what is commonly called by most astronomers the hot Big Bang. But CBR actually does more to disprove the idea that the universe really was at one point a singularity than it does to prove it. They say CBR has been in the universe since the Big Bang and came into existence because of the Big Bang, but it is actually far more likely that it was just in the universe, without a Big Bang, that is, without the universe ever having been a singularity.

If we disallow the concepts of both gravity and background expansion (two necessary Big Bang concepts) the creation of the various bodies in the universe, whether very large like super-clusters or very small like quarks, can be explained far more easily with the law of self-organisation. Obviously, Jeans conceded that gravitational instability could occur if the wavelength of the density fluctuation surpassed a critical point, one that was thereafter affectionately called the Jeans length. But when we add in a hot Big Bang, as well as the coexistence of background radiation and background expansion, it complicates things substantially.

When we also remember that matter exists in this supposedly *slowly expanding* background we end up with a top-down and bottom-up approach to explaining how the universe exists the way it does. The problem is this model needs dark matter, dark energy, adiabatic or isothermal fluctuations, and all manner of other uncertainties to make sense. Ultimately, it ends up producing both a top-down and bottom-up system, which overall only really makes sense if we disallow gravity and background expansion. Within the scientific community certain opponents to the Big Bang theory, like myself, mainly exist due to these sorts of inconsistencies. Most of them, again like myself, are usually Steady State theorists. Steady State theory being based on three early Einsteinian assumptions: (i) that the universe will be on average in a kind of rest-balance (or Islam) at any given moment in time, (ii) that the universe is a closed and curved structure (an aspect that I personally disagree with), and (iii) that the universe as a whole is static.

No doubt, Einstein later abandoned his own assumption of a static universe when Georges Lemaître, a Belgian priest and astronomer, proved through the effects of red-shifting that the universe was expanding; but he still maintained the other two assumptions as do most cosmological theories today. The red-shifting galaxies basically proved to the scientific community that these galaxies were moving farther away from earth. From here Lemaître formulated, what is now commonly called the Friedman equations, whereby he suggested that the universe was expanding, on the one hand, and that at one point in time it must have therefore been extremely small (a singularity) and extremely dense (producing heat and radiation), on the other. Thus was developed the theory that a Big Bang (or hot Big Bang) must have taken place at the beginning of time (or time-space), eventually leading to the cosmos reaching its current state through the process of development over time.

Nevertheless, the James Webb Space Telescope has already begun to unravel most of these generally accepted ideas. Firstly, it has discovered the existence of black holes dating back to 200 million earth years after the assumed time of the Big Bang. With such being the case the implications are numerous towards destroying the vast majority of Big Bang models. Essentially, if the universe really had so many internal black holes while it was still itself in, what the various Big Bang models encourage us to believe was, a relatively quantum sized state, then what kept these black holes from combining to form into super black holes, thus consuming the entirety of the still quantum sized universe? Moreover, the black holes they actually discovered using the James Webb Space Telescope were themselves so massive in size that they were forced to dub them monster black holes; thereby again, giving them further potential and capacity to have consumed the entire universe while it was still quantum, or relatively quantum, sized, that is, if we accept the universal singularity delusion.

All this thereby, definitively, invalidates the current models based on the age of the cosmos being 13.797 billion earth years of age. Basically, we are already aware that stars can live for hundreds of millions of earth years. Therefore with the James Webb Space Telescope looking back to portions of the universe that would have developed 200 million earth years after the perceived and accepted date of the Big Bang and discovering black holes (entities that are mainly produced in the universe by the death or consummation of a former star), maintaining the popular dating of the Big Bang to the timing of the development of cosmic background radiation (CBR) has effectively been falsified. Though some physicists may still cling desperately to the Big Bang as a theory, this revelation alone could essentially prove to be its demise.

Historically, there were, or have been, only three main and major evidences accepted that support the Big Bang theory: (i) the red-shifting of the lightwaves coming to earth from distant galaxies – red-shifting that could only occur if the lightwaves from those galaxies were being stretched towards the longer spectra of wavelengths (something that they appreciate would only happen if the galaxies were moving away from the earth); (ii) the estimates based on observations gathered through the Hubble telescope that the red-shifting and galactic retreat was occurring at a constant rate, successively named as Hubble's constant; and (iii) the discovery of cosmic background radiation (CBR) from billions of years in the past (again, estimated at about 13.797 billion earth years ago). All of these observations were used by Georges Lemaître to suggest to the scientific community the occurrence of a very hot and very explosive event that transpired at the very beginning of time, or time-space, that most scientists today affectionately call the hot Big Bang.

Yet with the invalidation of CBR being in any ways connected to the actual beginning of time, or time-space, the vast majority of beginning of time theories effectively fall apart. At this point, the only real remaining evidence to support and maintain the idea that there ever did occur an actual Big Bang is the common explanation provided for red-shifting of the lightwaves. Nevertheless, another, more probable explanation for the red-shifting of these lightwaves that have been coming to us from various distant galaxies is the fact, actual, proven, well-known, scientifically validated, documented, and appreciated, that all galaxies go through their own cyclical motions and orbital movements.

Accordingly, these galaxies are not moving away from the earth in the sense of expanding into a deeper (Blank?) They are essentially rotating and revolving around various points in the universe. Further, our own galaxy is itself rotating, revolving, and going through orbital motions, as is our globular cluster, and our star-system, and our own planet. All these motions are therefore far more probable reasons for the red-shifting and the rate of red-shifting (Hubble's constant) observed by Hubble and his colleagues. Not that the universe is or ever was expanding but that the galaxies were moving farther from earth and the earth, its star-system, its globular cluster, and it galaxy were moving farther away from them, the confluence of each producing a constant rate of orbital motions.

Consequently, the idea of an infinitesimally small universe (singularity) is so easily and undeniably disprovable that even

Nobel Laureate Roger Penrose had to admit that the probability of our universe coming into existence based on any Big Bang model (even those that he himself subscribed to) was 1 in 10 to the power of 10^{123}. Now just to inform those that are confused by this assortment of numbers: 10^{123} or 10 to the power of 123 is a 1 with 123 ciphers behind it. Consider now that it is 10 to the power of 10^{123}, where 10^{123} is in fact the exponent, and you have an astronomically mind-boggling number. Then add to that the discoveries just provided from the James Webb Space Telescope and they are all effectively dead in the water.

Obviously, there are new theoretical arguments that have been starting to gain ground as a result of these recent developments. The most popular being that the Big Bang did not occur 13.797 billion earth years ago but 26.7 billion earth years ago. This is a relatively conservative theory, maintaining Big Bang orthodoxy, and thereby not challenging the scientific establishment, but readjusting its models to improve the accuracy and coincide with empirical data (the evidence). Nevertheless there are still a lot of scientific questions to be answered, especially considering that the Big Bang theory itself was only really respected as a credible theory due to its coinciding with the evidence of the CBR. Without its connection to CBR, which is and has been definitively dated to 13.797 billion earth years ago, it is unnecessary and completely inefficient as a theory. In fact, as Penrose's mathematics has already shown, it proves to be far too problematic for its uses.

There is effectively a far higher probability of an arrow being shot from earth and reaching the sun than of the universe coming into existence by any of their Big Bang models. Such is what happens when things are left to chance. However, when you add in an intelligent being, be it Allah or an organic universe, suddenly the odds rise dramatically. Further, if the universe was at one time infinitely small, where did it dwell? Is there another universe that contained our smaller universe before the Big Bang? If there was, is that universe infinite? What are its laws? Such questions are actually nonsense and just show how shallow the common discussion of Big Bang really is.

IV

The last universal law we will discuss here is the weakest of the universal laws of existence; however, as the universal laws of existence are the most powerful laws in the universe it is still therefore more powerful than any other physical law. The twelfth universal law of existence is the law of interrelation (or relativity). To explain this it must first be stated that this conception is more in the physical sense than in the metaphysical sense, therefore in this section various classical debates will be revived. Firstly, in Newtonian physics and the sciences before him they suggested that time was absolute (Newton 1999). Well, time is a social construction created by humanity to measure, estimate, calculate, understand, and assist. The central form of measuring time that has been used over the centuries is the earth's rotation around the sun. The understanding was, if time was absolute then the universe would be static and all the motions of the moons, planets, stars, and galaxies, would be constant and theoretically even eternal.

However, Einstein showed that time changes with the location and speed of the object, i.e. time is variable, or more commonly, time is relative. The current definition adds to this the understanding that it is actually the interrelations between the various bodies and forces within time-space that are relative. Also, time and space are not only relative based on indices like location, light, and acceleration but based on scale too. First of all, if we consider the very big like stars or planets, they can live for millions of years, galaxies for billions. Then if we consider the very small like protons or electrons, they can exist for femtoseconds (one quadrillionth of a second), quarks for attoseconds. Yet if time is interrelated to scale as well as place, position, and speed then being infinitely bigger would make planets existence appear to be for only femtoseconds, while being infinitely smaller would make quarks existence appear to be for billions of billions of earth years. Thus the relativity and relationality of time-space is and has always been completely total.

To explain this further let us use as an example a thought experiment. Returning to the original thought experiment devised by Einstein himself but with a simple twist: instead of lightning striking simultaneously in two places yet being perceived differently from the perspective of two spatially different observers, let us do the same experiment from the perspective of scale. Let us say lightning comes from the sky and from the earth simultaneously in two completely different places (lightning can come from the earth during a thunderstorm as the earth has its own electrical field). Let us say one observer is a 10ft cow elephant who sees these phenomena as simultaneous, and let us say a male lizard happened to be standing directly under her head when this simultaneity happened. His size would make what appeared simultaneous to her seem somewhat delayed to him. Basically, as we all know, an electromagnetic wave can only ever travel at the rate of 670,616,629 mph so the speed of an electromagnetic wave must always be constant. We also know that almost nothing in the universe can ever move faster than the speed of electromagnetism. Accordingly, their difference in size creates either a time dilation or time contraction as potent as those created by distance and acceleration.

Consequently, as we know, atoms only really exist for femtoseconds, thus an electron wave moving through a cloud of probability around a proton wave could only do this for attoseconds before they die. The speeds that they produce are thus undetectable at our scale of observation. But at a smaller scale their speed would not be faster than the speed of electromagnetism. What we can see from all this is that: (i) The speed of electromagnetism is constant and is therefore without change. (ii) If a person was the size of an atom they would see the speed of an electron at a relationally different time from someone at human size, therefore time must be relational (relative) based on scale as well as distance and acceleration. (iii) This relationality of time for the very small must also apply to the very big so that the larger one gets the more accelerated time should be proportionately. (iv) This further means that proportionately time decelerates the smaller the object and accelerates the larger the object, though its acceleration or deceleration does not affect the actual speed of electromagnetism. (v) Not only is time relational but time-space as a whole is also relational as the size of an object can accelerate or decelerate time proportionately.

Seven implications can be derived from this: the time-space continuum is infinitely large; the time-space continuum is also infinitely small; actual time is interrelated to size as well as to speed and location; time contraction is what causes bodies that are large to seem to be moving fast yet appear to be moving at snail's pace speeds; time dilation is what causes bodies that are small to seem to be moving slowly yet appear to be moving at attosecond speeds; the acceleration of a body caused by an electromagnetic force will always be finite; and the deceleration of a body caused by an inertial force is able to be infinite. Based on these observations we see that time seems to move faster for the very large and move slower for the very small. Moreover, the reason bodies that are planetary in size seem to be moving so fast in spite of having greater inertial force is that time moves differently for larger bodies. Accordingly, it is not acceleration that causes large bodies to move at incredible speeds it is time contraction.

Effectively, if a body is large time for it is normal but for bodies that are smaller, that same time moves slower making the body seem to be moving faster while appearing to them as moving slower. Even so for bodies even smaller than that, for them that same time moves infinitely slower so the body will seem to be moving infinitely faster while appearing to be moving infinitely slower. A clear example of the relationality of time being based on size can be found in our own lives. When we are young time goes by so much slower; whereas when we become adults time speeds up. Now we attribute this to an affectation of maturity and the gaining of knowledge, but what if it is not? What if there is a genuine reason for this vagary of perception based on the size of the observer? Still, this is admittedly a weak argument.

Infinitudes are not that much fancied by most modern scientists: to say the universe is both infinitely big and infinitely small is anathema. Measurable numbers are far more greatly preferred. However, numbers are themselves social constructs created by humanity to measure, calculate, computate, assist, and construct; and even they can be said to be infinite. Numbers are nothing more than symbols we have given value to. But what if the universe has no real numerical value? The universe could be shown to be eternal by the first law of thermodynamics – the law of conservation – and the universe can be shown to be infinite by this law of interrelation.

This all brings us right back to the Cartesian question of atoms and corpuscles. The Cartesian argument was over whether substances could be continually divided *ad infinitum* or whether there was an undividable substance (an atom) that was the primordial substratum. It was believed in the early twentieth century that Einstein had discovered the atom. Then they divided the atom (the undividable) or split the atom into protons and electrons. Though we split the atom we then believed that protons and electrons were now the undividable substances, until we divided them too. What stops us from splitting even smaller *ad infinitum* is lack of technology not lack of ability.

However, some would argue that the universe is constantly expanding therefore it must have a limit, how then can it be infinite? The simple answer: it is expanding into something, produces a simple response: the laws of physics would cease to apply outside of our universe. This is how physicists get into trouble. The laws of physics already cease to apply in our own universe at the quantum level, it is no surprise therefore that they cease to apply at the cosmic level too – as above so below, as they say. Nevertheless, there are laws at both levels, laws that we have not yet discovered, though not for lack of imagination.

The truth is, if we were infinitely smaller phenomena like the Double-Slit test would make perfect sense to us, and the intricacies of their mysteries would be abundantly clear. The same with the so-called expanding universe: if we were infinitely bigger we would have understood its intricacies all along, and that the universe in fact has no limits. We would also know the laws of the infinitely big or infinitely small depending on the scale we choose. But perhaps we are reaching the limit of what we can know from observation at this scale. Perhaps the universe is too vast for us to ever fully know all its intricacies. Perhaps, "There are more things in heaven and earth, Horatio, than are dreamt of in your philosophy."

Still, it cannot be denied that since the days of Kepler the question has been stated thusly, "If the universe were really infinite then there would be an infinitude of stars, this would thereby make it impossible to have a dark night." Most modern scientists, however, believe that the universe can be spatially infinite due to the fact that the light from galaxies at prohibitively far distances simply does not have the time to reach the earth due to the finite speed of electromagnetism. As Frank Shu put it, "There is a spherical surface, the cosmic event horizon (roughly 10^{10} light-years in radial distance from the earth at the current epoch), beyond which nothing can be seen even in principle; and the number (roughly 10^{10}) of galaxies within this cosmic horizon, the observable universe, are too few to make the night sky bright" (Shu 2023; quoted in Britannica 2023: Cosmos).

Again, these concepts are not simply being made to justify Steady State theory as such, they are being made to explicate the theory of an organic universe. It is thereby that the current theories are distinguished from Steady State and Big Bang. As stated, the Big Bang theory is based on the idea of an ever expanding universe. Herein, the theory states that if the universe is ever expanding then there must have been a point when it was extremely small and extremely dense. From these beginnings it must have grown to become what it has become. Nevertheless, as also noted earlier, a hot Big Bang has a far greater probability of not producing the universe than it does of having produced it.

Moreover, the idea of a time before time, space, energy, and matter existed – a time that is implied in most Big Bang models – proves somewhat of a ridiculous idea that contradicts the first law of thermodynamics. However, this simple contradiction is not what should cause this notion be rejected; but more so that the actual infinitude of time, space, energy, and matter is itself far more likely than all the various incomplete and incompatible Big Bang models attempted thus far. Yet, even in spite of this understanding the idea of just throwing away the entirety has rarely occurred to any of the theorists of our time, who instead seek to maintain, yet adjust, it. But why is this so?

The real problem dates back to the great debate and splitting of theoretical physics in the early twentieth century based on various contributions made to the sciences by Einstein. First, Einstein's discovery of "atoms" through Brownian motion began the process of looking at the very small. As the atom (a Greek word meaning undividable) was eventually itself divided it thereby birthed research and study into the subatomic world, and thus birthed quantum physics. The second and third major Einsteinian contributions were special relativity and general relativity. These two contributions themselves birthed research and study into the cosmic and astronomical worlds, and thus also birthed astrophysics. These two camps within theoretical physics have been in conflict ever since, while, at the same time, still trying to develop a singular model that will ultimately unify theoretical physics again.

The Big Bang theory in itself only really exists within the world of astrophysics. Though not exceptionally necessary, it has been helpful and useful for explaining the accepted expansion of the universe, or what was believed to have been the expansion of the universe. At the same time, quantum physics is somewhat adverse to it and only accepts it due to the scientific orthodoxy. A lot of what is known today in quantum physics actually defies relativity theory, at least in its current form, and defies the theory of a Big Bang, of universal expansion, and of a primordial singularity.

Again, astrophysics teaches that the vast majority of space is vacuum space, but quantum physics explains that vacuums, at least as currently defined, are an unlikely possibility. Due to inherent quantum fluctuations the concept of vacuums (spaces within our universe in which nothing could possibly exist but gravity) and true vacuums (spaces within our universe in which nothing could possibly exist including gravity), are impossibly fictitious fallacies of perception and imagination that have no substance in this actually existing universe. Even in artificial vacuums energy and matter in fact fluctuate at zero point energy and zero point matter. It is through this method that the vacuum is able to remain a vacuum, while, at the same time, existing within a universe in which its laws and principles determines that such an entity should not and cannot develop a natural existence. This fact and truth further defies the astrophysics theory that there could ever have been a state of pure nothingness.

Effectively, every vacuum – or the various cosmic or artificial states of nothingness – actually has energies and particles (mass/matter) constantly appearing and disappearing (decaying) within femtoseconds. These particles and energies take no proper shape and so, while still remaining nothing (the mathematical equivalent of zero), are also yet something. Essentially, nothingness is merely a collection of zero point energies and zero point masses appearing, neutralising each other, and then disappearing through annihilation. These never become actual bodies; never take on form, shape, or definition; and only fluctuate in and out of existence based on the principles existing at quantum level. It is here that Max Planck's theory that all matter only exists due to the influence of independent and autonomous forces that themselves possess their own consciousness and intelligence, if not then of an independently and autonomously conscious and intelligent All-force that interconnects the universe. Planck believed these forces or this Force were or was the central component(s) of a quantum information field.

Conversely, within this theory was further assumed that the quantum information field was what allowed phenomena like supersensory communication, vision, and influencing to transpire. Planck also believed it to be a realm from which all matter and energy emerged and was sustained. Finally, he understood that it also interconnected all things in the universe to all other things in the universe. All this, thereby explained why a substance like thought is currently the only thing known to science that actually, not only moves faster that the speed of electromagnetism, but potentially has simultaneity, appearing anywhere or everywhere at the exact same time.

Many modern scientists, also building on Planck's initial theory, further speculated that information is one of the few physical entities that cannot be created or destroyed. Moreover, they further conceded that the speed of thought, being instant and simultaneous, was the only substance in the universe that is actually faster than electromagnetism. Regrettably, however, all these quantum physics theories only further disconnected it from all its colleagues in astrophysics, whose own various Big Bang models only muddle their effectiveness. Hopefully, it is hereby that can be seen how an organic universe theory is able to exist within a revolving universe theory that also includes a concept of double-ended universal infinitude. Still, the organism of the universe does not simply imply a universe that is infinite, it also technically implies a universe that is eternal. This is why the corollary to the law of interrelation is that it is also an eternalist law.

The theory of eternalism itself standing in complete contradiction to the theory of presentism, a concept articulated in classical, or pre-Einsteinian, physics. J. M. E. McTaggart posited the theory in the early twentieth century based on the understanding in those days that time was a series: it moved from 1, to 2, to 3, et cetera. "That the units of time ... form a series, the relations of which are permanent, is as ultimate as the fact that each of them is present, past or future. And this ultimate fact is essential to time" (McTaggart 1908: 124). Yet, McTaggart explained presentism and eternalism as two different kinds of series, the A series of time and the B series of time respectively.

McTaggart provided an example to explain the A series of time or presentism, "this characteristic of presentness should pass along the series in such a way that all positions on the one side of the Present have been present, and all positions on the other side of it will be present. That which has been present is Past, that which will be present is Future" (McTaggart 1908: 114). Further on he then provided an example for understanding the B series of time or eternalism, "Take, for example, the adventures of Don Quixote. This series, it is said, is not an A series. I cannot at this moment judge it to be either past, present or future. Indeed I know that it is none of the three. Yet, it is said, it is certainly a B series. The adventure of the galley-slaves, for example, is later than the adventure of the windmills. [So] a B series involves time" (McTaggart 1908: 145). Another way of saying this is that a novel or a movie can be seen as representing a B series of time, having a beginning, middle, and end all contained within a complete story.

While the A series of time takes into consideration the lived present, to the B series of time past, present, and future all exist at the same time, so if everything in the universe exists within the B series then every entity that has been or ever will be has already come and gone and only ever will come and go. Each individual time-space, though interrelational, therefore proves infinite. In other words, the reader's story has already been written along with the earth's, the star-system's, the galaxy's, and every cell's and atom's. Yet as mind blowing as that may be, this is exactly what the relationality of every single time-space proves. What Einstein revealed to us was that there is no substantial universal present or simultaneity, there is only the illusion of a universal present and simultaneity. The truth is, we all exist in an infinite number of interconnected time-spaces. Time for me will be very different from time for the reader, though our clocks and watches may give us the illusion of simultaneity.

Consequently, even if there is no universal present, and only an infinitude of interconnected presents, that does not necessarily mean we do not experience any present at all – and thereby substantiate the B series of time. However, that present is still an illusion: whether the eternal present or the specious present, any present in time automatically assumes time, which itself cannot be explained without again assuming time. Remember, time is an instrument of measurement created by humanity to measure, calculate, computate, and understand. Outside of humanity it has no substantial existence. Nonetheless, just because time is an illusion and simultaneity is an illusion that still does not disprove the reality of the moment. To this it could be said, yes, but only from our perspective.

If we take, for example, Tony Stark to be a real person, then to him each moment he lived was the present. From growing up in the Stark family, to getting sent off to boarding school, to his parents death and him taking over the company, to his becoming Ironman, to the experiences of each of the solo films, all would have been past, present, and future to him, yet to us they were all technically past. At the end of each adventure they would have all also been past to him, and at the beginning of each film they would have all been future, and each moment itself would have been to him present. Now all that is before we get into the crossover films like the Avengers films, or Civil War and Homecoming. Even so, our lives are groupings of interrelational stories; though rather than there being three, or ten, or multiple stories in which to tell each of our stories, we have one big, long, interrelational story which is contained within one specific genre.

Add to this the fact that with the digital construction of various advanced and deeply complicated virtual realities, and the algorithmic encoding of various autonomous, self-aware, and emotionally sophisticated artificial intelligences – and we are all left with the deeply difficult to swallow notion that we ourselves may in fact be nothing more than highly complex artificial intelligences living in a highly advanced virtual reality. This notion is called within the philosophical community, simulation theory. Essentially, the understanding within theoretical physics of a fine-tuned universe has sometimes been used by the advocates of this theory to explain the occurrence of certain inexplicable phenomena in the universe.

For example, as noted earlier, within quantum physics there is the concept of a quantum information field. This field, like a computer hard drive, stores, processes, and delivers data. Furthermore, within the computer sciences concepts like data structuring – which is a way of organising data – can be used to explain the various operations and functions of the universe itself, even as it is currently used to explain the various operations and functions of a computer. Again, if we consider that the common operations and functions that we respect all exist in the universe right now, such as: indices, matrices, codices, axioms, laws, constants, equations, logarithms, and of course the almighty algorithms, we can see how these terminologies have been becoming excessively more common within digital linguistics than within cosmological.

To give an even deeper dive we will now explore the most popular term within the computer sciences: the algorithm. By definition an algorithm is nothing more than a coding or codex applied to achieve the optimal result for a particular operation. Or, using a less insider heavy definition: an algorithm is a kind of methodology designed to achieve the best possible outcome for a particular task. Because most modern algorithms are currently based on computer codes and codices, todays algorithms are, generally speaking, methodologies used within a computer that are essentially codes designed by a programmer to achieve a certain result on or with their computer. The best algorithms are therefore those based on codes that are able to either solve problems or achieve results faster and easier than any others. This is a concept called within computer science and digital physics, optimisation.

If we were now to combine all these ideas we could thereby theorise that, maybe instead of simply perceiving our lives to be a written and complete *Book of Life*, or even generic film, we should, even more interestingly perceive them as a kind of video game. Through this methodology, although recognising that the paths of our stories have been already written – as with the stories of our families, our communities, our cities, our countries, our planet, our star-system, our galaxy, and even our universe – we still have a small level of agency in how our stories actually play out. True, to us it may be happening moment by moment and event by event, but in the eyes of the universe it has already been written and our path determined.

This idea coincides with the theory that we all possess a level of agency even if within the confines of a broader story or narrative – this theory is that of negotiable fate. According to Dach-Gruschow et alia., negotiable fate should be differentiated from insurmountable fate (which leads to complete determinism) and conquerable fate (which leads to the existentialist theory of total freedom): "Unlike insurmountable fate, which holds that all events are predetermined by fate and are therefore unalterable, negotiable fate entertains the possibility of bringing about desired outcomes through agentic actions. Unlike conquerable fate, which boasts the ability to allow one to self-determine one's course of action and considers outcomes to be unconstrained by external agents and circumstances, negotiable fate recognizes fate as a powerful causal agent" (Dach-Gruschow et alia. 2011: 34).

Within this idea is thereby the understanding that though our will is relatively free there are still biological, psychological, societal, historical, environmental, and physical constraints that are able to impede our choices. However, while these impediments may seem real to us in the moment, they could technically be considered a result of the "programming" we have received and the world we have been brought into. Whether we put that programming on our parents or some divine programmer, every one of us has been born with certain limitations (obviously some with more than others) and certain unfair advantages (again, some with more than others).

To maintain the perception of absolute freedom is a little delusional, but to accept that we all possess both limitations and advantages given to us in a life we played no part in designing is to have a measured knowledge and acceptance of truth. The most obvious of these limitations would be those of: self-motivation, self-organisation, self-destruction, evolution, devolution, inter-subjectivity, and self-similarity. Herein we are able to also see the organic nature to our "programming," that what gives us life and organism, what defines us as living, organic, and biological beings may in fact be nothing more than the coding given to us by a programmer.

Not to mention the further conceptions of theoretical physics that are even better applied and explained by simulation theory: those of cosmological constants. In physics constants themselves are no more than basic mathematical functions and operations that appear as algorithmic, logarithmic, axiomatic, or equational applications. Appreciably, the most popular constants in physics today are those of: the speed of electromagnetism; the force of electromagnetism between two separate charges; the magnitude of force between two mass bodies; the level of modification to an electromagnetic field when insulation is introduced; the amount of heat and pressure present at the state of equilibrium in a phase transition; the dimensions of energy per degree of heat; and the very charge of an electron. Within computer science, however, these kinds of data points could easily be programmed and determined using what is defined as priority queues. All priority queues is the various indices, matrices, and codices programmed into a computer to produce consistent and optimal results, every single time. As can be seen, such a function is exactly what a constant performs and is supposed to perform, every single time.

If we now acknowledge then, that as was said before, the quantum information field is itself based on a great ocean of consciousness – a cosmological constant determined by the application of the law of intersubjectivity – then we can appreciate how our human consciousness could be perceived to in fact be nothing more than a kind of sophisticated and highly complex AI algorithm that merely interfaces with a super-computer that has generated for us this virtual reality that we believe to be a physical universe. Herein we can now see the reason why all the other universal laws are more powerful than this eternalist law. Effectively, though the eternalist law is technically based on the total relativity of the time-space continuum; every ecosystem within the universe, *ad infinitum*, has its own personal time-space through which all these laws operate.

Conversely, the basis of the eternalist law: that though the past, present, and future have already happened and we all exist within a B series of time, our individual actions and choices will subjectively be somewhat autonomous. Further, as the eternalism of the universe, and of everything in it, does not negate the existence of choice and responsibility for an entity, concepts like the pleasure principle, the law of intersubjectivity, the law of self-organisation, the law of opposition, and the law of repetition will each therefore remain more powerful than the eternalist law. Accordingly, though the universe is infinite and eternal and time only really exists as an illusion within the mind of humanity, still each choice that a mind (human and non-human) makes will have consequences within their own personal time-space and the time-spaces of those minds with whom they share a close connection.

McTaggart (1908) explained all this as part of the C series of time. Unlike the A series, which works on a Linear-Chronological Model (LCM) of time the C series works by what could be called the Event Sequence Model (ESM) of time. The ESM is based on the idea that history has only actually been based on acausal and non-linear events. This sort of understanding should be clear to anyone who has ever written a history, as opposed to a historical fiction. An author of historical fiction may be compelled to use the LCM to tell their story. However, an author of history usually abandons the LCM and uses the ESM instead relating in a somewhat linear fashion various non-linear events in a sequence. In this sense, even though our own story may have already been written, we still play a major part in causing the events of our destiny within that story, which idea is figured into the first eleven universal laws.

Nevertheless, every story is really just the narrative of an essence moving through time, evolving, devolving, organising, reorganising, and eventually transitioning into another form. The job of a godbody is to uncover the narrative story of a natural body, and, while it may be impossible to know their whole story, to know as much about their personal story as is required. A good godbody theorist, through the methodology of mechanical analysis, should be able to know the aetiology (beginning), eschatology (ending), and teleology (destinations) of a natural body's story. Basically, they should be able to take any natural body and learn the details of their narrative at any particular chapter: whether the first chapter (aetiology), the last chapter (eschatology), the third chapter, the ninth chapter, the hundred and tenth chapter, or any other chapter before or after the then present moment (teleology). Any time in the body's story should be accessible to a godbody theorist through mechanical analysis.

Even so, the job of a godbody psychologist, sociologist, anthropologist, or historian should be to learn the biographical or ethnographical story of the one they are studying. So, though we have said that the meaning of life is to receive pleasure and remove pain, one can still inject a deeper meaning into their life by giving their story a theme. Seeking the one, two, or three things have shown up in their story consistently that also gives them pleasure. By making that thing or the intersection of those things the theme of their story their personal *Book of Life* or virtual *Game of Life* will fill them with deeper meaning. Again, sex is not the only thing that gives us pleasure: as Freud (2002) said we humans are able to sublimate our sexuality and find high levels of pleasure in an art, a science, a philosophy, or some other activity. To improve our story all we need to do is give our story a title, a genre, and a theme and our lives will be that much sweeter.

One of the main problems with certain stories is that they may have too many themes at once, or they have no theme at all, so it is hard to know what the Author was trying to get across with the story. The same can happen with a godbody's life story. The genre of most modern life stories is urban drama, rural drama, or historical realism; but what is its theme, its central theme. There may be several subthemes that can be found at the overcoming

60

of each difficulty, but the central theme, the main theme unifying all other themes, must be clear for their story to make sense. We can also look at the pains, trials, and problems of most life stories as the subthemes that make their central theme that much more interesting. Again, life would be boring if we had no problems to overcome. An easy life with no suffering or problems is a boring life. By deciding on a title, genre, and theme for our story we ensure our lives do not fall victim to what is called in the author world: narrative disorder.

V

From all these ideas we can see that the question of Allah and of his theophany is a very complex one to consider. For this cause, the best way to define Allah is either as libidinal energy, as the universe, or as a *tawhidi* principle. Yet, if we wish to define Allah without the need for all these spookisms we have to understand that he will need to be embodied, and such an embodiment can be found in none other than we Original people – all non-White people are the Original people. Herein we find that we Original people represent more than just the *imago Dei* but in fact become the *vere Deus*. Based on this definition Allah is thereby defined as a collective of Original people, both male and female, that exist beyond all time-spaces and have attained *omnivision*, omniscience, omnipotence, and omnipresence.

At the same time, we are also able to see, that a true godbody theology should itself be based on this kind of natural theology: the finding of the theophany, not only in Original people, but also in the entire universe. Just to be clear, though, what is here being stated is that the godbody theology should not attempt to be an exegetical theology as such, but a natural theology based purely on mathematical, physical, historical, and psychological facts. Furthermore, as we still find the theophany in Original people, and as we also see social science as a natural science, our natural theology should not only include a study of the physical sciences but also of the social sciences.

The main reason we say only Original people should be categorised as embodiments of Allah is that White people already embody their own god and that their god is at variance with Allah and his universal laws. The main reason we say all Original people have the potential to become embodiments of Allah is that we are unable to be blinded by White privilege to the many racial shortcomings, visible and invisible, of the actually existing systems of modernity. Accordingly, White privilege blocks most White people from ever attaining to Black divinity. However, supreme mathematics and mechanical analysis opens the door for those of us within the Original nations to attain to Black divinity – or, at least, to a form of omniscience.

But this brings about a simple question: what then, in itself, is omniscience? Does omniscience mean to know everything? To this it could then be asked, does someone who knows everything also know how to create a calculation that even they themselves are unable to solve? If not then they hardly know everything. But even if they did then they would have effectively undermined their ability to know everything by having created something that even they will never know. So from that moment on they will cease to know everything. Basically, the traditional theory of omniscience is essentially delusive, even impossible. For omniscience to actually be scientifically observable it must be quantified and demystified, thereby it becomes measurable.

Indeed, true omniscience is not some spookish, hokey, Harry Potter type wizardry. It is measurable through diagnosis (knowledge of an entity in-depth), prognosis (knowledge of an entity's destiny), and epignosis (knowledge of an entity's history). However, the current book is far more confident in exploring the ideas of social diagnosis, social prognosis, and social epignosis. Therefore, when it speaks of Original people attaining to a form of omniscience what is really being implied is a form of social omniscience: that is, having access to social diagnosis, social prognosis, and social epignosis, which can only really come about by adding supreme mathematics to social mechanics.

But one of the main problems with this mathematising of social science is that "frequently one is offered not proofs but mere assertions which are really no better than the same assertions given in literary form" (von Neumann & Morgenstern 2004: 5). Moreover, at this early stage of mathematisation "application serves to corroborate the theory. The next stage develops when the theory is applied to somewhat more complicated situations ... Here theory and application corroborate each other mutually. Beyond this lies the field of real success: genuine prediction by theory" (von Neumann & Morgenstern 2004: 7). Or said another way: in the first phase words are replaced with numbers, in the second phase numbers are used to create theories and applications, and in the third phase theories are used predict events.

Unfortunately, supreme mathematics at current features mainly the very first phase with a few touches of the second, that is, it has mathematical assertions with only a small few theories. It awaits one with greater mathematical knowledge than myself to find more and better applications and to develop newer and better predictions based on those applications. Yet through supreme mathematics we have been able to turn what could have possibly become infinite matrices of numbers into three easy rows: internal potential, external potential, and eternal potential. At the internal level are knowledge, wisdom, and understanding represented here as k, w, and u. At the external level are freedom, power, and equality represented here as f, p, and e. At the eternal level are God, build, destroy, and born represented here as G, B, D, and $\forall$, with the $°$ to signify a cipher.

Obviously, many literalists may complain that such a mathematics is unsound as it lacks empirical evidence. To those who say such it must be reminded that mathematics itself is not as objective as they have come to accept it as. First of all, numbers themselves are fictive symbols we use to define, measure, and calculate. Second, number theory has manifested itself in many different forms based on the introduction of new hypotheses and new revelations. There have historically been natural numbers, real numbers, rational numbers, irrational numbers, complex numbers, hypercomplex numbers, magic numbers, et cetera. Well, supreme mathematics is based on organic numbers that are here used to define and measure the interactions that exist between and within organic beings.

If we now, however, move on to social mechanics: the social potential of a social body is based on inertial forces. Any social body that is inert and remains in stasis will be proportionately disempowered in relation to any larger body, which corresponds to Newton's first law of motion and the universal law of repetition. As social forces start to act upon an inert social body they will begin to resist their disempowerment with a social movement to either increase their power in relation to the larger body or to completely separate from it. The level and strength of their resistance will be proportional to the strength of the social forces they have acting upon them, which corresponds to Newton's second law of motion and the universal law of interaction. The resistance of the people, the disempowered people, will also be met with an equal and opposite reaction from the larger body, a reaction that comes due to the inherent forces of the larger body and can affect any part or aspect of the social movement. This corresponds to Newton's third law of motion and the universal law of opposition. All social changes are produced by social movements, whether they be by resistance or by reaction; but it is the strength of the force of the interaction, and not the size of either body that determines which side will ultimately succeed.

In this, the methodology of social mechanics bears stark similarities to Marx's dialectical materialism with some key differences. Marx's dialectical perspective was a huge triumph of social science due to the fact that he was, unwittingly, applying Newton's third law of motion to society. Firstly, the study of the contradictions of society (in Marx's case, between classes; in our case, between social bodies) is compatible with the analysis of resistance and reaction in social systems. Secondly, Marx's understanding that the key to social change (in his case the interaction between productive forces and productive relations; in our case between social forces and social bodies) was, again, unwittingly, an application of Newton's second law of motion to social relations.

Nevertheless, if we hope to gain a better understanding of how a godbody can use mechanical analysis to understand the collective conscious and unconscious of various social actions and act-species certain definitions must of necessity be considered: an unacknowledged or unconscious dream, wish, or vision is a form of *phantasmic* act-species; while an acknowledged or fully conscious dream, wish, or vision is a form of fantastic act-species. The *phantasmic* can be either exorcised, *phantomised*, incorporated, or resurrected. Still, the spook nature of the *phantasmic* means that they are forces that will always seek concretisation, otherwise they will haunt and traumatise like a dark obsession. All unnatural forces, which are all forms of electromagnetism, are capable of becoming a *phantasmic* spook, thereby haunting can take place on any level but the natural. That is it can take place with strong, radioactive, bonding, astral, social, global, environmental, terrestrial, solar, globular, galactic, superclusteral, or cosmic forces which all could potentially become a *phantasmic* spook haunting their respective subjects.

To ensure that the *phantasmic* had no power over an individual Freud created the psychoanalytic perspective. Freud saw the psyche or the self as divided into three intrapsychic structures: the id (or instincts), the ego (or self-identity), and the superego (or ideal-self). The id being based on our urges, the instinctual self; the superego being based on our ethics, the ideal self; and the ego being based on our identity, the personal self; the first two being primarily *phantasmic*. It is also in the *phantasmic* that our ego gets haunted by forces, spooks, and psycho-affects, all seeking to control it. The ego is therefore compelled to fight off these forces, spooks, and psycho-affects before they become for it an obsession.

Following Freud we can surmise that the first psycho-affect developed in all infants, whether male or female, is libidinal interconnectedness. This interconnectedness is first developed while still in the womb but through post-natal intimate interactions can ultimately develop into an intersubjective ego. At this stage of the infant's neurological development their nervous and circulatory systems start producing in abundance the empathy hormone oxytocin. This hormone effectively sends electrical impulses through their infantile dopamine neuro-transmitter to produce in their infant soul feelings of love, care, and empathy, and also the ability to be decentred from a personal perception into a universal perception.

Then, continuing on with Freud's definition, we can establish that the second psycho-affect an infant gains is the death drive, or what Adler called the striving for power. This striving then works in concert with their libidinal desire to produce the infant's urges. Both of these psycho-affects would be produced via the slow but potent development of the infant's hormones, neurons, and neurotransmitters in their circulatory and nervous systems. With the very early development in all infants of both the sex hormones, testosterone and oestrogen, effectively sending electrical impulses through their dopamine neurotransmitters, the infants receive instant pleasure sensations from the various environmental cues that have triggered them. *It must, however, be stated at this point that the existence of infantile libidinal triggers is not to be taken as a justification for any form of perverted paedophilic aggression.*

From that point, the third developmentally produced psycho-affect of an infant, as we discover à la Freud, is self-differentiation, through which their self-identity is distinguished from those of their primary caregivers. This thereby creates for the child a sense of primordial ego and alterego (alterego is here defined as any ego Other to self). It is at this point in the infant's development that the awareness hormone norepinephrine, which sends electrical signals through the adrenal neurotransmitters, produces within the infant an overall sense of alertness and consciousness that ultimately develops, through interaction with the dopamine neurotransmitters: cognition, self-cognition, and self-differentiation.

The fourth psycho-affect created from here within the mind of an infant is aggressive delimitation expressed through idealised objectification. The aggressive object becoming idealised thereby produces within the child an ideal-self, or what Freud called, the superego. Also at this stage the sexual drive that was developed by the early stage production of both testosterone and oestrogen hormones, begins to get sublimated (or purified) by societal and cultural standards – prescriptions and proscriptions – that thereby produces within the child the so-called depressive position. This reality can easily be traced to the higher levels of cortisol production that would be taking place at this particular stage of their development.

Finally, the fifth developmental psycho-affect a child acquires is supersensory potential. All infants, again both male and female, are able to develop high levels of emotional, sensual, and spiritual potential due to the tryptophan aminos and melanin proteins in their bodies absorbing all the sunrays, and any other forms of electromagnetic energy throughout the day. These first get secreted in the pineal gland throughout the day to be sent through the serotonin neurotransmitter to become melatonin at night. While this process is continued in all infants, it has a longer, stronger, more refined, and better history with the children of

Original people than with those of the unmelinated. (This is in spite of the current standard of mental normality being so far based mainly on White people, whose pineal gland usually calcifies by the age thirteen). If any of these five stages of psycho-affective development get interrupted by a trauma it could potentially cause the astral forces of the child to go through a transmutation from affective forces into spook forces that essentially derail their psychological wellbeing.

By adulthood a person's conscious determinations will purely be the result of their self-identity. There is even another, rather interesting, phenomenon that occurs with regard to the astral bodies of humanity: as both oestrogen hormones and melanin proteins are known to send electrical signals through the serotonin neurotransmitter, they ultimately produce in us high levels of what could be called mastery and intuitive sensation. At the same time, whenever the testosterone hormone sends electrical signals through the same neurotransmitter the only known aftereffects of this action on, what would essentially be, the nervous systems of unmelanated males, has consistently been aggressiveness and competitiveness.

Conversely, our unconscious mechanisms prove themselves to be the result of an interaction between our ideal-selves and our urges. These two – the ideal-self and the urges – effectively war within our unconscious producing one of four outcomes: when the urges are dominant over the ideal-self a person can become an exhibitionist. Their sexual energy will also be liberated possibly even allowing for the development of supersensory behaviours and perceptions. When the urges and the ideal-self are in equitable balance then their sexual energy gets sublimated into progressive behaviours and perceptions. When the urges are inhibited by the ideal-self then their sexual energy gets transmuted into neurotic behaviours and perceptions. Finally, when the urges are prohibited to the point aggressiveness on the part of the ideal-self, then their sexual energy will get transmuted into psychotic behaviours and perceptions.

These four are the outcomes of the astral forces that define a person's subjective reality. When the reality is the collective perception of an entire, or the majority of a, social body then they are social forces. However, when the collective perception is shared by the majority of a nation or racial group then they are global forces. I must, however, warn the reader at this point, before they continue on into the next section, a section that considers the study of social forces in particular, the section will get quite complicated, maybe even prohibitively so. If that is the case, and it becomes too difficult to understand then just skip ahead to section VII and read on.

VI

Within godbody sociology all social bodies can be activated by social forces, which themselves get activated by a social body entering into a kind of electromagnetic field called a social field. All electromagnetic fields store two kinds of forces: (i) the impressed forces which are based on the velocity that generates acceleration and (ii) the inherent forces which are based on what happens after a body recovers from acceleration as a result of its elasticity. Electromagnetic fields are effectively what keeps all the bodies that are on earth attached to the earth, unless of course their impressed forces reach escape velocity, in which case they will simply orbit the earth, or, if they have enough force, orbit the sun. The same is true for social bodies too. Social fields are what keep all the astral bodies that are in a social body attached to that social body, unless their own impressed astral forces reach escape velocity, in which case they will simply orbit that social body, or with enough force, orbit their closest global body.

Inherent social force contains potential energy and is that inertial force within a social body that keeps the astral bodies within that social body moving at a constant rate; even driving

69

them to resist change. All social forces continually exhibit both social velocity, which is based on the libidinal drive in its rawest state, and socio-elasticity, which is based on the superego of that social body. When two or more bodies interact they produce a field, which delivers both the inherent forces that keep the bodies within the field and the impressed forces that drive the new body they have thus created, to new movements and destinations. Thus a social body that has attained inertia due to socio-elasticity is at that time being driven by an inherent social force, while also interacting with other bodies to determine the potential for a new social movement.

Now, let it be known that all forces: be they astral, social, global, or otherwise, will henceforth be referred to as impressed forces unless indicated. Basically, it is the impressed forces within a field that cause both forms of acceleration (attractive and repulsive) to occur between all the bodies within that field. At the same time, the inherent forces within that field keep the bodies within the field intact and are therefore the adhesive forces that hold all bodies together. For example: the impressed astral forces of an astral field are also the inherent social forces of the social body that the two or more astral bodies within that astral field have thus created; while the inherent social forces of that social body generated by that astral field will keep each individual body within the field intact.

Furthermore, when social body x_1 interacts with another social body it will generate a social field and increase the impressed social force within that social field. The impressed social force thus produced is also that inherent global force that is generated by social body x_2, or even by an astral body, and produces a reaction to social body x_1 within the social field that will either attract or repel social body x_1. All social movements are established by the impressed social forces – which are also the inherent global forces – within a field. The other parts of that

70

field will be characterised by the attractive or repulsive properties of the bodies in their field.

Social fields themselves are nothing more than the figurative spaces between a social body and another body. One that either attracts or repels it. Again, impressed social force is caused by a social body moving through a social field. When a social body interacts with another social body it generates a social field. That field, again, may attract or repel the other body. Thus in a social interaction between x_1 and x_2 one of three things will happen: they will be attracted/drawn, they will be unified/connected, or they will be repelled/separated, either way it is the centripetal force that we call electromagnetism which causes all this to transpire.

Herein all forces are appreciated as being electromagnetic, and that it is the level of inertia of the bodies they interact with that will determine the type of force they are on paper. Again, all bodies have forces that generate electromagnetism as all bodies contain forces that draw them to a mathematical centre. When that centre is of its own body then it will be centripetal, when it is of another body, which can only happen through the force of interaction driving it to pursue that aim, a centrifugal force may take effect causing it to either revolve around the body in question or to escape the electromagnetic field it has thus created.

Due to the strength of a body's electromagnetic field nothing within that field can affect the inertial force of any of the bodies within its field in any serious way or shape. However, a body from outside the field, say, a social body from an entirely different global body, if it interacts with social body x_1 could potentially cause social body x_1 to come to either growth, disintegration, or displacement from its mathematical centre. Every single body has a mathematical centre (its core concepts) that are indispensable to it. All other concepts of that body will be drawn towards these concepts. They ultimately set the body's direction and are to it its *principia prima*.

When social body x_1 interacts with body x_2 the interaction will always produce a reaction from body x_2 as both bodies are within a global field. Say body x_2 was faster or stronger at the time, the reaction to the force of social body x_1 will invariably be the same measure of force as that which it exerted. If social body x_1 is itself not strong enough to handle the force of the reaction it may cause either disintegration or displacement. Essentially, a body outside of social body x_1 can cause disintegration or displacement if it has more force than social body x_1 can handle. Notwithstanding, if it has less force than social body x_1 can handle then social body x_1 will react with a force equal and opposite to the force exerted on it. And though not always the case, larger bodies do tend to have more inertia so are less likely to disintegrate.

To explain all these ideas mathematically we shall now go into Maxwell's (2013) mathematics, and as God Allah Shah said, "Nothing comes close to the science of living mathematics" (The Five Percenter Vol 22.4; 2016: 4). So anyone who has studied magnetism should know the following mathematical equation for reduced momentum:

$$\left\{ \begin{array}{l} X = \dfrac{d}{dt}(Lu + Mv) \\ Y = \dfrac{d}{dt}(Mu + Nv) \end{array} \right\}$$

Well, based on this equation I have found the following for social mechanics:

$$x_1 = (Eu + Fv)$$
$$x_2 = (Fu + Gv)$$

Where velocities u and $v = \dfrac{d}{t}$, $E =$ coefficient based on the magnitude of x_1, $G =$ coefficient based on the magnitude of x_2, and $F =$ relative effect of x_1 and x_2.

Using more of Maxwell's mathematics: on a graph where the revolutionary displacement curve is between x and y in a three dimensional graph it produces this equation for social forces,

$$\left\{ \begin{array}{l} \dfrac{d\delta z}{x} - \dfrac{d\delta x}{y} = \alpha(xy) \\[2ex] \dfrac{d\delta y}{y} - \dfrac{d\delta z}{z} = \alpha(yz) \\[2ex] \dfrac{d\delta x}{z} - \dfrac{d\delta y}{x} = \alpha(zx) \end{array} \right\}$$

By then adding in exponentials, due to the logarithmic non-linearity of social variability, in the place of this equation for displacement we instead get this equation for social force:

$$v\left(\frac{x_1^n}{x_2^n}\right) = \alpha$$

Where x must always be ≥ 1. This is because x must always be greater than or equal to a whole. At the same time, as it is a social force x^n must always be anything from x^{10} to x^{19}; or in the language of supreme mathematics x^{10} to x^{1V}. Also, due to potentials x^o to x^V always being variable, the fact that the number for velocity is always constant, and the fact that exponentials are always based on self-similar and logarithmic bodies, each force elevation decreases the exponent by x^{10} thereby making it easier to graph.

Again, in equations where a body interacts with a body larger than itself, phenomena occur that may seem different but are not. In all cases of smaller bodies interacting with larger bodies, the larger body must invite the smaller body to interact with it or the smaller body must force itself into the larger body's company for them to interact at all. If we further consider this situation mathematically: the number 100,000,000,000,000,000,000 could be written as 10^{20}, as 100^9, as $10,000^5$, or as $100,000^4$.

Either way it is the same number. Even so with these forces, due to the simplifying expedient of exponents their overall inertial potential when featuring interacting bodies that have radically different potentials must match the force of the exponential with the higher exponent while it still maintains the same number: in the example above the number would be the 10^{20}.

Or take as a better example a social body interacting with a global body, it is really just another social body within a collection of social bodies so they would actually be interacting within a global field and not a social field, however, the global body will still have to be made compatible with the social body. In this case, these types of interactions will always produce an inherent global force at $\beta \geq x^{20}$. Or, again, take an astral body interacting with a social body, it is really just another astral body within a collection of astral bodies so they would actually be interacting within a social field and not an astral field. But the social body must be made compatible with the astral body. In this case, the force that body produces, no matter how strong that astral body's impressed force, will always be $\alpha \geq x^{10}$.

Also, when an astral body interacts with another body or within a larger body than the two bodies, then both bodies within their field must always be x as the other body will still contain the astral body within its own body. For example, a woman interacting with a feminist social body is still within the feminist global body therefore they are not written as x and y, they are always written as x_1 and x_2. The impressed social forces of a social body also allows all social bodies within its social field to move, develop, and change with time.

It must also be appreciated that impressed social forces are the product of the acceleration generated by social velocity, even as social reactions are the product of the deceleration generated by socio-elasticity. Still, social velocity is based on electromagnetism, which itself is generated by a social body entering into a social field. Yet because most bodies do not make *great* leaps without interacting with larger bodies, the larger exponential in any force equation must always be the dividend (numerator), while the smaller exponential in the force equation must always be the divisor (denominator). Moreover, contrary to the methodologies of standard mathematics where, say, in $\left(x^{17}/x^{13}\right)$ the quotient is x^4, due to self-similarity and the logarithmic nature of supreme mathematics $\left(x^{17}/x^{13}\right) = x^{14}$ or $\alpha = x^f$, where $\alpha \geq x^{10}$. Remembering also that forces only transform from quality to quantity through the increase of their potential, which itself only rises through interaction with abstract bodies – that generate a field. While a body remains in a social field it remains at $\alpha \geq x^{10}$.

How this works on a solar level is take our own star-system, all the planets inside our star-system are attracted to the sun, not by a gravitational field as such but by what is believed here to be an electromagnetic field. To explain this idea let us take two magnets: as they are both magnetically charged they will repel each other as they are brought closer together. The field of force repelling the two magnets being almost centrifugal causes the magnets to go in a curvilinear direction rather than a direct-linear direction. The cyclical motions they make are similar to those of the planets. As each planet produces electromagnetic energy they are all like electromagnets. Well, the sun is the strongest electromagnet within our star-system, producing enough electromagnetism to reach as far as Pluto. The electromagnetic charge from the planets is repelled by the electromagnetic energy from the sun, while, at the same time, being drawn by it. This causes the centrifugal effect of the planets' rotations. Thus, all the planets are effected by the electromagnetic field of the sun and the solar force of the interaction between the sun and the planet, even though Pluto itself is no longer a planet.

But how then can we explain the correctness of Newton's law of gravitation? As we know: $F = \dfrac{G\,(m_1 m_2)}{r^2}$. The truth, however, is that Newton's law is only an approximate law and does not take into consideration feedback loops and perturbation. In fact, what we are coming ever closer to understanding is that based on the three body problem, Newtonian gravitation turns out to be excessively optimistic. It is the best we have but is still excessively optimistic. The three body problem was known even to Newton himself (Newton 1999) and basically says that his law of gravitation only works with two bodies, add a third body and the gravitational mass, gravitational force, and feedback of the third will cause drastically chaotic results. Now consider that the various star-systems of the universe each have several bodies and it becomes even more complicated. Indeed, from the time Einstein first presented his theory of general relativity to the very present there has yet to be seen a single indisputable sign or signal that a gravitational wave or graviton particle even exists. In fact, the results of using Newton's gravitational equation are like those of using a *camera obscura*: the picture is clear but not real. We actually gain a far more realistic picture of the universe by discounting Newtonian gravitation than by maintaining it.

Again, they did not know the depths of magnetism back when Kepler first laid out his laws of planetary motion like we do in our time. We can now see that electromagnetism explains planetary motion far better than gravity. Electromagnetism also produces the social movements that all the social bodies within an electromagnetic field undergo. In that sense, the social forces that interact with social bodies are all electromagnetic forces. Yet no social movement can continue indefinitely by itself: all social movements must have a purpose and therefore have an end (no social movement, regardless of how courageous, can endure beyond its own natural limitations) therefore the aim of a godbody sociologist must be to find its natural limitations. Written as an equation this amounts to: $Lm > g$.

Nevertheless, a social movement's success is determined by neither its size, nor wealth, nor smoothness, nor scalability, nor durability, nor medium, nor cunning, nor any other spatial factors. Social movements are caused by and succeed through the social forces they have acting on the social bodies – thus whether they will succeed or fail can be determined by whether they are able to maintain the consistency of their social force, hence: $\exists(\alpha > Lm) \to g \nearrow$. Finally, social movements (whether they be resistance or reaction) become completely inert as new systemic boundaries and societal limitations begin to replace older ones, thus causing the social forces to decelerate, or:

$$\exists Lm \to \alpha \searrow +g \searrow$$

For a more complete explication of social movements: the process of stasis of a social movement begins when the social movement has reached its natural limitation and remains constant and predictable, and when there are no external social forces driving it to instigate change, hence:

$$g(Lm) \leftrightarrow \alpha \searrow o$$

When a social movement has generated greater levels of inertia to become a systematised social body all narratives that describe the process of its development and continuance will be fictive and therefore require intersubjectivity:

$$\exists(\alpha \searrow o) \to x^u > g.$$

These two axioms apply to all social stases and the study of all socially static bodies. When a social body has become inert these axioms will begin to take over. Basically, as Everlasting Life Wisdom Cipher Allah said back in 2017 "Math is law and order" (The Five Percenter Vol 22.11; 207: 4).

Different axioms apply when social bodies interact with other social bodies. Freud said on the subject, "it is precisely those communities that occupy contiguous territories and are otherwise closely related to each other – like the Spaniards and the Portuguese, the North Germans and the South Germans, the English and the Scots, etc. – that indulge in feuding and mutual mockery. I called this phenomenon 'the narcissism of small differences'" (Freud 2002: 50). From here we can trace out a new axiom for social dynamics: when two or more social bodies interact it will always be repulsive or divisive unless social cohesion is achieved:

$$x_1 + x_2 \rightarrow na$$

Social cohesion between two or more social bodies cannot be achieved until the natural limits, the systemic boundaries, between them have been abolished or amended:

$$x_1 + x_2 \rightarrow pa \leftrightarrow Lm \searrow$$

If consistent pressure is not exerted any abolished or amended limitations will revive, taking on new formations of the old which thereby become inherent:

$$pa > Lm \rightarrow D \leftrightarrow pa \searrow$$

Social change comes from social movement and social movements come from impressed social forces, hence: $g \propto a$. The impressed social forces that move social body x_1 would most likely come from body x_2 which could either be an astral body, a social body, a global body, an environmental body, or a terrestrial body. All social forces are the resultant forces derived from the social potential and social velocity of a social body. The social potential of a social body is based on the exponential inertia of that social body while the social velocity of a social body is based on its sexual drive; thus the unconscious is both the social potential and the social velocity. If a social body is collectively neurotic or collectively progressive in their unconscious, in their consciousness it is what they are striving for, or what they plan to do when they reach their potential, that allows a godbody sociologist to assess their social aetiology. What is their ideal?

If a social movement is neurotic or psychotic a godbody sociologist should be able to see from the beginning but if what that social movement attains if it comes to power is harmless, which would be unlikely if they had real neurotic or psychotic behaviour, then they can be left to fulfil their *phantasmic* dreams. A progressive or exhibitionist social body, on the other hand, will most likely produce a harmless social movement or even a transformative social movement, in which case it is up to the godbody sociologist to decipher whether the social movement is genuinely progressive or whether it will lead to a *cul de sac*. In either case, the godbody sociologist must read both social potential and social velocity to come up with a social aetiology, a social teleology, and a social eschatology – and as all social movements are curvilinear the social aetiology can be used to find the social eschatology as well as the calculus of a social teleology.

True, all the drives are for the purpose of getting pleasure, but the sexual drive is the drive that motivates all life. Sexuality is the pleasure principle in its most natural estate. Orgasm is life's prime want, though it is prefigured by aggression, hunger, sleep, excretion, and sociality. Pleasure comes in many forms especially the libidinal, thus motivation and velocity are the libido's central act-species; and as sexual energy always leads to empowerment, written as a formula it becomes:

$$v(g) \rightarrow emp.\,g$$

This is where Black demodernisation becomes marginally sophisticated.

There is an erotic element in Black demodernisation that leads to a kind of libidinality that sexually tempts one out of vain activities and into activities that can liberate the total person. Liberation here includes also the spiritual: therefore Black demodernisation *should not* only be seen as a philosophical outlook, it should also be seen as a kind of new age outlook too. Effectively, ethno-demodernisation is, in itself, a form of ethno-thearchy. Indeed, the age of iGod is a postsecular age as much as it is a sexual age. Here, just as the "African worldviews [tended] not to make a distinction between sacred and secular realities" (Douglas 1999: 132); even so, most of the people on the planet today consider themselves to be a part of some sacred tradition (in fact, more than half of the world's population) and those that do not are not necessarily atheist either, but fall into the category of belonging to what Lonergan et alia. called faith-based organisations, denoting such: any "organisation with ties to a religious institution and/or an underpinning faith ethos" (Lonergan et alia. 2021: 507).

VII

Having come this far someone may now ask the question: does any of what has been said really match up to the godbody teachings? To this it could be said, none of what has been said goes too far from the ideals of the godbody movement, and as Born King Allah said, we as godbodies, "received Allah Mathematics as our foundation before receiving any of the lost found Muslim lessons. Allah gave us Muslim lessons so we would not have to be Muslim to get the lessons" (The Five Percenter Vol 20.9; 2015: 3). The cultural traditions he passed down to us godbodies have allowed us to thrive as a movement and become one of the few Black movements that started in the 1960s to survive into the new millennium, and also look set for many millennia to come. Therefore this disclosure of the Black Godbody Theology reveals the intricacies of the movement and how it has, in effect, a natural theology.

When James Cone created the classical model of Black theology in the 1970s it was mainly to analyse the Black experience theologically. To Cone, "A community that does not analyze its existence theologically is a community that does not care what it says or does. It is a community with no identity" (Cone 2020a: 9). Indeed, he designed Black theology to be a kind of exegetical theology, using the exegesis of both the Bible and the Black experience to understand God's self-revelation. Classical Black theology is also a systematic theology, in that Cone (2020a) systematised Black theology into the study of God, of anthropology, of Christology, of ecclesiology, and of eschatology. Finally, it is also a practical theology, in that it centres on this world and a this-worldly experience.

Yet due to Cone's indoctrination into the teachings of Barth he also shared a dislike for natural theology, believing same to lead either to pantheism or a belief in the divine right of people (read White people) over the world. Cone further acknowledged, "Every student of theology knows of Karl Barth's merciless attack on natural theology, which he believed failed to take due notice of the infinite qualitative distinction between God and the human being. God is God and human beings are human beings and there *is* a difference, according to Barth" (Cone 2020a: 51). Thereby, Cone developed Black theology to be a systematic theology without being a natural theology, which to the end he believed was dangerous. It is here that Black godbody theology distinguishes itself from Black liberation theology.

The godbody model of Black theology is designed to be, first and foremost, a natural theology, in that it uses natural sciences to prove its theological points. Second, it is a practical theology, in that it uses psychological and sociological ideas in order to interpret theological behaviour. Third, it is also an ethical theology as we believe fundamentally in teaching and practicing righteousness. These accordingly define our Black theology, even though to Cone, "The task of [a] theology, … is to explicate the meaning of God's liberating activity so that those who labor under enslaving powers will see that the forces of liberation are the very activity of God." Conversely, "its sole reason for existence is to put into ordered speech the meaning of God's activity in the world" (Cone 2020a: 3, 1). With these statements Black Godbody Theology also agrees and takes up the mantle of studying and explaining the activity of God in the world. However, godbody theology sees God in Black *people* therefore godbody theology also includes a godbody sociology.

Cone's exegetical theology was furthermore based on *his* interpretation of God, as he stated, "It is important to note in this connection that the righteousness of God is not an abstract quality in the being of God, as with Greek philosophy. It is rather God's active involvement in history, making right what human beings have made wrong" (Cone 2020a: 2). But Cone's method was to distinguish the theological from the ideological – to allow the theological to function in its own right (Cone 1997) – we, however, do not make this blunder. Theology, as with any science, must build upon the shoulders of both its descendants as well as its predecessors. Ideology, according to Heywood (2017: 10), is "a more or less coherent set of ideas that provides the basis for organized political action, whether this is intended to preserve, modify or overthrow the existing system of power."

In this sense, Cone's (2020a) understanding that the White American society had a theology that denied the humanity and personhood of the racialised Other was very much so an ideological understanding. Again, Cone could not abide White American theology and sought to overthrow it academically with his writings. As he said in 1970, "American white theological thought has been 'patriotic,' either by defining the theological task independently of black suffering (the liberal northern approach) or by defining Christianity as compatible with white racism (the conservative southern approach). In both cases theology becomes a servant of the state" (Cone 2020a: 4). This is true thereby delineating the purpose of demodernisation. Herein, godbody theology is not only a natural theology but must also remain a practical theology and an ethical theology teaching a godbody sociology.

Godbody sociology as defined here is based largely on a redemption of Comte's (1986) original plans for sociology: the study of social change, social stasis, and social interaction. Social change is caused by social movements, and the science of understanding social movements is social kinetics. Social stasis comes about due to social boundaries, and the science of understanding social boundaries is social statics. Social interaction is a process of social resistance and social reaction, and the science of understanding social resistance and social reaction is social dynamics. Though these ideas are profoundly different from what Comte had in mind they still serve to continue on his method.

But one may now undeniably say: if all this is the case then can a godbody sociology really be based on scientific neutrality or can it only be based on dogmatic commitment? To this it could be said: it must be based on commitment, while still maintaining its scientific authority and having scientific standards. Even the functionalists, Marxists, interactionists, feminists, and postmodernists maintain their own scientific standards based on the presuppositions of their methodologies. Godbody sociology is no different, maintaining presuppositions within its own methodology of mechanical analysis that distinguish it from various other scientific perspectives. True, mechanical analysis is still in its infancy, but the following chapters will try to explicate to the existing sociological and theological schools some of its deeper qualities through an in-depth study of the age of iGod. Indeed, as we move out of the Industrial Age and into the Age of iGod the questions and theories articulated throughout will become more pertinent to those who experience its subtleties.

The Deification of Blackness

"1. Who is the Original man? The Original man is the Asiatic Black man. The maker, the owner, the cream of the planet earth. The father of civilization and God of the universe" (Student Enrollment).

Based on what has been said so far some would no doubt ask the question: what are the godbodies – Négrotheists, believing that God is the Asiatic Black man; or scientists, believing that God is the Higher Intelligence found within the sciences? To this I would say doctrinally we godbodies are both, the real question therefore is: which element is valued more? In this case, though many of us highly value the Négrotheist concept, we also claim to be neither pro-Black nor anti-White but instead pro-righteousness; this has meant that we have each chosen to add-on to our Négrotheism: either scientism, moralism, humanism, womanism, ecologism, naturism, or monism. I for one add theocentric-monism to my Négrotheism; but as a godbody I am inevitably a Négrotheist. Whether Afrocentric, Hebrew, Christian, Muslim, Rasta, humanist, womanist, ecologist, or scientist, a godbody must be primarily Négrotheist, but I believe personally that we would do well by adding-on theocentric-monism to our Négrotheism as it leads to a greater depth of universal understanding.

Indeed, the tradition of monism includes movements as vast as: Taoism, Buddhism, Sufi Islam, Gnostic Christianity, Kabbalic Judaism, Vedic Hinduism, and the ancient Egyptian philosophy also known as the Shetaut Neteru. We also know that Orthodox Judaism teaches monotheism, but also teaches prognostication and propitiation; and that Orthodox Christianity teaches monotheism, but also teaches trinitarianism and, either moralism or liberalism, based on personal interpretations of the Bible; and again, Orthodox Islam teaches monotheism, but also teaches legalism and moralism. Well, we teach Négrotheism, but can also teach scientism and monism together with that Négrotheism.

Obviously, there are many who believe that calling anyone God but Jehovah, or Jesus Christ is the epitome of blasphemy. However, if the Black man truly is God, which I am confident he is, then to call the Black man anything other than God is in actual fact the blasphemy. The very ones who say the Black man cannot be God may actually be the true blasphemers of God. Even those who say that the Black man cannot be a God because he is a man, only say such based on a Western misconception of the actual concept and person of God.

The concept of God existed long before both Moses and Abraham. In fact, in ancient Egypt (ancient Kemet) a civilisation existed that held all the initiates to be gods and goddesses. While admittedly, they had various spookish gods and goddesses too, they also accepted that people could become divine through knowledge of self and knowledge of the universal order of things. Basically, the original teachings about God were that the Black man could very well become a God through knowledge of self, which is exactly what we godbodies teach. It was effectively understood back then that God was personified and embodied in all initiated people, and that calling those initiated people anything other than God was in fact the real blasphemy. So who then are the real blasphemers: those who say the Black man is God or those who say the Black man could never be a God?

I

Black godhood was a very well respected understanding of ancient times, particularly in ancient Egypt, as they painted all their deities Black. The idea of Black gods, or of Black people attaining to divinity, may remain challenging ideas until one learns of these ancient interpretations, and that Black people were always held as divine, especially by non-Black people. This divinity was further complemented by the relationship between ancient Egypt and ancient Ethiopia (ancient Kush) in which Egypt was the daughter and Ethiopia was the mother: an ancient understanding that has been backed up by Greek historian Diodorus Siculus,

> *"They ... say that the Egyptians are colonists sent out by the Ethiopians ... For, speaking generally, what is now Egypt, they maintain, was not land, but sea, when in the beginning the universe was being formed; afterwards, however, as the Nile during the times of its inundation carried down the mud from Ethiopia, land was gradually built up from the deposit ... And the larger parts of the customs of the Egyptians are, they hold, Ethiopian, the colonists still preserving their ancient manners. ... Furthermore, the orders of the priests, they maintain, have much the same position among both peoples; for all are clean who are engaged in the service of the gods, keeping themselves shaven, like the Ethiopian priests" (Siculus quoted in Ashby 2005a: 8).*

To be clear, when Diodorus Siculus used the word Ethiopia here he was most likely speaking of Nubia in the area that today we call the Sudan. "The term[s] 'Ethiopian,' 'Nubian,' and 'Kushite' all relate to the same peoples who lived south of Egypt. In modern times, the land which was once known as Nubia ('Land of Gold'), is currently known as Sudan, and the land even further south and east towards the coast of east Africa is referred to as Ethiopia" (Ashby 2003a: 12). But for continuity I shall be referring to all the land south of Egypt as *ancient* Ethiopia, including the Sudan, South Sudan, Eritrea, Somalia, Djibouti, and Ethiopia. Again, when one understands the interrelation between Egypt and the Dogon tribe of Mali it becomes even clearer that an ancient school must have arisen that taught both Egypt and the Dogon their traditions. This school, when viewed from its historical perspective, must have been from none other than ancient Ethiopia.

The fact is, even if we make believe that the ancient Ethiopians and the ancient Egyptians were not Black, as many modern Egyptians and Egyptologist claim, they still painted all their gods and goddesses Black, therefore they still worshipped Black people. They even painted themselves and their Pharaohs Black, showing that they saw themselves as Black. How some Egyptologists get around this is by claiming that the colours they used were symbolic. But they painted them with human hues and not with alien or cartoon hues. Where is the blood red Pharaoh or the baby blue god? *These* colours definitely had more symbolic value to the ancient Egyptians than the Black hues by which they painted themselves and their deities.

Indeed, all the colours of the rainbow had symbolic value to the ancient Egyptian initiates. It would have easily been better for them to paint themselves any of these colours – just like the Hindus painted Krishna blue and Ganesha pink – if they were really only meant to be taken as symbolic. Some of these modern Egyptologists in turn explain that the dark red by which they painted themselves was obviously symbolic in that no actual race is really dark red(?). The truth is, they painted themselves a reddish brown clearly to resemble mahogany and there is definitely today a race that is mahogany. Basically, the modern Egyptologists appear to be presenting a kind of racial denial, as they obviously know the ancient Egyptians painted several different racial groups. They clearly do not believe the colours of these other racial groups were symbolic. When they painted the Asians sandy brown, which colour they happened to be, and the Oromo Ethiopians jet black with braided hair, which is clearly true of them, they recognise that they were clearly being very faithful in how they coloured them. Yet these Egptologists assume that they were not being faithful in how they painted themselves and their deities for, *Reasons*(!).

Then again, the modern Egyptologists may now pull out the only real dog they have in this fight and claim that Ausar was painted pale green so as to symbolise his death. Of all the multitudinous deities of Egypt the only one whose colour was symbolic was Ausar(!) and even he is painted jet black in many of his pre- and post-death paintings. The truth is, the arguments of these Egyptologists are all based on ideas postulated by the French anthropologists concerning the Leucoaethiopians, a supposedly Caucasian race that either migrated to or inhabited East Africa and birthed the ancient Ethiopians and the Egyptians. Such a ridiculous, and, indeed, racist, idea has produced the current misconception among modern Egyptians and Egyptologists; but their paintings of themselves, their gods, and their goddesses as Black cannot be denied or overlooked. If we genuinely wish to honour the ancient Egyptians we must honour them how they saw themselves and their divine beings, and they were all seen as Black.

Now, as these Original Black men ascended up the Nile till they reached ancient Egypt they carried with them their Ethiopian traditions. And though I said Black men, in this case I also meant Black women. In fact, the times most likely to have been the times of ancient Ethiopia's rise to power were actually matriarchal times. In this, the Black woman held most of the power. Not that the Black man had no power, but that his power had to come through the Black woman. Like Auset she represented the throne: for the Pharaoh to rule he had to rule with her permission. Conversely, ancient Ethiopia and ancient

Egypt were not gynaecocracies where women ruled in the sense of men ruling today – although in the Congo such tribal relations were not uncommon – in Kush and Kemet they practiced a co-regency. So these early Black people travelled from ancient Ethiopia to ancient Egypt at a time when the pre-dynastic tribes were still matriarchal.

These again, were the Original people as Diodorus further related, "Now the Ethiopians, as historians relate, were the first of all men and the proofs of this statement, they say, are manifest" (Siculus quoted in Ashby 2005a: 7). Even so, the fossils of the first human-like creatures were found in Afar (Ophir), which is in Ethiopia. These Hominidae would have further evolved into the Homo erectus at about 1.8 million years BCE. The ancient people of Kemet, being themselves very educated and intelligent, would have no doubt learned these truths of history and anthropology from the ancient Ethiopians. Ancient Ethiopia was even where they discovered the fossils of the earliest Homo sapiens sapiens man, a man that has been called in our time, Idaltu (elder). His fossils were apparently also discovered in the Afar region of Kush and dated back to 160,000 years BCE. From this beginning the Homo sapiens sapiens people clearly migrated up the Nile Valley to engulf the rest of the world.

All these Original Nilotic people were not Leucoaethiopians (Caucasians) – as some anthropologists would have us believe – they were Black: pure and simple. Their skin was Black, their hair was Black, their culture was Black, and most importantly, their religion was Black. They held the image of the deity to be Black because they saw no other possible images for God. There were no White people until the Homo neanderthalensis. And as all Whites have a small percentage of Neanderthal blood in them, these races could not have been the Original people as the Homo erectus predates them by thousands of years. (These Neanderthal came from the area of the Caucasus Mountains in Eastern Europe, where the Aryans and the Ashkenazi also came from).

With White people living in caves throughout most of the Pleistocene epoch their definition of the prehistoric caveman is quite accurate. However, this does not hold good for the Nilotic Black people as during the last glacial age they were living in a semi-tropical climate in Africa. As Dr. Ashby also noted, "Egypt existed much earlier than most traditional Egyptologists are prepared to admit. The new archaeological evidence related to the great Sphinx monument on the Giza Plateau and the ancient writings by Manetho, one of the last High Priests of Ancient Egypt, show that Ancient Egyptian history begins earlier than 10,000 B.C.E." (Ashby 2005b: 26), which is a time deep into the Pleistocene epoch. Consequently, glacial ages are not total occurrences experienced everywhere on the planet. Glacial ages are patches, though arguably large patches, over different intervals of time and space. To be sure, as Pyotr Kropotkin (2006) himself argued we still have glacial ages going on in Greenland and Antarctica.

About the time that the Homo erectus was evolving into the Homo sapiens sapiens in Africa and the Homo neanderthalensis in Europe two groupings began to occur, Black people and White people. True indeed, though the Neanderthals had larger skulls than the proto-humans, even as most White people today have larger skulls than most Black people, this was not to denote intelligence: they were still cavepeople adjusted to the cave life and the cave world. Further, I know quite a few White people today who have massive heads but are just not that bright. Thus, using a science like phrenology to judge these proto-humans is actually a bit absurd; and as Means also pointed out in his research, "If large heads were the symbols of intelligence, elephants would rule the world. Their heads are large enough but unfortunately, they contain no grey matter, and [are] often used for the seat of [their] master" (Means 1945: 5).

In ancient Ethiopia, nevertheless, the Black people "developed wild plants into tamed fruits and cereals. The Cushite was the only race that could have performed this service, for the other races in historic times despised agriculture." "These indefatigable men domesticated wheat, barley, oats, rye and rice, in fact all the staple plants of our civilization were fully developed so far back in the distant ages, that their wild species have disappeared" (Houston 1985: 55, 56). Not only so, but these events may have also coincided with the historical founding of a Kingdom in ancient Kush known as Ta Seti.

Indeed, Bruce Williams of the Institute of Chicago affirmed that this kingdom, in around about 26,000 BCE – not that long after the final extinction of the Homo erectus, and while the last glacial age was still at full strength – was somewhat renowned for this owned paradise of conquerors in East Africa. Even today in Kolo Boyo, Sudan there are carvings in stone from this ancient civilisation, each going back to over 20,000 years BCE, deep into the pre-dynastic times, and long before there was a Sumer, a Turkey, an Arabia, or even an Abraham (father of the Arabs). The fall of Ta Seti, which itself corresponded with the general ending of the Pleistocene epoch, would prove to have a lot to do with the mass migrations occurring from South to North by these ancient Kushites.

Conversely, the ancient Kushites would further go on to master the making of clothing from flax and cotton weeds, thus producing linen- and cotton-wares in abundance. These "Ethiopians [also] developed long staple cotton, millet, kaffir and Soudan grass" (Houston 1985: 57), allowing them to produce an advanced civilisation during the Pleistocene epoch at a time when the rest of the world was going through their intervals of glacial and interglacial ages. When the fully developed African people finally entered the caves of Europe during the last glacial age, wearing their fine spun linen and cotton clothing, smelling of perfumed oils and incense, with their shaved and lotioned bodies, dazzling jewellery, braided wigs, made-up faces, scraped tongues, with fresh breath, the European cavepeople were so amazed that they worshiped them as deities.

Culture came to Europe from Africa, mainly from Kemet, and the Europeans thus hailed the Africans as gods and goddesses, as noted by Herodotus. Their original traditions all evolved into polytheistic traditions from this start of admiring the ebony rulers and nobles that brought them civilisation. Born King Allah also qualifies all this, saying, "Once the whiteman … escaped the hills, mountains and caves of Europe he saw … to be a fact in this life with his own two eyes … [that we] are the Fathers of Civilization who had left signs and symbols of our ability to build from the Great Pyramid of Giza to Adam's Calendar. Adam's Calendar is one of the oldest manmade structures on the planet that most people don't even know about. It is positioned along the same 3-degree longitudinal line as the Great Zimbabwe structures and the Great Pyramid of Giza" (The Five Percenter Vol 22.2; 2016: 3).

Furthermore, as Drusilla Dunjee Houston continued, "The Great Pyramid [itself] contains ninety million cubic feet of masonry. It stands on the thirtieth parallel facing the four cardinal points with geometrical exactitude. … Petrie believes that the stones were cut with tubular drills fitted with jewel points. The lines marked upon the stones by the drills can still be seen, with evidence that not only the tool but the stone was rotated. The machinery with which the latter was effected is still unknown. The Egyptian carved the hardest granite, regarded now as impossible to work, as … though it was so much soapstone." Indeed, "Our best modern steel, with difficulty carves even plain letters in granite" (Houston 1985: 89, 88).

Not only so, but "Sayce described the statue of Khaf-Re in the museum of Gizah as a living portraiture. There is a sublime charm about it. The work is of exquisite finish; yet it is carved out of diorite rock, the hardest of hard stone. The stone mason of today possesses no tools with which to work it" (Houston 1985: 80), and these are all Old Kingdom artefacts. Moreover, a number of geologists have come to appreciate that the Great Sphinx itself has been water weathered, in Egypt(!), a country that has not seen rain for millennia. This pushes the building of the Sphinx, and thereby of the pyramids, to before the start of the current interglacial period. Again, according to palaeontologists interglacial ages usually last for around about 15,000 years, and our current one has lasted for approximately 10,000 years already. This pushes the building of the Great Sphinx and of the pyramids to sometime before 8,000 BCE.

Nevertheless, a brief comment must be made before we go any further with this line of thought that John Baldwin pointed out, "Cushite colonies were established in the valleys of the Nile and of the Euphrates, which in subsequent ages became Barbara, Egypt, and Chaldea. Its beginning could not have been later than 7000 or 8000 years before Christ, and it may have begun much earlier. The Cushites occupied India, Western Asia to the Mediterranean, and extensive regions in Africa. In this period they brought to full development that knowledge of astronomy and of other sciences, fragments of which have [even] come down to us" (Baldwin 1874: 97). Thus the source of science itself was in all likelihood ancient Kush, and as mentioned earlier 8,000 BCE was just about the time of the ending of the last glacial age, so that while these Kushites were mastering sciences, the rest of the world was surviving by living in caves. Houston also said on this subject, "At the beginning of the historical period of Egypt [7,000 BCE] most inhabitants of the earth were rude savages. In western Europe and northern Asia the half-human Neanderthal lived in caves under overhanging ledges and fed upon the untamed products of the wild. … In Africa we find no evidences of this slow progress of man up from the barbaric state" (Houston 1985: 54).

Moreover, as Dr. Ashby continued, "The Ancient Egyptians lived for thousands of years in the northeastern corner of the African continent in the area known as the Nile Valley. The Nile [River] was a source of dependable enrichment for the land and allowed them to prosper for a very long time. Their prosperity was so great that they created art, culture, religion, philosophy and a civilization which has not been duplicated since" (Ashby 2005b: 25). Indeed, the Europeans, during the time of pre-dynastic Egypt, all learned civilisation from these early Africans. Yet, as Rodney also exclaimed, "As far as Africa is concerned during the period of early development, it is preferable to speak in terms of 'cultures' rather than civilizations" (Rodney 2018: 36). Basically, these cultures of Africa at that time brought culture itself to Europe.

Obviously, Rodney (2018) felt that culture had a heavier connotation of the way a people behaved and practiced a lifestyle, including within its definition how they dressed, how they walked, how they talked, how they treated women and children, how they socialised their young, how they laboured and traded, what they ate and how they produced it, and what they thought of death and aging. Furthermore, in the ancient African cultures "the predominant principle of social relations was that of family and kinship associated with communalism. Every member of [the] African society had his position defined in terms of relatives on his mother's side and on his father's side. Some societies placed greater importance on matrilineal ties and others on patrilineal ties" (Rodney 2018: 39). Patrilineality and matrilineality also played a huge role in the establishment of both patriarchy and matriarchy, thus while there was a lot of patriarchy in Africa, there was also a lot of matriarchy in Africa too.

Accordingly, from pre-dynastic times to deep into the Old and Middle Kingdoms Kemet was most likely matriarchal. (True, they became more patriarchal at the start of the dynastic times, but maintained a kind of matriarchal system until the Hyksos invasion; and even after that time they still had female Pharaohs). Now matriarchal systems are usually focused excessively on culture, aesthetics, creativity, acausality, beauty, sensuality, and non-linearity; whereas patriarchal systems tend to be more focused on dogma, analytics, objectivity, causality, strategy, rationality, and linearity. Patriarchal systems are masters of war, but following war they have no means of bringing peace or pleasure to their people. This is because they suppress the woman and the feminine side of their nature.

Still, ancient Kemet did not learn culture from the sky. The God to them was more than just Shetaut initiates and certain key principles of nature. The main gods to the ancient Kemetic people were their ancestors, and to be sure, they knew that all of their ancestors came out of ancient Kush. The open reality of the Kemetic honour of the ancient Kushites as their fathers and mothers is shown in the title that they gave to their land: Ta Neteru (meaning: land of gods and goddesses). Again, we must also remember the undeniable truth that Hereen further pointed out: "The Ethiopians were distinguished from the other races by a very dark or completely black skin" (Hereen 1850; quoted in Houston 1985: 31).

To the ancient Kemetic people Pa Neter, the only one, was the principle that made the Neteru as his attributes; it is here Dr. Ashby said again, "While the Divine may be referred to as the male aspect, God, it may also be referred to as Goddess. Thus, we have striven to correctly translate the word 'Neter' as 'Divinity' instead of 'God,' and 'neteru' as 'gods and goddesses' instead of just 'the gods.' In Ancient Egypt women enjoyed complete equality in society. They had the same rights as men. This cultural righteousness was reflected in the practice of religion as well or it might be said that the practice of righteousness in religion supported the practice of righteousness in society" (Ashby 2005b: 68).

Moreover, "The Ancient Egyptian word 'neteru,' which is loosely translated as 'gods and goddesses' … actually means 'cosmic forces engendering creation' – it is the etymological origin of the Latin word 'natura,' and Anglo words 'nature' and 'natural.' The neteru (plural) emanate from Neter (singular meaning [Supreme] Being-Supreme essential power). Thus, the neteru have mythical references to nature and mystical references to human psychology which lead to greater understanding of the origins and destiny of human existence" (Ashby 2005b: 74). Indeed, the title of Neteru was given to ancestors, to interactive forces, and to the Pharaoh and his fellow initiates in the Shetaut (mystery schools), "Ultimately, all the divinities are referred to as Neteru and they are all said to be emanations from the ultimate and Supreme Being" (Ashby 2005a: 21).

According to Dr. Ashby, "The idea of classifying the neteru or gods and goddesses comes about as the Sages of ancient times sought to explain the manifestations of the Divine in nature as well as in human psychology. However, they should not be understood as divinities, but as cosmic forces and principles, their forms denoting the special qualities of those forces" (Ashby 2003a: 65). In all actuality, the Neteru concept itself could be likened to the yang and yin concepts in Taoism or like the lingam and yoni concepts in Tantra. It is effectively the Kemetic concepts of masculine and feminine enlightenment, signifying both male and female enlightened ones.

The great masses, however, received only elementary learning in these sciences of Kemet, which themselves, remember, all came from ancient Kush. Indeed, in Kush these secrets were no mystery, they were taught in the tribal religions in plain sight of all. We can even see from the Narmer palette that Hethor, one of the most important female deities of ancient Kemet, second only to Auset, was a Kushite goddess long before the dynastic times. We can also see from the Narmer palette pre-dynastic worship of Horu existed in Naqada, Kush for centuries; herein as Ashby also exclaimed, "traditional Egyptologists … have refused to accept the evidence of a Predynastic period in Ancient Egyptian history contained in Ancient Egyptian documents such as the *Palermo Stone, Royal Tablet at Abydos, Royal Papyrus of Turin,* the *Dynastic List* of *Manetho,* and the eye-witness accounts of Greek historians Herodotus (c. 484-425 B.C.E.) and Diodorus. These sources speak clearly of a Pre-dynastic society which stretches far into antiquity" (Ashby 2005b: 26). Having actually seen the Narmer palette for myself, I can say conclusively that Horu and Hethor were the most likely images being represented there, though the conservative Egyptological view is that they are other than, or at least that the cow image is other than.

II

It is of course a godbody claim that the Black man is God (which as the reader has hopefully seen the ancients also believed) but to achieve true divinity the ancient initiation rituals were markedly different to the examinations of the Gods today. The older Gods challenge the "newborns" based on the supreme mathematics, the supreme alphabets, the twelve jewels, and all of the lessons contained in the Honorable Elijah Muhammad's Supreme Wisdom lessons. If they pass then they instantly knowledge 120 and come all the more closer to 360° knowledge, wisdom, and understanding. No God can claim to knowledge 120 without having been examined, and to do so they need an examiner. They also need an enlightener, one who teaches them the Black man's science. As I myself was a newborn in America I know little of the actual process of initiation into the higher levels of the godbody movement, but from what I do know I have developed a means for our further progression as a movement.

To be sure, the lessons we teach in the godbody are currently closer to those taught in the Nation of Islam than to those taught in the Shetaut Neteru. However, what we teach in the godbody does bear some similarities to what was taught in the ancient Kemetic schools. That which is 1 in the supreme mathematics is also knowledge, the sun, and the divine Black man; while he who was Ra in the Shetaut Neteru was also knowledge, the sun, and the divine Black man. That which is 2 in supreme mathematics is also wisdom, the womb for the cream of the planet earth, and the Asiatic Black woman; even as, in the Shetaut Neteru, Hethor, who comes from the right eye of Ra, was the goddess of wisdom, the womb for the king of the planet earth, and the divine Black woman.

Again, within the system of supreme mathematics that which is 3 is also concerned to represent understanding, the five point star, and the divine Black child; while from the womb of Hethor came Horu, who in the Shetaut Neteru also represented enlightenment, a young sun, and the divine Black child. In all this, we can hopefully see how the mathematics of the godbody bears some similarities to the mysteries of ancient Kemet. Moreover, as Sabu Supreme Allah once said, "They are living lessons and living mathematics. You live it, walk it and talk it and it becomes you" (The Five Percenter Vol 22.10; 2017: 4). So let us further consider now some of these ancient lessons of the people of Kemet to see how they interrelate to those of the godbody.

First of all, the ancient Kemetic people developed their sciences based on lessons taught to them by the ancient Kushite people. But as these Kemetic people began to get more and more patriarchal, which began during the later dynastic periods, they lost a lot of their connections to the astral realms and began seeing things more and more from a materialistic point of view. In this sense, the undeniably more patriarchal Persians and Greeks – who themselves started off as matriarchal through the lessons they gained from Africa – were then able to conquer them. Once the Black man loses his connection to the astral plane, which usually comes to him via the Black woman, he is easily defeated. The astral plane, where dwell astral forces (which the ancient people used to call angels and *jinni*), was a plane we used to dwell in more than any other race. Materially we may have been poor but in the astral plane many of us were rich. Not that we should therefore give up on the material altogether; Kemet was as much a material paradise as it was an astral one. It simply means we should not put our *emphasis* on material demands.

Kush may not have had the great monuments and delicacies of Kemet, yet it was still called by the people of Kemet "Ta Neteru." Based on this we can guess that what the Pharaohs and initiates were doing within the higher echelons of Kemetic society; the Kushite tribes were doing at all levels of society. According to Dr. Ashby, "The sages of Kamit instituted a system by which the teachings of spirituality were espoused through a Temple organization. The major divinities were assigned to a particular city. That divinity or group of divinities became the 'patron' divinity or divinities of that city. Also, the Priests and Priestesses of that Temple were in charge of seeing to the welfare of the people in that district as well as maintaining the traditions and disciplines of the traditions based on the particular divinity being worshipped" (Ashby 2003a: 44). In similar vein, Born King Allah said concerning the Nation of Gods and Earths, "Not only were we making Allah world manifest we made New York the **CITY OF THE GODS** and everybody knew it." Indeed, "the Gods were not the first to call Harlem, Mecca [there was also] the Harlem Renaissance and luminaries such as Hurbert Harrison, W.E.B. Du Bois, Marcus Garvey, Zora Neale Hurston and Langston Hughes", as Divine Prince also explained (The Five Percenter Vol 20.9 2015: 3; Vol 22.4; 2016: 4).

Furthermore, each city in ancient Kemet relayed a knowledge tradition necessary for its own environment and deity, and each had their own narratives and symbols. The initiate in that particular city would meditate on the mysteries of their particular temples to unlock their secrets to divinity and immortality. Indeed, the Kemetic masters were also master engineers whose temples and pyramids were feats of advanced engineering accomplishments. Dr. Ashby stated concerning these ancient metropoles, "The Mysteries of Anu are considered to be the oldest exposition of the teachings of Creation and they formed a foundation for the unfoldment of the teachings of mystical spirituality which followed in the mysteries of the city of Hetkaptah through the Divinity in the name Ptah, and the Mysteries of Newt (Waset or Thebes), through the Divinity in the name Amun" (Ashby 2005a: 51).

Even so, as Houston mentioned, "The early population of Thebes was [undoubtedly] Nubian" (Houston 1985: 69); and not to flog a dead horse, but, "Keane says the Nubians [excelled] in moral qualities. They are by his description obviously Negroid, very dark with full lips and dreamy eyes" (Houston 1985: 34). Consequently, the most important mystery school in Kemet at the beginning of the dynastic era was not the one in Thebes but the one in Annu (which the Greeks called Heliopolis). To the people of Annu the centre of worship was Tum, the self-engendered autoerotic god who becomes Ra Atum. The Paut Neteru of Annu (in English: *the company of gods and goddesses of Heliopolis*) were all derived from this divine being. Again, "The Pyramid text of *Pepi II* determine the Company of gods and goddesses of Anu to be: Tem, Shu, Tefnut, Geb, Nut, Asar, Aset, Set and Nebthet" (Ashby 2003a: 108). Based on this list of the Pauti can be put together the Kemetic definitions of psychological development: Tem – the Creator, Shu – the perfectionist, Tefnut – the generous, Geb – the influential, Nut – the romantic, Ausar – the overseer, Auset – the mother, Setekh – the adversary, and Nebthet – the peacemaker.

The Paut Neteru also symbolised psychological states that had to be mastered to achieve the divine nature. As everything in ancient Kemet revolved within a cipher, the process of overcoming these psychological states had to be repeated annually to allow for the internalisation of godhood. Each title represented the god or goddess (though it would be better translated as the astral force or principle) who guarded those who lived out their trait. From February 21 to December 20 one was to train themselves up in mindfulness, meditation, and speech, to show themselves divine. From December 21 to December 24 they were then to consider the past year and stand trial before the fourteen judges (the Kemetic grandmasters or *Sebis*) who would decide whether they had attained divinity that year or not. It was a difficult process but by December 25, when the sun reappeared in the sky over Kemet, many had been acknowledged as divine Neteru.

It was study of the ancient books that allowed these initiates to attain to their divinity. An obvious example would be the Book of *Em Dwat*, which revealed the mysteries of the underworld and the secrets to immortality. Surprisingly, the Kemetic people did not believe in death but believed in the transitioning of the body from one form to another in the astral plane; thus immortality and divinity played a huge role in the Shetaut Neteru. The secret of divinity was contained in Ra and the secret to immortality was contained in Ausar. Thereby, it was believed that when these two gods united to become one it would be the end of this dispensation of life and the beginning of a brand new dispensation of life. Interestingly enough, these two gods would unite every night at the sixth hour of the night according to the Book of *Em Dwat*. This symbolic uniting of the two gods at what was symbolically meant to be the darkest hour of the night, and their symbolic uniting at what was further considered to be the darkest hour of winter (the winter solstice: December 21) have vague though discernible similarities.

To take this idea a little further, the initiates of Kemet would have also understood that just as the cycle of the earth on its axis produces physical ramifications (day and night), and the cycle of the earth around the sun also produces physical ramifications (the four seasons) even so, the great cycle of our star-system around the twelve zodiac must produce its own physical ramifications (which they considered to be four ages: from golden age, to silver age, to bronze age, to dark age – with the dark age being the winter). In our case, the winter solstice of the ages has apparently occurred in recent millennia, which means that Ra and Ausar have already been united and the secrets of divinity and immortality are now ready to be revealed.

When the lessons of the Book of *The Elevation of Ra and the Overcoming of Apop* meets the lessons of the Book of *Prt m Hru* – which is a name that translates to the Book of *Coming into Spiritual Light*, or the Book of *Going Forth as Enlightened*, or the Book of *Turning into a King* – then can true godhood in all its glory be attained. Again, the Kemetic people did not believe in death as such, they held that the soul was immortal. Their progressive salvation would come from the soul escaping the cycle or cipher of death and rebirth: that is, going into oblivion only to be reborn as a blank slate. When they died they wanted to remain in their then current state forever. This was immortality to the Kemetic people and only the initiate, the master, or the grandmaster could ever hope to achieve it.

Now based on these ideas we get a glimpse of the Kemetic spiritual system: the Book of *Em Dwat*, the Book of *Gates*, and the Book of *Prt m Hru* were to be studied till mastered in order to overcome release from the body and transition to another body. The key hope of all initiates was to enter the hereafter in a state of bliss: one either spent in Pet with Ra or in the Dwat with Ausar. "A righteous person has the choice to go to the Djed and abide in Asar, to merge with him, or they can await the time when Ra traverses through the Duat … illuminating it as He passes in his Boat. If they choose Ra, they will be picked up and be loaded unto the boat where they will merge with Ra and experience peace, bliss and happiness for all time. … If they choose to stay in the Duat, they will lead a life in the astral plane similar to that on earth but with very important differences" (Ashby 2005b: 129).

One of the unfortunate realities of ancient Kemet was that it was only the initiates, masters, and grandmasters that had any hope of attaining a life hereafter this congenial, or of even getting the choice to be united with Ra or Ausar. In order to prepare for the hereafter the initiates were also bound to the weighing of the heart ceremony in which the initiate stood before the fourteen judges to be tested on forty-two principles by chanting the *Nezemt* (or forty-two declarations of innocence): declarations that were not easy to make, as the standards of Kemet were such that nobody could have in all honesty passed; thus measuring the person's closeness to the divine standard. That is not to say, "I have not exaggerated," or "I have not prejudged," but, "I have not *unjustly* exaggerated," and "I have not *unjustly* prejudged" in that they have lived according to the ways of Maat (order, justice, and reciprocity) regardless of whom or what.

Again, if given a thorough interpretation no one would have honestly been able to pass the *Nezemt*, but the test was not whether one had or had not actually committed sin, but whether one could see the justice in spite of the sins they had committed. Thus the weighing of the heart was the weighing of guilt. The heart heavy with guilt would manifest itself even if the initiate tried to hide it. If failed the test would have to be taken again the following year to be one with Ausar, who was himself without guilt and innocent in all his ways. These examinations performed in ancient Kemet were not taken lightly either. The initiate had to train their body, their mind, their breathing, their posture, their words, and their tone. However, to any initiate in the Asarian mystery schools becoming one with Ausar was the ultimate goal.

In the Annuvian mystery schools it was a little more subtle, one became one with Ra through Khepru (or elevation). Herein the process was to train the mind, the body, and the soul to be free from the dominion of the Paut Neteru. Once free from the dominion of the Paut Neteru, the initiate would have been under the rule of only one God, Neb er Tcher (or Lord of All). Ra, himself the Most High God, was merely the aspect of Neb er Tcher that personified the sun in its circuits. Dr. Ashby wrote of this symbology when he said, "In Ancient Egyptian Mystical Symbolism the Journey of Ra is symbolic of the journey of the soul. Just as the sun is born in the east, traverses the sky and then dies in the west, a human being is said to come into existence (birth), live life and then die as well. Thus, it is beneficial to go to the west and stay there because this is the abode of the blessed. … However, those who are not ready to remain in the west due to their previous actions (karmic entanglements) and spiritual ignorance will be reborn again. Therefore the aspiration or desire is not to go to the east because the east symbolizes the land of reincarnation" (Ashby 2005a: 223).

But Ra was not considered to be the fulness of Neb er Tcher, he was only considered an aspect of him. Indeed, all the gods and goddesses were understood to be Neb er Tcher, that is, God-Collective. Hereby, the coincidence of Ra with Ausar in Neb er Tcher can be seen in this verse from the Asarian Mysteries: "Neb-er-tcher saith, I am the creator of what hath come into being in primeval time. I had union with my hand, and I embraced my shadow in a love embrace; I poured seed into my own mouth, and I sent forth from myself issue in the forms of the gods Shu and Tefnut" (Ashby 2005a: 48). The whole Annuvian drama is here given an Asarian makeover. True indeed, the Annuvian gods and goddesses, the Paut Neteru, were made one in Neb er Tcher, who himself was Pa Neter. Any individual only under the rule of Pa Neter was automatically considered a Neteru themselves, just like any Pharaoh who was only under the rule of the last dead Pharaoh was automatically a Horu. However, to be a god, just like to be a king, you had to be born into privilege, though not in ancient Ethiopia. In ancient Ethiopia you just had to be a part of the tribe and of the right age to acquire all the tribe's secrets. Here the tribesman who asked more questions would gain deeper knowledge of the traditions.

The current emphasis of the godbody here is on the Blackness of God and on God-Collective being in actuality filled primarily with Black people. This lesson is what separates us from the Nation of Islam and connects us to the people of ancient Kemet. Like our predecessors we have an initiation system, like our predecessors we have a symbolic mathematical system; and like Fakim Allah exclaimed, "You see the culture in us by the way we walk and the way we talk. Once a person gets knowledge of self, you'll see a drastic change in them" (The Five Percenter Vol 20.10; 2015: 4). But unlike our predecessors we currently do not view the Black woman as a Goddess. This systematic misogyny will be challenged in Chapter 5, but for now suffice it to say we are not currently a matriarchal system like the ancestors were in the golden age of these Nilotic schools of divinity. Still, the godbody represent a connection to the past: our initiation system has allowed us to also see self as divine and to appreciate the divinity of our fellow initiates even as in the ancient culture.

III

In Kemet the priests of the city of Annu taught that the gods and goddesses (the Neteru) all came from *the* God (Pa Neter) and that the God was Neb er Tcher, who they usually represented in the person of Tum. Within the search for divinity the most important thing one could learn was the knowledge of Tumu or self-creation. Self-creation to them was therefore central and essential in any form of a quest for divinity. The Absolute, the *Brahm*, the creation in and of itself, was Neb er Tcher, who to the citizens of Annu was personified in Tum, even as Tum himself was made up of the *Aakhu*, the *Ba*, and the *Ka*.

Accordingly, we can see how divinity begins in the mind with astral forces but it further expands to include social conditions. Once the mind is free the body will also seek to be free. Yet in order for us to identify the mechanisms of the mind more readily it will help again to return to the teachings of Freud. That which Freud called the id is very close to what the ancient Kemetics called the *Ba*. The *Ba*, like the id, was said to reside in the brain, and particularly in the hypothalamic region of the brain. However, according to Freud the id represented a predelineated, ahistorical, amoral, and instinctual aspect of our psyche that was driven purely by the pleasure principle.

The next aspect of the psyche that Freud called the superego the ancient Kemetics spoke of as the *Aakh* or *Aakhu*, which to them resided in the heart. Modern psychology is only now starting to catch up with this theory, even as Hedges said on the subject, "it is estimated by researchers that a sizable number of cells in the heart [themselves] are neurons, the same kind of cells that are found in the brain" (Hedges 2014: xxix). In fact, it has been estimated that there are up to 40,000 neurons in the heart, which perhaps explains why the heart is the most powerful electromagnet in the human body. Indeed, the electromagnetic energy in the heart is 5,000 times stronger than in the brain.

These two elements, the *Ba* and the *Aakhu*, both made up what the Shetaut Neteru, and makes up what godbody sociology, called and calls the astral force. The initiates in ancient Kemet also said that both of these elements reside in the *Ka*, which to them represented the astral body or psychic twin/double. The concept of the *Ka* is very similar to, though distinct from, Freud's own conception of the ego. Furthermore, as both the brain and the heart reside in the physical body, so both the *Ba* and the *Aakhu* theoretically resided in the astral body. This is how the unconscious and the conscious were unified in the *Ka*. Yet all three ancient Kemetic ideations were symbolised as embodied, whereas all these Freudian conceptions are far more abstracted. This current theory prefers to use the ancient Kemetic variation as it makes symbolic representation easier and less complicated.

However, instead of calling it the *Ka* it is called here the astral body.

This is also particularly helpful when considering the visualisation of the *Ka* fighting off unnatural *jinni*. As both the *Ba* and the *Aakhu* are unconscious level thought processes the *Ka* gives image to these entities and their interactions. The image of the *Ka* itself is the astrally projected double of the person; yet the *Ka*, in order to be perfected, must evolve (*Khepera*); and the best means of evolution is through self-creation (or the manifestation of *Tumu*). Consequently, in the process of evolution Tum mortified his flesh, or what the Kemetic people called the *Khat*, with masturbation, meditation, and yoga so as to escape the various trappings of carnality.

Masturbation, this act of self-satisfying and self-copulating, is utterly fruitless but to satisfy the flesh; while, at the same time, depriving it of the pleasures of actual sexual intercourse. According to Dr. Ashby, "Tum (Atum) is he who came into being (through Himself) in Anu. He took His phallus in His grasp that he might create joy in Himself, emitting the twins Shu (air, dryness, space, ether) and Tefnut (moistness)" (Ashby 2005b: 78). Thus his process of self-creation features masturbation up to the point of co-creation until there is finally procreation. Therefore, sexual congress is an act of divine love manifesting itself beautifully in the deity Atum, who, from the moment of masturbation, became Ra Atum, that is, the self-created God. This God loves so much that though there is no other being or object in the universe other than himself, he must copulate with himself in order to manifest that love. He cannot help but manifest his divinity as he cannot help but manifest libidinal love; and as he is wholly complete, self-sufficient, God fully and totally, he manifests that libidinal love to himself alone in order to begin the process of creation. Thus, Tum as Ra Atum is the divine self-creator.

Not only so, but in the ancient Kemetic mystery system it was Tum who birthed god, i.e., from Tum came Ra. Tum is Ra and Ra is Tum. Without Tum there can be no god and no godhood. At the same time, Tum, through self-creation, also became Nefer-Tum, that is, he became the beautiful self-creator. Nefer-Tum was the son of Ptah born in the origin out of the chaos of Nu and rising upon a lotus flower. It is easy to see from here the Kemetic valuing of meditation. This divine Nefer-Tum ultimately attained his divinity through meditating on self and on self-organising principles. The story works in this way: Ptah forms a thought in his heart (the most powerful electromagnet in the body), he then speaks forth through words of power (*hekau*) the thoughts he was thinking. First, he creates a mound to sit on, then he creates a body for himself, then he creates the lotus flower, which itself rises upon his lap, and from the midst of the lotus arises Tem who sits on it.

This initiation system of these Nilotic Black people is very reminiscent of that of the godbody, being immersed in meditative and mindful practices. Like with ancient Kemet, meditation and mindfulness are the key to our knowledge of self. Now within meditative and mindful philosophy there is what is called a great ocean of consciousness, and within the Kemetic story of creation there was also a great primordial ocean. Dr. Ashby explained the story as such, "The Ancient Egyptian Creation Myth tells of the emergence of Ra out of the Primeval Ocean. The ocean was unformed, undifferentiated matter. The emergence of Ra was synonymous with the coagulation of matter into various forms. In so doing, Ra established Maat (order) in the place of chaos" (Ashby 2005a: 219). Now the god Nu was the primordial chaos even as the lower stages of consciousness are internal chaos. Through meditation and mindfulness one learns to control or elevate beyond these lower stages, and like Tum, to self-create.

Tum, in himself, did not represent righteousness but he did represent the Highest Self, the union of *Ba* and *Aakhu* to form a

Self even higher than that of the *Ka*. Tum or Tem came into being by saying his name (or by Ptah saying his name). In other words, creation was birthed by vibration, and from vibration came waves. Atoms themselves are waves of neutral charge, each containing both positive and negative charges. As meditation and mindfulness allow for the production of thought, these thoughts go on to create brainwaves, which in turn are waves of electrical energy that essentially vibrate through our brain. Tum, the self-creator, was born from the great ocean of Nu bringing forth light out of the darkness. The light he called Ra and the darkness he called Apop. Tum chose the light over the darkness and so became Ra Atum. Thus Tum attained godhood (or Tum became Ra Atum) through meditative and mindful thought and yogic and symbolic action.

According to certain other Annuvian explanations Ra Atum was alone in Nu so he breathed out Djehwti, who was symbolic of his word, and he created Hethor and Maat as his two eyes. Maat and Djehwti then coupled and created the Dwat, Pet, and Ta. They themselves then dwelt in the Dwat, or astral-space (the realm of visualisation), Ra Atum and Hethor dwelt in Pet, or phase-space (the realm of causality), but no one dwelt in Ta, or time-space (the realm of physicality). Then Ra Atum's hand embraced his penis and from his masturbation came Shu and Tefnut, that is, wind and moisture respectively. From Shu and Tefnut came Geb and Nut, that is, soil and sky respectively. From Geb and Nut came Ausar and Auset, that is, the masculine and feminine of vegetation respectively; and Setekh and Nebthet, that is, desert and matriarchal civilisation respectively. Then, from the eyes of Ra Atum came human beings. All these dwelt then in Ta until certain changes occurred that caused each of the gods and goddesses to relocate into new locations.

Ra Atum's further use of yogic practices also helped him to develop an interconnection to the universe around him. We too, through yogic interaction with our environment, can develop an interconnection to those things that we best identify with. True, in time those things we are interconnected with will soon become bonded with us so that we all develop a level of interdependence with each other. The closer we draw to our prescribed destiny, the more interconnected we will become to it, and the more powerful and traumatic a force or entity it will take to sever that bond. The act of self-creation is thereby *Tumu* and to create self as god is Ra Atum. In order to begin this process one must first cut oneself off from the world and the worldly; primarily devoting oneself to Egyptian Yoga or Sema Tawi. Dr. Ashby said on the subject, "The Ancient Egyptian equivalent of yoga is: **'Smai.' Smai** (Sma, Sema, Sama) means union, and the following determinative terms give it a spiritual significance, at once equating it with the term 'Yoga' as it is used in India" (Ashby 2005b: 40).

Egyptian Yoga was effectively practiced in ancient Egypt long before Indian yoga was practiced in India; as Dr. Ashby further continued, "The Ancient Egyptian language and symbols provide the first 'historical' record of Yoga Philosophy and Religious literature. The Indian culture of the Indus Valley Dravidians and Harappans appear to have carried it on and expanded much of the intellectual expositions in the form of the Vedas, Upanishads, Puranas and Tantras, the ancient spiritual texts of India" (Ashby 2005b: 41). Yet in a technical sense these traditions even predated Egypt as they can actually be traced all the way back to the ancient Ethiopians, "The Dravidians in ethnic type are Ethiopian and are the race of India from which her civilization originated" (Houston 1985: 223). Houston (1985) also continued that these Ethiopians who migrated to India were the very people who founded the Vedic and Yogic traditions of India; thereby showing that the link between Indian Yoga and Egyptian Yoga is because both shared the same origin in ancient Ethiopia.

Dr. Ashby then went on to inform us, "Yoga in all of its forms was practiced in [Africa] earlier than anywhere else in our history.

This unique perspective from Africa provides a new way to look at life, religion and the discipline of psychology. Perhaps most importantly though, Egyptian mythology, when understood as a system of Yoga, gives every individual insight into their own divine nature" (Ashby 2005b: 40). Here, Sema Tawi becomes the ancient Egyptian concept of yoga, a concept developed by the ancient Ethiopians and passed down to the people of Abdu in Egypt. Again, whereas in the Annu tradition Tem was the Highest Self, in the Abdu tradition Ausar was the Highest Self.

Ashby said concerning Ausar, "Asar is also an Avatar, a divine incarnation into time and space, the incarnation of the … Self, the Soul, into the realm of time and space" (Ashby 2005b: 85). Even so, as he continued, "In ancient times, Egypt was divided into two sections or land areas. These were known as Lower and Upper Egypt. In Ancient Egyptian mystical philosophy, the land of Upper Egypt relates to the divinity Heru (Heru), who represents the Higher Self, and the land of Lower Egypt relates to Set, the divinity of the lower self. So *Smai Taui* means 'the union of the two lands' or the 'Union of the lower self with the Higher Self'" (Ashby 2005b: 41).

Sema Tawi in the Abdu tradition was Sema Horu-Setekh and developed from these basic ideas. Ashby related a case in point, "There is a picture, related to the Ancient Egyptian epic story of *The Ausarian Resurrection*, which shows the character[s] Heru … and Set … as sharing one body with two heads, that of Heru and that of Set. The Heru-Set figure leads us to understand that Heru and Set are not two separate individuals, but two aspects of the same character. The entire story of the Ausarian Resurrection hinges on this very point" (Ashby 2005a: 218). There is also a picture featuring Horu and Setekh standing together and tying down the Sema hieroglyphic symbol, which "symbolizes the union of Heru and Set [and] is a mystical code for the uniting or harmonizing the lower and Higher Self in the individual human being. It means achieving inner harmony and peace with the universe, the culmination of the Ancient Egyptian injunction: *Know Thyself*" (Ashby 2005a: 218).

Now for those who do not know, Ashby also related the main story of the Abdu tradition, which was known as the *Asr Uhem Ankh* (the Asarian Resurrection): "The central and most popular character within the Ancient Egyptian Religion of Asar is Heru, who is an incarnation of his father, Asar. Asar is killed by his brother Set who, out of greed and demoniac (Setian) tendency, craved to be the ruler of Egypt. With the help of Djehuti, the God of wisdom, Aset, the great mother and Hetheru, his consort, Heru prevailed in the battle against Set for the rulership of Kemet (Egypt)" (Ashby 2005b: 41). Even so, the Kemetic story of the Contestation of Horu and Setekh represented the subjecting of Setekh to Horu and was likened to the subduing of the flesh and subjecting it to the Highest Self of Ausar or Atum. This was the goal of most of the yogic traditions in Kemet.

Effectively, "Mythology and spiritual symbolism were never intended to be understood as factual events which occurred in a particular place in time exclusively. Rather, they are to be understood as ever recurring principles of human life which need to be understood in their deepest sense in order for them to provide humanity with the benefit of their wisdom" (Ashby 2005b: 28). So as "Heru [eventually] prevailed in the battle against Set for the rulership of Kemit (Egypt). [Even so,] Heru's struggle symbolizes the struggle of every human being to regain rulership of the Higher Self and subdue the lower self" (Ashby 2005a: 38). In like manner, "When the wisdom teachings are studied deeply and the mystical implications are understood, a special form of transformation occurs which leads to the discovery of the highest spiritual truths within one's heart. Discovering this glorious truth of your true nature. This is the goal of yoga and all mystical philosophies" (Ashby 2005a: 96). But to complete the process of yogic development the self must ultimately mortify the flesh, that is, the *Khat*, transcending it through masturbation, meditation/mindfulness, and yoga.

IV

There is an even deeper explanation, coming from the Annuvian mysteries, for the process of awakening the Highest Self; still, in order to understand it we must explore it piece-by-piece. Essentially, in this narrative the story begins with a *benben* stone arising from the primordial chaos and carrying with it a *benu* bird. The importance of these ideas may be easily overlooked at first; but to the Kemetic people the word *benu* could be translated as the modern word phoenix. Basically, the *benu* was that mythical bird symbolic both of the *Ba* and the bird form of Ra, showing and carrying many deep meanings to the Kemetic people. Remember, the *Ba* was supposed to symbolise those instinctual drives that motivate our unconscious. The *Ba* of Ra being the divine drives was always painted as a phoenix – which itself was a *benu* falcon. This meant that, in the process of self-creation we can reach a point when our instincts are driven by the deity. This is the whole ideological adjustment theory. The theory states that we are not born with hate or love, we learn them as we enter into adolescence and adulthood. Neither our sexual fetishes nor our racial prejudices are predetermined, they are learned through experiences, and anything you can learn you can also unlearn.

When somebody's *Ba* is completely right and exact their *Ba* becomes like the falcon to the Kemetic people, which soared through the sky and apparently never landed. The falcon dwelt in the heavens alone, that was its home, just like the sun – also symbolic of Ra. But a phoenix also brought healing in its wings. Hence, the self-created Ra could also help organise others towards their own self-healing. Here the *benben* stone also symbolised a mound or mount from which a master or grandmaster could share their lessons. It could even represent a platform from which a teacher or preacher could give their message. Ultimately, it was significant only inasmuch as the divine man or divine woman used it. Hence, it was the platform from which the Medu Neteru (hieroglyphic symbology) was taught. "These writings were inscribed in temples, coffins and papyruses and contained the teachings in reference to the spiritual nature of the human being and the ways to promote spiritual emancipation, awakening or resurrection" (Ashby 2005a: 41).

But bringing enlightenment and self-creation into one's environment (thus making oneself god of or to that environment) reinforced personal self-creation too. The more we guide others toward self-creation the more we show them how to manifest divinity. The more we make others divine the more divine we ourselves become. Just like the positive energy radiated from yogic practices so is the positive energy radiated by positive co-creation. And just like, "The goal of yoga is to promote integration of the mind-body-spirit complex in order to produce optimal health of the human being. [Even so, this] is accomplished through mental and physical exercises which promote the free flow of spiritual energy by reducing mental complexes caused by ignorance" (Ashby 2003a: 59).

Hence, "If you study, rationalize and reflect upon the teachings, you are practicing *Yoga of Wisdom*. If you meditate upon the teachings and your Higher Self, you are practicing *Yoga of Meditation*. If you practice rituals which identify you with your spiritual nature, you are practicing *Yoga of Ritual Identification* ... If you develop your physical nature and psychic energy centers, you are practicing *Serpent Power* ... *Yoga* (which is part of Tantric Yoga). If you practice living according to the teachings of ethical behavior and selflessness, you are practicing *Yoga of Action* (Maat) in daily life." (Ashby 2003a: 23). Basically, Ra Atum, as the central sungod and the phoenix, organised not only the inner self through masturbation, meditation, and mindfulness, but also the cosmos and the environment around him through yogic interaction and teaching.

But according to tradition the phoenix usually died at night-time being consumed by its own flame, before it rose from the ashes to take to the skies again. This was the price of its existence as a form of Ra Atum: so long as it was Ra Atum it had to self-organise, self-create, and become absolute and absolutely God. But this absolutising would become all-consuming and included all that was close to it and all that came close to it. Ra Atum was not and could not be satisfied with just meditating, mindfulness, and yoga. Ra Atum also had to make all things divine, and thus had to free all things from self-destructive existence.

Here a master through meditative and mindful thinking, and through interdependent yogic action, could prove themselves divine by taking and tolerating and accepting death. Like the phoenix they would die willingly knowing that they would rise again in the morning. Even without this knowledge they would still accept death as a means of attaining or proving divinity. This is the sacred step and where refinement would begin: the sacrificing of self to attain to the broader Self. But refinement by self-sacrificing love was never easy, so Ra Atum became an expression of more than simply self-mortifying humiliation, he also became an expression of a self-denying master or initiate.

In the Annuvian traditions Ra Atum, after creating himself, then created Hethor, not only to be his right eye but also to be his hand. The two of them then embark on a co-creation expedition of the elemental forces of nature: fluids, liquids, solids, and lucids. Without interaction Ra Atum would have been stuck at self-creating/self-sacrificing mode. He created Hethor by imagining her there, then interacting with what he had imagined. She was not real – though she was the mother of kings – but for the fact that God had willed for her to exist. Thus, through visualisation Ra Atum began the process, not only of self-creation – which he already completed when he became Ra Atum – but also of co-creation.

Therefore, in the process of co-creating one's universe it always remains important to remember the effect that Other will have on self and that self will have on Other. This is particularly important with regards to how we define ourselves and how we join together like with like through self-organisation. Sometimes resistance to the merger may occur at either or both ends of the unifying. These instances of self-destructive and abortive tendencies may block co-creation and unification if they are not quenched by all co-creative tendencies in the earlier phases. At these moments a reassessment of core self-defining concepts will be necessary. Co-creation occurred for Tem when he produced Hethor, but its initial phase was when he became Ra Atum. All things of necessity adjust and self-organise not all things, however, are able to acknowledge their own divinity.

Unrefined man coincides with unrefined woman so that co-creation effectively produces self-destruction. However, if the woman is refined and exhibits the qualities of the divine nature then life itself will sever any relationships that are self-destructive. Her nature alone will bring likeminded people into her company. This is when we see divinity manifesting itself in her life, for the Gods and Goddesses that come into her life from the time she devotes herself to refinement will themselves be refined and will admire her refinement. But to maintain the unique quality of divinity they will have to abort certain relationships in their own lives that may prove unfruitful moving forward.

In Annu it took a studying of these types of mystical lessons for one to become a proper adept. Different variations of the lessons applied from city to city but the goal was always the same: to conquer the lower self and gain alignment with the Highest Self. Back then, Ra was the personification of godhood and was translated: the enlightened one. Thus Ra represented that being of higher consciousness and the level one reached through meditative, mindful, and yogic practices, thereby becoming one with creation. At this state of enlightenment, the *Ka* would merge with the Tem (the Self or the self-creator/self-created) to allow Tem to transform it into what it was supposed to be. Accordingly, the *Ka* stopped struggling and trying to preserve what little self it had and allowed the broader Self to take full control. There was no rule, no power, no force, just the easy letting go and allowing the Self to dictate what path one went in.

Dr. Ashby further informed us again, "When you aquifer true insight into the nature of the Self ... it means that you have glimpsed into eternity, your own eternity, your own divinity. This is true knowledge, born of your own experience of the Divine" (Ashby 2005a: 121). Enlightenment was essentially considered oneness with the Divine, or Neb er Tcher. It was the throwing away of a false self-identity and the adopting of a true and real and living self-identity. Through transcendence of the sensational world one could begin the process of turning their *Ba* into a *Benu*. This transformation was called Khepru or evolution. But the transformative process had to be performed through interaction. Ra was the *Benu* bird but he was also the central sungod. The significance of the light of the sun with regard to enlightenment is here undeniable. The sun provides light, life, healing, and warmth, just like the *Benu* bird, and the *Ba* of those who are enlightened. But the sun can also be powerful and destructive just like any powerful being that lacks knowledge of self.

V

The city of Net Djehwti, which was called by the Greeks Hermopolis, developed an entirely different theology based on the god Djehwti. According to Dr. Ashby, "Djehuti is the god of learning, writing, mathematics and language. Djehuti is referred to as Thoth by the Greeks. In Ancient Egyptian mythology, he is the scribe of the gods. He appears as the record keeper of the dead in the *Books of Coming Forth By Day*. He is the patron of learning and of the arts. He is the inventor of writing, and in the specific theology related to him, he is also seen as the Creator of the universe" (Ashby 2003b: 78). Within this tradition Djehwti was the father of the Khemnu (Ogdoad) whom he created by stirring the ocean of Nu with his *Sekhem* (Caduceus).

The Khemnu of Net Djehwti were eight Neteru that appeared from the chaotic vibratory waves before anything was ever manifested: Nun and Nunet (the male and female equivalents of formless energy, respectively); Heh and Hehet (the male and female equivalents of infinity, respectively); Kuk and Kuket (the male and female equivalents of darkness, respectively); and Amun and Amunet (the male and female equivalents of astrality, respectively). Then, "Suddenly, with a burst of creative energy." As Tyldesley recounted, "the Mount of Flame rose out of the [vibrations]. A lotus bud pushed through the mound. Opening, the blossom revealed the sun god in the form of a child" (Tyldesley 2011: 55). Thus, in the Shetaut Net Djehwti it was Djehwti who set the creation epic in motion with the power of his Caduceus.

So the question now becomes, who was Djehwti to the people of Net Djehwti? "Djehuti is the master teacher who initiates the aspirant on the spiritual path of wisdom. In teaching others, the priest or priestess [thereby assumed] the role of Djehuti" (Ashby 2005b: 95). Moreover, "He was also called the lord of the truth … and the thrice great … from this last description, the Greek writers derived the word Trismegistos since he is the greatest of all theologians, the greatest of all scientists and philosophers and the greatest of all royals" (Seleem 2004: 75). Djehwti was also considered the first of the beings to honour Pa Neter, and to teach the Neteru and people of Kush how to honour Pa Neter.

According to Dr. Seleem, "The ancient Egyptians believed in one almighty God, who has no form, shape, gender or name. *Tehuty* (Hermes), the founder of this spiritual system and the original author of The Book of Life, said,

None of our thoughts are capable of conceiving God, nor any language of defining Him. That which is incorporeal, formless, invisible, cannot be grasped by our senses. That which is eternal cannot be measured by the short rules of time. God is, accordingly, ineffable" (Seleem 2004: 11).

Djehwti, in that sense, could be called the first true theocentric, who wrote several books to humanity that were part of the original Kemetic canon. These books are now lost to history but spoke on various sciences, arts, mathematics, philosophies, ethics, poetry, technology, architecture, and yogic disciplines. "Some classical writers, like Clement of Alexandria, said that forty-two of the books of *Tehuty* were kept in the Library of Alexandria but were burned when the Romans entered Egypt in 30 BC and burned one wing of the Library of Alexandria" (Seleem 2004: 76). Now as we have noted Djehwti was a *Sebi* (grandmaster preceptor) that taught both astral and physical beings. This he did via both of the forms of the Medu Neteru (words of the divinities). See, the Medu Neteru were not just divine words when spoken, when written down they were also always written as hieroglyphs.

Conversely, as Dr. Ashby was not slow to mention, "Djehuti [was] the spiritual preceptor of two important Kamitian Divinities, Hetheru and Heru. [In both stories he] fixes their faulty vision, i.e., he enlightens their intellect" (Ashby 2003b: 82). With regard to Hethor he tells the story thusly, "One variation of the story holds that the Eye left Ra and went to Nubia in the form of a lioness (Hetheru, in her aspect as destroyer of evil and unrighteousness). When Ra heard this, he sent the Nubian god *Ari-Hems-Nefer*, a form of Shu and Djehuti to bring the Eye back. ... The Eye refused to leave because it had learned to enjoy its new existence. It was destroying those who had committed sins (plotted against Ra) while on earth. Djehuti [then] worked his magic on the Eye and brought it back to Ra" (Ashby 2005: 94). While there were many versions of this story: some featuring Maat as the Eye and others featuring Sekhmet as the Eye, it was always Djehwti who ultimately solved the problem.

Now the goddess Sekhmet (who was Hethor in her destructive manifestation), herself had a name derived from the word *sekhem*, which meant power, force, and was also an electromagnetic body to the people of Kemet. In this sense, Sekhmet was similar to the Hindu goddess Shakti, who is the kundalini goddess. Shakti, like Sekhmet, is the dynamic form of Shiva and her name meant power and force too. Sekhmet herself was always hungry for power and fed on energy. She loved to destroy, hurt, and punish. Indeed, Sekhmet on her own was raw, unbridled power as can be seen in the story of the destruction of the world at her hands. But when she was focused and channelled in the right direction she was the greatest of healers, warriors, protectors, and defenders. In like manner the taming of Sekhmet was similar to the rising of the kundalini to Samadhi. But before the kundalini can rise it is necessary for it to first awaken.

According to the Tantric arts there are four main ways to awaken the kundalini: (i) Yoga – this could be hatha yoga, kriya yoga, raja yoga, or karma yoga. In fact, any form of yoga could be used to awaken the kundalini if practiced regularly and with patience. Kemet also had their own yogic systems in Sema Tawi which each led to the awakening of the kundalini (the *arat*). (ii) Mantras – this could be chants, affirmations, or word spells. In Kemet these were called *hekau*. (iii) *Tapasya* – this word means purity and to the Tantrics it means holiness. It is the living of such a holy and devoted life that kundalini easily awakens within the yogi. In Kemet this was called *abu* (purification) and it was an arduous process. (iv) *Maithuna* – this word means literally the "sacrifice" of sexual intimacy. Not that one gives up on having sex, but that one prolongs the pleasure of the sexual experience by sacrificing the discharge or ejaculation. Sex to a Tantric is sacred and it is one of the fastest ways to awaken the kundalini. In Kemet it was called *an-sti* (literally: no ejaculation).

Any one of these methods could awaken the kundalini causing all kinds of supernatural/supersensory experiences to transpire. But in the Tantric arts it is also beneficial if one also goes through three other awakenings before the kundalini. First, what the Tantrics call the *ida* and *pingala nadis* have to be awakened and cleansed. The *nadis* are like channels or pathways for energy to flow through. The *ida nadi* controls the mental process and the right hemisphere of the brain; the *pingala nadi* controls the life force and the left hemisphere of the brain. These two spiral up the central shaft of the spinal column called the *sushumna nadi*. In Kemet the *ida* was called Nekhbet, the *pingala* was called Wadjat and the *sushumna* was called the Sekhem Arat. All three were called the Arati.

According to Dr. Ashby, "There are three most important channels through which the Serpent Power flows. In India these are known as: *Sushumna, Ida and Pingala*. These are represented by the Egyptian Caduceus of Djehuti which is composed of a staff which has two serpents wrapped around it. Thus, in the Kemetic mystical system, the three main channels of Life Force energy of the Serpent Power may be understood as being presided over by three divinities" (Ashby 2005b: 124). These were Sekhem, Wadjat, and Nekhbet, respectively. The second awakening would be of the seven chakras, which were called in Kemet the Sefekh Ba Ra (seven divine channels), each one unlocking further supersensory potential. The third awakening would be of the *sushumna nadi* or the Sekhem Arat. Then, finally, the kundalini or Sekhmet would be awakened. If the first three awakenings did not occur before Sekhmet, then she would be a destructive force that would destroy not only the individuals one interacted with, but also the mental stability of the one who had awakened her.

Djehwti, as the wise *Sebi* instructor, guided Hethor through all of these awakenings by teaching her the Medu Neteru. Again,

Hethor was called the Eye of Ra, but when the Eye was awakened by one who was not guided by a master, it could easily turn out to be destructive. Dr. Ashby was very clear about this, saying, "the plight of the Eye and its subsequent restoration through the teachings of Djehuti in the *Udja Hetheru* text as the transmitter of wisdom, embodies the principle of the teacher-disciple relationship [through] which spiritual knowledge is transmitted" (Ashby 2005b: 95). Basically, the Eye (*Wdjat*), was symbolic of supersensory perception, particularly astral vision. When this is acquired without the guidance of a genuine master it is not only destructive but potentially produces nothing but wickedness and corruption. Only through a genuine *Sebi* or Guru is one able to learn how to use supersensory abilities wisely and justly, and not for one's own sake or in ways contrary to the will of God.

Dr. Ashby also noted, "The same teaching of the Eye is to be found in the story of Heru and Set where Set (ego) tore out Heru's Eye. It is Djehuti who restored the Eye through the power of magic (wisdom teaching). In this context, the whole teaching of wisdom which Djehuti applies (*Hekau*) to the Eye causes it to remember its essential nature and its glory as the Eye of Heru" (Ashby 2005b: 95). Thus Djehwti was also the *Sebi* of Horu and *his* guide in the teachings of the Medu Neteru. Moreover, in the sense that Djehwti was the Neter of magic, whenever he used *hekau* (magic words) they were also considered to be Medu Neteru (divine words).

Even though to the initiates of Net Djehwti: just as Djehwti could bend reality with his *hekau* (magic words, commands, or words of power), they also believed that they could bend reality and perform the supersensory by mastering *hekau*. Not only so, but to the initiates of Djehwti history itself was bendable and changeable through *hekau*, thereby making the Net Djehwti initiates not so much foretellers as forth-speakers speaking and creating their own reality. These initiates were the *Shemsu Djehwti* but as *Shemsu* (followers, travellers, pilgrims) they held to a high code based on self-knowledge and righteous living. A *shems*, to the Kemetic people, was one who was an initiate in the mysteries. Thereby a *shems* or *shem* always followed a path.

Moreover, a *shems* was devoted to the path they followed, living completely according to its principles. Dr. Ashby (2003: 165) also noted that in the hieroglyphic language of the Medu Neteru the word "*Shems* [was depicted as] a staff with a package attached to it and at the top of the package there [was] a knife. The determinative ... of legs facing forwards, provides the ideal of 'movement towards' ... The legs are conscious effort to move in the direction of what is truth, to follow the divine where it leads. *Shemsu* ... are followers. There [were] two types of followers, ... *shemsu neteru* – 'followers of the divinity' and the ... *Shems-ab* – 'followers [of the] desire of one's heart, greed, lust, wishes.'" Basically, the *Shemsu Neteru* were the followers of the Shetaut Neteru who spoke the words of the Medu Neteru. In the Net Djehwti theology, therefore, to be a *Shemsu Neteru* was akin to being of the Paut Neteru (God-Collective). Effectively, as Djehwti taught the Medu Neteru, so the *Shemsu Neteru* also taught the Medu Neteru.

VI

In the Abdu traditions initiates sought to be one with Ausar, thereby becoming wise and not arrogant or hungry for power. When elevation went wrong the *shems* was not on the path to Ausar consciousness but on the path to Setekh, i.e. the lower self. In Abdu, Setekh was seen as more guided by his passions than by a desire for wholeness. Yet, "When the lower self (Set) is mastered and placed in the service of the Higher Self (Heru ...), then spiritual realization is assured" (Ashby 2005a: 145). In Abdu, Ausar represented the Tum principle of the Highest Self. Accordingly, "Discovering the Self within your heart [dispels] the malady of ignorance about the contents of the universe. Having discovered the Self within your heart there will be nothing left to discover. All that is to be known will be known" (Ashby 2005a: 122). The self can gain alignment with the Self through learning to attach itself to those who are also seeking enlightenment. Through interaction with them an Ausar can be free from fruitless and useless interaction and bring guidance to the lost.

The Abdu traditions did, however, contain some differences – mainly related to the trinity of Ausar, Auset, and Horu. The Abdu mysteries taught that unity with Horu was only a preliminary step of initiation; the final position aimed for was unity with Ausar, the father of Horu. To become a Horu the Pharaoh had to rule wisely and combat the forces of tyranny, injustice, and disorder (an-Maat) personified in Setekh and in his wiles. In like manner, the initiate (*shems*) had to confront Setekh and his ways of unrighteousness by standing against social and public wrongs in society. Those who practiced unrighteousness (an-Maat) were the children of Setekh and were opposed by the initiates, who sought unity with Horu. But the initiates were also protected by Horu and Ausar from the forces of Setekh. Still, defeating Setekh meant more than defeating external unrighteousness, it meant a complete devotion internally to righteousness. This was making the choice to practice spiritual principles in one's daily life. The life devoted to spiritual principles was the life that would ultimately gain access to greater knowledge of the divine and how to attain to divinity. This was a Horu, an initiate (*shems*) devoted to godliness.

So what is the importance of these Abdu traditions of Ausar and Setekh to us modern Black people? It cannot be doubted that the murder of one's brother leaves a formidable impression on the psyche. Here Freud is ever so helpful in his recollection of the murder of the primeval father, the ancestral Oedipus conflict; though in the Abdu tradition it is not the father that is murdered, it is in fact the brother. But from where has Freud conjectured his ancestral Oedipus conflict? And can psychic representation be a reasonable replacement for actual facts? Well, we can never know with certainty the actual occurrences of antiquity. However, there are left to us traces in the mythological traditions, here Greek mythology assists us further with the odd but significant repetition of patricidal incidents.

First, Chaos, who is done in by his son Uranus. Then, Uranus is castrated by his youngest son Kronos. Then, Kronos is done in by his youngest son Zeus. It is easy to see that the Greeks had a longing, indeed, a lust, to do away with the father figure. Thus, what to the people of Kemet was signified as the murder of the brother and perpetrated by "lower level" individuals seeking personal glory out of jealousy and greed, to the classical Greeks was more the murder of the father and was perpetrated by the aspiring to obtain release from an oppressive figure. It is clear to see that the Black and White did not share the same psychic connection as the traditions of the classical Greeks and the ancient Egyptians were significantly different. Where the Greeks, and thereby the Whites, have Oedipus; we Blacks had Horu. Horu does not murder his father and marry his mother. Horu is raised by the mother and avenges the father, not on the mother, whom he loves, but on the uncle who murdered him.

This has implications. Whereas Oedipus has no significant moral compass other than the search for knowledge, Horu is moved forward by a desire for justice. As Dr. Ashby stated in his book *Egyptian Yoga: Volume 2*, there are always "unconscious impressions which are formed as a result of one's actions ... These impressions can be either positive or negative. Positive impressions are developed through positive actions by living a life of righteousness and virtue (Maat). This implies living according to the precepts of mystical wisdom or being a follower of Heru (Horus) (*Shemsu Hor*) and Aset ... These actions draw one closer to harmony and peace, thus paving the way to discover the Self within" (Ashby 2005a: 124). The Horu construct actually existed in the male initiate from early childhood and continued with him into adulthood. Though Horu meant light, day, and enlightenment, it also meant above, chief, and king in the proper and actual senses of the word, and every boy in ancient Egypt therefore was a potential Horu in the symbolic. But the Horu-child had to confront injustice and be taught by his mother (or, indeed, his father) spiritual principles.

At once every Black boy becomes a potential Horu as they face injustice from early youth and are in all cases taught spiritual principles from their mother. However, these alone do not define the Horu-child, the Horu-child must come to terms with the death of his father(s). And by a modern interpretation it is beyond doubt that the Black boy is of all people most subject to injustice himself and the injustice committed against his forefathers by the system he was born into. Yet to become a Horu he must also appreciate how these spiritual principles apply to him and his people. He must consider how to make sense of his plight and the plight of his people and his ancestors without sacrificing himself to the hands of the system. The system that killed his father will try to kill him too; therefore he must consider ways to defeat the system through those spiritual principles.

Horu is the Black man/boy while, at the same time, being the divine king/prince. Horu was a Neter of enlightenment just like Ra: thereby showing he was and is the personification of every male initiate, and, at the same time, the principles they had to follow to become an initiate. Every Horu may have wanted to be one with Ausar, but every boy wanted to be one with Horu; and to be a Horu meant one lived by spiritual principles. This Horu construct also had its counterpart in the Hethor construct: here the feminine qualities were distinguished from the male. The Hethor Black woman/girl was also the divine queen/princess. Hethor was the Netrit of femininity and the goddess concept personified. Both male and female had both constructs in them from early childhood and both had to be navigated effectively to reach the place of elevation (*khepru*) beyond them. The Horu construct is represented today when the hypermartial inclinations of the lower self are directed towards fighting injustice and tyranny. The Hethor construct is represented today when the hypersexual energies of the lower self are put under our own self-control and directed towards the uplifting of self and kind.

The Black boy becomes a Horu and develops his Horu construct as he grows and learns more spiritual principles. The same with the Black girl, as she gains more spiritual knowledge her Hethor construct develops. But I go deeper into these constructs and the ancestral Ausar in my first book in series *Black Divinity* if the reader wishes to learn more about these subjects. Again, Horu was also a king, thus it was a high honour to be called one with Horu; and this honour did not come easily, it came at a cost. Only the initiated could have access to the books to learn the mysteries. Only a priest, one born into the priestly family, or one proven to be wise, could learn the mystery lessons unless of royal blood. The hierarchy of Kemet was set in stone and only those who could afford the books or were found worthy to enter the mysteries were able to acquire the lessons.

Not so with the public. They were denied the lessons of the mysteries and so to them the secrets of ancient Kemet were just that: a mystery. It appears that the forces of injustice and inequality counted only so far as heredity was concerned. The son (or daughter) of a priest, a king, or a *Sebi* could acquire the mystery lessons but not the average worker in the country. This inequality explains why so many Egyptologists believed that the people of Kemet, with all their knowledge of science and technology, were a primitive group of idolaters with a primitive mythological system.

Not much has changed historically and initiation orders still reserve the higher honours for those who master their lessons. The public at large are, however, denied the opportunity to learn any of the secrets of the order and are kept completely in the dark as to their symbolisms. In this, the Kemetic mysteries are very similar to the Supreme Wisdom lessons of the Nation of Islam, and the Kushite tribal system is matched by the godbody ciphers. Any and every member of a Kushite tribe had access to the lessons of their tribe and it seems that the entire tribe was literate and well trained in the arts, such that their land could be called Ta Neteru. Even so the godbody: we all have access to the lessons and we have a very able and literate following. Only, unlike Kush, who taught Kemet their lessons, we godbody gained most of our teachings from the Supreme Wisdom lessons of the Nation of Islam.

VII

In considering now some more prominent ways in which the ancient Nilotic Black people were similar to us godbodies we must, first of all, appreciate how they defined the divine Black people. By the standards of ancient Kemet the divine Black people were those who were equal to Maat. Now, "Maat is the daughter of Ra, and she was with him on his celestial boat when he first emerged from the primeval waters along with his company of gods and goddesses. She is also known as the *eye of Ra, Lady of heaven, Queen of the earth, Mistress of the Netherworld and the lady of the gods and goddesses* ... In the form of Maati, she represents the South and the North which symbolize Upper and Lower Egypt as well as the Higher and lower self. Maat is the personification of justice and righteousness upon which God has created the universe, and Maat is also the essence of God and creation" (Ashby 2005b: 104).

What we can see, therefore, is that if the Black person becomes equal to Maat then they not only get access to divinity but also to the union of the lower self and the Higher Self respectively. In this, the Black person, through the doctrine of the godbody, becomes a *Shemsu Hor*. This is where politics and politicking also come into play. The Gods politick at ghetto parliaments where we discuss issues facing the godbody movement. As the young Black man grows he understands that

128

these parliamentary discussions are an open door to revealing injustices within the Black community and various means to combat them. If social justice issues are not discussed at these parliaments and only celebratory back-patting then the godbody become merely a useless group of intellectuals who can and do effect no change to the system that corrupts and imprisons their kind. Justice cannot be just if it does not confront injustice, and godbodies cannot be Gods if we do not confront ungodliness.

The universal laws were thereby known by the *Sebi* of ancient Kemet, however, these *Sebis* also fought to keep their people in ignorance, for the central reason that they were too ignorant(!). The people of Kemet were predominantly idolatrous, superstitious, and sun-, wood-, stone-, metal-, and nature-worshippers. The *Sebis* of Kemet knew and taught the lessons only among themselves and among the various *shemsu* (initiates). Moses grew up in this tradition, which obviously disgusted him, so he started his own tradition and taught the Shetaut lessons to slaves, the lowest of the low, in complete defiance of how things were done in Kemet. Moses, having reached the age of forty, was effectively worthy to be an actual *Sebi*, and very likely even passed the ordination process to be an actual *Sebi* of the Shetaut Amun.

Furthermore, according to Dr. Seleem, "The initiates of the ancient Egyptian religion included Moses, Abraham, Plato, Pythagoras, Solon, Homer, Thales, Buddha, Huang-Ti, Hu and Ceridwin (the founders of the Druids). Indeed, the Gnostics, Kabalists, Mazdeans, Taoists, Druids, Buddhists and Australian Aborigines also embraced [their] concepts" (Seleem 2004: xvii). While it is doubtable whether all these men were actual *Shemsu* of the Shetaut Neteru − despite their own affirmations to the positive − considering how secretive and exclusivist they were with their own people let alone with foreigners. Still, we can be very sure that all these men at least came to Egypt and studied from the Library of Alexandria the vast collection of scientific books they had stored. Again, the modern equivalent to the

Library of Alexandria could be either the British Library or maybe even the Amazon bookstore. Either way, one does not need to be a part of an order like the Masons to learn and master the sciences of today. That said, as all the sciences of Kemet were based largely on monism, those that studied in Kemet definitely at least headed in that direction, even if not all of them became actual practicing monists.

Nevertheless, while concepts like the universal laws of existence may themselves seem somewhat falsified by the historical and physical evidence, such is only from a short or extremely short range view of the evidence. However, the *Sebi* of Kemet did not get their books and concepts from self-contemplation, or even from deep meditation. The books and concepts of Kemet came from the teachings of the people of Kush, who themselves had learned from accurate testing, observation, contemplation, and records stretching as far back as thousands of decades all the way to the ancient kingdom of Ta Seti. Remember, as said earlier, Ta Seti was a civilisation built by the people of ancient Kush in 26,000 BCE.

The ancestors of Ta Seti passed down their lessons, sciences, and methodologies through the ages so that by the time of Dynastic Kemet the people of Kemet called them Neteru (gods and goddesses). This was mainly because what was only known in Kemet by the Pharaoh, the *Sebis*, and the *Shemsu* was known by all the people of Kush. Their sciences were not time tested by centuries like ours is, but were time tested by millennia. So when the people of Ta Neteru began to teach the people of Kemet, Arabia, Sumer, and India about concepts like karma, evolution, self-creation, and timelessness; they were doing so based on millennia's worth of research and scientific evidence.

Moreover, while the true founder of Ta Seti was most likely the historical Setekh, or a *Shemsu Setekh*, there was very likely a revolution by the *Shemsu Hor* under the guidance of either the historical Djehwti, or *Sebis* of ancient Ta Seti that was empowered by the teachings of Djehwti. It is said concerning the historical Djehwti, "He founded all human sciences, chemistry, physics, anatomy, literature, oratory and mathematics (arithmetic, geometry, music, stereometry and astronomy)" (Seleem 2004: 75). Whatever the history of this real or imagined Djehwti, he guided the revolution of the *Shemsu Hor*, thus turning Ta Seti into a scientific paradise: knowing the astronomy of the stars and the science of civilisation from deep into that time, around about 26,000 BCE, to the time of pre-dynastic Kemet, around about 8,000 BCE. Effectively, to the people of ancient Kush, from the time of the revolution in Ta Seti; and to the *Sebi* of ancient Kemet, from around pre-dynastic times; knowledge, that is, science, was the key to godhood.

Perhaps this is the biggest similarity between ancient Kemet and the godbody: the question of knowledge. Knowledge to the ancient Kemetics was the only means to attaining divinity in the truest sense: Ra. To become Ra or a child of Ra (*Ramsu*) one had to learn, study, and master the mystery lessons of their particular temple. The more one knew the closer to Ra one became. In like manner we Gods have the 120 lessons. These are no mysteries; the lessons are open for any who join, as we are taught, "What is the duty of a civilized person? The duty of a civilized person is to teach the uncivilized people – who are savage – civilization, righteousness, the knowledge of himself, and the science of everything in life, which is love, peace, and happiness" (Lost Found Muslim Lessons No. 2: 18). But the knowledge one gains from 120 hardly accounts for what was learned in ancient Kemet and ancient Kush. While their sciences were time tested over millennia, our sciences deal with more modern and Western influences. The ancient Nilotic sciences, those of ancient Kemet and ancient Kush, have been neglected and so are lost to us. And to be sure, the ancients had a much better grasp of what accounted for divinity than the modernists do.

The dilemma of what form of knowledge to spread in a cipher is not a common one. We Gods have our lessons and it is unlikely that we will be changing them any time soon. Starmel Allah said, "In this culture, knowledge is always the foundation. Knowledge of our self and our environment is the reality we had to be aware of before we can begin to actually be aware" (The Five Percenter Vol 20.9; 2015: 8). The tenacity of we godbodies towards our culture and the fervour with which we defend it against all outside influences is admirable. However, for the lessons to adapt more to the Afro-chic trend the world seems to be heading towards we must embrace a more open-minded view to the teachings of the ancients. These men and women studied longer and harder the actual facts of the universal order of things than the Honorable Elijah Muhammad. The truth is, as a movement we are far from the divine manifestation transmitted in ancient Egypt, or even that transmitted in the modern church or mosque, even though we say that the church and the mosque have corrupted the truth of divinity and taught only a mystery god, one closer to illusion than to reality.

What has transpired historically in our effort to understand the mysteries of the astral plane has been that we have identified the ancients with this illusory world. Indeed, ancient Egypt did have as much of an illusion as we Gods claim Christianity and Islam does today, yet to the masters and grandmasters there were no illusions, they studied the lessons of their temple until the secrets of the universal order of things were revealed. The masters learned the knowledge from the *Sebis* of Egypt; *Sebis* elevated beyond master level when they came to appreciate the realm of the astral that included both Pet (the causal world) and the Dwat (the fantasy world).

Dr. Ashby said concerning the Dwat,

> *"It is the realm where those who are evil or unrighteous are punished, but it is also where the righteous live in*

happiness. It is the 'other world', the spirit realm. The Duat is also known as Amenta since it is the realm of Amen (Amun). The Duat is where Ra, as symbolized by the sun, traverses after reaching the western horizon, in other words, the movement of Ra between sunset and sunrise, i.e. at night. Some people thought that the Duat was under the earth since they saw Ra traverse downward and around the earth and emerged on the east, however, this interpretation is the understanding of the uninitiated masses. The esoteric wisdom about the Duat is that it is the realm of the unconscious human mind and at the same time, the realm of cosmic consciousness or the mind of God" (Ashby 2003a: 95).

For the godbody the idea of a Dwat is somewhat laughable as after death there is no hereafter; the mind simply returns to the Essence. Heaven and hell are not in some life hereafter, they are in this life, here and now – heaven is what you make it and hell is what you go through. These ideas are highly monistic. Even so, there is, or at least once was, a tradition within the godbody movement that spoke of a persecution that was to come upon the Black community, and particularly upon us godbodies. It was believed that this event would be instigated by the United States government thus eventually leading to our internment, isolation, torture, and even murder. Well, such an event may be transpiring before our very eyes right now with the current destruction of Black lives.

Yet even despite this tradition we in the godbody presently lack a formal or universally recognised doctrine of death; let alone an understanding of it or of its intricacies. Not that this book intends to explain or unravel any of its mysteries; nonetheless, as a contribution, or at least a beginning, so as to lead the way towards the future development of a much more comprehensive adaptation, this book suggests that we borrow

133

and reimagine from the super-gang culture our own, "Divine Army Chant:"

"If I should die, feel no shame; my soul will enter,
the astral plane.
So put the peace sign, across my chest;
and tell the ciphers, I did my best."

While this may be a rather simple, and even simplistic, chant originally created by the Crips due to the ever present reality of death among those in the gang culture; it still contains a lot more subtlety than we or they have ever appreciated. Therefore, at least as a beginning to a much more comprehensive and satisfying understanding on our part: of death, life, and the afterlife, it is here being suggested that we adopt this ritual to be expressed at the close of all our ciphers and parliaments. This should also hopefully prepare us for the development of an authentically godbody funerary interpretation, as a God or Goddess enters the astral plane to dwell among the ancestors being themselves now one of the ancestors (regardless of their age when they pass).

Conversely, at current within the godbody understanding there is an aversion towards the astral, or any type of engagement with the astral. While most of us accept that there is an astral plane we refuse to consider it valuable enough to ever learn about it. Yet, if we consider the ancient Egyptian interpretation: as mentioned before, "From a higher level of understanding, the Duat is the unconscious mind and Asar is that level which [transcends] the thinking processes ... its deepest region. It is the level of consciousness that is experienced during deep dreamless sleep". "When the body dies, it returns to the earth from whence it arose [and the soul] returns to the ocean of consciousness, as represented by the Duat, and if it is not enlightened, returns to this Physical Plane of existence to have more human experiences" (Ashby 2005a: 79, 96). Such a conception of death may not be common in our movement, but it would be more comprehensive than simply seeing the mind or soul returning to the Essence from whence it came, which happens to be the current standard conception we predominantly have.

So far what we have discovered is that the system of the godbody is comparable to the system of ancient Ethiopia, which comes to us via ancient Egypt. The godbody, like the ancient Egyptians, also attached a high level of importance to the concept of the Self. To us it represents that highest state of consciousness that comes by studying and understanding the 120 lessons. Having identified several Egyptological reference points through Dr. Ashby's keen eye we can come to a place where we can recognise certain markings for an understanding of the ancient Egyptian people, particularly in reference to their mystery schools, affectionately called by them the Shetaut Neteru. Dr. Ashby, who I feel has one of the greatest grasps of the spirituality of the ancient Egyptian *Sebis*, disregarded the popular interpretations of the modern Egyptologists and treated the Shetaut Neteru as a living reality.

At the same time, the current godbody emphasis on the material world in no ways negates this ancient Egyptian spirituality and emphasis on the astral world, it actually complements it. To fully appreciate the ancient Egyptian spiritual system one needs to comprehend the world of the material. With concepts like Ra, Tem, Ausar, Auset, Horu, Hethor, Amun, Setekh, and Neb er Tcher in the ancient Egyptian vocabulary the spiritual (that is, the astral) world was never far from the imagination of the ancient Egyptian citizen, let alone the ancient Egyptian priest or *Sebi*.

The godbody may not formally consider the spiritual world to be of importance enough to base an entire system on, nevertheless we do hold that the astral plane exists and contains all the spooks and spectres that affect the physical plane and the way we perceive the physical plane. We are also willing to acknowledge that the third eye can open the mind to see these realms of the astral plane which the ancient Egyptian people called Pet and the Dwat.

Ultimately, what we have discovered is that the godbody fascination with the *concept* of divinity and how it interrelates to Black empowerment is not a backward or schizophrenic pathology (dysfunction), though some may call it archaic; it is a continuation of ancient ideas carried long ago by a people whose civilisation and scientific excellence no learned scientist would dare question. There may be a current propagation of ancient Egyptian backwardness but it is actually of more recent times in an attempt to humiliate what is coming to be accepted as an undeniably Black people. In times past the anthropologists, to relieve themselves of racial complexes over the greatnesses of ancient Ethiopia and ancient Egypt invented the idea of Leucoaethiopians in the fear of not being the Original people or the fathers and mothers of civilisation. They separated the Ethiopians and Egyptians from the rest of the so-called Negro population by effectively calling them White.

The true reasoning of the ancient Egyptians, the Kemetic people, was based on their spiritual interpretations, and what race is more deeply spiritual than the Black race? (I say this tongue in cheek). The spirit world features so heavily in the Black worldview that it is a more primary world than even the physical. The spirit possessions and dark arts practiced on the African continent are testament to the value given to the astral plane in the minds of the African people. Obviously, Africa is not alone in this, most of the Orient (the Muslim world, India, Indo-China, and Southeast Asia) all hold mystical and otherworldly beliefs and superstitions, but if we were to compare them all it would be relatively easy to conclude an African predominance in the world of the spiritual. This predominance suggests that the Black relationship with the astral plane is not the amateur investigations of the European, but the complex interactions of highly sophisticated adepts. Culturally, Black people all over the world study the spiritual systems of their tribe, group, or community, and master it, even so with the ancient Kemetics.

Finally, just like how the soul to the godbody is the self and the self must connect with God-Collective to achieve true enlightenment, so this was exactly how the conception of the soul was understood by ancient Kemet. The godbody of today are very concerned with the soul of the Black person as it is through learning about our Black soul that we can attain to Black divinity. There is a genuine reverence for the Black soul in the godbody outlook that should never be overlooked. We respect the existence of an astral plane and the idea of spirituality, we just do not acknowledge these as central to human existence. To the godbody the aim of human life is to escape the temptations of devilishment and live a righteous, civilised, and refined existence, thus proving oneself divine. Again, in Egypt was also a people that believed that righteousness and refinement were proof of divinity, understanding that the soul, when it is entrapped by the desires of temptation, can never find either peace or contentment.

The ultimate maturity of the godbody beyond the hood and into the mainstream may happen through identifying the concept of the Self as a basis on which to build our system. In building and adding-on to this psychological basis I will be laying out further descriptive formulae in the hopes that these may be adopted by the Gods and Goddesses for the purpose of elevating us to the next level, beyond the streets of the American ghetto and a few middle-class American suburbs into the global metropoles of Europe, Asia, Australia, and Africa (or West, East, and South Asia respectively to a godbody). I say this not to ridicule our beginnings but to expand on them; we are the continuation of the teachings of Kush and Kemet and as such we have unimaginable potential, but we must accept the challenge to expand to larger territory with great enthusiasm for it to be a success.

In the age of iGod Black theologians will either have to accept the godbody conception of God not only as respectable but as the original conception of God or they will have to abandon the God concept altogether. To get to a point that our philosophy is accepted by these types of individuals, who we godbodies for the most part have rejected out of hand, we must meet them where they are – generally speaking most of our Black brothers and sisters are in the church, the mosque, or are liberals – that means considering the world as it actually is and not how we would have it if all Black people had knowledge of self. To give all Black people knowledge of self we have to meet them in their current estate just like Allah did with us.

We are the heirs to Allah's message and his example; Allah did not simply retransmit the message of the Nation of Islam to us he expanded it. My own expansion follows the Black man through his own psychological and sociological development showing and proving how history has gone full circle with the Black man returning to his own divinity. We are the completion of Black psychological development and must rise above petty squabblings over doctrine to appreciate that. In the long run what the ancestors laid out all those thousands of years ago we have taken up and now it is up to us to answer the call of destiny and re-civilise our lost brothers and sisters in the science of Black civilisation.

Shaitan's Way of Getting Us Back

> *"2. Who is the colored man? The colored man is the Caucasian White man. Yaqub's grafted devil of the planet earth" (Student Enrollment).*

One of the first things that becomes clear to anyone who studies the godbody movement in a systematic way is that in order to demystify the devil concept we use the figure of the White person. As Born King Allah said, "Almighty God Allah gave us knowledge of God and the identity of the devil so we could see the reality of both good and evil" (The Five Percenter Vol 20.12; 2015: 3). But in claiming all White people are the devil some people may assume that that makes us a racist movement as to literally demonise another race like this carries huge racial implications. The fact, however, is that our conception of the devil is extremely different from the Christian. To us godbodies, as long as White supremacy exists in the world White people will remain the devil, as the devil is not an absolute evil as much as a power who uses lies (or *trick knowledge*) to promote the idea of his superiority.

I will shortly present my evidence that the discourse of White superiority has turned White people into devils, but first I will comment on the divide they created (pitting the White, good, upright, civilised, paternal, and sane against the Black, bad, deviant, savage, infantile, and mad) that has been maintained from the enslaving, to the lynching, to the segregating, to the colonising, to the criminalising, and to the excluding of Black people historically, even to the point of taking on apocalyptic implications. Not only so, but based on Fanon's (1969) articulation their discourse of White superiority – fused heavily with this apocalyptic language – is even given an air of inevitability. It is no wonder that the godbodies now subvert the same apocalyptic language against them making White people the devils and Black people the Gods.

Eventually the West became so saturated with these systems – as the words themselves are systems in their own right – that they became internal within the White race long before they even became, in the genuine sense, a race. Dalal explained how one of the central processes of the ideology of White supremacy – mythology – was essential for demoralising the Black person: "Mythology consists of several elements, one of which consists of the day-to-day sayings that are perpetuated through unthinking repetition. Examples of these are the well-known ones of blacks as bad, noisy, stupid, dirty and so forth. The power of mythology and gossip is such that it becomes part of the belief system of those that it denigrates – and it is repeated and perpetuated by them too" (Dalal 2010: 93). Yet the ideology and the mythology associated with it caused an equal and opposite reaction to occur within the global White unconscious. Within the current global unconscious of the White race one of the three general symptoms of neurosis exist, these are: phobia, depression/hypersensitivity, and megalomania/superiority complex.

The manifestation of some White people's global neurosis is through phobic or anxious/phobic thoughts towards racialised Others manifesting as xenophobia, Negrophobia, or Islamophobia; in other White people it is through depressive or hypersensitive feelings concerning their own privilege –

140

otherwise known as White guilt; and in still other White people it is through megalomaniacal feelings and beliefs towards all things White, which creates a White superiority complex. Each of these reality distorting perceptions come from one source: the discourse of White superiority. Again, White supremacy and White privilege are not socio-economic in nature, they are reinforced by socio-economics but are not based on it. White supremacy is based on invisible, unacknowledged, systems that create the conscious and unconscious perception that to be White is to be better than Other.

Most White people's mishandling of racial issues is not based on ignorance, it is based on neurosis: the pathology (dysfunction) of White superiority. A re-examination of White cultural dominance causes us to see that it has always been a façade created by trick knowledge and pseudoscience: the phantasm of dominance through the denial of opposition, "Dominant ideologies ... represent their dominance, to themselves and others, as a state of things independent of human choices: deviants and dissidents are relegated to an arbitrary under-world of personal pathology and emotion which alone can explain their futile actions" (Littlewood 2006: 31). Worse still, "It is in the name of the spirit ... the spirit of Europe, that Europe has made her encroachments, that she has justified her crimes and legitimized the slavery in which she [has held] four-fifths of humanity" (Fanon 1969: 252). Hence, colonialism and racism can theoretically be considered the conscious and unconscious basis of the perception of White supremacy.

Racism actually even existed in Europe during the time of the Middle Ages, spurred on by religious pride and social jealousy. Dalal explained how race first became a classification through a poem by a man named William Dunbar as late as the sixteenth century. After this "the term race appears as a generalized descriptive category in the informal discourse of travellers' tales.

However, its appearance is rare, much more frequent are references to Blackes, Moores, Negroes, apes, Aethiopes and the like, attached to whom were attributes of devilishness, monstrousness, lasciviousness, debauchery, and so on" (Dalal 2010: 12). As if the Church during those times was the pinnacle of piety. The clear implication Dalal (2010) here provided was that racism existed long before the classifications of race and racism gained any predominance. Still, while this may explain the racism of the expressly racist ancestors to the modern Whites it does not explain how this racism is now currently unconscious within White people today or whether racism has, indeed, become unconscious at all.

There are many reasons that Dalal said, the "ephemeralness [of racist actions] is used by some to flatly deny the existence of racism" (Dalal 2010: 29). A claim that may harbour offence in some minds relief in others and bears stark similarity to the claim by Thatcher that there is no such thing as society. The denial of the existence of racism creates a blame the victim mentality that, to justify itself amid the claims that it does exist, has to resort to further racism, or, for those of the race in question, a kind of autophobia (irrational fear of self and kind).

But the necessity of this idea may be called into question: surely if we are genuinely living in a post-racial world then it is neither racist nor autophobic to claim that racism no longer exists. The question, however, remains, how does one measure whether racism exists or not in a world which has already denied its existence? The fact of the matter is that in no time in White history was it ever considered wrong to mistreat, enslave, lynch, segregate, colonise, incarcerate, or humiliate non-Whites, particularly Blacks, until after the non-Whites fought for their rights within their generational movements. It was not considered racist or negative to call a Black person an animal or property or nigger until after Blacks began to demand their humanity. Whites, even Christians, would not dare challenge the status quo but a few, who were themselves influenced by their Black colleagues and associates.

I

For us to understand the history of White relations with non-Whites we shall start with a quote from Born King Allah, "The natural goodness of original people was about to cost the Indians everything good they had ever known. As all original people do Indians allowed the devil to come amongst them and do trading. The Indians taught the devil how to survive[,] they taught them how to fish and get food out of the water. They taught them how to till the land to grow their food out of the land and just did not understand the devil wanted all the land. So in return the devil gave the Indians a Book of death followed by diseased blankets and bullets to the head. ... The Indians knew whites were different they just didn't know they were devils and it cost them everything. The thanks given for all the good Indians did was pure evil genocidal murder" (The Five Percenter Vol 20.12; 2015: 3).

That is White people's history with the Native Americans, we Blacks, on the other hand, have experienced the historical enslaving, lynching, segregating, colonising, criminalising, and dehumanising of our people. Born King Allah said, in words very similar to those of de Beauvoir, "Slaves are not born they are made from suffering, cruelty and deprivation." Indeed, "Using trick knowledge and lessons on how to master the original man [White people] made slaves out of the original people" (The Five Percenter Vol 20.10; 2015: 3; Vol 20.12; 2015: 3).

Not only so, but even after their revolutionary war to gain independence White people still denied Black people their independence and humanity: "A difficult and critical sticking point at the Constitutional Convention was how to count a state's population. Particularly controversial was how to count

143

slaves for the purposes of taxation and representation. If slaves were considered property, they would not be counted at all. If they were considered people, they would be counted fully – just as women, children and other non-voters were counted. Southern slave-owners viewed slaves as property, but they wanted them to be fully counted in order to increase their political power in Congress. After extended debate, the framers agreed to the three-fifths compromise – each slave would equal three-fifths of a person in a state's population count" (The Five Percenter Vol 20.10; 2015: 3). Thus they effectively dehumanised Black people in language that barely recognised our personhood.

These are the beginnings of the racial difficulty in America. As the devil has thus far defined Black people and set the standard for the dominant culture it is inevitable that they will have a vastly different interpretation of race and racism to what Black people have. Indeed, no less an authority than Abraham Lincoln had this to say concerning Black-White relations during the American Civil War:

> *I will say then that I am not, nor ever have been in favor of bringing about in any way the social and political equality of the black and white races ... and I will say in addition to this that there is a physical difference between the white and black races which I believe will forbid the two races living together on terms of social and political equality. And inasmuch as they cannot so live, while they do remain together, there must be the position of superior and inferior, and I as much as any other man am in favor of having the superior position assigned to the white race (Lincoln 1964; quoted in Cone 2021: 11).*

Good 'ole honest Abe, for obvious reasons they kept that out of the movie. Ultimately, we see that the disparity between Black and White has, at least in the mind of White people, placed the

Black as the inferior and the White as the superior, particularly since the days of the Renaissance.

But this discourse of White superiority has also affected how Black people see themselves. We do not look at ourselves and see past triumphs and greatnesses, we are forced to look at ourselves through the eyes of White superiority, which means looking at ourselves as inferior. Not only so, but many Whites have no idea how prominent their opinion is in the minds of Blacks – even the nationalist Blacks – which can lead to the ridiculous idea that the current power relations are fair and just the way they are or that we should deny the concept of race in our time as race has been superseded by more "important" issues like nationality and ethnicity. True, the idea and conception of race is not a popular one as it recalls the racism of the pre-1980s, but hiding is not solving. As mentioned before, the avoidance mechanisms encouraged by White guilt only exacerbate the problem. To come to the final resolution of racism it must be challenged by more effective means than to deny its existence or to ignore its historical and current mechanisms, both its internal and its external ones.

It seems to be a habit among White Westerners to exalt their race and culture and avoid or deny any racial problems that may arise in society. They have had their history rewritten by their ancestors to make them out to be the intellectual, the philanthropist, the civiliser, the explorer, the conqueror, the warrior, et cetera., while all that were categorised as non-White were "relegated to an arbitrary under-world" (Littlewood 2006: 31). However, the question of how the White person viewed ideas of race provides an interesting answer. As Dalal stated, "In the earlier period 'the Negro' and various 'Others' were not as yet admitted into the category of humankinds, and this allowed them to be treated as beasts. Over time, the progressive collapse of this division under the weight of accumulating evidence, leads to the Negro gaining entry into the category humankind" (Dalal 2010: 13).

Two problems arise from this statement: as Black people in Africa at the time of their dehumanisation by the Europeans were far more advanced, educated, and sophisticated than the Whites of Europe, they had to, first of all, pass off a more developed, civilised, and scientific people as savage, uncivilised, and primitive and, secondly, underdevelop a people with far more advanced knowledge and technology. To do both they employed the use of trick knowledge; and to be sure, our Black ancestors were not innocent in all this.

One of the central arguments was to denigrate an, at that time, advanced people; the methodology they used was to over-glorify self and kind and present Other as a poor facsimile. Now, during the Middle Ages religion played a very important role in how they accomplished this task. Monogenesis, that is, the theory that human life began with an Original couple, represented a perfect beginning to this denigration. Because based on *their* Adamic interpretation the first couple were White – hence the multitudinous paintings of a White Adam and Eve – the White race considered themselves an advanced, pure breed while all other races must have biologically morphed into their present colour through sin.

The idea of an Original man, monogenesis, having been colour coded by the White man to be just that – a White man – was advanced not based on scientific discovery nor on a desire to find the truth, but as a means of reinforcing racialised views and internal opinions of superiority; in other words, it was based on mythology. As Dalal noted "The proponents of *monogenism* argued that the variety of races were the outcome of degeneration of the first perfect race, and that the colour spectrum from white to the yellows and browns ending with black, reflected the degree of degeneration. It was [also] proposed that this degeneration must have taken place very rapidly in order to give rise to such disparate varieties of humans" (Dalal 2010: 14). The precautionary methods used to justify this pseudoscientific – though given the veneer of genuinely scientific – proposition do not in any ways make the claim less precarious.

The scientific language used to authenticate this opinion was, at that time, challenged by another school that came into existence as a result of the three-fifths argument, as Dalal continued: "The *polygenists* argued that there was not enough time for the degeneration to take place and so the different races had to have begun separately. In saying that the races were different species, they were saying that they were quite literally different animals" (Dalal 2010: 14). The scientific quantifying of these arguments is quite deceptive. It makes the current debates of evolution quite diabolical; especially when one considers that the origins of humanity have now been traced back *legitimately* to East Africa (to what has come to be accepted as a Black man).

Seeing as how the White race could not prove their superiority by saying they were a first, pure race, they had to fall back on claiming they were superior by being a more developed (evolved) form of humanity. Same song different generation. But the fact still remains that Black people are most likely the Original people, though Whites are still, unsuccessfully, looking for evidence to disprove it with their views concerning Greek civilisation and the Leucoaethiopians. The question of the origin of the races and of civilisation shows how far Whites are willing to go to be separated and divided from the other races. But it is not a question of now unifying what were once divided; the system they have created with the unthinkingly natural prerogative of superiority must be dismantled first.

II

We can see thus in effect a White society set in place by the social forces of White supremacy and empowered by astral forces that have been encouraging White superiority and White separateness. These two ideas were further crystallised during the colonial era when it was the White man's burden to civilise the non-Whites amid huge resistance from the people. The psychological infrastructure thus determined the sociological superstructure of the world. The medium between this psychological infrastructure and the sociological superstructure was the ideological structure of the colonial system. Not content with having power externally through the barrel of a gun White people also took power internally through spreading the myth of White superiority via their various media.

Nevertheless, social forces affect social bodies far more than social bodies affect them; also social forces influence the sociological superstructure, which itself has its basis in the psychological infrastructure. To prove this I will present the example of a psychoanalytic experience recounted by Atwood and Stolorow:

> *"A good illustration of this situation is provided by an incident that occurred in the treatment of Fritz Perls by Wilhelm Reich (described in Perls, 1969). One of the critical factors in Perls' childhood development concerned a deeply troubled relationship with his father, who was experienced as emotionally withholding and relentlessly critical and judgmental. It appears that many of the dominating issues around which Perls' subjective life was organized concerned his need to separate himself from the powerful negative influence of his father, with whom he also became closely identified. In his autobiography Perls describes his relationship with Reich in predominantly positive terms and reports one incident that captured his imagination. This was Reich's conclusion that the man who had raised Perls was not his actual biological father, but rather that Perls was the product of relations between his mother and an uncle who was the pride of the family.*

148

Although Perls never became firmly convinced that Reich's idea was sound, he remained intrigued and confused about the possibility for the rest of his life. In view of the intense struggle to become liberated from the influence of and identification with the father, it can be easily understood why this suggestion would have struck a responsive chord, notwithstanding the fact that there was no actual evidence to support the proposition. Indeed, Perls states that he never had any idea how Reich had arrived at this conclusion.

The offering of the reconstruction becomes intelligible once we consider the historical circumstances under which the structure of Reich's subjective world crystallized. Reich's life was also dominated by a need to dissociate himself from the influence of his father, whose authoritarian and sexually repressive values had played a central role in provoking his beloved mother to kill herself ... It was Reich's allegiance to his father and identification with his values that led him at the age of 13 to betray his mother's sexual infidelity. The father's discovery of her adultery precipitated her suicide. Reich's drastic regret and guilt over this betrayal and its tragic consequences gave rise to his lifelong struggle to overthrow authoritarianism and affirm the value of sexual freedom and spontaneity. This situation was also the source of Reich's need to deny the significance of his father in his own life, a need that culminated in his conviction that he could not possibly be his father's son" (Atwood & Stolorow 2014: 39).

From this story of the personal psychology of Fritz Perls, a German psychiatrist, and his experiences with Wilhelm Reich, a prominent psychoanalyst, we see certain world changing actions transpiring. Regardless of the astral forces affecting Reich personally and the realities that brought them into his world, he and his psychoanalytic theories went on to change the social world despite what he himself had been through with his father in adolescence.

People change the world more than the world changes people, which undermines the White perspective on the subject of racist discourse in the following ways: First, it shows that White internal mechanisms concerning racism are best found through psychological routes rather than sociological, which only explain but do not define. Second, it reveals that as the Whites are considered the standard and the norm, to define the White social norm is to simultaneously define the standard social norm. Third, it affirms that institutionalisation is the inverse of internalisation, producing a hardening of sociological realities, particularly with regard to identity (which includes White identity). Fourth, it confirms that it is White astral forces that eventually become White global forces so that we can see where change must begin for the transforming of the White global unconscious. Fifth, it shows that all the power relations of White society have many social forces behind them that must be exorcised in order for them to free their society.

Though we understand in our time that the idea of psychic degeneration within the White racist is very true, if racist forces have institutionalised racism into the existing global ethic of White society then not only has racism become an unconscious mechanism within White society, it has also rendered degenerate actually existing White society. This subject and discussion may be a very delicate issue though and may leave the reader feeling a little uncomfortable, but we are working through years, decades, centuries, of avoidance and ignorance. The global ethic of White society must be dealt with at length to finally be surpassed so that we do not indoctrinate another generation into these pseudo-integrationist/pseudoscientific ideas that have their basis in the racism of the modern system.

Sigmund Freud was the first known theorist to attempt to scientifically unravel the world of the unconscious through his theory of psychoanalysis. The first thing that must be understood about Freudian theory is that it has its basis in the vicissitudes or divisions of the mind: the id, the ego, and the superego. According to Freud all three of these make up the internal intellectual infrastructure. In Freudian analysis the unconscious is made up mainly of two of these sections: the id or sexual/aggressive instincts and the superego or ideal-ego. This superego is the internalisation of the properties and characters of someone admired by the individual: an internalisation that may lead to various psychic inhibitions and constraints.

All this takes place because the superego personifies the "master" of the unrestrained instincts. Or, as Dalal recounted, "One of the functions of the superego is to constrain and modify the uninhibited expression of the sexual and aggressive instincts" (Dalal 2010: 39). Obviously, this also fits into what Littlewood said concerning *psychohistory* "analysts examined cultural change through the individual conflict between instincts and social constraint" (Littlewood 2006: 23) or in a social context: between social resistance and social reaction. Starting from here it could be theorised that White racism either comes from an instinctual aggressiveness or from a social constraint forced upon future generations by culture. Therefore, racism may either be biologically instinctual to White people or was sociologically forced upon White people by White culture.

To help us to better understand how our internal astral body can affect social and global bodies Freud explained how, "One can justifiably maintain that the community too evolves a super-ego and that the development of civilization takes place under its influence. [Indeed, anyone] who is conversant with different civilizations may find it tempting to pursue this equation in detail" (Freud 2002: 77). To which Littlewood also added, "Freud had argued that the critical passivity of [a] crowd was a return to archaic patterns by a leader who took the place of the developed 'superego' (parental values internalised in childhood) of each follower" (Littlewood 2006: 27). Accordingly, the social superego replaces the parentally developed superego, and defines for the social body its ethics and its values.

Further, while the social force of a social body determines its success, it is the social superego or ideal-ego that determines the social potential of the social force. But the social superego itself is not an amalgam of each crowd members' general superego, it is instead the internal superego of the crowd leader, i.e. the ideal-ego of the group's ideal personality. Thus the social constraints or social reactions of a crowd or social body would be the same constraints or reactions of the group leader, and this is the cause of all social stases. Though it is not always the case, what tends to be the case more often is that individuals deny their developmental, parentally enforced, social controls for social acceptance when within a crowd or social body – making clear that crowd pressures have the potential to lead the crowd with irrational ideas and methods so long as they are accepted by the largest number of people. It takes a strong character to go against the crowd and maintain an identity based on originally developed superego.

Freud maintained, "Some manifestations and properties of the super-ego can … be recognized more easily by its behaviour in the cultural community than by its behaviour in the individual" (Freud 2002: 78). So, to understand the social statics of the racist mechanisms in both astral and social bodies we must return to Freud's theories of the mob, "All mobs forget their inhibitions, their critical judgement and their superego controls, and borrow for a time the superego of their leader … The psychopathology of the mob leader that propels him to antinomian leadership in crisis now releases and mobilises the hidden psychopathology in each mob member" (La Barre 1970; quoted in Littlewood 2006: 27). The theory thus states that unconscious behaviours that would otherwise be considered antinomian (lawless) in the sense that they are reprehensible to practice with or in one's own family, when they are socially accepted, get internalised from the mob leader's superego into the superego of the mob members.

Whereas individually, based on parental socialisation during the developmental process of child-raising, one may not necessarily allow their own unconscious racism to be expressed, in a racist mob or social body they will release whatever negative feelings they have towards another race; at which time the more complex reality of the mob comes into play. The obvious example of this is the type of mobs that incited the lynching of a Black person, for example:

> *When a mob in Valdosta, Georgia, in 1918 failed to find Sidney Johnson, accused of murdering his boss, Hampton Smith, they decided to lynch another black man, Haynes Turner, who was known to dislike Smith. Turner's wife, Mary, who was eight months pregnant, protested vehemently and vowed to seek justice for her husband's lynching. The sheriff, in turn, arrested her and then gave her up to the mob. In the presence of a crowd that included women and children, Mary Turner was 'stripped, hung upside down by the ankles, soaked with gasoline, and roasted to death. In the midst of this torment, a white man opened her swollen belly with a hunting knife and her infant fell to the ground and was stomped to death.'"* (Cone 2020b: 120.)

These sorts of lynchings were not only acts of extreme mob passion, they were also acts of premeditated planning, as Cone (2020: xiv) also noted, "In its heyday, the lynching of black Americans was no secret. It was a public spectacle, often announced in advance in newspapers and over radios, attracting crowds of up to twenty thousand people." But how could such spectacles have been tolerated by a people who claimed to be civilised and cultured? Dalal, answered this, saying, "in a racialized society there would be little or no guilt to inhibit the venting of the instincts against racialized objects, because in attacking something apparently bad, one would be doing a good thing" (Dalal 2010: 40). Again, these sorts of lynchings happened not only in America, but also in the Caribbean and Europe, as Peter Fryer (2018) explained in his phenomenal opus *Staying Power*.

III

What we know of history is that White people initially followed their unconscious racist drives from the Middle Ages into the twentieth century. The social constraints they developed against racism were not there until after Black people began to fight for change and drove to guilt certain members within the White power structure. Not that racism was not an unconscious drive in all other races too, but White people used their racism as the basis of their power structure, whereas other races, through social self-constraint, either allayed racial stratification or adopted, in time, the White racist opinions about themselves and other races and thereby became corrupted. Overall, the psychology of White superiority led to the ideology of White supremacy, to produce a sociology of White privilege. "Dem's the breaks."

Having said that, it does create a kind of ticklish situation: I myself can feel the irony of it in the present endeavour. We godbodies are at current teaching exactly what could be considered the obverse of what the White racists taught during colonial times – that history began with Black people, that Black people are the Original people, that civilisation was developed by Black people, and that White people are uncivilised savages and devils. How are we any different? How are we any better? While I agree, we are not that much different with regard to our doctrine, and again, ours is based on relatively pseudoscientific ideas, most of our general theories are provable, while those of the colonial regime are constantly getting undermined by their own empirical evidence.

Obviously, that does not negate what could be considered racist undertones, but racism is based a lot more on power relations than on object identity. The supposed racism of the powerless, like Fanon said concerning anti-colonial violence, is a response to the avalanche of racism that has been historically used to oppress and exploit us, and as Fanon said concerning colonialism, it "is not a thinking machine, nor a body endowed with reasoning faculties. It is violence in its natural state, and it will only yield when confronted with greater violence" (Fanon 1969: 48). By replacing the word violence with the word racism we see that, "While 'the master's tools will never dismantle the master's house,' as Audre Lorde rightly points out, prudent use of the master's tools may certainly help one to understand the subtleties of the master's house" (Douglas 1999: 19).

Still, the social aetiology (social cause) of White racism has been somewhat of a mystery. From a Freudian perspective, as has been articulated, it could be said to be based on the internalising of mechanisms into the superego that – like with Perlz internalisation of Reich's psychoanalytic discussions – belonged to a leader's superego. At the same time, Dalal also noted that racism may have a more general social aetiology, one that is found in the concept of envy: "The amalgam of various psycho-social tides (two of the most important being Christianity and the Enlightenment), inculcated the repression of the passions (particularly sex and aggression) in the European Christian. These repressed elements are bound to be split off from consciousness and projected into a territory which is designated as similarly repellent in some way (enter the racialized Other). The racialized Other is now experienced as containing not only something desirable, but being desire incarnate" (Dalal 2010: 44). To which Freud also concurred suggesting how, "Experience shows that most of the people who make up our society are constitutionally not equal to abstinence. Whoever would have fallen ill under less severe sexual restrictions will do so more readily and more seriously under the demands of today's civilized sexual morality" (Freud 2002: 95).

To continue with this theory Dalal used Fairbairn to demonstrate how the libidinal drives of the id can produce within the ego of the individual this kind of contradictory conclusion, "The exciting object, which was initially a part of the internalized bad object, is projected onto the Other. The different relationships that the two repressed egos have with this object complicate matters: the libidinal ego desires the Other, and the anti-libidinal ego attacks it because it contains the tantalizing" (Dalal 2010: 55). Or, in other words, a bad situation within selfobject relations: selfobjects being friends, loved ones, possessions, places, et cetera., but particularly caregivers; could result in the bad object being projected onto the racialised Other. Thus while being repelled by them, being the bad object, one could still be drawn to them through them being based on selfobject.

Yet, as Fairbairn continued, the death drive also has a relation to the issue of racism. Dalal could not but agree when "Fairbairn adds the intriguing dimension that the 'us' is threatened by both love and hate. Hate and aggression threatens the 'us' from within through fragmentation, and libido threatens the 'us' either by attaching itself to a lower level of organization (a version of splitting), or by absorption into a bigger 'us'. In summary identity is threatened by hate towards the self and by love towards another" (Dalal 2010: 54). This being the case would make the conflict between libido and anti-libido the cause of racism; which in fact only takes us right back to the unconscious: White people have allowed their unconscious racism to determine the societal superstructure they created. The fact is, psychoanalysis cannot go beyond this basic summation, which, as Dalal (2010: 65) said, "seeks to look for the *causes* within biology (the vicissitudes of the instincts) and *individual* development (the vicissitudes of the developmental process)", both relating to the unconscious, the id and the superego.

Nevertheless, in searching for the social aetiology of White racism let us move now from psychoanalysis to group analysis; Foulkes, who was originally an exponent of Freudian analysis, left the school to forward the more radical idea that psychological states are a result of social processes. Foulkes basically took Freud's theories of the mob and expounded on them. According to Dalal, "Foulkes and Anthony [claimed] that in 'the most asocial and antisocial individuals, one can discern the wish [for empathic connection], which is tantamount to saying that, fundamentally, man is a group animal'." (Dalal 2010: 112). Basically, "Foulkes is saying that the fundamental drive [within humans] is not as Freud suggested, instinctual discharge, but the drive to belong" (Dalal 2010: 112).

The Foulkesian conclusions on racism, in Dalal's mind, were thus simple: "According to Foulkesian theory, the idea that skin colour [as] a signifier of belongingness, must of necessity be located in the social unconscious – which by definition, is *unconscious.*" So again, we come to the same conclusion that, "all one could say is that instinctuality has been blackened and expelled from the conscious part of the psyche, or one could say that instinctuality has been projected *into* blackness" (Dalal 2010: 118, 119). Basically, what we have discovered so far shows that racism, being embedded in the internal nature of White people, was at some point in their history given free rein to determine their sociological superstructure. According to Foulkes and Dalal, and also according to Freudian analysis, the basis of racism can therefore be found in the group matrix of the social body and is related to the unconscious: though in Freud it is the superego, in Fairbairn it is the ego interacting with the unconscious, and in Foulkes it is the unconscious projection of instinctuality onto the racialised Other. We shall next explore the validity of this "unconscious racism" theory by trying to answer the question of why, although being dormant within all other people, the phenomenon of unconscious racism occurred historically within the White race.

IV

In continuing with Dalal's theoretical progression: from Freud, to Fairbairn, to Foulkes, the next theorist he evaluated was the eminent sociologist Norbert Elias. From Elias Dalal concluded that the social constraints of the superego come about due to the power structure of the society: "Elias says that every social relation is a power relation" (Dalal 2010: 121), which does not necessarily mean that the existing power structure *is the same thing as* the societal superstructure, but can more generally mean that the power structure is the *basis* of the social superstructure. Dalal considered Elias' theories to be of social aetiological value because they answered, for him, what the psychoanalytic theorists could not: why the social forces of White social bodies allowed for racist conscious and unconscious behaviours to be accepted at all by those White social bodies. Dalal said concerning Elias, "His window on to this complex space [of social aetiology is] a novel one, through a kind of social anthropology, which consist[s] of the analysis of the changing history of etiquette in western Europe over the last millennium" (Dalal 2010: 122).

Elias began his analysis by explaining the difference between the German concepts of *kultur* and *zivilisation*. Then he went into the transition of the West from behaviours that we would consider uncivilised to civilisation. Elias said, "*Courtoisie* originally referred to the forms of behaviour that developed at the courts of the great feudal lords. Even during the Middle Ages the meaning of the word clearly lost much of its original social restriction to the 'court', coming into use in bourgeois circles as well. With the slow extinction of the knightly-feudal warrior

158

nobility and the formation of a new absolute court aristocracy in the course of the sixteenth and seventeenth centuries, the concept of *civilité* was slowly elevated as the expression of socially acceptable behaviour" (Elias 2014: 87).

"In a very similar way in the course of the eighteenth century, the concept of *civilité* slowly lost its hold among the upper class of the absolute court. This class was now for its part undergoing a fairly slow process of transformation, of bourgeoisification, which, at least up to 1750, went hand in hand with a simultaneous courtization of bourgeois elements." So "Like the concept of *courtoisie* earlier, *civilité* was now slowly beginning to sink. Shortly afterwards, the content of this and related terms was taken up and extended in a new concept, the expression of a new form of self-consciousness, the concept of *civilisation*. ... The concept of *civilisation* indicates quite clearly in its nineteenth-century usage that the *process* of civilization – or, more strictly speaking, a phase of the *process* – had been completed and forgotten. People only wanted to accomplish this process for other nations, and also, for a period, for the lower classes of their own society" (Elias 2014: 88).

Thereby from the feudal courts of the mid-Renaissance to the early-Reformation came the term *courtoisie*. Then, as towns and cities were starting to form; which were at that time given the names berg, burg, burgh, and *bourge*; so came the bourgeois into existence. This bourgeois class, due largely to the fact that they dominated city life, were called the civil after the Latin word for city. Therefore, White society effectively evolved from courteous, to civil, to civilised; which also represented the development over time of social manners with regard to the upper classes. "However," as Dalal noted, "those of lower rank continually emulated the habits and behaviours of those in the higher echelons of society, and in the process blurred the lines of distinction. This in turn set off a counter movement in the privileged circles – the progressive refinement in their manners to maintain their distance from the common folk" (Dalal 2010: 123). Basically, if we were to look at Western history we would be able to observe over the years how manners caused them to inhibit certain instincts at certain times so as to avoid shame or guilt. The inhibition has always been to appease that drive which Foulkes believed to be chief of all human instincts, the drive to be social.

Starting from the *courtois* times of the Renaissance we see individuals living according to the social manners prescribed by more distinguished individuals. The upper classes basically set the standard for what was accepted, as in the social dynamics of the group matrix they possessed all the power. But who defined who was in the upper classes? Surely, as Elias noted, the feudal knight and courtly noble represented the upper class of *courtois* times; then in the times of *civilité* the royalty and aristocracy were the upper class with the bourgeois slowly breaking through; finally, the bourgeoisie started to represent the upper class in the more "civilised" times.

A significant figure to rise from the non-noble intelligentsia during the transitional phase between the Renaissance and the post-Reformation was Erasmus of Rotterdam, who, in writing his book *De civilitate morum puerilium*, set the standard for what would be classed as civilised. The broad conception of manners, at that time, was such that many things that we now take to be immodest were taken for granted by them. According to Elias:

> *"Everyone, from the king and queen to the peasant and his wife, [for lack of the utensils] eats with the hands. In the upper class there are more refined forms of this. One ought to wash one's hands before a meal, says Erasmus. But there is as yet no soap for this purpose. Usually the guests hold out their hands and a page pours water over them. The water is sometimes slightly scented with chamomile or rosemary. In good society one does not put both hands into the dish. It is most refined to use only three*

160

fingers. This is one of the marks of distinction between the upper and lower classes" (Elias 2014: 50).

Again, "with [regard to] the exposure of the body. First it became a distasteful offence to show oneself exposed in any way before those of higher or equal rank; with inferiors it could even be a sign of good will. Then, as all become socially more equal, it slowly became a general offence. ... Precisely because the social command not to expose oneself or be seen performing natural functions now operates with regard to everyone and is imprinted in this form in children, it seems to adults to be a command of their own inner selves and takes on the form of a more or less total and automatic self-restraint" (Elias 2014: 118).

What Elias was basically saying was that customs that in the West seem, and have seemed for some time now, natural and normal, had their actual genesis, not in scientific or religious advancement, but, in the class relations of the power structure existing in medieval Europe.

Elias said that "The *De civilitate morum puerilium* of Erasmus ... stood in many respects ... entirely within [this] medieval tradition. Almost all the rules of *courtois* society reappeared in it. Meat was still eaten with the hands, even if Erasmus stressed that it should be picked up with three fingers, not the whole hand. The precept not to fall upon the meal like a glutton was also repeated, as were the direction to wash one's hands before dining and the strictures on spitting, blowing the nose, the use of the knife, and many others" (Elias 2014: 61). From the omnipresent nature of European manners in the world today it may seem strange to read that instructions needed to be given not to expose one's naked body, and on how to blow the nose and eat a meal tastefully, but the truth of this necessity, up into the eighteenth century, at the height of the Enlightenment, reveals the realities of Europe's not so propagated history.

On the subject Elias continued, "In the earliest stages the need for restraint was usually explained by saying: Do this and not that, for it is not *courtois*, not 'courtly'; a 'noble' man does not do such things. At most, the reason given is consideration for the embarrassment of others". "Later on, a similar rationale was used above all: Do not do that, for it is not 'civil' … Or such an argument was used to establish the respect due to those of higher social rank"; "this sensibility and a highly developed feeling for what was 'embarrassing', was at first a distinguishing feature of small courtly circles, then of court society as a whole. … Then, at a certain point, this behaviour came to be recognized as 'hygienically correct', i.e., it was justified by a clearer insight into causal connections and taken further in the same direction or consolidated" (Elias 2014: 97, 98).

The people of late modernity would surely feel more comfortable hearing differently, as Elias also explained, "[T]hey expect to find the elimination of 'eating with the hands', the introduction of the fork, individual cutlery and crockery, and all the other rituals of their own standard explained on 'hygienic grounds'. For that is the way in which they themselves in general explain these customs. But as late as the second half of the eighteenth century, hardly anything of this kind is found as a motivation for the greater restraint that people impose upon themselves" (Elias 2014: 97). The fact is, the upper class played a vital role in the development of Western manners and customs to a level of refinement, through social pressure. Dalal took this premise, that through the internalisation of certain key social ideas which came about due to the social dynamics between the upper class and the lower classes – which again he broadened to the European and the non-Europeans – and reconsidered how the social aetiology of White racism came into play.

Dalal, now explaining the social aetiology of White inhibition, related that, "Over time we witness the progressive disappearance of some behaviours not only from the public domain, but also from the treatise on etiquette themselves. Through the ages, subjects that were allocated entire chapters to themselves become progressively shortened and eventually disappear altogether. The reason for this apparent evaporation is a shift in the location and method of social control – it has moved from the external world to the internal world, and the family has replaced wider society as the means of instilling the restraints" (Dalal 2010: 125). Thereby bringing to light both the process of socialisation in the European developmental process, and showing how the developmental inhibitions within Western children came about historically. These inhibitions were instituted at moments in time from a relatively less inhibited social milieu.

From here we should see the interrelation between history, socialisation, and developmental personality; what we may not see is the effects these may have on individuals. As these prohibitions got relegated more and more to childhood, during the developmental process, they would become mystified and mythologised by the time the child reached adulthood. Basically, when the proscriptions and prescriptions of etiquette finally became consigned to the world of socialisation they gained psychological meaning. Dalal said it better, "It is at this moment that the prohibitions take on the appearance of something natural and self-evident[,] because they 'are associated with embarrassment, fear, shame, or guilt, *even when one is alone*' ..." Moreover, "at a later time these same mechanisms [were] also critical [for] the manufacture of races, which [were] born out of similar imperatives" (Dalal 2010: 126, 123).

V

It is at this point that Dalal (2010) ventured into Barthesian semiotics to discuss the mechanisms by which Black people became subject to the categorical prejudices we currently endure. Rather than following suit in this particular area I shall instead use Foucauldian archaeology – despite my disliking of many of his other conclusions – as it continues the theme of historical recovery. As we have already noted, Erasmus was a man of the Renaissance who redefined etiquette for the Europeans, but the Renaissance did more than change people's opinions and beliefs about behaviour. According to Foucault, "The dawn of madness on the horizon of the Renaissance is first perceptible in the decay of Gothic symbolism; as if that world, whose network of spiritual meaning was so close-knit, had begun to unravel, showing faces whose meaning was no longer clear except in the forms of madness" (Foucault 2001: 15).

Thus Foucault here showed that the defining of madness was becoming far more refined during this *courtois* phase of European history, moving beyond a purely spiritual definition (possession by *daemons*) to become, to some, a more social reality. Yet to all Europeans alike, "Madness, [represented] the values of another age, another art, another morality [calling] into question, but ... also [reflecting] ... all the forms, even the most remote, of the human imagination" (Foucault 2001: 26). Herein lay the redefining of madness by *courtois* – that is, mid-Renaissance to late Reformation – standards. That which was Other, whether in historical, aesthetic, or moral terms, was relegated to the position of mad.

Then, in the 1600s, at the dawn of the times of *civilité*, began a wave of confinement practices in Europe to keep undesirables from ruining the name and reputation of a country. In England the Poor Laws articulated that any who were not willing to work were to be confined in one of the country's houses of correction until such a time as they were willing to do so. In France it was the Hôspital Général that would confine and remove all undesirables. Foucault acknowledged, "The first houses of correction were opened in England during a full economic recession. The act of 1610 recommended only joining certain mills and weaving and carding shops to all houses of correction in order to occupy the pensioners. But what had been a moral requirement became an economic tactic when commerce and industry recovered after 1651, the economic situation having been re-established by the Navigation Act and the lowering of the discount rate. All able-bodied manpower was to be used to the best advantage, that is, as cheaply as possible." At the same time, "When the Hôspital Général was created in Paris, it was intended above all to suppress beggary, rather than to provide an occupation for the internees. It seems, however, that Colbert, like his English contemporaries, regarded assistance through work as both a remedy to unemployment and a stimulus to the development of manufactories" (Foucault 2001: 48, 49). It is here that sanity and morality were both equated with civility. That which was considered uncivil was to be removed from vision, and the highest form of civility, to the European, and particularly to the Englishman, was work.

With work being the highest standard of morality and sanity those who refused to work were thus deemed immoral and insane so that when Other, say, the slave, chose not to work for the master she was relegated to the position of immoral if not of insane. "And it is in this context that the obligation to work assumes its meaning as both ethical exercise and moral guarantee. It will serve as *askesis*, as punishment, as symptom of a certain disposition of the heart. The prisoner who could and who would work would be released, not so much because he was again useful to society, but because he had again subscribed to the great ethical pact of human existence" (Foucault 2001: 55). These days of *civilité* or absolutism were times in which etiquette, morality, and employment determined a person's level of sanity. Those who were civil, moral, and employed were considered sane while those who lacked in any one of these would be removed and confined until such a time as they were deemed sane based on their willingness to work. Hence, "Unreason was hidden in the silence of the houses of confinement, but madness continued to

165

be present on the stage of the world – with more commotion than ever. It would soon reach, under the Empire, a point that had never been attained in the Middle Ages and the Renaissance" (Foucault 2001: 65).

Racism could come into play because the European standard of etiquette, morality, and employment only worked for the European. It could be argued that as civil Europeans interacted with non-Europeans they saw them as uncivil, and therefore insane, because they did not live up to European standards of civility. The European therefore developed an air of distinction making him (or her) feel superior to the non-European. Having been spoon-fed this narrative of distinction the pan-European who encountered the non-European automatically unconsciously felt superior to them. It was beyond their control, the narrative created the racism. The fact that the average uncivil European was removed from sight, and that the culture of the non-European was unfamiliar to them made their insanity appear truer than ever.

According to Foucault, "James's Dictionary expressly urges us to consider as delirious 'the sufferers who *sin* by fault or excess in any of various voluntary actions, in a manner contrary to reason and to *propriety*; as when they use their hand, for example, to tear out tuffs of wool or in an action similar to that which serves to catch flies; or when a patient acts against his custom and without cause, or when he speaks too much or too little against his normal habits; if he abounds in obscene remarks, being, when in health, of measured speech and decent in his discourse, and if he utters words that have no consequence, if he breathes more faintly than he must, or uncovers his private parts in the presence of those who are near him. We also regard as being in a state of delirium those whose minds are affected by some derangement in the organs of sense, or who use them in a fashion not customary to them, as when, for example, a sufferer

is deprived of some voluntary action or acts inhabitually'"
(Foucault 2001: 93; emphasis mine).

What we gather therefore is that behaviour that was originally
considered normal practice, nearing the end of absolutism and
the days of *civilité*, began to gain an air of the medical about them.
Medical terminology and justification replaced argumentation by
reason of etiquette and morality. Indeed, those once considered
immoral were now considered mentally ill, bringing about such
absurdities as a "slaves' desires to run away from bondage …
being rationalised by medical opinion as an illness –
drapetomania or dysaesthesia Actheopis" (Gilroy 1999: 21), so
they said. Basically, Black people were never considered uncivil,
immoral, or insane due to some natural disposition but because
the definitions of civility, morality, and sanity only matched up
with the ways and actions of White people.

This knowledge of difference then morphed into the trick
knowledge of distinction as the narrative of pan-European
distinction began to become unconscious in the minds of most
Europeans. This narrative of pan-European distinction soon
itself morphed into a discourse of White superiority during the
civilising process. But as the Europeans began spreading their
version of civilisation, they, of course, encountered resistance:
resistance that was condemned as being based on the uncivilised,
immoral, and insane natures of the non-Europeans, now
becoming the non-Whites. Ultimately, it would not be their
cultural distinctions that would make White people the devil but
the tricknology that corrupted that distinction into superiority.

Thus, what we have discovered so far is: the unconscious
reality of the superego demonstrates that, as ideology is the basis
of the sociological, and psychology is the basis of the ideological,
so the psychology of the leader influences the social body, which
in turn develops social constraints that inhibit their social
activities. Moreover, we can conclude that Dalal's theory of the
social aetiology of Europe's narrative of cultural distinction is,

in his estimation, the basis of racism: that what was uncourteous to the noble and the knight in *courtois* times, and uncivil to the lord and the aristocrat during the days of *civilité*, was inhibited by social constraints manifested in the superego of the child during bourgeois times.

Effectively, Dalal's theory of racism can be summarised as such: the basis of Europe's racist global ethic is the collective unconscious of the social body of the European upper class, and the feelings of superiority they felt towards those of their own race were translated into superiority even more so towards those of any other race as they began to interact with non-Europeans. The feelings of disgust that the upper class felt towards behaviours like loudness, aggression, sexuality, exhibitionism, and rudeness were projected onto the natives of different lands so as to distinguish the European from the "savages" even as they were originally projected onto the lower class Europeans during earlier phases. Thus it could be said that the social kinetics of trick knowledge represented narratives and discourses that were developed when Europe was coming into its own.

Yet, all this hardly makes for a convincing excuse, as anyone who does a little research will be informed. The Europeans of the late Renaissance who learned etiquette from Erasmus of Rotterdam did not know that Erasmus learned etiquette and cleanliness from the French royalty. Going deeper one finds that the French royalty usually married into the Spanish royalty and were thus influenced by them (Apicella 1990). However, this is where the story becomes quite diabolical: the Spanish royalty and nobility learned etiquette, refinement, and cleanliness from the Moors of Mauritania, Mali, Senegal, and the Maghreb who had conquered Spain from the 8th century. For this cause we shall now have to leave Dalal (2010) and consider the work and research of Walter Rodney (2018) in order to discover the thriving civilisations that existed in Africa from the times of ancient Kush up into the time of the Renaissance, when Europe began to distinguish itself.

VI

The civilisations of Africa during the European Middle Ages were not primitive hunter/gatherer or even barbarian tribal groupings but were advanced empires. In fact, for most of its history, from ancient times onward, Africa had thriving empires of advanced cultures. In North Africa there were the Fatimid and Almoravid empires; in West Africa there were the Ghana, Mali, and Songhai empires; in Southern Africa there were the Zimbabwe, Mutapa, and several other Bantu empires; and in East Africa there were the Meroe, Axum, Amhara, and Zagwe empires. Effectively, Africa had powerful, wealthy, and well-educated populations from the time of Kush up into the time of the European Renaissance.

Rodney (2018) noted that Africa had two main stages of economic organisation before the modern era: communalism and feudalism, without advanced slavery in-between. Not only so, but Africa was even able to develop different forms of manufacturing from those of the Europeans. "African manufacturers have been contemptuously treated or overlooked by European writers, because the modern conception of the word brings to mind factories and machines. However, 'manufactures' means literally 'things made by hand,' and African manufacture in this sense had advanced appreciably." "It was [only] at the level of scale that African manufactures had not made a breakthrough." Indeed, "By the fifteenth century, Africans everywhere had arrived at a considerable understanding of the total ecology – of soils, climate, animals, plants, and their multiple interrelationships. The practical application of this lay in the need to trap animals, to build houses, to make utensils, to find medicines, and above all to devise systems of agriculture" (Rodney 2018: 46, 47, 44).

Rodney painted an interesting description of the feudal culture of the major African empires in his masterpiece *How Europe Underdeveloped Africa*. For one, he started from the premise that the Africans were culturally advanced and not backward, as many White scholars had painted them. In his description of feudalism in Egypt he noted that, "Although feudalism was based on the land, it usually developed towns at the expense of the countryside. The high points of Egyptian feudal culture were associated with the towns. The Fatimids founded Cairo, which became one of the most famous and most cultured cities in the world. At the same time, they established the Azhar University, which exists today as one of the oldest in the world" (Rodney 2018: 56). Moreover, at a time when literally 99 percent of Christian Europe was illiterate the Fatimids also built the Dar al-Ilm (House of Knowledge) library in Cairo which became world famous for housing more than 100,000 bound books and quite a few unbound; while the Azhar library housed more than 9,000 books and almost 600,000 manuscripts. The Khaza in al-Qusur beat that, housing more than 1.5 million books and booklets.

The Fatimids were a vibrant people – who existed prior to the European Renaissance in medieval Africa – that took North African culture beyond the communal phase and brought them to the phase of feudal existence. "Under the patronage of the Fatimid dynasty (969 A.D. to 1170 A.D.), science flourished and industry reached a new level in Egypt. Windmills and waterwheels were introduced from Persia in the tenth century. New industries were introduced – papermaking, sugar refining, porcelain, and the distillation of gasoline. The older industries of textile, leather, and metal were [also] improved upon" (Rodney 2018: 56). Thus we can see how Egypt thrived even during the Middle Ages and did not completely devolve after the fall of ancient Kemet. While many things may have definitely gone backward from that great civilisation, improvements were significantly still being made.

Yet Egypt was not the only place in North Africa to thrive pre-Renaissance:

> *"In the eleventh century, the armies of the Almoravid dynasty gathered strength from deep within Senegal and Mauritania and launched themselves across the Strait of Gibraltar to reinforce Islam in Spain, which was being threatened by Christian kings. For over a century, the Almoravid rule in North Africa and Iberia was characterized by commercial wealth and a resplendent literary and architectural record. After being ejected from Spain in the 1230s, the Maghreb Muslims, or Moors as they were called, continued to maintain a dynamic society on African soil. As one index to the standard of social life, it has been pointed out that public baths were common in the cities of Maghreb at a time when in Oxford the doctrine was still being propounded that the washing of the body was a dangerous act"* (Rodney 2018: 62).

This Almoravid Empire, from whence we get the Moors, had distinguished Black and Brown representatives who brought culture to Europe during Europe's Dark Ages. Indeed, "in the 10th and 11th centuries when Europe had no public libraries and only two significant universities, the Moors gave Spain more than 70 public libraries, built Spain seventeen famous universities and established an observatory at Serville" (Karenga 1989: 65).

Next, concerning West Africa, Rodney continued that "references to the Western Sudan in early times concern the zone presently occupied by Senegal, Mali, Upper Volta, and Niger, plus parts of Mauritania, Guinea, and Nigeria. The Western Sudanic empires of Ghana, Mali, and Songhai have become [emblematic] in the struggle to illustrate the achievements of the African past. That is the area to which African nationalists and progressive whites point when they want to prove that Africans too were capable of political, administrative, and military greatness" (Rodney 2018: 65). (And to be sure, when Rodney here said the empires of Ghana and Mali, he was not speaking of the Republics of Ghana and Mali that were created in 1957 and 1960 respectively, but the medieval Empire of Ghana and the medieval Empire of Mali which inhabited large sections of West Africa from the Niger River to Senegal and Mauritania).

Again, Rodney went on to explain, "The origins of the empire of Ghana go back to the fifth century A.D., but ...reached its peak between the ninth and eleventh centuries. Mali had its prime in the thirteenth and fourteenth centuries, and Songhai in the two subsequent centuries. The three were not in exactly the same location; and the ethnic origin of the three ruling classes was different; but they should be regarded as 'successor states,' following essentially the same line of evolution and growth" (Rodney 2018: 65). Rodney even went so far as to say that cotton manufacturing in these empires reached a height unlike any other medieval culture with varying degrees of specialisation and industry.

Within the Empire of Mali was also Timbuktu, which was known as the City of Gold due to the vast amounts of gold they had acquired through trade. Rodney continued, "During the centuries of Mali's greatness, extensive mining of gold began in the forest of [modern-day] Ghana to supply the trans-Saharan gold trade. The existing social systems expanded and strong states emerged to deal with the sale of gold. The merchants who came from the great cities of the Western Sudan had to buy the gold by weight, using a small accurate measurement known as the *benda*" (Rodney 2018: 68). Indeed, the gold trade had reached such sophistication in the Malian Empire that Mansa Musa, the Emperor of Mali at the time, was able to depress the value of gold in Egypt for approximately twelve years by being so generous with it. More importantly, Musa also built the University of Sankore in Timbuktu, which had a library housing at least one million manuscripts and made the value of knowledge in his empire priceless.

As far as feudal southern Africa goes, "Much has been written about the buildings which distinguish the Zimbabwe culture. They are a direct response to the environment of granite rocks, being built upon granite hills and of flaked granite. The most famous site of surviving stone ruins is that of Great Zimbabwe, north of the river Sabi. One of the principal structures at Great Zimbabwe was some 300 feet long and 220 feet broad, with the walls being 30 feet high and 20 feet thick" (Rodney 2018: 77). Moreover, "Their floors were constructed from cement made of crushed granite. [...] There were numerous drains and dadoes. At its height in the fourteenth century AD, the city 'was as big as mediaeval London' accommodating 18,000 people. The name Zimbabwe [itself was] derived from the Shona *Zimba Oye* meaning Great Revered House" (Walker 2011: 513).

Also, "Scholars have debated the possibility that the builders of Great Zimbabwe possessed highly sophisticated mathematical and astronomical knowledge, in addition to their better known engineering skills. Some writers suggest that the Temple contains structural features that display mathematical and/or astronomical alignments – as has been claimed for the Great Pyramid of Giza" (Walker 2011: 525). Furthermore, from the foundation of ancient Zimbabwe through to medieval Zimbabwe there was great prosperity and wealth in the land due to their abundance of goldmines, as Walker also stated, "The early miners of the gold belts displayed great efficiency and industriousness. They [thus] exhausted the empire's 4,000 gold mines" (Walker 2011: 524). Again, this industriousness in goldmining continued deep into the fourteenth and fifteenth centuries, when Zimbabwe hit its Golden Age, an age that was maintained during the time of the Mutapas.

Walker wrote concerning them, "Before the imperial rule of the Mutapas, the kings were just rulers of Great Zimbabwe." But,

"From the period of Mutapa Mutota, Great Zimbabwe stopped being the administrative capital of the region. The new capital of Munhumutapa was at Mount Fura, much further north" (Walker 2011: 520, 523). Moreover, this was no simple city-state tribal confederacy, "Since there are stone-built forts in the Johannesburg region, Ingombe Illede, and Manikwene, we conclude that the Mutapas held sway from Ingombe Illede in Zembia, to the north, to Johannesburg in South Africa, to the south. The empire ruled as far east as Manikwene in Mozambique, near to the coast of the Indian Ocean. It was already one of the largest empires in Mediæval Africa" (Walker 2011: 521). Thus after the fall of Great Zimbabwe Mwenemutapa became a great empire in feudal southern Africa, having its origins in the fifteenth century, at just about the beginning of the European Renaissance.

Rodney also continued, "The Rezwi lords of Mutapa did most to encourage production for export trade, notably in gold, ivory, and copper. Arab merchants came to reside in the kingdom, and the Zimbabwe region became involved in the network of Indian Ocean commerce, which linked them with India, Indonesia, and China. One of the principal achievements of the Rezwi lords of Mutapa was to organize a single system of production and trade" (Rodney 2018: 81), allowing gold to be traded in abundance during this reign of the Mutapas. It is even said that tens of millions of tons of gold were extracted from the 4,000 mines in the region which allowed the people of Mwenemutapa to cover virtually everything they had with gold, including "thread to weave into cloth, golden chains, golden wire of various gauges, golden beads with fine microscopic chevron decorations, and gold plating to cover objects. They covered statues, arrowheads and battleaxes with beaten gold" (Walker 2011: 524), even their headrests were covered with gold foil.

Finally, in East Africa culture and civilisation existed in other forms. First, "The Ancient Kushites of the Sudan ... became famous for the production of very high quality iron. This led a modern writer to describe the Kushite city of Meroë as the 'Birmingham of Africa'. The Kushites, at this date, traded through a road that led to two ports on the Eritrean coast called Azab and Adule, the latter became a centre of the world trade with contacts with the Far East, Greek-ruled Egypt and India. In 100 BC the city of Axum became the new capital for the Ethiopians" (Walker 2011: 460). The Axumite Empire was a thriving and bustling enterprise that created great glory and wealth for the people of feudal East Africa. The merchants of Axum were world famous as were their monuments. Massive granite obelisks and multi-storey structures covered the city, as did imports of silk and various metals.

Moreover, Walker noted that, "As well as ivory, the Axumites traded gold, rhinoceros-horn, hippopotamus hides and teeth, exotic animals, frankincense, emeralds (originally from Nubia), and slaves. These exports paid for the importation of silk, cotton, swords, wine, and glass drinking vessels. ... Gold and silver became transformed into plates. Gold and bronze were fashioned into statuary, some to a towering height of 15 feet. They fashioned weapons of steel. They also made lacquerware, military cloaks for the elite and olive oil. They had trading links with Kush, Egypt, the Roman provinces, the Mediterranean, Arabia, India, Sri Lanka and China" (Walker 2011: 461). Thus this was an empire of renown that made a powerful name for itself across both the Red Sea and the Mediterranean Sea.

But not only were they known for their trade and wealth, or even for their merchants and enterprise, they were also known for their culture and artistry as Graham Hancock noted, "Their sophisticated and prosperous culture mobilised large groups of labour and enough wealth to build great edifices – monumental architecture that survives to the present day. These massive buildings and towering stone sculptures are eloquent witness to a high level of artistic ability and engineering and mathematical skills" (Hancock 1996; quoted in Walker 2011: 460). In other words, they were no fools. Their intelligence in these matters was no small feat, yet we are told that the Ethiopians and East Africans were uneducated and ignorant. This is the danger of the discourse of White superiority.

Accordingly, not only was culture and wealth abundant in the Axumite Empire but "In 940 AD Judith, a Falasha conqueror, seized the throne and proclaimed herself Queen. [Thus ending] both the thousand-year supremacy of the city of Axum, and also an era of Ethiopian history. Succeeding her were the Zagwe Dynasty, who ushered in a Golden Age" (Walker 2011: 467). Indeed, though "Some authorities have suggested a Falasha origin for the Zagwes ... among the splendours of their building programmes, are a series of eleven rock-hewn *churches* in their new capital. Emperor Lalibela (*c.* 1150-1220) built these strikingly impressive engineering marvels in the late twelfth and early thirteenth centuries" (Walker 2011: 467). The economic and architectural abilities of feudal East Africa cannot be denied even if modern East Africa is currently known for its poverty.

What we see therefore is that all this took place in medieval Africa, long before the European Renaissance and before the days of *courtoisie*. So these Africans were not in the jungle swinging from trees before the White man came to them, but were actually far more cultured and prosperous. Basically, the social aetiology of White racism should not be sought for in Black people's lack of culture, as Africa had sophisticated cultures and intellectuals, such that many White people even attempted to emulate. The social aetiology of White racism should actually be sought for in something different that must have taken place during the Renaissance, as that is the time when the European narrative of distinction began to be propagated. So what was so significant about the Renaissance? Why was it then that White people began denigrating Other, and particularly the Black?

Because the enslaving of Black people from Africa began in Portugal and other pockets of Europe during the Renaissance.

Effectively, the only way White people could enslave those who at that time were far superior to them in philosophy, art, science, technology, cleanliness, purity, spirituality, and warfare; and enslave a race whose image was the original image of the Madonna and Child – and perpetuate that slavery amidst the vast evidences that Black people developed great civilisations and cultures, and had built thriving cultures from ancient times up into the Renaissance – was through spreading trick knowledge and saying that Black people were savages. They basically had to create the lie of our primitiveness and the lie of their own distinction to perpetuate their enslavement of these advanced peoples. Indeed, when most people think of the Renaissance they think of beautiful works of art; all I think of is Pope Eugene IV giving Europeans the right to enslave Africans and thus sanctioning the slave trade in 1442. This was the beginning. This was when tricknology was created to free European minds from any guilt over the enslaving of Black people.

Rodney also continued, stating that, "no people can enslave another for centuries without coming out with a notion of superiority, and when the color and other physical traits of those peoples were quite different, it was inevitable that the prejudice should take a racist form" (Rodney 2018: 102). This racism became the basis of European and American codes and how they saw themselves and compared themselves to Other. Thereby we can see that the internal contradiction, the problematic that created trick knowledge, was slavery. Trick knowledge was the system used to justify slavery, and as Rodney went on to say, "Nor was it merely a question of how the individual white person treated a black person. The racism of Europe [and America] was a set of generalizations and assumptions, which had no scientific basis, but were rationalized in every sphere from theology to biology" (Rodney 2018: 102).

Moreover, the international trade in slaves and the products of slave-labour also perpetuated European interests overseas as Europe turned economic and legal advantages into pivotal strengths (Rodney 2018). Not to mention that in any place where "the original European advantage was not sufficient to assure supremacy, they deliberately undermined other people's effects" (Rodney 2018: 97), whether through creating legal strictures that prevented non-European competition, or by using their first mover advantage to provide technological and financial support to existing industries. "Outstanding examples are provided in the persons of David and Alexander Barclay, who were engaging in slave trade in 1756 and who later used the loot to set up Barclays Bank. There was a similar progression in the case of Lloyds – from being a small London coffee house to being one of the world's largest banking and insurance houses, after dipping into profits from slave trade and slavery. Then there was James Watt, expressing eternal gratitude to the West Indian slave owners who directly financed his famous steam engine, and took it from the drawing board to the factory" (Rodney 2018: 98). Effectively, slavery helped, and in some cases even funded, European, and particularly British, development.

But not only so, also America, and even East Coast areas as prestigious as New York City, gained substantially from slavery. According to W.E.B. DuBois, "The city of New York has been until of late (1862) the principal port of the world for this infamous commerce; although the cities of Portland and Boston are … second to her in that distribution" (DuBois 1954; quoted in Rodney 2018: 100). In fact, the East Coast trade in slaves and the products of slave-labour stimulated maritime commerce, shipbuilding, and urbanisation in America (Rodney 2018).

What we therefore see is that slavery allowed for modernity to advance by providing commercial and industrial revolutions in Europe and America. So while a few White scholars love to remark that slavery was incapable of stimulating economic growth and therefore capitalism came to replace it, any unbiased analyst would know that most of the entrepreneurial heroes of early capitalism received their start as slave traders, slave owners, or were heavily funded by slavery, and that many of the rules of capitalism were developed during slavery. Indeed, Adam Smith's *Wealth of Nations* was written in 1776, long before slavery, or even the slave trade, had been abolished. Basically, the rulers and beneficiaries of capitalism would not have maintained a system for centuries they saw no value in; thereby linking capitalism, indivisibly, to slavery (Rodney 2018).

We now come to the final summation: is it fair to call White people devils? I would say yes. Why? Because due to the system created by White civilisation White skin has come to signify more than just a tonal coloration. It signifies power, privilege, prestige, respectability, importance, purity, honesty, et cetera., not just to White people but to *all* people. In sum, to be White is to be better than Other. Their skin colour does not stand in the world as innocent. It is highly signified and highly positioned; and there are also psychological connotations inherent in what their skin colour signifies, not just for other White people but for *all* people. At the risk of gross generalisation: *all* people inherently accept the discourse of White superiority, and the aphorism that to be White is to be better. It is no less real due to the pockets of resistance against it, from both White and non-White people. There are, indeed, many who see through the lies of this trick knowledge and fight against it; however, the vast majority have just come to accept it, or actively fight to preserve its constituencies. So what makes White people devils? The fact that the locus of devilishment is internal to them. For the non-White the locus of devilishment is external to them and will always remain so.

Moreover, if we consider where devilishment came from in the first place we get an understanding that what caused the devil to fall at the origin was a superiority complex: the devil felt superior to God and fell, or the devil felt superior to Adam and fell. Whatever way you look at it it was a superiority feeling that led the devil to become a devil. Well, White superiority and White supremacy are the current conclusions of devilishment. Obviously, it could be argued that devilishment thereby predates the days of the European Renaissance making the current definition somewhat useless. However, devilishment in its current form is that which we are to exorcise to remove the current tricknology haunting White society.

Tricknology in its current form is the basis of White supremacy. It is a discourse that creates all White social projections and social denigrations. These social projections in turn cause White behaviour towards Other, which thereby produces the result of a global White neurosis, on the one hand, and White devilishment, on the other hand. As we have seen, the root of the ideology of White supremacy was the social kinetics of the Renaissance. The manners of nobility, which they indirectly learned from the Moors, soon became common among the masses and those masses soon used that as an excuse for their feelings of superiority to the non-Whites, who through trick knowledge had been denigrated by the upper echelons of White society to the position of the savage.

VII

The ideology of White supremacy has not gone away in our time. It has instead gone through a radical transformation since decolonisation and desegregation. Late modernity has produced three responses from the global community: secularism, Charismatism, and Islamism. Secularism (of the post-structuralists, post-colonialists, and postmodernists type) surrenders to three very obscure forms of existentialism: for the post-structuralist an anti-discursive existentialism, for the post-colonialist an anti-Western existentialism, and for the postmodernist an anti-science existentialism. All three represent three versions of neoliberalism and all these see truth in subversion and inversion (by the standards of what they are opposed to). On the other hand, Charismatism (of both the Catholic and Protestant type) represents both an evangelical and eschatological response to late modernity. Both of these are neoconservative: the reactionary patriotism drawn from the merging of Christian morality and traditional values with political ideology and modern technology. Finally, Islamism (of the Sunni, Shi'i, and Sufi type) is the Islamic response to White supremacy in the form of neofundamentalism. Not all Islamists are terrorists, but all Islamists are Muslim fundamentalists. Both Islamism and fundamentalism have become dirty words post-9/11 but they need not be. A fundamentalist, of whatever sort, is merely a true believer, while an Islamist is merely a revolutionary Muslim.

To be clear, none of these positions can be considered left-wing therefore we have moved into a new ideological permutation: the right (whether New Right or Alt Right) has basically won for now, so be it. What we need to do at this point is find the synthesis between the neofundamentalist high conviction and the neoliberal low conviction. That synthesis is in anarcho-Islamism – or what *could* (and I emphasise could) be called neo-Islamism. It is the balance between high conviction leading to neofundamentalism and low conviction leading to neoliberalism. It is a personal conviction leading to anarcho-Islamism. Such is what the godbody movement introduces. Whereas conviction can be inhibiting, anarchism must, by definition, be liberating. Anarchism delivers one from the curse of the law, while allowing them to fulfil the law being led by a new conviction – a conviction based on integrity. Here legal, judicial, and penal institutions no longer become necessary as we have become a walking tablet, a living law, even, God demystified.

Nevertheless, anarcho-Islamism must produce its own contradictions, therefore as anarcho-Islamism grows its opposition will also grow causing a reactionary counter-revolution to occur in those places that institute anarcho-Islamism. Moreover, as the state is complicit in oppressing and murdering the Islamic, whether psychologically or bodily, Islamism must remain anarchistic. Marquis Bey (2020) took this argument even further, stating, "Destruction of the State, which is understood robustly as being attended by racial, gendered, and imperialist baggage, is an attempt at moving toward an anarchist society" (Bey 2020: 50). There is something inherently rebellious, even villainous, about anarchism; and those who seek to create an anarchist society thereby get infected by this association with all the negativity included in the terminology. Not only so, but anarcho-Islamism is also haunted by the spectre of Islamism, a spook currently feared and persecuted in the West. Anarcho-Islamism, or neo-Islamism, is therefore rebellious, and makes no bones about being rebellious.

Again, while it could be said, "Black anarchism can be found – or sometimes be glimpsed – in movements like that of BLM, or Anarchist People of Color, or Critical Resistance, or the Audre Lorde Project, and in a range of other formal and informal groupings" (Bey 2020: 103); there is still a power in identification, and in collaboration. Nevertheless, though movements like Critical Resistance and the Audre Lorde Project may not be as popular as the international movement against the destruction of Black lives, they are just as important. Here a unity of struggle shows that we are one anarchic whole. This struggle of anarchic identification must at once be anti-state as it is the state that creates institutions like prisons, patrols, and patriarchy to punish the transgressive, i.e. the Other. The state also creates a power dynamic that favours the rich, the male, and the White; a power dynamic that is outdated and worn.

To be sure, as can be seen by their association with the state and with power, neither neoliberalism nor neoconservatism, the New Right proper, are free from their own gendered and racial undertones. Still, as Born King Allah explained, "The devil had planned but Allah planned best and would not be stopped in giving the truth crushed into the earth back to the people who it was stolen from." "When Allah found us we were in a world that despised and kept us apart from their social equality ... Allah made it easier for us to see the atrocities and crimes they committed against us as the work of the devil ... Allah revealed that the devils['] old world had an expiration date and that the new world he would build through us represented the kingdom of God on earth" (The Five Percenter Vol 20.9; 2015: 3). Also, "Allah had proven we were not pro black or anti white. His teaching of Azreal was the proof of that statement. Birthed named John Kennedy, Azreal was a young white man Allah taught and helped while in Matawan" (The Five Percenter Vol 20.12; 2015: 9).

So some may now ask the question, how can you call White people devils and yet still believe that you are really not anti-White? To those who think thusly it must be reminded, very few of us actually consider White people to be the devil ontologically, however, we must, for the sake of sanity, empowerment, and unity, consider them to be the devil strategically. This philosophy effectively keeps us from being anti-White as we expect nothing from White people but to be devils. We are thereby not surprised or defeated by any racism they may manifest, unconscious or otherwise, and do not hold it against them. Trans model and Black activist Monroe Bergdorf summed up the Black struggle with White supremacy in a nutshell when she said, "The most ridiculous thing is that you call out racism and they respond with more racism, it just doesn't make any sense." When you understand that White supremacy and the White superiority complex has turned White people into devils then you expect nothing more from them than to behave as devils.

Indeed, when White people behave other than devil you are genuinely shocked. You never see it coming. It also gives you the ability to empathise with White people no matter how racist they are, as you know that they could never possibly understand what racist behaviour is without you explaining it to them. We also do not hold their racism against them, as frustrating as it is to constantly keep on having to explain it to them, as we expect no better from them. Now, this does not let White people off the hook, or give them a free pass to behave like devils, this gives Black people another layer of protection against their inevitable devilishment.

Again, whereas the current ideologies of the New Right perpetuate trick knowledge thereby corrupting them, we godbodies expose the devilishment of the trick knowledge and teach them knowledge of self, thus liberating them from this corruption. Indeed, as White supremacy and the doctrine that to be White is to be better are both forms of tricknology, the only cure for this trick knowledge, in both the White and the non-White, is knowledge of self. For White people knowledge of self leads to a humbler position, for non-White people it leads to a more exalted position. It was once said, "whosoever exalteth himself shall be abased; and he that humbleth himself shall be exalted" (Luke 14: 11).

Thus, what the Black theologian must accept in this, the age of iGod, is that White people have been corrupted by trick knowledge, which has turned them into the embodiments of devils. The White theologians, on the other hand, must accept that the sociological constructions of White supremacy have produced in their psychology, as well as in the world's, the ideation that to be White is to be better than Other. Therefore they will either fight against their own White privilege or they will remain contributors to this White supremacist system that has turned them into devils.

Consequently, men like David Cameron now go about saying things like Black people should just "get over slavery." You mean to say you tortured us, murdered us, kidnapped us, branded us, hung us, butchered us, some you threw overboard in the Atlantic to claim the insurance money from, and the rest you took to labour on your fields until they died of overwork replacing them with freshly bought slaves from Africa when they did, and you expect us to get over it. Just to let you know, Mr. Cameron, we will not just get over it and WE WILL NEVER FORGET.

Moreover, it is incumbent upon all us Black people to never forget, and to thereby fight to overthrow the current system of White supremacy they and their ancestors have created, having its destructive foundation in tricknology. This tricknology affects all sections of society causing both familial and governmental institutions to be beholden to its power. It is for this very reason that we godbodies oppose the state and the government, being ourselves the "ungoverned" and "ungovernable." Yet while such an idea may seem disorderly, even threatening to some, as Bey continued, "To be ungoverned is, yes, disorderly. Many castigate this yearning, [asserting] the utility and, indeed, value of order. But the order they speak of, and the order the ungoverned reject, is the order of the present society, a society ordered by virtue of its violent quelling of all those deemed disorderly. But ours is an order that arises by way of ungoverned disorder, an order that is more accurately a harmony, a beautiful ensemblic swarm that supplants the order of the State" (Bey 2020:31).

We godbodies for our part can help bring about the order of the ungoverned by creating new forms of Black revolutionism (*thawra*), even as Allah encouraged us to use *thawra* (revolutionism) in order to fight against *zulm* (oppression). Conversely, we have thus far chosen to fight against the *zulm* of White supremacy using illegalism as acts of rebellion against those who made the legal system. This has been relatively ineffective as it has put many Gods and Goddesses in prison with no means of legitimating their critique. The following argument is to expand Black revolutionism beyond underclass methods and to incorporate working class methods as more effective means of bringing social crisis to the White establishment. The most glorious method of working class revolutionism is the general strike, as Tom Brown said, "Every advance by trade unionists, or even by unorganised workers has been gained by a strike or the threat of a strike ... Even an individual threat to quit the job is an application of the strike weapon. Trade unions owe their birth and growth to the strike" (Brown 1990: 11). Following Brown we will now consider a list of the various strike methods and how to use them so that they can be employed as forms of Black revolutionism to cause social crisis to White devilishment.

The first and most notorious method of striking that Brown spoke of was the lightning strike: "The lightning strike, not [only] because of its speed, but also as a result of the time and place of its blow, is usually more effective than the orthodox, long drawn-out affair, played according to a set of rules almost as traditional as those of chess. It is particularly effective on a small scale, as in a single factory or group of factories" (Brown 1990: 87). How one works is basically a strike is called and initiated immediately without preparing the bosses or alerting the trade unions. It is purely a workers' action. "Almost equally important is the 'guerrilla strike,' to wage a struggle in any section of an industry, in any locality or even in a single factory, whenever conditions may be temporarily favourable" (Brown 1990: 12).

These forms of working class revolutionism (*thawra*) should be incorporated into godbody forms of Black revolutionism. Though many godbodies have illegal occupations there is a large number of us who have legal and legitimate occupations. Surely we godbodies can agitate those in White-owned, or predominantly Black, workplaces into strike action to raise their confidence in their own self-worth. "Many ingenious strike tactics have been invented by the French Syndicalists. Of these, the work-to-rule strike of the railmen is, perhaps, best known. When, under nationalisation, French railway strikes were forbidden, their Syndicalist [fellows] were delighted to urge the railmen to carry out the strict letter of the law. Now French railways, like those of most other countries, are governed by thousands of laws, most of them unused and ignored, their place being taken by commonsense and experience." "One French law tells the engine-driver to make sure of the safety of any bridge over which his train must pass. If, after personal examination, he is still doubtful, then he must consult the other members of the train's crew. Of course, trains ran late" (Brown 1990: 88). It is interesting to see how creative the mind can be when devising ways of rebelling against the system.

Whether we use a lightning strike, guerrilla strike, or work-to-rule strike, any form of strike is a mass action far more effective than selling illegal substances; and though the reason behind selling illegal substances is primarily to feed oneself and/or family, the fact is, a godbody is far more useful at the workplace agitating the workers into bringing about a social crisis than on the streets committing illegal activities. Though agitating for strike action can still be as dangerous as committing illegal actions, such strike actions can be organised when Gods and Goddesses go to the modern factory – the business, corporation, or organisation – and meet with a few key Black people there. Indeed, these meetings should be held in secret, just like the plotting of a slave rebellion, so as to keep the Black workers from being fired. Any form of social revolutionism (*thawra*) has its dangerous element; however, if the end result is the *deshackling* of Black people the ends can justify the means.

Furthermore, according to Bey (2020: 93) "To deshackle oneself marks a radical act of freedom in the broadest sense, a way of living not in defiance but in refusal and subversion of the

State." This is why we must understand, though we will be fighting the bosses, managers, and companies, the main opposition we will face will come from the state. The state is currently the central power of society and will seek to remain so for as long as possible. By the Black workers taking up their power, and exposing the extreme powerlessness of the state, the state will retaliate with shows of force and other means to demonstrate that it is worthy of maintaining its existence.

This will be the second form of danger presented to the Black workers who take a stand against the system. I will say, however, that it was dangerous for Harriet Tubman to guide those slaves through the Underground Railroad. It was dangerous for the anti-colonialists to wage armed struggle to free themselves from colonisation, and it was dangerous for the Civil Rights activists to sit at Whites Only diners during the era of the Klan and the noose. Revolution (*thawra*) entails danger as the system will seek to maintain its existence, and change is always hard, but in our case it is also necessary.

Nevertheless, if a godbody does seek to agitate for strike action they "must change [the] strategy from that of the General Walk Out Strike to that of the General Stay In Strike." Accordingly, "The workers, instead of walking out and leaving the factory or other plant in the hands of the employer, stay in and lock out the boss. This at once prevents the factory being used for Blacklegging and protects the strikers" (Brown 1990: 69, 89). The stay in strike is basically an occupation of the workplace by the workers of that workplace thereby causing a massive crisis in the fabric of White society.

To occupy a workplace is to effectively take all power away from the bosses and owners and show them how powerless they really are; the example being the Italian Occupy Strike of 1920: "Not a skull was cracked. Not a safe. ... Commotion everywhere, except in Italy. It is true that, day by day, more and more factories were being occupied by the workers. Soon 500,000 'strikers' were at work, building automobiles, steamships, forging tools, manufacturing a thousand useful things, but there was not a shop or factory owner there to boss them or to dictate letters in the vacant offices. Peace reigned" (Seldes 1935: quoted in Brown 1990: 91).

However, one of the major problems with any occupy strike, particularly a Black occupy strike, is that once the bosses and owners see the power of the workers they will seek to curtail it. For this cause it is unwise for a business, corporation, or organisation that has been taken over and occupied by the workers to ever give the company back to the owners. Whatever the reason for which the workers of that business, corporation, or organisation began an occupy strike, the end cannot and should not be the gaining of that, or that and several other, concession(s). The owners and bosses will regroup and recuperate after their failure and only begin a round of job depreciations and layoffs (coupled with a few bribes) to make future occupy strikes less likely or at least less effective.

If Black workers choose to use this, the most effective weapon in their arsenal, the end must be to buy out the company. Of course, the bosses will call in their lawyers and the trade union leaders but all that is just smoke and mirrors, they are powerless against an occupy strike if sympathetic workers from other industries supply them with food, toiletries, and inspiration. They will, however, as soon as they begin the occupy strike, need to hire their own lawyers, those who specialise in proxy fighting, and start making plots on what, in the business world, is called a hostile take-over of the company. Everything will basically be easy for them so long as they put all the profits they make into a communal fund to pay-off the lawyer, thereby turning their current place of employment into a co-operative.

Nevertheless, another key aim after the occupy strike has begun will be arming and creating a Black militia for protection against counter-revolutionists and police. This should also be organised by the Black workers as soon as the strike begins. Any employed God or Goddess must organise the non-White workers into a body, and arm and train them to protect themselves and the movement. In this case, the example is Spain: "In the Spanish Civil War of 1936 the Workers' Militia was largely based on the squad of ten men known to one another and choosing their own squad leader or delegate. The squads of ten men were united into centurias of one hundred men and seven or eight centurias formed into a column, all on the federal principle." Indeed, "The Spanish Militia of 1936-37 had no officer caste or badge of rank, no privilege or special ration, no saluting. The ranks were filled, not by conscription, but by the revolutionary knowledge and enthusiasm of the workers" (Brown 1990: 60, 62).

Brown (1990) also suggested the forms of units that can be used (shipyard, dock, and seamen for naval; bus, lorry, and truck drivers for land and transport; chemical workers, engineers, and arms dealers can use their skills to help and arm the workers). Yet he was also very earnest, "For the defence of the Revolution there must be no new regular army, or police force, or officer caste, but the arming of the workers." "If a new police force were created to arrest counter-revolutionists the policemen would naturally try to preserve their new jobs even when the old regime had been crushed" (Brown 1990: 63). It is incumbent upon the godbodies who practice these working class forms of social revolutionism to remember their anarchic leanings. Indeed, "the overarching claim of anarchist ideology is that any kind of coercive, dominative oppression is to be quashed" (Bey 2020: 12).

Always also remembering, "anarchism is a kind of abolitionism." Still, "As I think explicitly about [abolitionism], I am using as its definition, simply, the political strategy of *eradicating* rather than *reforming* systems, discourses, and institutions that structure life" (Bey 2020: 94, 91). This is what anarchism is and does, it abolishes and demolishes the systems, discourses, and institutions of what has been called by those seeking to sound intellectual: biopolitics. The abolition of biopolitics, and, indeed, all politics is one of the central aims of anarchism, and though not currently an aim of the godbody, it identifies with our general theories. The current system is overrun with trick knowledge and has caused the doctrines and ideas of White supremacy to become embedded into the structures of life. These structures must be washed and rinsed clean from these systems of White supremacy, and the discourses and institutions that accompany them.

Yet if we godbodies truly wish to overcome trick knowledge and the White supremacy it creates we must adopt new tactics: tactics that have the overall aim of bringing massive social crisis to White supremacy, recognising that such an ask is an exalted one. It is White supremacy that has turned the White man into a devil and it is White tricknology that has allowed them to create a system where they feel supreme. It will be acts of Black revolutionism, like the organised general strike of all predominantly Black or White-owned businesses, corporations, and organisations that will cause a huge and crippling halt to their ideology of White supremacy. Notwithstanding, after the occupy strike has begun the Black workers will have to make preparations to hostilely take over the business, corporation, or organisation, which will be most possible if it is done in the context of a Black general strike. While at first sight such may appear dangerous, the truth is, if we godbodies begin going to various White-owned, predominantly Black workplaces, agitating the Black workers toward mass action the end result *will* be a mass strike; but it will not happen overnight.

Ultimately, we can see how Black revolutionism (*thawra*) has a severe handicap if it is purely left in the hands of the underclass. We underclass are strong but we do not have the power of the working class. That is not to say that workers are the most revolutionary section of society: many workers are unwilling to risk their jobs or their money to fight for ideal societies. It is just to say that we underclass godbodies need to open up to the working class Black community more. These are what we godbodies call the 85 percent and so leave in the hands of the devils. But they could actually be a strong force to fight against the devils and exorcise their devilishment. When the Black workers have formed a mass of co-operatives as a result of various occupy strikes we will be in a position of power and no longer dependent on White bosses and White owners. There will thus be a turn, from Black people being the victims of a White oligarchy to Black people overthrowing the White oligarchy and initiating a Black thearchy.

Vampyrism and the 10 Percent

"15. Who is the 10 percent? The rich, slave-makers of the poor, who teach the poor lies to believe that the almighty true and living God is a spook and cannot be seen with the physical eye, otherwise known as the bloodsuckers of the poor" (Lost Found Muslim Lesson No. 2).

It is impossible to consider the culture of New York City today and not notice the influence of the godbody on virtually every aspect of the Black mind. Those that are not godbody still hold to godbody definitions and interpretations, or use godbody idiom in their expressions. As Black culture in America has always been an appendage of White culture the intellectual shift towards an anti-modern perspective has taken hold in their sciences. The effect this has had on the Black world has been profound if one considers the Christian Charismatics of the West. However, the godbodies are far more invocative of scientific elements with their show and prove injunctions than their Charismatic counterparts.

The question of whether the godbody is a modern or anti-modern culture may seem rather unimportant; however, if we are to decode their position in relation to the Black world, and particularly the Black bourgeoisie, we must see things from their perspective. The first thing we need to know is that anti-modernism does not necessarily mean anti-technology, or even anti-American. Anti-modernism means anti-American*ism*, as Americanism is the basis of modernism. Indeed, two things distinguish the anti-modern from the postmodern: (i) anti-modernism is when the postsecular meets the post-democratic to form a thearchic answer to modernism, and (ii) whereas postmodernism is generally anti-essentialist anti-modernism uses intersubjective essentialism to overcome imperialism, racism, classism, sexism, heterosexism (commonly called homophobia), and cis-sexism (commonly called transphobia).

The second thing we need to know about the godbody perspective is that godbodies for the most part use modern science to decipher the mysteries of the Black place in the world, and to show and prove that the Black man is in fact Allah. Now whereas such an expression has proven to be surprising, even shocking, to some minds, to a godbody it makes perfect sense. We godbodies see the revelation of Allah as Science, therefore if the Black man masters everything about a specific science that should prove the Black man's omniscience in that particular science, thereby making him the embodiment of Allah for that science.

The reason we godbodies also call ourselves Five Percenters is that it is generally understood that 85 percent of the Original people are easily led in the wrong direction and hard to be led in the right direction, they are the humble masses, mentally deaf, dumb, and blind to the truth about themselves and the world in which they live; 10 percent of the Original people understand much of the truth but use it to their advantage to keep the 85 percent under their control through religion, politics, entertainment, economics, and other methods; and 5 percent of the Original people are the enlightened divine beings, having repossessed knowledge of the truth regarding the foundations of life and of oneself, and seek to punitively liberate the 85 percent through education. Accordingly, we teach that all human beings are not only interconnected to the Supreme Being, but that all human beings are also Supreme Beings in their own right, manifested in four descending levels of righteousness: Divines, babies, vampyres, and devils.

Allah was the one who taught the first of us these kinds of lessons; though, as rich with content as they are, we were not able at that time to fully reach our greatest potential. Nevertheless, the lessons took us from humiliation, degradation, and mental savagery to the height of civilisation. Lord Jamel Born Akbar U Allah said, "The father broke down the knowledge and wisdom of all the sages that had come before him into little ABC's and 1-2-3's so even little kids in the hood could understand it" (The Five Percenter Vol 22.2; 2016: 4). And Born King Allah continued, "He chose us to become the all wise who the true and living God is to free us from the belief in a mystery god that enslaved generations of our people including our parents" (The Five Percenter Vol 20.9; 2015: 3). We had no knowledge of self until Allah brought it to us, now we can see ourselves as the true and living God and not as the devils have painted us.

But these lessons are also controversial on several levels, even for Black people – who for the most part hold to the interpretation of a White God; or some enlightened ones: of a Black God – to say that Black *men* are actually Black *Gods* is an unsettling idea at its best. Again, most Black Christians would be offended to be classified as babies, that is, as mentally deaf, dumb, and blind; let alone as vampyres, that is, as Black snakes or bloodsuckers of the poor. It could be asked: what is to be gained by smearing our Black brothers and sisters by saying this about them?

Obviously, to the godbodies the 10 percent are those Black bourgeoisies who have learned the lessons of devilishment from the devils and have been disseminated among the Black masses of the Black community to perpetuate the lie of White supremacy. But the Black bourgeoisie are not our enemy, the American world system is our enemy. White supremacy is our enemy. Yet, according to Born King Allah, "Using God as a weapon, whites have tricked black people to unconsciously worship them in the flesh. Diabolically, they have been able to get the enslaved black populace all over the world to fall in love [with] and worship their God that looks like them" (The Five Percenter Vol 20.10; 2015: 9). Basically, the spook god most Black people worship is a product of White trick knowledge that the devils have planted in the Black community to deceive us.

An example of this is found in some of those who love to ask the question: "Why can't Black people seem to pull themselves up by the bootstraps?" Explaining that the world is a fair enough place to reward anybody who works hard and earns it, they ask, "Why don't Black people just work hard and God will find a way to reward them?" Finally, they point to the Ashkenazi and say, "Look at all they suffered and look at how they pulled themselves up and are now in a position of power all over the world."

Well, on the one hand, the Ashkenazi trial with the Nazis was from 1933 to 1944, a bitter eleven years of torture. On the other hand, the Black struggle with pan-European slavery began in 1442 when Pope Eugene IV legitimated the enslaving of Africans throughout the European nations; continued on into 1553 the time of the first maroon rebellions among the slaves, and lasted, some say till 1834 when Britain abolished slavery throughout their Empire, some say till 1848 when France abolished slavery throughout their Empire, some say till 1865 when America abolished slavery throughout their country, and some say till 1888 when Brazil, the last stronghold of slavery, finally abolished slavery throughout their country.

But the abolition of slavery was only a farce as in 1885 the European powers met in Berlin to discuss the dividing up of Africa between them. Not that none of them had colonies in

Africa before the Berlin Conference, just that before the Berlin Conference they had colonies by the barrel of a gun, after Berlin it had been legitimated. Not a single African leader was present at the Berlin Conference so it was an act of theft and an act of aggression, but the continent was subjugated to European powers for another seventy, eighty, ninety, and in South Africa's case another hundred and nine years.

Basically, the eleven years the Ashkenazi suffered were hardly strong enough to affect their self-identity. They were rulers and powers before the Nazis came to power and they went back to being rulers and powers after the Nazis expended themselves. Black people never got a break: from slavery to segregation, from segregation to neo-segregation, or from slavery to colonisation from colonisation to neo-colonisation. Indeed, since the days of segregation and colonisation the US began using trumped up charges and false statements to arrest and discredit so many of our Black leaders: such as Maulana Karenga, Dr. York, and Dr. Sebi in America; and Economic Hitmen to bride and incapacitate various Black leaders in Africa.

I

In the last chapter we used Dalal's (2010) theories of race to help us understand where White racist behaviour came from, both internally and externally. However, we left out a significant aspect of Dalal's theory of race that we shall now explore in this chapter: his interpretation of Frantz Fanon's racial theories. Dalal (2010) investigated Fanon and developed an interesting explication of the psychology of the racially oppressed. Nevertheless, Dalal also presented a caveat that we must appreciate before going any further, "Although much of what Fanon describes is from a different age and place, its pertinence lies in the fact that he is describing a legacy that we are still firmly in the grip of" (Dalal 2010: 93). Such a caveat is quite telling for two reasons: (i) such a caveat is rarely made for Aristotle's theories in spite of the pro-slavery influence of some of them, or for Hegel's theories in spite of his racist proclivities, and (ii) the fact that he has to write it all the more validates exactly what he is trying to say.

To start with Dalal (2010) pointed to the pathological (abnormal, dysfunctional) tendencies that existed for the Black people of Fanon's time, "Fanon says 'With the exception of a few misfits within the closed environment, we can say that every neurosis, every abnormal manifestation … in an Antillean is the product of his cultural situation' … And by cultural situation he means the colonial situation" and to be clear, "the colonialist's world is a Manichaean world that is rigidly divided into two absolute regions – good and bad, white and black, colonizer and colonized" (Dalal 2010: 92, 95). What therefore was used to oppress the colonised Black person during the days of colonisation, is now used to undermine the bourgeois Black person during these days of late modernity.

These bourgeois Blacks, who have perpetuated the doctrine of trick knowledge among us, are to us another opposition within the Black community. Dalal (2010) noted that during colonialism the neuroses of the then colonised Blacks came mainly in three distinct forms: inferiority complex, tribalism, and obsessive violence. Yet in our time these three have evolved into three new forms of reality distorting neurosis: autophobia, prosperity theology, and pseudo-nationalism. Those Black individuals who subscribe to any one of these new forms have allowed the devils to deceive them into believing that the current world standard not only works but is the best system we could possibly have. This deception has corrupted them, having them bow down to either the White political system (pseudo-nationalism), the White spiritual system (prosperity theology), or to the White superiority discourse (autophobia). No matter how you look at it, all three for a Black person are forms of acculturation manifesting for them a deep-seated psycho-pathology.

As it is today, the unconscious assumption among *certain* White anthropologists, White sociologists, and White psychologists that Black is equated with the primitive, the criminal, the infantile, or the insane produces tensions within the bourgeois Blacks' self-definitions and interrelations with their own kind. Far from seeing self and kind as capable of potential greatness, they see self and kind as destined to regress, fail, or rebel. When one is bought up to believe, based on overwhelming evidence, that they and their loved ones are inferior, the psychological response is tripartite: regression into a repressive state of self-loathing and autophobia; digression into a depressive state of inhibited morality and materialist greed; or transgression into an obsessive state of social resistance and anti-social behaviour. These self-defeating mechanisms have been developed in the minds of the vast majority of Black bourgeoisies.

True indeed, most of we Black people start the race at a disadvantage. For us to even come close to empowerment we must start the race at an even footing; but this is very difficult at present as we have already been fed almost 550 years of inferiority and have for the most part accepted it and so followed suit. We became the child, the insane, the criminal, and thus degenerated into the caricature of our simplicity, our materialism, or our resistance. The less we identified with ourselves and our ancestors the more we became a pseudonoir, not Black but going through the motions of what we believe to be Black based on what we have been shown by this misrepresenting system of White supremacy.

Acculturation for the colonised occurred when the Black or ethnic individuals or social bodies accepted as truth the trick knowledge given to them either from a White person or from other Black or ethnic people. Acculturation is the losing of one's traditional and ancestral culture to adopt the dominant culture: and during colonialism this was White culture. Dalal (2010: 96, 97) explained it far better when he said, "The fact that everything of consequence is white, means that the colonized has to do everything in his power to make himself white, inside and out." Indeed, "Fanon counters the charge that the Negro makes himself inferior, by saying that he is *made inferior.*" There is, effectively, for the Black person an "internalization – or, better, the epidermalization – of this inferiority" (Fanon 2008: 4).

Yet White culture itself was the amalgamation of all ideas and standards acquired during the Enlightenment and the Great Awakening. The Enlightenment transpired when the European nations co-opted theoretical perspectives based on scientific and philosophic mastery. The Great Awakening was a reaction to the Enlightenment that took place in the American colonies, espousing the idea that the Bible was inerrant and the Protestant tradition was the foremost authority in interpreting it. These two, European scientific snobbery and American Protestant pietism, would further complicate the doctrine of tricknology that corrupted them as a people into buying into the idea of White superiority.

Then, to paraphrase Dalal (2010), White people began to educate some Black and ethnic people into the lessons of tricknology, as the threat of an intelligent or charismatic one inspiring Black or ethnic groupings to revolt was too imminent. Consequently, "when [a] black man is accepted it is 'on one condition: You have nothing in common with real Negroes. You are not black, you are "extremely brown"' … These constant 'reminders' [then contributed] to the creation of [their] inferiority complex" (Dalal 2010: 98). So these White people supervised the elevation of certain ethnic people into higher positions in the metropolitan centre only as this was beneficial for them in the keeping down, not only of the other races, but also of the more radically inclined within their own White race.

The distinction between inferiority complexes and autophobia is that while both are in their turn neurotic manifestations, inferiority complexes come from the incorporation of the White Other into the Black unconscious. Autophobia, on the other hand, is the irrational hatred and terror of self and kind. Yet how can this be when a phobia, as defined by Hesnard, is "a neurosis characterized by the anxious fear of an object (in the broadest sense of anything outside the individual) or, by extension, of a situation"? (Hesnard 1949; quoted in Fanon 2008: 119). Dalal helped us understand this better by saying, "In the normal course of events a phobic will distance themselves from the thing that they are phobic about. But here the black person does not have the possibility of withdrawing from their black skin and this in turn leads to alienation. [It then further develops as] the black person [looks] in the white man's eyes to give himself substance, to find himself, but instead of himself he finds the white man's perception of himself. In effect, he is torn asunder" (Dalal 2010: 97).

The depth of this racially motivated autophobia can be distinguished in the vampyres' pattern for what Anna Freud called identification with the aggressor. They internalised from Whites the "best" means of understanding themselves, and with Black ancestral culture being now antiquated and primitive to them, they are told that their ancestors were godless worshippers of stone, wood, the sun, and nature, and that their ancestors were underdeveloped and nowhere near as advanced as modern science has allowed White people to become. In reality, however, the opposite is true: our ancestors were far more advanced than modern science has allowed White people to become, and their technologies were far more spiritually and environmentally stable.

It is true that as godbodies we take most spiritual beliefs to also be forms of trick knowledge, especially those based on the mystique of invisible deities. Yet, the falsehood of religions based on a mystery God or mystery gods is not too distinct from the general acceptance in the godbody *ciphers* of a Universal Intelligence that we call Allah. What distinguishes tricknology from righteous teachings is the conception of waste and the systematisation of deceit, as, "the devil is a liar." The incorporation of deceit, whether it is self-deceit or group-deceit, is what defines trick knowledge. This is interesting as the climax of Western indoctrination occurred in the 1960s at the beginning of the Western Black Power movement and the height of the global anti-colonial movement. Since then Western religions and Western sciences have come seriously under question.

Nevertheless, to further explicate the psychopathology of the autophobic Black and ethnic person we must now consider the illness itself. First, we shall examine the component indices of the malady. According to Dalal (2010: 96), "Fanon ... asks the interesting question – how does the Negro become abnormal when 'very often the Negro who becomes abnormal has never had any relations with whites' ... He answers, that the abnormality is caused by a *collective catharsis*." Or, in Fanon's own words, "In every society, in every collectivity, exists – must exist – a channel, an outlet through which the forces accumulated in the form of aggression can be released" (Fanon 2008: 112).

These channels, according to Fanon, provide society with a cathartic release by projecting negativity onto the Other. "In the magazines the Wolf, the Devil, the Evil Spirit, the Bad Man, the Savage are always symbolized by Negroes or Indians; since there is always identification with the victor, the little Negro, quite as easily as the little white boy, becomes an explorer, an adventurer, a missionary 'who faces the danger of being eaten by the wicked Negroes.'" Indeed, "The black schoolboy in the Antilles, who in his lessons is forever talking about 'our ancestors, the Gauls,' identifies himself with the explorer, the bringer of civilization, the white man who carries truth to savages – an all-white truth.

There is identification – that is, the young Negro subjectively adopts a white man's attitude" (Fanon 2008: 113, 114). Effectively, what is an innocent catharsis to White people becomes a false catharsis for Black people.

Dalal further explained that with the self-identification of the Black person now redefined in accordance to the White person's gaze, for the Black person to not seek to flee from such a representation would itself be pathological. Basically, the ultimate conclusion is "you're damned if you do and damned if you don't." Yet, as Born King Allah articulated, it is their "acceptance of [the] white mysterious super God ... [that] switched chattel slavery into religious slavery" (The Five Percenter Vol 20.10; 2015: 9), thereby placing the bourgeois Black in a very difficult position: how can they condemn the evils of White people when religiously they are worshipping a White man. So then, far from equalising with the White man they adored him, and made his victory all the more diabolical by surrendering to his culture at the cost of their own. But such must always be the case within a system that has glorified and adopted White mythologies and White symbologies – that we here consider to all be forms of trick knowledge – into its power structure.

The tricknology of the devils has now become the bread and butter of the vampyres, who, not content with adopting the White man's mannerisms, superseded White people in their love for the systems. They became more outlandish, more over-the-top, more hyper-real; if not more bourgeois, more modernising, less sympathetic. Their own struggles in the world made them consider the non-aspirant to be lazy, impotent, and retrograde. The psychological traumata of having experienced any opposition in this White world system inspired them to desire never to go through that sort of experience again. The accommodating mechanisms in their minds all too easily forgave the White man and blamed their own Black people for their feelings of pain. Thus the devil became the authority, the parent, the obsession; such that their vampyrism deferred to the devil and psychologically retrogressed their followers to the position of an infant.

In considering deeper the acculturation of these vampyres, which manifests itself through the epidermalisation of such; it becomes imperative that we look more in-depth into its social aetiology before trying to diagnose a cure for it. Fanon has already said that what is taught the Black child during the process of socialisation contributes substantially to the Black child's psychological development. If a Black child is taught a form of tricknology – like the predominance of White superiority – it can be certain that child will have a form of inferiority or acculturating epidermalisation by their adult life. This is not only so for an astral but also for a social body.

Doctrines like democracy, as opposed to "primitivism," were heavily touted by the West as the most stable and sensible forms of indoctrination. Far from it, the West seemed to advance democracy for Whites and dependence and exploitation for Blacks. Racism was an unequivocal manifestation of Renaissance thinking. The racist represented an ideology, a White ideology of White civilisation, while oppressing the non-White people in the world and calling that civilisation. The non-Whites in Europe and America all seemed to be second or third class citizens. Thus modernism, the system that created racism, also allowed for White supremacy within the metropole.

White standards of morality, sociality, justice, and freedom did not match up with their history of violence, sexual abuse, exploitation, and theft. Some Blacks in the West and Blacks in the colonies understood that White standards were illegitimate for them: they only worked to subjugate the mass of non-White people. For these Black people the question of legitimacy and what made Western values better than non-Western were most pertinent. At a stand, the West has no right to lecture anybody on corruption as the nations they usually criticise as corrupt usually have no power. The powerful West in all its corruption forces itself where it does not belong and forces other nations to bow down to its standards of governance, justice, morality, and civility. Western corruption far outweighs non-Western corruption as the West has the military power to do what they want and the media power to justify it.

Where legitimacy fails to win the day is in the minds of the godbodies. We see the West forcing their form of governance on weaker countries and it reminds us of colonialism. What gives the West the right to impose their standard of governance on non-Western countries? Or to be even more blunt: What gives White people the right to force their standards of civility, morality, justice, and governance on non-Whites? The more we investigate with these sorts of questions the more we see that the question of White supremacy will not die until modernity has been properly superseded by a true postmodernism, where this legitimacy question is not just happening in non-Western countries but goes on in the heart of Western countries by both White and non-White people. The Black Power movement was the first in America to do so. They challenged the entire power structure of the White world declaring that White power had to be confronted by Black Power. That is, the glorification of all things Black.

Still, the devilishment within Black vampyrism has effectively created a reality that undermines us Blacks. The mechanisms they put in place translate, firstly, in the psychological with the discourse of White superiority, then in the ideological with the structure of White supremacy, and finally, in the sociological with the systems of White privilege, all leading to the progression of the White race. Therefore the overthrowing of White power begins in the psychological and ends in the sociological. The best therapy we can provide for the epidermal pressures acculturating their Black culture, and the astral traumata of obsessing on White culture, is to be recultured back into a Black culture, as relatively undefined as it may be. Following that comes indoctrination into a Black ideology for Black people (a Brown ideology for Brown people, a Red ideology for Red skinned people, a Yellow ideology for so-called Yellow people, and maintaining a White – though more congenial – ideology for White people).

Of course, being a godbody I would want the new ideology for all non-Whites (and even for Whites) to be the godbody ideology. In this, Lord Jamel Born Akbar U Allah said "with these teachings we should be able to go to different ciphers and come out God. We are lord of all worlds. We go to synagogues, mosques, NA, churches, and come out God" (The Five Percenter Vol 22.2; 2016: 4). However, if they are not convinced from this book to join the godbody movement I am happy for the non-White, and particularly for the Black vampyres among them, to be indoctrinated into another non-White ideology. Following indoctrination a former Black vampyre will be reconnected to the Black masses and will be in a position to change the Black communities they used to reject.

II

Dalal (2010) spoke of another way that Black people can become acculturated that is very pertinent at this time: "Fanon [chastized] the national bourgeoisie for not educating the masses, and instead encouraging the activation of ancient rivalries." Again, "Religious as much as 'racial' rivalries are activated to this end" (Dalal 2010: 107). Effectively, the national bourgeoisie, or in our case, the Black bourgeoisie, used religious philosophies and religious systems as lightning rods to galvanise the colonial community into competition or outright conflict with opposing religions. Dalal emphasised that in the writings of Fanon religious ideas were technically understood to be an opiate for the masses, "Fanon [was clear] that another way of avoiding the expression of rage and despair [was] by turning to religion and superstition as a way of making the situation more bearable" (Dalal 2010: 99).

Accordingly, if we want to help Black people, even today, we must meet them where they are, and a lot of them are in the Black Church. For this cause, a unity with the Black Church, instead of treating them like they are the enemy, could create an exponential and inexorable growth in Black development. The Black Church, however, is currently being used by their leaders to keep the masses poor by motivating them to give all their money to the progression of the church and church projects. Therefore, in our time, the central place of opposition to our movement will come, not from the Black Church as such, but from the prosperity preachers who lead many of these Black churches.

Black prosperity theology in itself is a form of acculturation and psychopathology turning many Black preachers into vampyres. The spook god they worship and teach others to worship is a fabrication created by tricknology to perpetuate their position. Not only so, but even the Jesus they worship and teach others to worship is a fabrication designed to maintain the illusion of their humility. He is not the actual Messiah who died thousands of years ago, and, according to the tradition, ascended or vanished never to be seen again. He is a fabrication that must be exposed. That said, the accomplishment of such a tumultuous endeavour, that of exposing the false teachings about the Messiah, will be pursued in greater depth in Chapter 6.

The prosperity theology that spreads their false message is based on a delusion that has created a poor ideal-self for Black people, causing them to sacrifice an ideal worthy of themselves for the ideal of a false messiah, that is, a false Jesus. Not only so, but the more they imitate and encourage others to imitate this false messiah the more damage they do to the ego of self and kind. Again, if we look deeper into this prosperity theology's effect on Black churches, which includes the Charismatic and Evangelical churches, we can see, "In these churches, prosperity, not only in things spiritual but also in the secular realm, is accentuated ... pauperism, destitution and slender means are simply interpreted as God's chastisement" (Ayegboyin 2011: 155).

To be sure, those prosperity theologians who use New Thought lessons to teach on the power of faith or the law of attraction are really just the pseudo-spiritual victims of tricknology. And as trick knowledge is a philosophy that perpetuates White devilishment, the overthrowing of it will assist in the overthrowing of the devil's system. At the same time, faith features heavily in prosperity theology, which teaches that God wants us all to prosper regardless of how righteous or unrighteous we are. Effectively, it creates a delusional bubble in which countless people are captive, believing that God is not wise but robotnic and mechanical, only able to abide by their misinterpretation of the law of attraction or law of manifesting (both amounting to the same thing in their misinterpretation).

This prosperity message is highly prominent in the Black community, further reinforcing in the Black community the position of the Black bourgeoisie. But if it all turns out to be just another form of trick knowledge then those bourgeois Blacks who preach prosperity will be nothing more than the vampyres we godbody oppose so harshly as the bloodsuckers of the poor. Furthermore, as "Paul Gifford observed concerning Mensa Otabil, the founder of International Central Gospel Church, prosperity preachers present themselves 'as entrepreneurs who have developed a successful enterprise and thus should serve as models for enterprising businessmen'" (Ayegboyin 2011: 158). So for the purpose of further understanding and elaborating the depths of their enterprising spirit it will be necessary for us to now study the thinking of one of the maestros of Black prosperity theology: Bishop Thomas Dexter Jakes Sr.

First, we shall evaluate the prosperity message as delivered by Jakes (2008: 14, 93): "Any resource that is related to value or wealth belongs to, comes from, and is controlled by God, our Father, who desires to bless *us*." "When we were quickened [saved by the Holy Spirit], all the wealth and spiritual blessings of Christ became ours." Accordingly, by being saved a Christian has access to the spiritual and material riches of God "who desires to bless us" (Jakes 2008). This is a respectable word, however, the social static of it creates an executive Christian elite cut off from the Christian majority, who themselves have no means of accessing the wealth and spiritual blessings he claims God wants to give them. To simply say, all wealth comes from a God who wants to bless us, "that God indulges himself in the luxury of pouring His grace upon our lives" (Jakes 2008: 51), without providing actual genuine help is just wishful thinking. Basically, sharing a positive message without providing a blueprint of how it can be actualised is just irresponsible. The Bishop effectively elucidates nothing more than positive words about God, negative words about the world, and fighting words about sin.

While I understand that Jakes does not see himself as a prosperity theologian, he must understand that to many of us common folk he is not only a prosperity theologian but is the definition of Black prosperity theology. Notwithstanding, my choice to quote from *Life Overflowing* is a matter of convenience as it is Jakes in his closest to prosperity theology. Furthermore, all the quotations I acquired from him are positive words and ideas: but they have no links to reality – which in itself is dangerous. Effectively, the message of prosperity has this dilemma: how does one transfer faith in the invisible realities of God into physical reality? That is one of the main problems with Black prosperity theology. The gap between the faith world and the real world is far too vast and the vast majority are unable to cross it. To simply say God has the power and desire to help you cross it evades the predicament, and disqualifies the answer.

This is where Bishop Jakes (2008) proves quite ineffective. As positive as his gospel message may be, positivity on its own is counter-productive. What is the Bishop's answer: "There are many believers who have old habits they need to break. ... But one by one, those habits must be changed." "Let me be very practical here. I have met people who tell me that they have no problem watching certain television programs that are filled with lustful and violent messages. As far as I am concerned, these people are giving the Devil the sofa in their living room. They are allowing him to occupy that place" (Jakes 2008: 248, 262). Now while these are not the words of a slave-maker as such, they are the words of an acculturated apologist.

Here Bishop Jakes endorsed the non-watching of certain programmes on television not because he was unable to enjoy them himself but because he was indoctrinated into a pathological position. He believed that the habits of the common person blocked them from attaining the riches of God, and the watching of certain television programmes was one of those habits. While technically it could be interpolated that watching television prevents one from participating in activities that could ultimately result in their success, such was not what Jakes (2008) had in mind. What he meant to say was, they are corrupted by watching television programmes into displeasing God, and that is why God does not bless them. Granted, Jakes (2008) provided no definitive method of unlocking blessings, whether spiritual or material, in his book, but it was heavily implied that blessings come from being pleasing to God and free from sin.

Accordingly, as Jakes continued, "Humanity is totally incapable of rehabilitating themselves. They cannot produce anything of sufficient value to reverse the sentence of death assigned to them, and they find themselves totally at the mercy of God. At the same time, God is angry with the wicked, and His holy nature will not allow Him to simply overlook their violations and declare man saved. He hates and must destroy sin, but he loves man. The mighty God resolves this problem by offering His Son, Jesus Christ, as a sinless sacrifice to be substitute for all of mankind" (Jakes 2008: 110). There are no two ways about it: humanity needs God to save them from sin, yet God needs humanity to stop sinning in order to bless them.

Thus we can see, in the case of the Black prosperity theologian, to paraphrase de Beauvoir (2009), they are not born they become a vampyre. A vampyre is made. They are told things like "when you are a child of God, you have the awesome honor of gazing upon the riches of your Father's wealth. And because you know what He has, your expectation from Him and your confidence in Him are enhanced." Indeed, "Understanding that Christ's riches are unfathomable frees us from many of the hazards of riches … the riches of Christ are inexhaustible, so we are free to share them and spend them without worrying about poverty tomorrow. These riches mean we are freed from jealousy, envy, and strife" (Jakes 2008: 13, 177).

To a godbody this is a delusional deception: not that God is impotent and impoverished, but because it reeks of superstition. Even Fanon also pointed out the superstitious manifestations of the time of colonialism, "I walk on white nails. Sheets of water threaten my soul on fire. Face to face with these rites, I am doubly alert. Black magic! Orgies, witches' sabbaths, heathen ceremonies, amulets. Coitus is an occasion to call on the gods of the clan. It is a sacred act, pure, absolute, bringing invisible forces into action. What is one to think of all these manifestations, all these initiations, all these acts? From every direction I am assaulted by the obscenity" (Fanon 2008: 95). All these superstitions of black magic may have been transcended in our time by prosperity theology but prosperity theology has its own superstitions in our time. An example of this is the idea that by sowing an offering you can raise your financial wealth. "They [therefore] admonish their adherents to give a variety of offerings – seed offerings, covenant offerings, breakthrough offerings, success offerings and the like" (Ayegboyin 2011: 161).

211

Thereby we see that not only are the Black masses deceived by these sorts of superstitious perceptions – and Black prosperity theology as a whole is a deception – but the Black prosperity theologians themselves are the victims of what could be called a neurotic disorder. This acculturation of Black prosperity theologians like Jakes, who have themselves adopted the tricknology of the White prosperity theologians, is not a result of weakness on their part, it is just that their epidermalisation of acculturation came about as a result of White global domination, thereby reinforcing their subordination. The 10 percent somatisation of tricknology led to this acculturation, which itself led to their vampyrism.

Yet in all their acculturation can also be detected an impairment of self-definition: "Moreover, in the context in which Paul is speaking to us in Ephesians, he is saying that even though I come from generations of heathen, I have just as much access to the Father as the Jew who has known and served Him for centuries!" (Jakes 2008: 138.) This word was so important to Jakes that he even used the exclamation mark to emphasise it. The generations of heathen in this case are his own Black ancestors, who, if considered more logically, had rich and vibrant cultures of their own. Jakes essentially denied the validity of his own people for that of another people. Though the situation is even more complex than that. […] It is in fact quite probable that those he called the Jews may in fact be converts from the tribe of the Khazars (Malcioln 1996) and that the original Jews may in fact prove to be the very people he condemned as heathen (Williams 1928).

The psychopathology of the Black prosperity theologians, in this sense, is not only a kind of self-hatred but also a self-denial: the unconscious denial of Black cultural expediencies perpetuated by White trick knowledge. This has kept men like Jakes blind to their own potential, which thereby creates the need for us godbodies to re-educate even the Black prosperity theologians, because they are just as blind as we used to be. God Allah Shah even remembered how he "was a savage until Gods such as Divine Prince and Justice Hakim pulled him in. There were plenty of institutions such as churches and the like, but it was God in the ghetto that got his attention" (The Five Percenter Vol 22.4; 2016: 4).

Some may say that my critique of Bishop Jakes was a little harsh or unfounded as all religious systems manifest what could be called abnormal behavioural practices. To call Black prosperity theology neurotic is unfair. That may be true to a small degree but one of the aetiologies of neurosis is identification with the aggressor, which is itself evident in Black prosperity theology as a result of acculturation. Ultimately, the social aetiology of Black prosperity theology's acculturation being an epidermalisation – the expulsion of Black culture and incorporation of New Thought culture – must be countered by a new self-identification.

Effectively, for these vampyres to escape from the epidermalisation of acculturation they must, first, effectively ameliorate the damage of socio-historical traumata through strong cords of empathic Black unity. Then, they must develop and internalise a Black ideology – again, for Black people, Brown for Brown people, Red for Red skinned people, Yellow for so-called Yellow people, and White for White people. As Prince Supreme said, "You have to love you first. This is the science of self-savior. Get to know your brother. Make a connection. We must come together. We're supposed to be one in the same. … It is problematic to think that you're greater than [your] brother" (The Five Percenter Vol 22.2; 2016: 4).

Yet and still, the violation of the non-White by the false representations and self-arrogance of the Whites, having redefined the world according to White fanciful phantasms, may offend some Blacks. The insanity of these Blacks in the eyes of the still acculturated vampyres is predicated on the ingesting by these acculturated Blacks of White stereotypes, as Littlewood made clear, "the White has ascribed to the Black, the epitome of worthlessness" (Littlewood 2006: 39). Basically, he expressed the reality of this phantasm as an essential reason for the growth of Rastafari in the Caribbean: "The image of the madman recalls the popular perception of the Rasta: indeed, for many middle-class West Indians, the Rasta is dismissed as 'mad'. If Rastafari can be taken as an assertion of those informal worthless characteristics which Whites have ascribed historically to Blacks, it is not surprising that many of the younger psychiatric patients in St Ann's [Trinidadian mental hospital] have adopted dreadlocks and Rasta idiom" (Littlewood 2006: 39). The same could also be said of those West Indian brothers and sisters who are not in a mental hospital.

The following of Rastafari by Black people is to authenticate their Blackness by becoming exceptionally Black. The Rastas represent that excessive Blackness dormant in the heart of every Black person: the return to Africa in culture, style, and mentality and the absolute rejection of the West and the White as Babylon. We godbodies share a similar rejection but to us the West is the poor part of the planet earth and the White is, ironically enough, uncivilised. If there is any biblical recollection on the part of the godbody it is more toward the land of Magog as prophesied by the prophet Ezekiel, the apostle John, and the Prophet Muhammad. Magog is the land of White authentication, it represents the empire of the Whites (Europe, America, Canada, Australia, New Zealand, and Russia). We godbodies, however, have at current very little identification with the Bible or the Quran but instead assimilate the ideas of science mainly into our doctrine and that is how we maintain our own standards of truth.

III

The third manifestation of psychopathology that Dalal (2010) spoke of in explaining the colonial disposition was violence,

"The fact of the matter is that not only is the colonizer venerated, he is also feared because of his power. Thus the aggression, which cannot be expressed 'upwards' because the consequences are too threatening, gets turned either inwards or outwards in a horizontal direction" (Dalal 2010: 99). When it is turned outwards it manifests as attacking your own kind. This can be seen in the anti-social behaviours in many Black communities. However, when it is turned inwards the expression is far more subtle. "Fanon ... describes how ... 'The Antillean has therefore to choose between his family and European society; in other words, the individual who climbs up into society – white and civilized – tends to reject his family – black and savage ... [so] the family structure is cast back into the id' ... Now the external structure is institutionalized in the psyche rendering the superego white and the id black" (Dalal 2010: 97). With the superego thereby becoming White the Black person's ideal-self becomes the White person, thus doing violence to the Black part of the self, which has been relegated to the "arbitrary underworld" of the id.

If the superego of a Black person thereby becomes a White person, or White people in general, then a complex drama transpires in which the "master" of the Black person's unconscious world is another force. This force, which has become incorporated as the Black person's superego, also becomes an aggressive presence in the mind of that Black person causing them to undermine and discredit self and kind. They can thus attack self and kind with ease due to this aggressive stranger dominating their mind. They also acculturate themselves from Black culture, thus making the Black thereby the opponent.

Yet this violence to self and kind can manifest in less aggressive manners. For example, the adopting of White ideals and claiming them for Black people. This pernicious form of acculturation and anti-Blackness is very prominent in those who claim political allegiance to White forms of society and

215

government like liberalism and conservatism, both being types of their form of nationalism. Belief in the established way of doing things, or even the Blackening of the established ways of doing things, effectively discredits the ancestors as Black and savage, while acknowledging modernity as civilised, whether White or Black – it is all White regardless. Again, such a perception does violence to the Black person by creating unconscious feelings of aversion towards what is Black and makes the unconscious master or ideal a White person, or White people in general.

The solution to all these situations is offered by Kohut in the form of selfobject transference, in which an individual (usually a child or infant) develops a healthy empathic connection with another individual (usually a parent). Atwood and Stolorow said, in explaining Kohut's theory of the selfobject, that, "A selfobject may be described phenomenologically as an entity that a person experiences as incompletely separated from himself or herself and that serves to maintain his or her sense of self" (Atwood & Stolorow 2014: 32). Transference, on the other hand, is the process of transferring pleasurable feelings from subjects to objects, and during the process of psychoanalysis, from patients to analysts.

Nevertheless, as Bernard Brandchaft (2010) was also quick to state, "Extensive experience with selfobject transferences have led me to conclude that it is a conceptual error to consider a selfobject transference as a *type* of transference characteristic of a certain type of patient. This error carries with it the implication that the analyst is presented at every turn with a sort of 'multiple choice' of types of transference. Instead, selfobject transference refers to a basic dimension of all relationships and of all transferences" (Brandchaft 2010: 35). The operation of selfobject transference, however, shows that the part of the analyst can be played by anybody (though it would be done better by a trained psychoanalyst) and a caregiver or superordinate superior or mentor, et cetera., could fill the role of the analyst. In these non-clinical interactions the intersubjective experience occurs when the superordinate is empathic and able to decentre themselves from their own subjectivity and immerse themselves in the subjectivity of Other (Doctor & Sorter 2010).

In these situations the power relation is not one-sided but reciprocal. It is thereby the responsibility of the superordinate to be for the subordinate a restructuring object that can heal any developmental difficulties that arose during socialisation, should there have been any, or culturally reorganise what would have biologically been their path, should they be genetically predisposed to pathological disquiet. One should also instantly be able to recognise from this that the personal development of any given individual is much more the result of both biology and sociology than of any one of these two individually.

An example of this can be found in obese parents giving birth to an obese child; it may not necessarily mean they will grow up to be an obese adult, though the odds are stacked heavily against them. Genes and culture play a role in how the child advances into adulthood. Genes carry information from generation to generation just like culture carries information from generation to generation. We can tell the potential or actual of the parent by looking at the child. Another example is found in Samuel Wilberforce living out his father William Wilberforce's dream of becoming a bishop. Genetically the child has the makeup that will drive and steer them towards a certain path – their upbringing also plays a part too – but other external factors may arise to regulate their culture thus preventing what would otherwise be inevitable (e.g. financial problems, a traumatic childhood experience, bullying, or any other developmental disruptions to the flow of genetic and epigenetic information). The sociological processes thus created, if they are developed, would reorganise their genetic constitution causing the individual and posterity to have an altered future.

Having thereby seen the social aetiology of the psychopathology of the colonised, so as to fully appreciate the context of the Black bourgeoisie, or the social consciousness and unconsciousness of these bourgeoisies, we should now move on to constructing a pathogenesis of Black impairment in a system that has only glossed over the fact of it. Nevertheless we must proceed in order to therapeutically alleviate the ever-present difficulties that have led to the degeneration of these Black bourgeoisies – which, though real, is also heavily under-represented in the Western media – and the best way to transcend the omnipresence of any Black degeneration, real or imagined, is to face these *jinni* and stop hiding from them. In facing these *jinni* we must get over them together in an intersubjective, that is, empathic manner. Alleviating selfobject needs, however, will only prove a primary step so long as there are no disappointments from within the therapy. All godbodies will have to take the place of the psychoanalyst – a difficult task, especially as we are not trained in counselling or selfobject identification.

In the classic selfobject relation – that between the mother and the infant – Wolf said on the subject "the infant experiences the parent and the parent experiences the infant as an essential aspect of the well-being of the self – as selfobject" (Wolf 1980; quoted in Atwood & Stolorow 2014: 54). The link between mother and child is so strong that Atwood and Stolorow believed there was even a synchronism and an almost choreographed harmony between the two. This kind of synchronism should be realised between the godbodies and the vampyres too, rather than condemning them as nothing more than our enemies and thus reawakening and solidifying feelings of inferiority, the godbody should seek an empathic link and connection with the 10 percent making them feel safe and valued. As Divine Prince said, "we are obligated to give our people the best that we have" (The Five Percenter Vol 22.7; 2017: 4). We Gods call this kind of enlightening and empowering lesson *understanding*, which is the backbone of our 360° system of cultural interpretation.

The vampyres, as Black people, underwent severe fundamental obstructions in their racial development that must be alleviated for them to move forward as a social body. They cannot progress until they receive some form of therapy for these psychological traumas they experienced from the developmental progression of our racial history. To deal with these traumas the vampyres have predominantly accepted several unhelpful solutions that only superficially alleviated the illness by removing some of the symptoms. Now, if we truly wish to be ghetto therapists to these lost Black brothers and sisters we must always try to remember these words from Bernard Brandchaft, "Each step of the way the analyst must take into account the intensity of his patient's fears of displeasing, offending, or alienating the analyst, fears that constantly threaten to bring the exploratory process to a halt by shunting it quickly into the more familiar groove of pathological accommodation" (Brandchaft 2010: 26).

An example of this pathological accommodation in social bodies is Dr. Martin Luther King's hope that Black Americans be integrated with White Americans. Although the idea in itself was not disingenuous any psychologist worth their mettle knows that poor self-other differentiation has a negative impact on developmental advancement, creating weak self-boundaries and an insatiable need to be all things for all people. Atwood and Stolorow said concerning this that,

> *"A requirement for the child's achievement and consolidation of self-other differentiation and of stable self-boundaries is the presence of a caregiver who, by virtue of*

a demarcated and firmly structured sense of self and others, is able reliably to recognize, affirm, appreciate, and pridefully enjoy the unique qualities and independent strivings of the child. When a parent cannot recognize and affirm central qualities and strivings of the child, because they conflict with a need for that child to serve the parent's own archaic needs, then the child will experience disturbances of self-experience in the area of unmirrored grandiosity, as Kohut (1971, 1977) has shown. We wish to stress that such pathogenic intersubjective situations in addition will seriously obstruct the process of self-other differentiation and self-boundary formation, as the child feels compelled to 'become' whatever the parent requires and thus to subjugate any striving to develop according to his or her own separate design" (Atwood & Stolorow 2014: 56).

Obviously, that is not to say that America should return to segregation. The actual solution to the predicament of Black-White relations in America was more ably found in the Honorable Elijah Muhammad's vision of a separation of the Black American from the White American into a land of their own chosen from between three and nine states in the United States. While such a vision seems unattainable now, had it have occurred back then the manifestation of poor self-differentiation and poor self-determination among those who now seek integration into White society, or who have sought historically to be integrated into White society, could have been avoided altogether. In the developmental histories of children this kind of situation is called the separation-individuation process and it must be experienced by all infants on the road to self-other differentiation, as Margaret Mahler pointed out.

That is not to say that self and Other must be separate in all things. True independence for a Black person, or for a Black nation within the Americas, is not only unlikely but is also unhelpful. There would need to remain an interdependent symbiosis between both groups based on a kind of selfobject relationship in place. Nevertheless, there are currently also plenty of Black people within America who have been able to recognise their racial identity as differentiating them from Whites and other non-Blacks and thereby have been able to structure self-identities based on ideas that coincide with ingroup histories. These self-identities have formed into cultural knowledge that gets passed on to succeeding generations to create racial and ethnic pride that reconfigures racial identity and the structuralisation of the ego, that is, the astral body.

Although, it could be argued that intersubjective philosophies and relations may themselves develop an obstruction that coincides with the development of poor self-determination and self-boundaries, the difference is that in intersubjectivity the self is not sacrificed for the sake of maintaining a relationship; in intersubjectivity superordinates learn to decentre themselves from their personal subjective perspective and explore the subjective reality of their subordinates, allowing them to see the needs of their subordinates, and allowing their subordinates to open up to them in ways which are both new and broad. There are no illusions of inherent homogeneity and no delusions of grandeur, there is simply the symbiotic working together of symbolically (though not subjectively) equal individuals. Thus we find altogether the semblance of a new ideological structuralisation that could reshape Black self-definitions and self-boundaries.

Though the Black bourgeoisie may currently see little incentive to being a part of a movement like the godbody, as we move deeper into the age of iGod such a position puts them at risk of being left behind and obsolete as the youth become more intrigued by our ideas. Ultimately, they will either be to these youths a Djehwti or a Setekh, but they definitely possess something that we godbodies currently lack, and that will be very

221

necessary for all of us to acquire in the future: freedom. The neurosis of these Black bourgeoisies belies their freedom, making them appear as vampyres when the truth is they are our brothers and sisters.

Indeed, when the 10 percent unify with the Five Percent then you actually have 100 percent of the Black population as it is the 10 percent that have corrupted the 85 percent. Not only so, but if we look at the supreme mathematics of the situation:

$$\alpha = v\left(\frac{x_1^G}{x_2^f}\right) = vx_3^u$$

Where α = social force, v = social velocity, x_1^G = godbody divinity, x_2^f = vampyre freedom, and x_3^u = Black social understanding, or empathic development. Ultimately, the freedom of the vampyres coupled with the divinity of the godbodies could allow the godbody to decrease its inertia substantially, while also allowing the vampyres to go to the next level in acceleration.

IV

A problematic does arise from this idea of uniting with the vampyres: how do we accept them into our communion without corrupting our civilised teachings? The message of righteous living must not be compromised for the sake of freedom, as precious as freedom is. Indeed, the danger of freedom is that it is also the freedom to be corrupted by trick knowledge. To prevent this we godbodies must be less free with our lessons and teachings, that is, become more dogmatic. Let me be clear though: I do not mean here the introduction of religious dogmas. What I mean is to set a demarcation point beyond which one either comes dangerously closing to leaving our system, or they compromise our self-identification and self-determination. While I recognise that dogma does have an air of religiosity about it which makes it just as dangerous as freedom, the truth is still the truth and to be dogmatic with the truth is to be free from the lie, whatever shape the lie comes in.

As German Marxist reformer Ferdinand Lassalle once said: "a party's weakness is its diffuseness and the blurring of clear demarcations; a party becomes stronger by purging itself" (Lasselle 1852; quoted in Lenin 2020: 43). We must therefore decide on what doctrine is formal godbody and what doctrine will not fly. This is the hope of Black Thearchism: to elevate the godbody movement into a formalised structure that is both credible and creditable; so that, even if we do unify with those who have misled the Black community to the point of denying their own culture and history, we will not be corrupted by them, and we will have several strong points on which we stand. Effectively, as the old aphorism says, "If you stand for nothing you will fall for anything."

While it may be true that godbodyism as it stands today already practices a high level of dogmatic discipline, we still currently do not have within our movement a fully and universally accepted interpretation or system that we all acknowledge and respect. For a start, we do not even have a current social or cultural signifier that distinguishes us from every other movement. To be sure, within the Fruit of Islam they have the suit and bow tie, within the MGTs they have their own outer uniform, within the super-gang movement they have their bandana and colours, within the Rastafari movement they have the Dreadlocks, and with the Afrocentrics they have traditional African clothing. We may say we ourselves have the crown and head-covering, but the truth is, these do not distinguish us as a movement. They were appropriated from Islam, therefore those who see us with our crown (kufi) or head-covering do not recognise us as a God or Goddess but instead see us as either a Muslim or an Afrocentric.

We need a distinguishing signifier, one that is ours and ours alone, not just for the purpose of identification but also for the purpose of branding. It is for this reason that I suggest as the first and fundamental practice of our movement the adopting by all members, male and female, young and old, of the wearing of the universal flag everywhere and at all times. To explain what I mean a little deeper: I do not mean the wearing of the universal flag as a tattoo or chain everywhere but the wearing of an actual universal flag bandana. Still, admittedly, even this move is not distinguished as such.

However, we can distinguish ourselves by how we wear the universal flag. Herein, the suggestion is that a rule be made for all godbodies, from the time we become newborns, that we tie the bandana of the universal flag around our left bicep and only around our left bicep. That means: it is never to be worn anywhere on the body of a God or Goddess but on the left bicep, not even on the left hand, shoulder, or forearm. This one practice will distinguish us as a movement and allow those in all the other Black movements to see that we are becoming more structured and more systematised. Again, all professional movements have a uniform or mark of distinction. As the universal flag is already of high value within our movement we should therefore express that value by wearing it everywhere. This distinguishing mark and the enforcement of strict discipline with regards to wearing it everywhere, will, however, only be a preliminary step.

It should be clear to those who currently follow our tradition that us not having a clearly defined stance on issues we profess to be important to us is inexcusable. We must therefore all have a substantive knowledge and understanding of our overall vision, and also on the objectives by which we plan to achieve our vision. Following Jim Collins and Jerry I. Porras: in order to find our vision and to find the objectives by which we plan to achieve our vision we must, first, answer three initial questions, then, answer three further questions. First, (i) what are our core and our adjacent values, (ii) what is our core purpose, and (iii) what is our BHAG as a movement. Then, (i) what is the Hedgehog Concept that will best explain our responsibilities as a movement, (ii) what is the flywheel we will have to turn to fulfil our responsibilities as a movement, and (iii) what is the 20 Mile March we will have to reach with maximum consistency to fulfil our responsibilities as a movement. While these may be figured out on an individual basis they must also be understood on a social body-wide basis too.

Based on the Collins and Porras ideas concerning various visionary companies that were built to last we can see that having a vision is fundamental to a company's stability and survival (Collins & Porras 2005). Using the Collins and Porras (2005) definition of vision: a vision is generally based on a company, corporation, or organisation finding its own core values, core purpose, and a BHAG to commit itself to. The same is true for a social movement/social enterprise; and as godbodyism is itself a social movement/social enterprise, we will therefore need, first and foremost, to find, know, and understand what Hofstede (2001) called our "deeply rooted values: things that are preferred by or desirable to the group." Yet, in order to find this we must before that define what a value actually is. According to Erdman, "American anthropologist Clyde Kluckholhn's concept of [a value], described [it] as 'a *conception* ... of the desirable which influences the selection from available modes, means and ends of actions.' In other words, values are thoughts and actions that are important to individuals within a society and are reinforced over time to define the group" (Erdman 2017: 36, 22; emphasis mine).

Based on the use of these kinds of terminology we can see that values themselves are basically specific kinds of conceptions or concepts that we have given meaning to. Hereby, if we wish to find, know, and understand our values, we must start by finding and understanding what our core, adjacent, and peripheral concepts are, within their own ideological morphologies (Freeden 2013). If we now consider the genuine morphology of our social movement/social enterprise then we can see how the core concepts of our movement should be the key values contained in the Black DREADS acronym: Black divinity, Black revolutionism, Black eroticism, Black astralism, Black demodernisation, and Black syndicalism.

At the same time, we should maintain as our adjacent concepts the key values of the LEADERSHIP acronym: L-look, listen and learn. E-evolve with education. A-accelerate with action. D-do your duty and fulfil your obligations as a civilized person. E-everything should be done with equality. R-respond with results and respect. S-set superior standards and provide selfless-service. H-have honest and open communication. I-input with intelligence and integrity. P-personal courage, positive attitude, and purpose. The reason I call these adjacent concepts and not core concepts is because they are more aspirational than already actively practiced. The core concepts are actually, for the most part, actively practiced within the current godbody culture. Finally, our peripheral concepts can be whatever the Gods and Goddesses consider to be important in the moment such as national consciousness and community control.

That said, with every movement there is also always decided their core purpose: something they believe worth fighting for, something they believe worth dying for, something that they are willing to spend their entire lives seeking to bring into the world. Based on our 120 lessons I think our core purpose should remain: to build a world of love, peace, and happiness. This must stay our Polaris and our true north, and, therefore, our overall purpose as a movement. A purpose that may not be fulfilled in the lifetime of many of those alive today, but that we will keep fighting for for another hundred, or even ten-thousand years. This is our dream, a dream that we will keep aspiring towards regardless of the oppositions and challenges that may arise to prevent its fulfilment. The difference between a purpose and a goal is that a goal may be fulfilled in our lifetime but a purpose may take hundreds or even thousands of years to be fulfilled. A world of love, peace, and happiness is a godbody dream worth fighting for and gives direction to our currently directionless movement.

However, we godbodies currently do not even have a universal goal that we all aspire towards. It is here, therefore, that I would like to introduce to us godbodies the concept of the BHAG (Big Hairy Audacious Goal) for our further progressive development. According to Jim Collins, who coined the term, a BHAG is a mammoth, even mountainous, goal that stirs and stimulates a team, unifying and galvanising them into action. I would like to suggest that we have our BHAG be to make the godbody ideology a world class ideology by 2040. Of course, none of this means that I am blind to the fact that it is still up for debate what form our ideology should actually take, whether Black Nationalist or Black Thearchist.

Obviously, I stand in the camp of the Black Thearchists: what I believe concerning the godbody is that our ideological positions must be based on the principles of the Black Thearchy, principles such as the divinity of Black people; the devilishment of White people; the vampyrism of the Black bourgeoisie; the eroticism of the Black soul; the righteousness of the Five Percent Nation; the trick knowledge of White superiority; the revolutionism of Black illegality; the refinement of civilised teachings; the spookism of religious teachings; the syndicalism of the godbody parliaments; and the constant striving for a world of love, peace, and happiness. This is Black Thearchism in the raw and the basis of our ideology must thereby be aligned with these principles; that is why as an ideology Black Thearchism is superior to Black Nationalism. It maintains godbody principles.

Moreover, one of the main problems existing within Black Nationalism is that at its core it is a form of violence to the Black soul surrendering too much of it to tricknology. While we gain a kind of Black empowerment from it in the form of converting the socio-cultural struggle into a socio-political struggle, we still remain disempowered by the internal mechanisms of the psychological infrastructures and ideological structures of society. Effectively, our ideological structures must come from our psychological infrastructures as Black people and not from our struggles for political acceptance.

Though it could be argued that we godbodies castigate most of the Black masses by calling them the babies and most of the Black bourgeoisie by calling them the vampyres; if we come to appreciate that some within the Black community have sold their divinity to the devil, metaphorically speaking, to become Black leaders, and that most other Black people have been led astray by these Black leaders, then we can avoid making the same mistakes. Again, whether they have sold themselves to the devilishment of the White superiority discourse or surrendered to the power of the White supremacy perspective, the Black bourgeoisie have become vampyres to us, feasting on the blood of the lost Black masses. Thus demarcating clearly to Black people that we are not just another Black Nationalist group is most important. We have various key doctrinal distinctions that separate us from the definitively Black Nationalist, and our ideology must reflect that.

Consequently, the question of whether to fight for Black Nationalism or Black Thearchism is far more important – as to the direction of the godbody – than has been appreciated. While such a question has been treated as meaningless by some there are others who argue that national consciousness is in fact vital to our struggle. While I agree that national consciousness is vital to the *Black* struggle, to the godbody it only means going backwards. We have already evolved beyond national consciousness and community control. We must therefore seek for ourselves and our people a kind of God consciousness, consciousness of the divinity of self and kind.

Nationalism on its own is too bourgeois, too modern, too liberal, even if it is a Black Nationalism. I am very passionate about this because bourgeois ideas and practices take from us the very essence of what makes us unique, and while certain bourgeois cultural niceties may be tolerable, and allowing certain bourgeois individuals to join our movement may be effective, if we surrender our ideology to the bourgeoisie, far from leading the people, we become the tail-end of the people. Our job and duty is to lead the people, not follow blindly the national struggle.

See, Black Nationalism comes in two forms: revolutionary and reformist. The revolutionary element want Black Americans to select certain states to occupy and then to secede from the rest of America, forming a United States of New Afrika, Ebonia, or whatever. Basically, a new country for Black Americans, led by Black Americans. They justify their right to have this separate nation with the exceptional circumstances under which Black Americans came to America and what they did in America after their kidnap. "Lincoln promised us forty acres," so they say. Well, if we added up all the descendants of slaves living in America and gave them each forty acres, then a land mass around about the size of Georgia and part of South Carolina would belong to this Black America. Therefore, they say they have the right to take a portion of the United States as their own. These Black Nationalists are also usually quite militant, at least in rhetoric, and want an end to White supremacy.

At the other end of the spectrum: reformist Black Nationalists are more for fighting to elect Black representatives in the US government, whether on a local or national level. The biggest victories to these individuals were the elections of Barack Obama as the first Black President, and of Kamala Harris as the first Indian Vice President. To these reformist nationalists change is possible within the United States and it is preferable to remain within the United States than to attempt to build a new country from scratch.

Both forms of Black Nationalism are bourgeois and based on bourgeois standards. We in the Five Percent have a far more complex and effective political theory, but there are some who wish to take us backward to national consciousness. The Father, however, did not believe in the national struggle, hence, why he told us not to marry according to the government. The only nation he believed in was the Nation of Gods and Earths. The national-state is thereby rendered useless to us. It is the national-state that sends its police to arrest and murder us, it is the national-state that uses its judiciary to tarnish our record, it is the national-state that makes laws to favour those that are against us, and it is the national-state that created a system so complicated that the children of White people get a superior education to the children of the ghetto.

Black Nationalism seeks to reinforce the national-state not abolish it, therefore it is of the utmost importance that we decide whether we will struggle with the Black Nationalists to teach national consciousness or rise above the national struggle and fight with the Black Thearchists to teach God consciousness. Following the masses and trusting in the spontaneous enlightenment of the masses rather than consciously bringing enlightenment to them will only degrade and dilute our movement. Black Lives Matter was powerful and important but we must guide the now nationally conscious Black people towards God consciousness.

To a degree it is a little opportunistic to say that the Black movement, in particular its manifestation as BLM, is better left to the spontaneity of the Black masses. The Black masses of the West are particularly indoctrinated into bourgeois nationalism from a young age. This indoctrination means that left to their own devices they will instinctively move towards nationalism, and reformist nationalism at that. Again, it is the devils and vampyres who have indoctrinated them into bourgeois nationalism; it is thereby the job of the godbodies to be more doctrinaire with regard to our teachings.

In this, while the Black vampyres of the 10 percent are predominantly bourgeoisies, and most of them reformist Black

Nationalists, it is our duty to educate, not only the Black masses of the 85 percent, but even the Black vampyres of the 10 percent. That means educating them in the concepts, purpose, and BHAG of our movement. As they get deeper in these lessons they will come to learn the vision they are to strive for and reach with consistency in order to move closer towards further fulfilling our destiny. The more dogmatic and doctrinaire we become concerning our vision and objectives, the less likely we are of being corrupted over the years, and the better chance we have of converting the vampyres into Gods and Goddesses.

There is also another danger inherent in making the target of our BHAG refining a nationally conscious vision and not a God conscious one; we may lose our credibility as leaders in the Black struggle. We have a duty to civilise Black people, guiding and directing them towards achieving our goal. Yet if our ideology is merely Black Nationalism and not Black Thearchism, then they can look to the vampyres, who have led them thus far already, and they will have all that they need. Truly, the vampyres make far more effective advocates of national consciousness than us.

Yes, we are already Black Thearchists, but I worry that this light subservience to nationalism may prove to be our downfall, making us undifferentiated from the other Black Nationalist groupings. Vampyrism comes in three main forms, and we cannot risk allowing one of those forms to turn us all into vampyres. At the same time, nationalism is a preliminary step for the Black masses; first, is racial self-consciousness (actuated in Critical Race Theory); second, is national consciousness (actuated in Panther and Decolonial Theories); and finally, is God consciousness (which is actuated in our own godbody theory).

Consequently, many of us love to claim that our duty is to educate Black people, thus seeing ourselves like a vanguard for the Black struggle. Well, as Lenin said in his own time, the other contingents must first recognise us as the vanguard otherwise we lead nobody. Imagine walking up to a bourgeois vampyre, and many of them are high intellectuals, and saying that our duty is to educate them. They will no doubt ask themselves, "Have we bourgeoisies not been educating the masses these many decades? Who are these upstarts who claim to educate us? What makes them any more educated than us? Indeed, we promote the national struggle more so than they do, and we have a firmer grasp of intellectual concepts. Their own intelligence notwithstanding, we far exceed them in our understanding of Black theoretical concepts, Black national consciousness, and the history of the Black struggle. We are also far better trained and have far more connections within the establishment. We will allow them this conceit in saying they are educating us, but for all, we shall continue doing what we have been doing all along." So if we truly wish to exorcise the vampyrism of these Black bourgeoisies we must share with them a different message from the one they have been sharing these many decades.

All that said, we will now need to consider the objectives we will have to perform in order to accomplish this vision. First, there is what Jim Collins called, again: the Hedgehog Concept. To explain this he shared the story of the fox and the hedgehog: the fox is crafty, cunning, quick, and dangerous, much stronger and far more sophisticated than the lowly hedgehog. The hedgehog, on the other hand, is dowdy, ugly, and much slower and clumsier than the fox. Usually the hero of most European folk tales, the fox wins every time. However, whenever the fox, with his multiplicity of moves and tactics, jumps in front of the hedgehog to catch him, the hedgehog just performs one simple move and the fox is defeated every time. Curling up into a ball, with spikes pointing in every direction, the fox stands no chance and has to admit defeat.

In order to find our own hedgehog concept we need to, first of all, understand for ourselves that as with every social movement/social enterprise we have an opportunity to build a franchise business model. This is important and it will be clear how important it is later on. Next, we will need to ask ourselves a very important question: what problems do we so effectively solve that would make anyone consider our social movement/ social enterprise worth funding? When we look at the situation from this perspective and *honestly* appraise ourselves through this lens then it becomes very obvious that for most of our existence as a social movement – while we may have been masters of helping other people to gain a knowledge of themselves – we have not really taken the time to know our own selves as a social movement/social enterprise.

While again, it could be said that our overall strength is that we have democratised divinity, what does that even mean to an ordinary person in the world? So how would *I* answer the funding question? I would say that the problem we solve is: we free people of all races, but particularly of the Black race, from any forms of mystification, misrepresentation, and victimisation that may otherwise prevent them from unlocking their own divinity. Understanding that, it should now become clear that we have the opportunity and responsibility to make sure we are paid for our service to the Black community, for our Allah Schools, and for two programmes I hope we can build in the future that I call the Allah College and the Allah Institute. The systems here expressed are fleshed out in greater detail in Chapter 6, which itself goes through the methodology by which we can organise and franchises our business model (ciphers, Squares, research facilities, parliaments, schools, colleges, and institute) and provides a systematic blueprint that can be rolled out suggestion by suggestion, in different communities across America and the world.

All this provides a great beginning as it can add deep levels of clarity and focus, allowing us to appreciate where we are most helpful and vital. From this beginning we now move up and on to the formalising and systematising of a brand strategy by which the practicalities of how we enact our business model on a regular basis can be understood. In our case, I would suggest our brand strategy be that of the iconic brand. Examples of iconic brands can be found in Red Cross, Red Crescent, and Nike. The practicalities themselves, however, can be found for us, not in the 120 lessons, but in the Build Allah Square lessons, as explicated by Sunez Allah: (i) Eat, (ii) Train, (iii) Read, (iv) Write, and (v) Share. Nevertheless, three of these in particular will be of interest to us here: train, read, and write. Admittedly, growing up in Brooklyn, New York I only really knew the training aspect of the Square: the fighting ring in which "punks jumped up to get beat down". At the same time, back then if anyone presented some unfounded information, or broke any godbody rules, at a parliament they may also end up in the Square getting "beat down."

But all this was done in love and for the purpose of training, so that if one of us was ever attacked they could defend themselves and their friends (a move that was especially helpful for the female godbodies, who themselves went into the Square with other female godbodies). The Square was thus effectively how we would train ourselves in various forms of mixed martial arts; and thereby gain strength, discipline, and confidence as we walked the streets of New York City. This was actually one of the main things I used to love about the godbody and is perhaps the best part of being God, that same confidence of knowing that if you were ever attacked you could fight back, and that even if you were winning in a fight and another God or Goddess saw you in the fight they would be obligated to jump in and help defend you in the fight.

Obviously, there can be detected in this an avenue towards our credibility, as our current use of violence is condemned by society with no proper understanding of its purpose or of its connection to martial arts training, which society currently recognises as itself a legitimate practice. Furthermore, can also be detected the analogy of an army nation; an analogy which is quite fitting as, like with any army, we ourselves are at war, our war is with the entire world system. Moreover, the band-of-brothers idea and reality also permeates our counter-culture. It is written in the Bible: "Hereby perceive we the love of God, because he laid down his life for us: and we ought to lay down our lives for the brethren" (1John 3: 16). Such an injunction may seem excessive and too difficult for most of the more squeamish members of modern Christianity, however, those in the military tradition live this principle every single day without complaint, resentment, or insubordination (at least for the most part).

Again, the analogy of an army for the godbody movement works well with the conception of our potential personal mission as presented earlier: to make the godbody ideology a world class ideology by 2040. And to be sure, we all know we could die at any time, therefore we must literally love our brothers and sisters in godbodyism to the point of being ready to die for them. Nevertheless, this is where the analogy ends, as in actually existing godbody ciphers and parliaments a captains' and a lieutenants' main duties are merely to guide the discussion and preside over the Build Allah Square, not to domineer over the soldiers nor any of the young Gods or Goddesses.

Remember also that the training element of the Square is not only for protection and confidence purposes, but also to keep godbody members from harbouring any bad or negative feelings towards their fellow brother or sister; this is because we need to be ready to die for these people should the worst go down. We *are* an Army Nation, and we usually exist within an oppressive nation that is at war with us. Notwithstanding, all godbody elders, older Gods and Goddesses, whatever their rank within the movement, should have a key position of leadership at our parliaments and ciphers based largely on their physical age.

Moreover, this training aspect of the Square actually and mainly works on three levels: (i) if somebody presents lessons or ideas that go against godbody lessons and ideas they may end up in the Square with six other Gods getting beat down for 90 seconds, (ii) if someone breaks any of the rules of the godbody they could also end up in the Square with six other Gods getting beat down for 90 seconds, and (iii) if a God has any kind of problem with another God for whatever reason: be it jealousy, humiliation, disrespect, fear, not picking up their phone when they called, or even looking at them funny, the two Gods would fight it out in the Square, one-on-one, in front of all the other Gods and Goddesses for 90 seconds, without needing to give the reason for wanting to go in the Square with that particular God. In each of these Square situations, no matter who wins the fight, who looks good in the fight, who looks weird or ridiculous in the fight, or who gets knocked out in the fight; when the fight is over all is not only forgiven it is also forgotten, and those same Gods were ready again to die for each other again, and that is literally die. The same was also true for female godbodies going into the Square with other female godbodies.

But though with regard to this training aspect of the Build Allah Square we should be as dogmatic as with everything else, we must still always remember its real life consequences in illegalism, violence, and in sexual train-running, which thereby challenge the moral status quo. Still, that is only because we currently tend to judge by White standards. Technically, if we throw away White standards our illegalism, violence, and sexual train-running could actually be an example to the people. As far as the train goes, we should not seek to initiate anyone into this practice while they are too young, but eventually they will still have to have sex someday. We can teach them the right way, with class and civilisation, even when running a train. This is the secret. Illegalism, if practiced as a form of social revolutionism, can be positive; violence, if practiced to defend oneself and/or loved ones, can be positive; and running a sexual train, if practiced with consent and responsibility, can be positive. Thereby, one can negotiate how one practices these godbody methods; without sacrificing the *realities* of the godbody lifestyle: which also includes these darker elements.

The main reason for the martial training aspect of this godbody lifestyle is to make sure that we all have genuine love for each other and not a fake, hypocritical, or delusional love for each other. Our lives are literally on the line in the street life so we have to literally be ready to die for each other. This means we have to be *willing* to die for each other, not harbouring resentment, animosity, or embarrassed feelings towards one another for whatever reason. While this darker aspect of the godbody lifestyle is real and visible, another element that was also quite real and quite visible was how well read most New York City thugs were. Those who were the biggest thugs in the street life were also highly intelligent. These were intellectual thugs who were autodidactic and deeply knowledgeable. Such a thirst for knowledge obviously had its origin in the godbody understanding that knowledge is infinite and that knowledge is the foundation, however, it also obviously had its roots in the read aspect of the Build Allah Square.

We, however, must now seek to develop this reading principle of the Square into a study and research principle for future generations. That means becoming masters of R&A. It also means developing facilities in our communities that rival those of the top colleges and universities. Not to say that we can rival the Harvards and the Princetons right now, but we have every reason to aim towards that destination. It is my heartfelt hope that we can see in ourselves the possibility of becoming not only intellectual thugs, but world class intellectuals. Period. Again, our research and analysis may not be limited to only reading but we must try to make it include reading as the more authoritative knowledge is usually found in books and academic journals. Of course, this will also obviously mean joining academic associations so as to keep up with the current knowledge of issues related to our area of research, but it will all be helpful.

Conversely, having university level research facilities may seem like a daunting task, but we call ourselves scientists so we must behave as scientists. All scientists do research and back up their research with evidence, so we must try to have our own research facilities at least by 2050 so that we can do so too. In order to get there we will have to do something very few of us have really had the stomach to do before, but will have to learn how to do if we wish to move forward as a movement: request donations from larger Black businesses and organisations. This sort of self-promotion will require the further building of our brand cache. As an example, Collins said quite provocatively, "Does Harvard truly deliver a better education and do better academic work than other universities? Perhaps, but the emotional pull of Harvard overcomes any doubt when it comes to raising funds. Despite having an endowment in excess of $20 billion, donations continue to flow" (Collins 2006: 25). Hereby, building research facilities in our ghettos may actually be a lot easier than we have so far thought, all we need to do is break it down into small simple steps that we can accomplish day-by-day.

Though this may all be fine and well, in our current form we have still failed to live up to the entirety of Sunez Allah's vision for the Square. There are currently too few godbody writings and too few godbody books. If we are to be truly faithful to the Square in its entirety we will need to write more and publish more. What I have done with mechanical analysis is provide us with a methodology on which to base our theories, but we must address new topics in society, the world, and in the sciences from our own perspective. This way we expand beyond knowledge 120 and move into wisdom 240. Publishing books and articles means we lead the Black community towards progress, empowerment, and divinity through our ideology. Whether we choose to publish through an academic journal, through Draft2Digital, through KDP, or through a traditional publisher, the godbody movement must aim to have no non-authors by 2040, NONE. Obviously,

238

if using Draft2Digital or KDP we should also be sure to go to Fiverr for our cover design, and to purchase David Gaughran's book *Let's Get Digital* so as to understand the full process of self-publishing. It is absolutely free and shows that getting a book published is not that difficult. Indeed, reading and research may be essential but we already do that more than enough, what we really need to do is write more and publish more.

As can be seen, these three central elements of the Build Allah Square play a major part in the application of our solution. At this point, it is all about discovering, based on this simple blueprint, what was called by Jim Collins "piercing clarity about how to produce the best long-term results [through attaining a] deep understanding of three intersecting circles: 1) what you are deeply passionate about, 2) what you can be the best in the world at, and 3) what best drives your economic engine." However, he also said, "Whereas in business, the key driver in the flywheel is the link between financial success and [an economic engine], I'd like to suggest that a key link in the social sectors is brand reputation – built upon tangible results and emotional share of heart – so that potential supporters believe not only in your mission, but in your capacity to deliver on that mission" (Collins 2006: 17, 25).

Having already discussed certain godbody general practices; and also presented these practices as solutions to common ghetto difficulties faced by the people; we can move on to the process of finalising our own Hedgehog Concept by consolidating all the information we have considered so far, plus using the three circles to achieve this end. It is thereby that I believe the best Hedgehog Concept for the godbody movement would be: we empower Black people intellectually, sexually, and martially, gaining greater brand equity per Build Allah Square initiated. This is and must remain our primary, central, and essential focus. Indeed, we may even have to learn to hyperfocus specifically on the fulfilment of these concepts, as Collins further noted, "exercising the relentless discipline to say, 'No thank you' to opportunities that fail the hedgehog test" (Collins 2006: 17).

Moving on, Collins further presented to us another principle from his theoretical framework for social movement/ social enterprise success: the flywheel principle. According to Collins, "In building a great institution, there is no single defining action, no grand program, no one killer innovation, no solitary lucky break, no miracle moment. Rather, our research showed that it feels like turning a giant, heavy flywheel. Pushing with great effort – days, weeks and months of work, with almost imperceptible progress – you finally get the flywheel to inch forward. But you don't stop. You keep pushing, and with persistent effort, you eventually get the flywheel to complete one entire turn. You don't stop. You keep pushing, in an intelligent and consistent direction, and the flywheel moves a bit faster. You keep pushing, and you get two turns ... then four ... then eight ... the flywheel builds momentum ... [Until] at some point – breakthrough!" (Collin 2006: 23).

For us in the godbody movement we fulfil this principle through the constant and consistent sharing of the message of What We Teach: (1) That Black people are the Original people of the planet earth. (2) That Black people are the fathers and mothers of civilization. (3) That the science of Supreme Mathematics is the key to understanding man's relationship to the universe. (4) That Islam is a natural way of life, not a religion. (5) That education should be fashioned to enable us to be self-sufficient as a people. (6) That each one should teach one according to their knowledge. (7) That the Black man is God and his proper name is ALLAH. Arm, Leg, Leg, Arm, Head. (8) That our children are our link to the future and must be nurtured, respected, loved, protected, and educated. (9) That the unified Black family is the vital building block of the nation.

Each of these essential ideas are helpful and can provide talking points for all godbodies, anytime we try to teach those in the Black community. However, there are other elements and aspects to godbody theory that were not mentioned there, and that is fine, the solving of the problems we fight to solve through sharing the message of What We Teach will ultimately be how we turn the flywheel. Even subject matters like White supremacy, devilishment, vampyrism, Islamophobia, autophobia, homophobia, transphobia, misogyny, and genocide must only be spoken of within the context of one of these: the general ideas of What We Teach. It is thereby that we maintain focus, unity, order, and consistency as a movement.

That said, the implications of all the ideas mentioned so far lead inexorably to the praxis of most of the lessons that have been delineated throughout this book: Leadership, Black people being the Original people and the fathers and mothers of civilisation; an education of one another in supreme mathematics and social science; a theology based on the godhood of the Black man; a nation that is an interconnected patchwork of families; becoming a world class ideology; and filling the world with love, peace, and happiness. If anyone holds to these sorts of ideas they should be considered a godbody regardless of whom or what. Yet these become mere trivialities and formalities if we do not enforce strict discipline with regard to our understanding of them. Without adopting a dogmatic approach to understanding the core and adjacent values, the core purpose, and the BHAG of the godbody movement, we are in danger of the dilution of our lessons over time. Nonetheless we all know that our lessons are of extreme value to the Black community.

V

The final objective that we as godbodies will need to develop is what Jim Collins called: the 20 Mile March method. To explain the 20 Mile March methodology Collins (2011) pointed out several indicators to determine whether a company was on its own 20 Mile March. Three of these will be of particular interest to our own social movement/social enterprise. Firstly, "A good 20 Mile March has *self-imposed constraints*. This creates an upper bound for how far you'll march when facing robust opportunity and exceptionally good conditions. These constraints should also produce discomfort in the face of pressures and fears that you should be going faster and doing more" (Collins 2011: 42). Having myself given this subject a lot of thought I have come to appreciate that for us this upper bound should be based on cautiousness over who we allow to franchise our movement and also receive our deeper lessons. This means not growing or accepting new members or new franchisees at a rate that is too fast for us to handle. There must therefore be a process, a long process, of preparation, probation, and qualification/ disqualification, before one can be an authentic godbody member.

If a person or franchise is disqualified they will then need to begin the process all over again from the start to have a hope of future acceptance but we should not deny anyone the right to start a godbody franchise on the basis of race, class, gender, sexual orientation, bodily transformation, physical ability, or religious identity. Herein we hereby protect and demarcate our movement from the potential corruption that may be employed by the allowing of members from all these various social groups, each having their own social agenda they wish to advance. Through this method we will be able to maintain and promote a dogmatic stance on our vision and the objectives used to fulfil it, while still being able to influence, interact with, and associate with those outside of our movement.

We must therefore determine within ourselves that we will have as our upper limit a decision that regardless of threat, bribe, promise, popularity, or governmental pressure (of both the positive and the negative type) we will not allow any new godbody franchises or godbody members to be recognised until they have been through first a preparation period, then after that a long probation period, during which time they will still be able to be disqualified and have to start the preparation process all over again: No questions asked. This will hopefully not mean that we become an elite within the ghetto, or that we overprice access to our franchise model. Historically the ability to join the godbody and learn the teachings has always been free or at least easy, and I do not in any ways seek to change that. However, what I do seek to do is make access to membership and the lessons a little harder to attain.

While that may seem or sound counter to the wishes and method of Allah, as I said, this should merely be adopted: Firstly, to keep us from growing too fast for us to control during the following years. Secondly, to keep us from being seduced and corrupted by wealth and power when it joins and becomes a part of our movement. Thirdly, to keep us focused on what our teachings are and not distracted by side missions and other agendas, as important as they may be. Finally, to develop within ourselves and within those on the outside a level of exclusivity for our movement; that it is not just some simple non-profit begging for members to join but an exclusive club only few notables will be able to join.

Some may now obviously say: how does what I am suggesting in any ways improve on what transpired in ancient Kemet with the Shetaut? To be fair, it does not in the least. True, Kemet may not have been perfect, but their system, as bad as it was, still lasted from around 8,000 BCE to around 30 BCE with minimal change; the largest in fact being the establishment of the monarchy. An establishment that even in its prime of patriarchy and class inequality still gave women a lot more freedom, rights, and power than most modern states do to this day; and gave to individuals of every class in society a much greater chance at class mobility than exists in this modern capitalist system.

Secondly, "A good 20 Mile March uses *performance markers* that delineate a lower bound of acceptable achievement. These create productive discomfort, much like hard physical training or rigorous mental development, and must be challenging (but not impossible) to achieve in difficult times" (Collins 2011: 40). Definitively, in employing the 20 Mile March method the godbody movement will have to choose a lower bound of performance that we must be sure, and do our utmost, never to fall below. That means setting up systems of criticism, correction, and punishment to prevent the potential abuse of the freedom that can exist within any movement. Again, having given the subject a great deal of thought I have come to appreciate that this lower limit should be based on our attendance at godbody meetings, which we call ghetto parliaments.

Just for the record, having ghetto parliaments does not make us a parliamentarian organisation. Remember, most of us tend to be anti-state and far closer to syndicalism than parliament-arianism. Here our parliaments are like councils designed to discuss any issues facing the godbody as a movement. This concept of using parliaments as councils to discuss politics, economics, and social issues for the Black and ghetto communities I have affectionately called Black syndicalism. Yet in declaring that these godbody parliaments are thus syndicalist meeting grounds I have also effectively given us another way to identify our own social movement with the anarchic tradition. Now that does not mean that I believe we godbodies should automatically identify ourselves as Black anarchists either. As Bey said, "One does not, in short, *need* to call oneself a Black anarchist to be doing Black and anarchic work" (Bey 2020: 9).

The title of anarchist means very little if it is not accompanied by anarchic work. Still, anarchic work is given far greater meaning when it is accompanied by the anarchist vision. I have therefore been arguing throughout this book for a kind of anarcho-Islamism, Black anarcho-Islamism, and believe the godbody to represent just that. Nevertheless, the godbody may not as yet see how they manifest these anarchist tendencies. Yet, Bey (2020) agreed that most Black people and Black movements possess these anarchic tendencies. Therefore, in taking unto ourselves the understanding of our anarchic tendencies, we godbodies can thereby feel a sense of duty in our godbody traditions and in our godbody parliaments. See, our godbody communities currently have ghetto parliaments designed like mini-syndicates where we discuss our communities, our movement, and our ideas for the future.

At the same time, an interesting suggestion could be made about our ghetto parliaments: that we would be of far greater value to the Black community by also developing monthly parliaments in godbody workplaces, neighbourhoods, and universities that I call workers' parliaments, consumers' parliaments, and students' parliaments, respectively (Albert 2003). Effectively, by organising workers' parliaments for all godbody workers in any godbody or majority Black business, corporation, or organisation; by further organising consumers' parliaments in any godbody neighbourhood; and by organising students' parliaments in any university where godbodies abound.

Again, this form of 20 Mile Marching effectively "imposes order amidst disorder, consistency amidst swirling inconsistency. But it works only if you actually achieve your march year after year. If you set a 20 Mile March and then fail to achieve it – or worse, abandon fanatic discipline altogether – you may well get crushed by events" (Collins 2011: 43). It is herein that syndicalism, as an economic system, creates a far more suitable counter to the economic systems of modernity, socialism and capitalism, than anything postmodernism currently offers. As Brown also said concerning syndicalism, "The Syndicalist method is not organisation from the top down but from the bottom upward" (Brown 1990: 12). Indeed, the fact is that if the godbody hope to reach the 85 percent who are not in leadership positions then syndicalism may be the only way to get to them. "Syndicalism declares for *industrial*, not craft unionism. All workers in one factory, all producing the same commodity, should be in one union; all crafts, the unskilled and the semi-skilled, the clerks, the technicians, the women, and the youth" (Brown 1990: 8).

It is quite plausible that the godbody would now ask why we should seek to infiltrate the workplace of majority Black or godbody owned businesses to set up workers' parliaments when trade unions already exist. The fact, however, is that a large number of unions are controlled by bureaucracy and struggle to get things moving. What I am suggesting to the godbody is that they instead lead and guide the Black workers to control themselves, to be their own saviours and their own managers. All this is in the tradition of anarcho-syndicalism, which "supports workers in a capitalist society gaining control over parts of the economy, and emphasizes solidarity, direct participation, and the self-management of workers. Additionally, anarcho-syndicalism has the aim of abolishing the wage system, seeing it as inextricable from wage slavery" (Bey 2020: 13). Indeed, workers would make far more effective managers of the work they have mastered doing than any newcomer who has only mastered the art of time management.

Furthermore, how this Black syndicalism would work would be similar to how anarcho-syndicalism worked when it did work. "The basis of the Syndicate [would be] the mass meeting of workers assembled at their place of work, factory, garage, ship, loco shed or mine. The meeting [would elect] its factory committee and delegates." "In the case of smaller individual shops, as these are usually found in groups (as grocers, chemists, butchers, bakers, etc.) about cross-roads or minor thoroughfares, workers from each shop would meet to elect their group committee" (Brown 1990: 35, 52). These committees could effectively co-ordinate with the neighbourhood consumers' parliaments in their locale to see what the consumers would like them to contribute to the social product based on their own qualifications and employment and what they are able potentially to contribute to the social product based on their capacity.

But these workplace workers' parliaments will not only be co-ordinating with the neighbourhood consumers' parliaments of their locale, they will also be co-ordinating with other bodies of workers' parliaments: "The factory Syndicate [should be] federated to all other such committees in the locality – textile, shop assistants, dockers, busmen and so on. In the other direction the factory, let us say engineering factory, [would be] affiliated to the District Federation of Engineers. In turn the District Federation [would be] affiliated to the National Federation of Engineers" (Brown 1990: 35), and we could probably squeeze a regional federation between the district and the national for workers', consumers', and students' parliaments too.

Finally, "A good 20 Mile March must be *achieved with great consistency*. Good intentions do not count" (Collins 2011: 42). So long as we attend these parliaments with consistency within our godbody communities, we will create far greater co-ordination and structure than currently exists within the chaotic market and far greater efficiency and functionality than currently exists within the lethargic state. Ultimately, we godbodies should have in our arsenal four kinds of parliaments: the weekly (which features the Square), and the workers', the consumers', and the students' parliaments. Obviously we should not seek to do things like running trains at any of these parliaments, though such should be encouraged and respected within our own communities. The eating and training aspects of the Square, however, should also only be practiced at the weekly parliaments. Still, the reading and writing aspects of the Square should primarily be practiced at our workers', consumers', and students' parliaments.

The psychic effect these parliaments would have on the vampyres would be to give them identification with their own

247

kind and not with the devils and their devil culture. It is undeniable that even those vampyres who do not identify with the devils or their Christian doctrine still identify with the Ashkenazi Jews more than with their own kind. Please understand what I am trying to say: there is no problem with identifying with another race, even a race that is aggressor to your own race, but not at the expense of your own race. That is like an Ashkenazi who so identifies with Germany for their civilisation, culture, and intellect that they praise the Nazis for almost exterminating their ancestors during World War II. As ridiculous as that sounds some Black vampyres tend to praise White Americans for slavery saying they saved the Black Americans from poverty and paganism in Africa.

The truth, however, is that the Europeans, through colonialism, brought poverty and a false messiah worship to Africa. I have already explained the effects of colonialism on Africa. As for the White Jesus, he is a false messiah and an idol: an historical anachronism. Therefore the worship of the White Jesus is the real idolatry and the real paganism. Then they say, "It makes no difference what colour the historical Messiah was, what matters is the forgiveness of sins: anything more than that is racism." But such a doctrine is just a regurgitation of something they learned from a White minister filled with White guilt or White hypersensitivity. They have taken the global neuroses of their White mentors and developed it into a Black neurosis.

Effectively, the acculturation of the vampyres is such that our movement may even appear to them to be less than disreputable. For example, when we hear a White boy from the British countryside say he cannot relate to something like rap music, saying it is arrogant and flashy, such is a bit hypocritical – the same could be said to be Mick Jagger's whole shtick. But when a thirty or forty year old Black person calls hip-hop culture (something very much influenced by the godbody movement) vile and arrogant, something is seriously wrong.

The fact is, hip-hop is the voice of the Black people from my generation just like Alt Rock and Grunge was the voice of White people from my generation, or Britpop was the voice of British people from my generation. When Punk Rock came out in England the adults could not and refused to understand their young, and for a country with such an historical predominance in youth rebellion it is a shame that many of their White indie fans fail to at least respect the existence of my culture – I speak here of hip-hop.

Most hip-hop artists may to you seem arrogant but the truth is, if you look beyond the arrogance you can find intelligence, politics, spirituality, hope, and compassion. When you listen to Biggie just to hear arrogance you can find it, but if you look deeper you can hear "Juicy," "Things Done Changed," "Everyday Struggle," or "Me & My B*tch." Even beyond Biggie there is A Tribe Called Quest, Brand Nubian, Nas, Rakim Allah, Big Daddy Kane, Public Enemy, Common, Cube, NWA, the Rza, the Gza, Raekwon the Chef, the Wu-Tang Clan, et cetera., all spitting knowledge. I actually hate it when my White friends feel so comfortable around me that they share their true feelings about rap with me as though I should agree with them, then end up with the shock of their lives when I defend hip-hop. But what is even more troubling is when Black Christians join in with the same critique to appease their White patrons.

This is the reality of Black vampyrism: realities that represent you and what your people experienced being dismissed as alien. But to make themselves or their White counterparts feel better they may talk about how spiritual reggae is and how it has a message. That is true, and the White person will agree that they have no problem with reggae just with rap. I suppose they are unable to detect the double standard here as dancehall reggae can be twice as violent and explicit as rap (at times). Not that I down dancehall – I love dancehall and all reggae – but growing up in New York my spirituality came mainly from hip-hop. I learned spirituality listening to Nas' *It Was Written* … and Tupac's "Heaven Ain't Hard to Find." One of the most spiritual rhymes I heard was while I was in prison: "Thugz Mansion" and that was after years of listening to Bob Marley.

As for politics, Dre's talking about the LA Riots in *The Chronic* album, the Gza talking about a fictitious Brooklyn battle in the *Liquid Swords* album, and virtually everything Ice Cube ever said on wax was political. Even Mobb Deep's *The Infamous* album which talks mainly about crime speaks to the harsh realities of what America forced on Black youths from the projects. By labelling us criminals they gave us the self-identity of a Black criminal. The fact that most of us were in poverty meant that the only way for us to make a dollar would be to resort to crime. The *The Infamous* album spoke of that crime reality. The world they left us in to kill ourselves, destroy ourselves, and waste our lives away.

I learned the codes of the streets from rap, I saw the glory given to Biggie Smalls in Brooklyn for representing us. I saw that glory turn to disgust when he refused to diss Tupac. I learned strength under pressure from that. True indeed, Biggie was never a real thug, and all those who knew Biggie personally will say he was never really doing that "thug shit" like he claimed. The fact is he repped our world. He was one of us. But to then hear a Black person talk about Biggie and Lil Kim as though they were vulgar and nothing more is deeply offensive. Lil Kim talking about all her sexual escapades may be vulgar to some delicate wimps but the fact is it was our world, we had young women who did that on a regular basis in New York. It was a part of our culture. Our culture may not be your culture but you have no right to denigrate it because it is different. New York City women are more sexually advanced than most women, especially New York City Black women; you should not look down on them for that but respect that that was not your experience and get over it. Conversely, while the majority of Black people, inside and outside America, either sublimate or exhibit their sexuality, Black vampyres usually inhibit their sexuality to the point that it is oppressed: $\exists (Lm > v) \rightarrow opp.\, g$.

Finally, the neighbourhood, university, workplace, district, regional, and national parliaments we create will give the Black vampyres the opportunity to converse with the hip-hop generation and understand our world. The two worlds can meet and delineate each of their realities. As the godbodies and the vampyres meet in these consumers' parliaments, workers' parliaments, or students' parliaments they can also share our message with the vampyres and hopefully reculture them. That is, remind them of the world they came from and most likely grew up in: a world that they deny and have conveniently forgotten. As Lord Jamel Born Akbar U Allah said, "We need to be in the parliament, connecting with each other making sparks on contact like the synapses in the brain. The activities we see in the electrical activity of the brain occur in life" (The Five Percenter Vol 22.2; 2016: 4).

No doubt, there is nothing we are unable to accomplish if we work together with each other and with our race. It is even as the old African aphorism says, "I am because we are." This kind of intersubjective experience will no doubt cause a selfobject transference to occur as the godbodies co-construct with the vampyres a reculturing and thus $x_1 + x_2 \rightarrow pa \leftrightarrow Lm \searrow$. As their new psychological infrastructure is being co-constructed during the process of their intersubjective communications all transpiring at these parliaments and ciphers then the Black person will soon turn from 85 percent or 10 percent to Five Percent having a knowledge of themselves and of their origins in the world.

Black vampyrism is neither evil nor ignorant it is just inappropriately empathetic toward the devils and not its own Black people or its own former Black culture. It spends so much time downing the violence and vulgarity of rap, or the arrogance and pizzazz of rap, that it misses the point: it is an escape, a ticket out of the hood, and not many people get that chance. When they do they therefore speak of the world they came from with a frankness that may be unpleasant to some but is a part of their reality, their culture, and they have a right to practice their culture without having it denigrated, just like Punk Rock and Grunge Rock also have a right to exist.

Pointing out the differences between Punk and rap or Grunge and rap to pontificate all the redeeming qualities of Punk or Grunge and the "so few" of rap is a cop-out. Rap has as much redeeming qualities if you look for them, and Christian Rock or reggae may be more spiritual but to be honest I think there is more spirituality in hearing Foxy Brown, saying, "Reminiscin' on how I fuck the best an' shit/Specially when I'm sippin' Bailys/don't give a fuck on how you move wit' dem other mamis/I push the Z/eatin' shrimp scampi with rocks larger than life/fuck them Reebok broads/you made it known who your wife was" (Foxy Brown 1996), than hearing someone sing "Jesus Loves Me" with a metal instrumental. And as Black female influencer Tee Noir also said, "It's taken Black female artists so long to be comfortable with vividly expressing their sexuality through their music" (Noir 2019); that Foxy Brown was a breath of fresh air in such a politically correct environment.

The Eclipse of Black Sexuality

> *"1. Who is the Original woman? The Original woman is the beautiful Asiatic Black woman. The receiver, the bearer, the womb for the cream of the planet earth. The mother of civilization and Queen of the universe" (Earth's Essence).*

As much as I love all women and want desperately for them to succeed as a gender I shall following be presenting a critique of feminism based on certain observations I have found to be true. Again, this in no ways means that I am against women's liberation. I just feel that as a movement feminism – and particularly anti-sex feminism – has many flaws that have remained unanswered, especially with regard to Black women. It is without question that one of the most marginalised groups on the planet is Black women. "They [are] embodiments of both a condemned gender and a condemned race." Indeed, "Black women are victimized by both of these cultural dispositions. They personify the intersection of race and gender interest" (Douglas 1999: 35).

To be sure, both terms, Black and woman, in our time, have come under serious scrutiny due to a wave of existentialist arguments that have agreed that both race and gender are social constructions that do not exist in any eternal, and, hence, essential, sense but only as social realities to undermine our human commonality. As both terms have been rendered by this school of thought as social constructions the necessity to deconstruct them has seemed imperative. Nevertheless, deconstructionism and godbodyism are two very different schools of thought. Effectively, in godbody sociology it is vitally important that we not sacrifice truth and rigour for the purpose of political correctness.

To begin this process of developing a godbody sociology of Black women I shall start with the concept of woman. According to de Beauvoir, "Woman is losing herself, woman is lost" (de Beauvoir 2009: 3). The question then becomes: how is she lost? De Beauvoir said it is because "she must take part in this mysterious and endangered reality known as femininity" (de Beauvoir 2009: 3). Yet even femininity as it is defined by the West is a social construction – one that has been used to determine normative and abnormal behaviours, performances, and bodily physiques for women – and if it is genuinely a social construction then she is the result of social forces, which in themselves are very spatialised and territorialised. The experience of a woman in college in Europe will be fundamentally different to the experience of a woman in say, rural Ghana or in the Pashtun tribe of Afghanistan. What a woman considers to be imperative to her survival or her wellbeing will differ immensely from one woman to another. A European woman, therefore, has no right or place to lecture a woman outside of Europe on how to live her life or what things to consider important, unless they are attempting to homogenise the female gender into one amorphous lump.

It is for this reason that African female activist Madhu Kishwa said "feminism, as appropriated and defined by the west, has too often become a tool of cultural imperialism" (Kishwa 1994; quoted in Kolawole 1997: 16). That is not to say there are no cases where non-White women are genuinely oppressed. However, in the history of Black people, Black women were the backbone of the Black Power movement, then came feminism, then Black women began fighting more against Black men than with them against White power structures. Thus Black power was divided, conquered, and reduced to nothing more than Black accomplishments in employment and business.

Sure enough, pan-European and Eurocentric feminists have felt the need to interfere in all women's personal, private, and public lives in order to make them more Europeanised and have used "women's liberation" as a beckoning call for women of other nations to follow them. The challenge of justifying and legitimising Black culture to the Black woman thus falls to the Black man, who has already been demonised within the feminist milieu as oppressive, sexist, misogynoirist, and a potential rapist. But when the Black woman refuses to respect Black men she not only compromises the Black family that all Black people highly value, she also puts herself at a disadvantage as Black issues will inevitably be prominent in her own life just as much as in his.

That is not to say Black women do not face forms of male oppression that are significant, or that there is not an unequal power relation between men and women in the Black community. What is being questioned, however, is the sincerity of the feminist movement with regard to their non-White sisters. I find it rather fascinating that second wave feminism arose in the 1970s in the heat of the anti-colonial conflicts and the Black Power struggle. I also find it quite fascinating that with the Black woman switching her focus from the nationalist struggle to the feminist struggle neither the African Nationalist nor the Black Nationalist struggles were effective at changing the discourse of White superiority substantially. The Black woman, who has always been a pillar in the Black community and the Black family, was no longer interested in securing a successful socio-political or socio-cultural superstructure but in exposing and preventing male dominance.

Looking at feminist discourses Mary Kolawole went into their basic premises, she first noted that: "Liberal feminism emphasizes the impact of legal strictures and custom on women's subordination and advocates gender justice" (Kolawole 1997: 12). Basically, liberal feminism fights for legal reforms to legislation to grant women greater levels of equality with men. Their overall perspective, however, is pretty much in line with the social philosophy of liberalism, hence, why some women simply call it liberalism in stilettos but not really that challenging to the patriarchal system. Their main understanding is that as the concept of woman is a social construction, she, in a general and genuine sense, is no different from a man and therefore is as entitled to receive equal benefits as any man within the current capitalist system.

Kolawole went on to say, "Marxist feminists maintain that gender justice is not possible while class stratification is not eliminated. [Marxist feminists] therefore blame capitalism for women's oppression" (Kolawole 1997: 12). True indeed, feminism is a product of a modern capitalist mode of production and civilisation, but which system takes priority to a Marxist feminist, capitalism or the patriarchy? Surely the answer will differ from woman to woman; nevertheless, both the liberal feminist and the Marxist feminist are just as much forms of White tricknology as their male bourgeois counterparts. At the same time, as Kolawole continued, "The role of patriarchy as it undermines women's sexuality is dominant in radical feminist discourse" (Kolawole 1997: 12). For these feminists the only solution to all the problems in the world is the institution of gynaecocracies.

But White women standing up to White men is not necessarily a negative thing, White women assuming that their struggle is universal and trying to spread their revolution to other women is not so beautiful. According to Kolawole, "Among the Asantes, many queen mothers founded dynasties, as we see in the examples of the Judan and Wenchi areas of Ghana." "In Uganda, women were prominent in the rebellion of 1928, in which the woman warrior Muhumusa played leading roles that made white colonialists dread her ... The role of women in Kenyan Mau Mau struggles are no less outstanding." "In the 17th century, a woman, Inkpi, also ruled the Igala people of Kogi state in the middlebelt area of Nigeria. This is not surprising since it is believed that the founder of the state was a woman." And "During the iron age, Zimbabwe was egalitarian and women enjoyed a high level of empowerment. Women in fact played dominant roles in the economy of that society. Power and wealth remained in the female line. Grains constituted the main food and women were in charge and were respected for feeding the community in addition to being mothers and wives" (Kolawole 1997: 49, 46, 45, 49). Not to mention the countless other Black women of Kush and Kemet, or those that took part in the anti-colonial struggles of Africa and slave rebellions among the Afro-Americans, Afro-Canadians, Afro-Caribbeans, Afro-Hispanics, and Afro-Brazilians.

It is for this cause that Hudson-Weems said, "While many academicians uncritically adopt feminism in its established theoretical concepts based on the notion that gender is primary in women's struggle in the patriarchal system, most Africana women in general do not identify with the concept in its entirety and thus cannot see themselves as feminists." Indeed, "African men have never had the same institutionalized power to oppress Africana women as white men have had to oppress white women" (Hudson-Weems 2003: 153, 158). The point is that the struggle is not the same for Black women as it is for White women; and while some Black women may find parallels between their personal struggle and that of the White woman, for the most part a lot do not.

That is not to say that no Black or African women have adopted feminism or a feminist critique of Black society and the

Black movement. But as Hudson-Weems also continued, "On the outskirts of feminist activity, black feminists possess neither power nor leadership in the movement … [Therefore] peripheral promotion of black feminists is only transient, as they will never be afforded the same level of importance as white feminists enjoy" (Hudson-Weems 2003: 159). On top of that, I question the motives of these second wave White feminists, particularly of the original ones, as their so-called hatred of the patriarchy and gender inequality seems to me to be just a matter of convenience that disappears at very strategic moments.

White women have always historically supported the White man in his endeavours: they stood with the White man when he beat both Black men and women during slavery (there was no sisterly solidarity then), they stood with the White man when he lynched Black men and women (there was no outrage over that during first wave feminism, which seemed to concern itself more with giving women – again, White women only – the vote), they stood with the White man when he colonised Africa, Asia, Latin America, and Australia (there was no connection made between patriarchal oppression and colonial oppression during the heyday of colonialism). But as soon as Blacks around the world began demanding the right to vote (for men and women), the right to national self-determination (for men and women), and the right to not be discriminated against (for men and women); then the Black man suddenly gets demonised as oppressing the Black woman.

As an example of female issues being used by White people to divide and rule us I will cite, again, from Fanon, "In the Arab Maghreb, the veil belongs to the clothing traditions of the [women of] Tunisian, Algerian, Moroccan and Libyan national societies. … In the case of the Algerian man, on the other hand, regional modifications can be noted: the *fez* in urban centers, turbans and *djellabas* in the countryside" (Fanon 1965: 35). According to Fanon, "In the colonialist program, it was the woman who was given the historic mission of shaking up the Algerian man. Converting the woman, winning her over to the foreign values, wrenching her free from her status, was at the same time achieving a real power over the man and attaining a practical, effective means of destructuring Algerian culture" (Fanon 1965: 39). The Algerian woman's condition and her veil were not held to be of any concern to the colonialist during the decades-long colonial rule of the French, at least not until during the anti-colonial struggle, then it was suddenly given chief prominence.

The circumstances under which the Europeans showed concern for the Algerian women and their veil were extremely suspect. All their "assistances" to the Algerian women were strategies of war, and it is a war they fought with extreme precision. The support of the White man or woman can thus be poison to the Black community as many of them are infiltrators. Fanon (1965: 38) also explained how, "Mutual aid societies and societies to promote solidarity with the Algerian women sprang up in great numbers. Lamentations were organized. 'We want to make the Algerian ashamed of the fate that he metes out to women.'" As though the European man was at that time – which was the 1950s – the epitome of gender justice.

It is for these reasons that I do not agree with either first or second wave feminism as first wave feminism (the suffragette movement) was concerned only with middle class White women and their issues, whereas second wave feminism (feminism proper) was more likely a tool to put a stop to the Black Power struggles in the West and the anti-colonial struggles in foreign. As can also be seen from examining their history, feminism's roots were quite diabolical, the example being found in the writings of suffragette leader Carrie Chapman Catt, who felt it necessary to, "Cut off the vote of the slums and give it to [White] women"; Catt sought to articulate, as she herself said, "the usefulness of woman suffrage as a counterbalance to the foreign vote, and as a means of legally preserving white supremacy in the South" (Catt quoted in Hudson-Weems 2003: 156).

The reality is, that which classifies as feminist can be highly suspect. Many second wave feminists may be offended to have a man speaking as I have thus far spoken against their ideology, but in its current form it is a tool of White trick knowledge with the intent of universalising the fight of the middle class White women of Europe and America. Not only so, but its very development transpired at a time when White women themselves were doing a lot better than their male counterparts of other races around the world, thus making the feminist critique look seriously dodgy. White women, who were oppressing foreign men and women, had the nerve to condemn foreign men as oppressing their women.

Then again, feminism's indiscriminate use of terms like gendering, objectifying, sexualising, pornifying, patriarchal, misogynist, and toxic masculinity – though they obviously do have a basis in reality, and in the various forms of mental, emotional, spiritual, bodily, aesthetic, sartorial, physiological, cultural, social, political, financial, material, institutional, and generational oppressions women have been suffering – has left them open for any person (particularly if they are female) to misuse these terminologies to undermine other oppressed communities. Of course, White women currently fight for justification due to the fact that White women have not really been justified within the White community as such (de Beauvoir 2009). Indeed, While Black women have a history, in Africa and the Americas, of strength, determination, and leadership in the Black struggle – though admittedly not always appreciated by Black men – White women have historically been subjugated and denigrated. In de Beauvoir's own words, "this world has always belonged to the men and … only today things are beginning to change" (de Beauvoir 2009: 10).

Though I find it rather arrogant for the White world and for a White woman to assume that because *White* men have for the most part oppressed them for so long that that is how it has always been for *all* women and for "this world". In this sense she justifies Fanon's statement; "The settler makes history; his life is an epoch, an Odyssey. He is the absolute beginning" (Fanon 1969: 39). Clearly, White people view themselves and their history as the absolute; there is no other. Therefore, when White women have men in their history who state things like, "A man's body has meaning by itself, devoid of meaning without reference to the male. Man thinks himself without woman. Woman does not think herself without man" (Benda 1946; quoted in de Beauvoir 2009: 6) too right women should stand against that notion. But that notion is in the history of *White* women, not Black.

Here Filomina Chioma Steady articulated the feelings of a large section of Black women towards feminism:

> *"Regardless of one's position, the implications of the feminist movement for the black woman are complex ... Several factors set the black woman apart as having a different order of priorities. ... Because the majority of black women are poor, there is likely to be some alienation from the middle-class aspect of the women's movement which perceives feminism as an attack on men rather than on a system which thrives on inequality." Furthermore, "For the majority of black women ... racism has [brought] the most important obstacles in the acquisition of the basic needs for survival" (Steady 1981; quoted in Hudson-Weems 2003: 154).*

Still, as Hudson-Weems also continued, "Africana women do, in fact, have some legitimate concerns regarding Africana men, [nevertheless] these concerns [should] be addressed within the context of African culture" (Hudson-Weems 2003: 159).

Ultimately, the issues of Black women are valid, but they are issues of the Black community and for the Black community to handle, not some White presence imposing their tricknology on us. Moreover, Black empowerment cannot truly come about while Black women are dependent on White women to help them find liberation. They have merely traded in one oppressor for another. For Black women to truly be liberated they must come to understand, first of all, that the White woman gains far more from the feminist struggle than they do. For this cause, Black feminism is a very problematic subject and the clear way out is to re-analyse some of the general conceptions held within their feminist theories.

I

For one thing, feminist theory condemns sexualisation while at the same time benefiting from the common White standard of sexuality and beauty, as Kelly Brown Douglas said, "The symbols of beauty in White/American culture ... bespeak whiteness" (Douglas 1999: 18). The common White standards of femininity and beauty have thus become the world standards:

$$\alpha = v\left(\frac{x_{Beauty}^k}{x_{White}^0}\right) = vx_1^k$$

where x_1^k = the White standards of beauty
According to Gentles-Peart this is due to the fact that "During the colonial period (between the sixteenth and eighteenth centuries), European travellers writing about Africa drew on and contributed to a European discourse on black womanhood that ascribed a big body to all black women ... [presenting] them as having monstrous (big), unwomanly bodies that were dangerously, aberrantly hypersexual, and not intended to be beautiful and admired" (Gentles-Peart 2016: 8). Conversely, in considering the social kinetics of the hypersexualisation of Black women Gentles-Peart (2016) traced its origins (social aetiology) particularly back to the hypersexualisation of Saatjie Baartman

(or Sarah Bartmann: commonly known as Venus Hottentot). "Her body was exhibited across Europe as the epitome of African and black female sexual abnormality" (Gentles-Peart 2016: 8).

Douglas went even deeper in explaining how, "In the early nineteenth century, Sarah Bartmann was a circuslike attraction across Europe. Her naked body was displayed so that Europeans could gaze upon one particular aspect of her physiognomy, her protruding buttocks. After five years of this dehumanizing exhibition, Sarah Bartmann died in Paris at the age of twenty-five." "The depiction of Sarah Bartmann is representative of the manner in which Black men and women were to be depicted by White culture. They were portrayed as lustful and passionate beings. That such a nature served as sufficient proof of Black people's inferiority, and thus their need to be dominated by White people, no doubt reflects the influence of the Western Christian tradition, which condemned human sexuality as evil" (Douglas 1999: 34). The reality of Bartmann's torture and humiliation at the hands of the White masses, male and female, began the process of the demeaning of Black culture as a whole, and of Black beauty and sexuality in particular.

Indeed, Gentles-Peart (2016: 16) continued the debate, stating that diaspora Black women, "cannot fully eschew European beauty sensibilities by simply inverting them, as they are a part of their histories; the inversion and co-optation of the 'thick black woman' do not erase or replace the colonialist and racist ideologies associated with the voluptuous black female body. In spite of being reclaimed and inverted, the 'thick black woman' ideology remains a tool used by colonizers to undergird ideas about black women's role and worth in modern society as reproducers and laborers." I agree with this premise most definitely: inverting the White stereotype of us will not bring about a *genuine* Black liberation. Further, it contributes to the White dehumanisation of our women's sexuality.

Nevertheless, as Douglas also pointed out, "the exploitation of Black sexuality is inevitable and, in fact, essential for White culture as it serves to nurture White patriarchal hegemony" (Douglas 1999: 12). In other words, regardless of what we do we will never escape the White stereotyping of our sexuality, it is inevitable. Further, "Attacks on Black sexuality seem intrinsic to White culture" (Douglas 1999: 13). White people will therefore never surrender sexual, or social, political, and economic power to Black people, they must be crushed into it. Now while such language may sound violent even the non-violent Dr. King said, "We know through painful experience that freedom is never voluntarily given by the oppressor; it must be demanded by the oppressed" (King 1986; quoted in Islam 2023: 239).

At the same time, Gentles-Peart (2016) was also right, White standards of beauty have caused the colonialist and racist to define Black women as nothing more than reproducers and labourers, thereby holding them back from social empowerment. Indeed, even if Black women (and men for that matter) behaved and became exactly like White people in every single way but our skin colour, that alone would be enough to make us deviant and thereby we would still be denied access to White privilege for:

$$x_1 + x_2 \rightarrow na \text{ as: } x_1 > x_2 \rightarrow (na)x_1$$

where x_1 = an oppressing group and x_2 = an oppressed group. Again, as Gentles-Peart (2016) said, the answer is not in inversion; rather the answer is in self-identification – knowledge of self and love of self – and such a venture will entail deviation.

Nevertheless, as Hardt and Negri also stated, "The will to be against really needs a body that is completely incapable of submitting to command. It needs a body that is incapable of adapting to family life, to factory discipline, to the regulations of a traditional sex life, and so forth" (Hardt & Negri 2000: 216); and rebellion against the traditional sex life can be in more than simply transgressive sexual preferences such as homosexual relationships. A transgressive sex life can also be found in hypersexual relationships.

Hypersexuality, which is how the Black body has thus far been socially constructed, is transgressive and therefore deviant. But while this may fall under the category of what Gentles-Peart (2016) called inversion it is not done for the sake of inversion, it is practiced as a result of self-love; and as Douglas said, "Self-love is the absolute first step to loving others" (Douglas 1999: 123). Moreover, Black hypersexuality should be understood sexologically as a form of sexual self-expression that gives us the freedom to love our own Black bodies; and as Douglas said again, "To be able to love our own bodies is to be able to accept God's love of us" (Douglas 1999: 123). It is also Black *men* and women who are currently hypersexualised so it is not a case of the Black female body being singled out. The Black male body is just as exoticised.

White women are just as capable of sexualising and "gazing" on the Black male form as White men are of sexualising the Black female form – the classic example being Frantz Fanon. On a commute Fanon could hear a child, saying, "Look, a Negro!" "Mama, see the Negro! I'm frightened!" What is the mother's answer, "Look how handsome that Negro is! ..." (Fanon 2008: 84, 86). This was dehumanisation by both commission and omission. She omitted confessing to the child his humanity and instead spoke of his body, his appearance, his sexuality. [...] Now I recognise how that may sound coming from a man when, as a man, I also tend to look at a woman's body, her appearance, and her sexuality; but I write this to point out the hypocrisy of many White women who judge us for it when they do the same thing, all the time, to Black men. This kind of fantasising over the Black male form is not new to the White woman either, hence the woman who cried rape scenario a number of Black male slaves fell into, not to mention Carolyn Bryant's fantasies about Emmett Till.

This opens up a wider debate: is it possible for a woman to be sexist? Obviously, this is a loaded question that would rarely, if ever, be asked due mostly to the existing power dynamic. But it does make sense to ask. What about female supremacy and female separatism? Are these concepts negative? In existing society, due, of course, to the power dynamic they are lauded and respected. Yet the same power dynamic exists also with regard to race. Ideologies such as feminism, and particularly radical feminism and difference feminism, are not considered female chauvinism due to the existing power dynamic. In fact, female chauvinism is considered any female who empowers men to perpetuate the male gaze. Yet Black racism and Black supremacy are insisted upon the Nation of Islam and Farrakhan due to their uplifting of the Black race.

Basically, what happens is that if a woman starts to resent men she gets called a hero or a champion in the cause of women's liberation. But if a Black person starts to resent White people they are instantly called a racist. Such blatant double standards exist not because Black people are any less oppressed than women but because society is blind to the oppression of Black people. (And in some cases willingly close their eyes to it). But this section has not been to completely deny women the right to critique sexualisation, just to challenge certain aspects of their critique in the hopes of liberating both male and female sexuality in the long run.

II

So now we come to the current feminist solution of desexualisation. I have no concern for the White feminists who use this currency as I personally believe they only use it to maintain White supremacy, as everyone knows that in the area of sexuality the Black man is king and the Black woman is queen. But to the Black feminists and womanists who use it, and I speak here especially to my aunty Angela Davis, who I love with the deepest love, I wish to solve the riddle of desexualisation as the words of Kelly Brown Douglas point to a clear area of necessary investigation for me. "Sexuality allows human beings to be in loving relationships that are inevitably life-affirming and life-producing. Women and men must then be able to celebrate, affirm, and experience their sexuality fully in order to know and experience who they are as children of God created in God's own image" (Douglas 1999: 121).

Not only so, but Black people have also faced the same issue with deracialisation that women face with desexualisation. So, using racialisation as my point of departure I shall now attempt to challenge the philosophy of desexualisation. The theory of deracialisation was created in part by Jean-Paul Sartre in dialogue with the Negritude movement. Rabaka commented on the Sartrean position as such, "In his efforts to explain Negritude to whites, Sartre took many liberties with the theory, producing his own unique existential phenomenological Negritude that greatly differed from Damasian, Cesairean, and Senghorian Negritude." Again, "Neither Damas, nor Cesaire, nor Senghor advocated, as Sartre did, 'a raceless society' as the end result of Negritude, but because (both Africana and European) scholars in the Francophone and Anglophone academic worlds have given greater attention and critical acclaim to Sartre's writings on Negritude (i.e., 'Sartrean Negritude'), he has, in a sense, become the go-to guy for knowledge on Negritude" (Rabaka 2015: 273).

Rabaka (2015) pulled no punches, he stated that Sartre's Hegelianising of Negritude was a completely paternalist and even White supremacist action from one who posed himself as a friend of Negritude. Sartre, in considering Negritude as an "anti-racist racism" missed the point. Negritude was the empowering of a disempowered people. It was neither the "negative moment" in the Hegelian dialectic nor the moment of the particular yet to become the universal. True, Black consciousness is a means, but it is a means towards a racially, sexually, and economically equal world and not simply an economically equal world. The Marxist desire for classlessness was effectively transformed by Sartre into a Negritude desire for racelessness. But that is not what Black people seek. When Blacks say that we want Black Power (empowerment) we are not looking for a world where racial issues are considered inconsequential, we are looking for a world in which we have power.

Born King Allah said on the subject, "Our beautiful black, brown, red and yellow hues are now denied and have been replaced with 'we don't see color' statement. That's fake because our blackness is real" (The Five Percenter Vol 20.8; 2015: 3). Effectively, this kind of colourblind racism seems to occur because White people fail to understand with Jackson that "race and race-thinking are not the problem. The problem is, rather, white supremacy and its commitment to racial hierarchy" (Jackson 2009: 20). Indeed, concepts like supremacy and superiority have their basis in some internal need to be better than, i.e. to compete and win. However, "The comparison of cultures presupposes that there is something to be compared – that each culture is not so unique that any parallel with another culture is meaningless" (Hofstede 2001; quoted in Erdman 2017: 36).

That perfectly well understood, I would still say with Jackson that though, "I concede that race is a 'social construct.' ... I am not convinced – scientific insinuations to the contrary notwithstanding – that this is enough to make it 'unreal,' any more than 'manhood,' 'beauty,' or 'kindness' are unreal. ... This is [all based on] a certain privilege of playing Big Brother ... in the sense of exercising a certain power of validation, an inscrutable ability to 'incentivize' others into seeing the world in a manner that confirms white sensibilities and interests. This ultimately translates into an all-encompassing false universal, where specific (read white) concretions of beauty, talent, intelligence, patriotism, even danger come to constitute the standard by which everyone must live" (Jackson 2009: 20).

This is the problematic with White supremacy, it creates a conscious and unconscious understanding that White standards and ways of seeing the world, beauty, talent, intelligence, manhood, womanhood, and danger are the only or the correct standard or way of seeing these things. Thereby their supremacy is implied in the standards they set and reinforce socio-politically, socio-culturally, socio-religiously, socio-symbolically, and socio-linguistically. Simply saying or accepting that race is a social construct is thereby not enough to rid society of the evils of racism and White supremacy. Again, Douglas also said on the subject, "When a White person remains silent in the face of White culture and [yet] reaps the benefits of that culture or nurtures and protects that culture in any way – even by denying its existence – that White person is fortifying his or her own sin" (Douglas 1999: 124) which is White supremacy.

Indeed, the popular idea is that because race, class, and gender are social constructs that need to be demolished, this should be the first aim of any true revolutionary. While this may be true, it is also true that class is an abstraction based on socially constructed relations; while race and gender are embodied realities and thus contain an element of embodiment about them that cannot be denied. And though it could still be said, "The radicality of God's love expressed in Jesus Christ means that God loves our very bodies" (Douglas 1999: 123), this also means that to deny our embodiment does a greater disservice to the genuinely revolutionary as it creates nothing more than a disembodied perspective of the lived-experiences of embodied individuals. Here Spivak helps us with her notion of "strategic essentialism" as Nielsen further explained, "the oppressed group, recognizing its need for group unity and a positive self-conception, intentionally promotes an essentialist identity" (Nielsen 2013; quoted in Rabaka 2015: 279).

To take this thought to a more ultimate place: essentialism itself can be rescued from racist, classist, sexist, heterosexist, and cis-sexist interpretations and made more intersubjective. This intersubjective essentialism is based not on a White cis-hetero-male sexualising a non-White and/or a female, it is based on empathic dialogue, interaction, and feedback loops. Such a variation of essentialism need not limit individual freedom either. People will be free to self-organise their own particulars within a larger essentialist unit. And as it is intersubjective essentialism the definition will constantly be changing in accordance with the times.

What I am clumsily trying to say is that deracialisation and desexualisation appear at first sight to be simple, linear, and straightforward but as we go deeper we see that deracialisation in a White supremacist world only frees White people from the embarrassment of their problematic past without either their punishment or a reward for non-Whites or both. Or, as Jackson said so much better, "the deracialization of whites (and blacks) can only reinforce the intractableness of [our] reality and postpone, if not subvert, efforts to come to terms with it. For coming to terms with what whiteness *has done* and *can do* requires not innocence and invisibility but sustained and vigilant recognition" (Jackson 2009: 21). The outcome is therefore that we non-Whites become the victims and White people the champions, but for what? For kidnapping, enslaving, lynching, segregating, colonising, and criminalising Black people, and for their orientalism, racism, classism, sexism, heterosexism, and cis-sexism against so much Othered groups – but hey, they put up a frowny face #gutted.

Even as Sartre was in no position to redefine Negritude so I am in no position to redefine feminism. Indeed, everything that I have said so far has been nothing more than the grossest form of mansplaining. Nevertheless, I do believe women have every right to fight for respect and empowerment in a world that denies them power and respect. All I am saying is that the ideal of desexualisation is merely the transferring to sexual politics Sartre's misinterpretation of Negritude. As Fanon said of the betrayal of Sartre, "I felt that I had been robbed of my last chance. I said to my friends, 'The generation of the younger black poets has just suffered a blow that can never be forgiven.' Help had been sought from a friend of the colored peoples, and that friend had found no better response than to point out the relativity of what they were doing." (Fanon2008: 102). If you wish to turn for inspiration to a theory that unconsciously betrayed the Black movement then do your thing but know it does you more harm than good.

"For Sartre, Negritude was merely a 'negative moment,' which was ultimately 'insufficient by itself.' What Negritude lacked, from the Sartrean point of view, was precisely what Blacks lacked: an openness to assimilation, which actually meant an openness to Europeanization parading under the guise of modernization, and a more in-depth understanding of Hegel and, especially, Marx, who, perhaps not unbeknownst to Sartre, were both – sometimes subtle, and sometimes not so subtle – white supremacists or, at least, extreme Eurocentrists" (Rabaka 2015: 276). Indeed, Marx himself was known for using the word "nigger" quite profusely (Skousen 2017) and definitely saw Europeans as superior to the colonised races (Said 2003). What we see therefore is that deracialisation in a White supremacist world is not the overthrow of White supremacy, it is the unconscious justification of White supremacy.

If the world were ever to deracialise without having abolished White supremacy then White privilege and Black inferiority would become naturalised and eternalised. Even so with desexualisation. To desexualise women without abolishing both misogyny and phallocentrism is to basically leave power with men. As a man I should have no serious problem with that but as a man who believes in female empowerment I do. With the power balance currently in the hands of men women's empowerment can only come by them taking their strongest weapon and using it to bring about their empowerment, not treating their greatest gifts as though they were a curse.

To finalise this point, no one is denying women's right to empowerment, what I am trying to say is sexuality is not the absolute evil the anti-sex feminists make it out to be. The sexuality as scapegoat position that haunts anti-sex feminism will be a difficult spook to exorcise. It is for this reason that Douglas (1999) stated the need for a sexual discourse of resistance in the Black community. Herein, as Douglas repeated, "A sexual discourse of resistance is necessary to call Black people back to their African religious heritage, which rightly views human sexuality as divine" (Douglas 1999: 122). The shadowy, dark, nightmarish, supervillain that anti-sex feminism has painted men as is therefore unhelpful to both genders in our struggle for sexual liberation.

III

The main problematic I personally have with feminism is its anti-sex narrative. A narrative which, according to Douglas, they developed, whether consciously or unconsciously, in response to their misinterpreting, or even maligning, of Black sexual liberality: "Carnal, passionate, lustful, lewd, rapacious, bestial, sensual – these are just some of the many terms that come to mind when thinking of the ways in which White culture has depicted Black people's sexuality. This practice of dehumanizing Black people by maligning their sexuality has been a decisive factor in the exercise of White power" (Douglas 1999: 31). Herein, by us considering now, in these times we are currently in, we may be able to see how this misconception of Black sexuality was essentially developed based on certain events that transpired during Victorian times.

272

All of this particularly culminated in the spreading of what I personally call, and will be continuing to call throughout, the Victorian monogamous patriarchal standard. Again, this standard was created during Victorian times, mainly as a result of the abolition of slavery throughout the British Empire. Even so, considering Douglas' conception that "sexuality is integral to power" (Douglas 1999: 22) we find that it essentially received its beginning during the British process of "civilising" their Caribbean ex-slaves initially called the Apprenticeship (1834-37). During this time, the British felt they needed to teach, train, and guide their former slaves into "respectable" and "decent" living and livelihoods. It was from this moment that "the exploitation of Black sexuality [became] inevitable and, in fact, essential for White culture [thus serving] to nurture White patriarchal hegemony" (Douglas 1999: 12).

The project of Apprenticeship would inevitably fail, a truth that was not fully appreciated until after the beginnings of the actual Victorian monarchy. Mimi Sheller (2012: 60) also went on to say of the misogynoirist cruelty of those days how, "Female apprentices were punished in large numbers for trying to assert and protect the limited rights they had won as mothers of the slave labor force during the period of so-called amelioration (an attempt to raise the birthrate among slaves following abolition of the slave trade). ... While British abolitionists focused on the cruel treatment of women, [the] women themselves took a major part in protesting the conditions in which they found themselves supposedly free."

Obviously, this all ended as soon as Queen Victoria ascended the throne (1837). From that time a new standard for the colonies was beginning to get promoted. Firstly, "Virtuous women [were] required to be pure, chaste and monogamous". Secondly, there began the propagation of "a phallocentric position that emphasises and legitimises the privileging of men's needs, desires and fantasies" (Nzegwu 2011: 254). Interestingly,

"When [the] new order arrived with the abolition of slavery in 1834, European writers like Anthony Trollope argued plainly that civilization would only proceed in the colonized world on the basis of 'a clear gender order with breadwinning husband and father and domesticated wife and mother'" (Sheller 2012: 95). Thus, was most likely created, if not at least further reinforced, the standard of the virtuous and monogamous patriarch.

The Victorian monogamous patriarchal standard was itself most likely developed due to the popularity of the mistranslated and misinterpreted King James Bible by various Anglican clergy, particularly with regard to the apostle Paul's statement to the evangelist Timothy, "This is a true saying, If a man desire the office of a bishop, he desireth a good work. A bishop then must be blameless, *the husband of one wife*, vigilant, sober, of good behaviour, given to hospitality, apt to teach ... One that ruleth well his own house, having his children in subjection with all gravity; (For if a man know not how to rule his own house, how shall he take care of the church of God?)" (1Timothy 3: 1-5; emphasis mean). Thus, with the spreading of this philosophy further afield, mainly, again, through the popularity of the King James Bible, and more so due to its being completely misread by various Anglican clergy and missionaries, thereby arose the Victorian monogamous patriarchal standard.

Moreover, "Catherine Hall (2002: 125) [has] especially ... shown how the abolitionist dream of a new post-emancipation society rested on a gender order in which 'black men would become like white men, not the whites of the plantations but the whites of the abolitionist movement, responsible, industrious, independent, Christian; and in which black woman would become like white women, not the decadent ladies of plantation society ... but the white women of the abolitionist imagination, occupying their small but satisfying separate sphere, married and living in regular households'" (Sheller 2012: 95). With the

Anglican clergy and missionaries also narrating, propagating, and imposing this general theory and outlook on the people of the African continent, it became very clear the need to somehow "expose the exploitative nature of [their] notion of sexuality [thus] feminist research on battery, rape, incest and child sexual abuse, prostitution and pornography [which all thereby] demonstrated that women within this European and European-derived sexual scheme [were] objects of pleasure rather than subjects who ought to have pleasure" (Nzegwu 2011: 254).

Basically, to empower the Black woman to become, not only a subject appreciating her own sexual value and right to enjoy pleasurable (read orgasmic) sexual experiences, but empowered sexual objects with autonomy and will; Nzegwu went on to talk about how, "Sexuality discourse in the *kpanguima* curriculum [currently] lays out the culturally approved boundaries of behaviour, the culturation of the natural body for sexual expression and the conditions under which sexual encounters can be pursued ... Because sexual pleasure is [actually considered] a social good, sexual desire is not subject to punitive laws unless one engages in practices that are deemed culturally unacceptable. [Furthermore, these types of Black] communities emphasise the right of women to enjoy sex. Students learn about the critical stages – pre-coital, coital and post-coital – as well as a range of techniques for the different phases" (Nzegwu 2011: 260).

In presenting her case for early Black forms of marital arrangement Nzegwu further introduced the concept of nuptial advisers, "The institution of [these] nuptial advisers ... emerged to facilitate pleasurable experiences, and to instruct young women and couples in the art of lovemaking. These advisors are found in different regions of Africa, and include the Sande *sowei* (Boone 1986) and the *laobé* in Senegal; the *nwang abe* of the Ubang of Nigeria (Uchendu 2003); the *magnonmaka* of Mali (Diallo 2005); the *ssenga* of Buganda (Tamale 2005); the *shwen-kazi* among the Banyankore in Uganda; the *tete* among the Shona of Zimbabwe; the *alangizi* of the Yao of Malawi and the *chewa* of Zambia; the *nacimbusa* of the Bemba of Zambia (Richards 1956); the *mayosenge* in parts of Zambia and the *olaka* of the Makhuwa of Mozambique" (Nzegwu 2011: 261).

Consequently, the Black love and hypersexuality of the ancient Egyptian people, both male and female, also allowed for a much greater level of sexual independence among the women of ancient Egypt. Nzegwu (2011: 257) even furthered this point when she wrote concerning the ancient songs of the Chester Beatty Papyri I, "The songs are [very] passionately charged declarations of love and intense sexual desire. They speak in smouldering erotic tones about the male whose 'heart is afire with desire for {his beloved's} embrace' (Obenga 2004: 598); or the female lover whose 'heart flutters hastily / When I think of my love of you / ... / It lets me not put on a dress' (Chester Beatty Papyri I)." These kinds of dramatic and erotic act-species essentially played a part in giving ancient Egypt a reputation and self-identification as a highly erotic, one might even say hypererotic, people. However, such a hypereroticism did not remain, and has not remained, exceptional to ancient Egypt. As Nzegwu also noted, "The pan-ethnic Sande and Bundu *kpanguima*, and all other similar sexuality schools, taught young women about the force of [their ability to give and receive erotic] pleasure" (Nzegwu 2011: 260).

In this, Nzegwu virtually gave herself a mission: to enlighten Black people, and Black women in particular, as to their own authentic Afrosensual heritage, so as to give to modernised Black women a pride in these kinds of Afrosensual schools. Also to remove from us the shame developed from the indoctrination of dehumanising, degrading, and derogatory ideas about ourselves from having lived and experienced persecution in a White society with a White outlook from a White gaze; especially in relation to our sexuality: "Because the [Black] theorisation of sexuality takes place in the context of producing a good society and healthy social living, [hence] Sande instructors work on firmly moulding girls into self-assured women. They induct them into community-wide fellowships of women and transform them into Sande *nyaha* or mature adult women, complete with an adult personal aesthetics and a female-identified consciousness" (Nzegwu 2011: 260).

Herein we can see the genius of what Nzegwu was hoping to restore to Black women, as she said again, "The [Black] discourse on sexuality typically begins from the standpoint of understanding, mastering and directing this powerful [sexual] energy ... It treats [it] as a critical dimension of not just life, but a seat of women's power. [This] force is [also] vital because it modulates man's propensity for aggression, acting like an opiate to produce calmness and equanimity". Though she still also recognised, "As [with] any skilled task, performers must acquire relevant knowledge and gain proficiency in the art of pleasuring. Students learn ... the art of igniting passion by means of gestures, the look, the walk, dance moves, spatial configurations, modes [of] dressing, food initiators [and even] knowledge of erogenous zones and rhythmic pelvic movements ... Lastly, they also learn coital sound stimulants or 'lovemaking noises' (Tamale 2005)" (Nzegwu 2011: 260).

This kind of sexual education is very different from that of the West. It is a fully immersive, completely interactive, and absolutely visceral experience based on seductive guidance, and sexual expertise come from training and guidance in the secrets of sexuality. This system itself can be traced all the way back to our Tantric ancestry in ancient Egypt. Though admittedly I am not a Tantric expert myself, I have still been trained in the Tantric arts and am very familiar with their lessons, some of which were enlightening and very inspirational. What do I mean by that? Two of the best and most game changing lessons I have ever learned I received from within the Tantric school I was initiated into.

The first thing I learned is: one of the main things that society needs to appreciate is that masturbation is not embarrassing but is in fact very normal. In what was called: the *Cosmo Report* written by Linda Wolfe, it was reported that 54 percent of the women who then masturbated had themselves begun at the age of 15; 32 percent began between the ages of 10 and 15; 17 percent began between the ages of 5 and 9; and 5 percent even confessed to having begun masturbating from before the age of 5 years old (Wolfe 1981). Indeed, it should be clear to anyone who interacts with any self-aware and self-assured women that they actually tend to be able to get far more sexual pleasure without men, whether through masturbation or homosexual experiences, than men are able to get without women. With this in mind most of the patriarchal systems developed during the Victorian times, which condemned any form of female sexual expression: from masturbation, prostitution, "fornication," pornography, lewdness, sexual dancing and gyrating, homosexuality, and hypersexuality begin to make a lot more sense.

The patriarchal fears over female sexual freedom or empowerment were very likely based, in large part, on this understanding within the minds of the Victorian clergy. Moreover, the transgenerational sexuality of the Black man, and especially of the Black woman, with her sometimes otherworldly irresistibleness – when she knows how to use it – and her orgasmic sexual aura, are exceptionally overt. It must have therefore placed a fear in the hearts of these clergies that either one of us would steal their White women away. Such a statement is not arrogant boastfulness or wishful thinking either. It is well documented, even to this day, the White man's feelings of sexual inadequacy in comparison to the Black man; add to that the sexual potential of a hypersexual homosexual Black woman and you get even greater reason to fear. This is what created the need, post-emancipation, to control Black bodies and Black sexuality, lest Western civilisation fall as a result of our free sexual expression and sexual potential.

Some might now say that such nonsense as the White Victorians designing the Victorian monogamous patriarchal standard in response to the threat of Black sexual potential goes against the democratic and Christianising vision of the Victorians. Also, this throwaway line of a "transgenerational sexuality" goes completely against scientific, and thereby provable, evidence. Herein I will therefore present as my evidence a statement articulated by Malcolm Gladwell, "Cultural legacies are powerful forces. They have deep roots and long lives. They persist, generation after generation, virtually intact, even as the economic and social and demographic conditions that spawned them have vanished, and they play such a role in directing attitudes and behavior that we cannot make sense of our world without them" (Gladwell 2008: 175)

Moreover, as he further continued, "Why is the fact that each of us comes from a culture with its own distinctive mix of strengths and weaknesses, tendencies and predispositions, so difficult [for our time] to acknowledge?" (Gladwell 2008: 221). It is herein that we understand the importance of an essential truth: men are pretty powerless against a hypersexual Black woman who is determined to seduce them. Indeed, men – even men – are able to have multiple orgasms during a single sexual experience, when triggered by a hypersexual woman, especially a Black woman. Accordingly, if the only orgasm someone receives during sex with a woman is at the climax of the experience: that is actually not a good thing. He has basically cut himself and his wife or girlfriend off from the truly amazing experience that comes mainly through transfiguring her; and the best way a transfiguration is inspired is through hypersexual behaviour, behaviours that *literally* come naturally to Black women. Effectively, the Black man and Black woman were again *literally* designed by their Maker to inspire ecstatic and orgasmic sexual experiences.

The second thing I learned through Tantric initiation was a little more controversial, in fact, it was so controversial that at first I did not accept it, I was unable and unwilling to wrap my head around it. They taught that there will eventually come a time, when one has mastered or come close to mastering the art of Tantric sex, when one will no longer even want or desire to discharge. When I first heard this word I immediately rejected it. Then I began having sexual experiences, sexual experiences in which I transfigured all Black women to such an extent that I not only had multiple orgasms, something I was already very capable of and skilled at; I had at that time become so orgasmic that I felt like I was about to explode in a theophany of pure erotic pleasure. I basically had to call it (before climaxing or ejaculating), though I definitely did not feel cheated or frustrated for not cuming. At that time, cuming itself would not only have been superfluous and unnecessary, but even a distraction or hindrance to the pure pleasure I had experienced.

Basically, by practicing what we in our day call "edging," we godbodies can experience heights of sexual ecstasy unimaginable. These levels of sexual ecstasy, these orgasmic levels of having reached what I call pure pleasure (and modern society calls "edging"), were not so much reached because of the women – though they obviously played a part through their turning me on to the point that I desired to transfigure them – but because my transfiguration of them at that time was not simply from the mind but also from the heart. Since then I have still had times when I ejaculate in sex, but for the most part I now seek, and have experienced quite a few more, moments in that ecstatic reality of pure pleasure. That is what I now go after in my sexual and masturbatory experiences, from the first time it has been tasted no lesser sexual experience will do. Indeed, if these kinds of lessons were taught during sex education and not the asexual garbage that is being taught today in most sex education classes, we would never have to worry about rape, incest, or paedophilia as no male, boy or man, would ever seek that lesser rate experience when he could have prime simply by being with someone he genuinely believes is worthy of transfiguration.

This, however, is the rub. This is where the sexual techniques taught to girls/women in the African sexual communities become very helpful. These effectively inspire the man to transfigure them. While, at the same time, the male must play their part and learn or understand the female body. It was in Tantric school that I learned that a woman's body is very sexually complex, while with a man we can reach orgasmic level within maybe two minutes, maybe even one, and thereby climax very quickly from the encounter; it can actually take a woman quite a while to reach that orgasmic stage, usually up to 20 minutes. This means, if the male really wants to pleasure her, that is, take her to the ecstatic heights of pure pleasure, he will have to do a lot of foreplay, especially with his tongue. The beautiful thing about a woman, though, is that once she has had her first orgasm during that sexual experience, it will be a lot easier to give her multiple orgasms throughout. Indeed, when the two master their sexual craft they will be able to give each other multiple orgasms during any single sexual episode simply by each other's touch, without any skill at sexual motion, movement, gyration, or performance.

Conversely, the desire should be to reach those levels where they need to beg their partner to stop gyrating and moving as their heart is already on overload and any further movement could result in explosion. To be clear, it will not be to avoid cuming, it will be to avoid a heart eruption into a mess of ecstatic pleasure that it, at that time, is literally unable to handle. It is at this point that they will realise there is nothing better than sex. I say this as one who used to smoke at least seven marijuana blunts a day; drink at least one 64 oz every day cause 40s were not potent enough; went to megachurches with the most "heavenly" choirs imaginable; became a gospel music aficionado; has even been in a "loving" monogamous relationship where I believed our love had taken me to "cloud nine" – and though I have never done cocaine, even that would feel like a step down. In fact, the levels of pure sexual pleasure I have reached through the arts of Tantric sexuality not only destroy all that other mess, the scale is so lopsided that I have come to see libidinal energy as the very face of Allah himself.

Now while I recognise that this idea may sound, seem, and feel daunting to most young people, particularly to young men, who now realise that they have to be so skilled at foreplay that they can take a woman to orgasm by it, then have to control their own body in such a way as to keep from ejaculating when they know that it is in the very sexual experience that they are completely out of control, and they even have to try to reach levels of sexual ecstasy where they can literally see the very face of God(!). However, before I provide an assurance to my young Black people, I want to speak to my more mature Black brothers and sisters, who currently feel that they are set in their sexual ways, and have no time, patience, or countenance for any new sexual ideas or methods.

First, the main thing you need to understand is based on a truth appreciated by Malcolm Gladwell, "researchers have settled on what they believe is the magic number for true expertise: ten thousand hours" (Gladwell 2008: 40). I say this because in many of your cases you have already stacked up well over ten thousand hours of sexual experience. In that case, all you need to do is seek to prolong the sexual experience, not out of duty, demand, or disengagement but based on a love so supreme that you can see the God/Goddess in your partner. As noted, this act of seeing the divinity in your lover, especially during the process of making love, is called transfiguration. Effectively, there comes a point in the sexual process, so long as you have been transfiguring your lover, when the mere touch of their sexual part, without them even moving or gyrating at all, will take you to such ecstatic heights of orgasm that you will be afraid that if you continue your heart will explode.

The first step is to prolong the sexual experience as long as you can (which modern society calls "edging"). During this process you should be able have multiple orgasms. Again, as hard as it may seem, many of you have already racked up your ten thousand hours of sexual experience, you just need to know where to direct your libidinal energy. The answer is simple: toward transfiguring your partner. Through learning about this possibility and this technique I myself, on the very same night it was taught to me, was able to prolong my own discharge (ejaculation) and thereby gain multiple orgasms during a sexual experience, all from the one act of transfiguring my lover. The same will be very likely for you too: now you know you can do it and how to do it it should be easy for you to get there.

As for you young people, I recognise how much pressure is on all of you to be good, especially in your first few times. It can almost feel like you have to climb an unclimbable mountain. There is pressure from society, pressure from your celebrity heroes, pressure from your friends, and pressure from the one you are about to have sex with. Now on top of all this pressure here I come giving you the added pressures of prolonging the sexual experience, having or giving multiple orgasms (can they even be given?), and transfiguring your partner in both your heart and mind. To add even more pressure there may also be the fear that if you are no good the first few times nobody will ever want to have sex with you, or worse, you will never get good enough at sex at all to ever give anybody pleasure. These fears are understandable and very natural. I think all of us more mature adults have had most, if not all of them, at some point in our lives. However, over time, and with practice, you will eventually rack up those ten thousand hours, even if you need to supplement some of those hours with masturbation. The thing is, as soon as you hit that ten thousand hour mark your body and brain will change. You will feel more confident in movement, action, technique, and capability. You will also find it easier to prolong the sexual encounter through transfiguration, thereby opening the door to multiple orgasms.

Effectively, even though the Victorian monogamous patriarchal "notion of sexuality has made tremendous gains in various parts of the world, this does not mean its view of the erotic is correct (MacKinnon 1989), or that it is the only appropriate way of thinking about the erotic" (Nzegwu 2011: 254). Moreover, through her own research into the different sexual-school communities of Africa Nzegwu mentioned how "it is necessary to establish what happens when women are positively affirmed; how our understanding of sexuality differs when the vagina is perceived as an important organ. At the very least, cultural songs and dances are [now] rich with sexual allusions to the power and strength of this organ. Cultural dances and contemporary dance moves, such as *makossa, mapouka, ndombolo, soukous* and *ventilator* speak of this power in fluid, circular gyrations of the hips and quick forward and backward thrusts of the pelvis. These dances can be energetically or slowly enacted, delivering the … sexually charged moves that suggest the penis will be devoured" (Nzegwu 2011: 263) Or in plain English, within Black pro-sex traditions the female has always had far more autonomy than in the Victorian monogamous patriarchal tradition, regardless of the screams of White feminism to the contrary.

Herein we see that by, "Placing sexuality (and erotic agency) at the center of our understanding of what freedom means and how it might be embodied and performed [we can develop] a breathtaking revision of traditional political histories" (Sheller

2012: 39), which includes those of Afro-Americans, Afro-Canadians, Afro-Hispanics, Afro-Brazilians, Afro-Caribbeans, and all indigenous Africans. True, it may be understood by many that inversion and deviation may not solve all the internal or external problems of the Black community, still public deviation has always been able to set off a chain of events that has brought about structural or superstructural change. Essentially, through self-identification with the low life, the vulgar, the worthless, we develop such a consciousness of self that we feel no shame over our past, nor any serious shame in public deviation. In this relation, "Cooper's tongue-in-cheek, yet serious, call for 'bottoms-up history' (Cooper 1993: x) reminds us of the 'pubic' that is the root of the word 'public' and the 'sexualised representation of the potent female bottom in contemporary Jamaican dancehall culture' [even if these are] nether regions that are not spoken of in polite/political society" (Sheller 2012: 42).

IV

Now, there is obviously a complaint that White women are quite capable of being oppressors too, which has also put a lot of Black women off feminism, as Delores S. Williams has stated: "Some black women had reservations about white feminist definitions of patriarchy as the primary cause of *all* the oppression *all* women experience. ... Most definitions of patriarchy provided in the USA were silent about white men and white women of every social class working together to maintain white supremacy and privilege" (Williams 2012: 61). As a Black man I can say it is unhelpful to the cause of feminism to treat all men as though all we are is craven sex monsters and dehumanisers. I for one believe in female empowerment, I also support and respect the womanist cause, but I am not a feminist and feel that our Black female warriors should take seriously the arguments made by womanism against feminism.

As Hudson-Weems articulated, "the prioritizing of female empowerment and gender issues may be justified for those women who have not been plagued by powerlessness based on ethnic differences; however, that is certainly not the case for those who are Africana women. Those Africana women who do adopt some form of feminism do so because of feminism's theoretical and methodological legitimacy in the academic community. Moreover, they adopt feminism because of the absence of a suitable framework for their individual needs as Africana women today – in the academy and the community" (Hudson-Weems 2003: 153). Yet within feminism Black women seem to be background figures, "It is quite obvious, for example, that bell hooks will never be elevated to the same status as either Betty Friedan or Gloria Steinem" (Hudson-Weems 2003: 159). It is also clear that a Susan B. Anthony and a Simone de Beauvoir will get more attention in feminist theory and history than an Ida B. Wells or an Ella Baker, but within womanism these and all Black women take centre stage. They have the leading role.

As an example of what I mean, Black people seem to play minority roles in most ideological movements: Black anarchism, Black Marxism, Black socialism, Black liberalism, Black conservatism, Black Republicanism, Black nationalism, Black feminism, and Black eroticism are all movements that require the qualifier "Black" in order for the Black presence to be acknowledged. In womanism, however, Blacks are the leaders. Womanism is one of the few movements that is our movement. Now a womanist is defined by Alice Walker as:

A woman who loves other women, sexually and/or nonsexually. Appreciates and prefers women's culture, women's emotional flexibility ... women's strength. Sometimes loves individual men, sexually and/or nonsexually. Committed to survival and wholeness of entire people, male and female. Not a separatist, except periodically, for health. ...

Loves music. Loves dance. Loves the moon. Loves *the
Spirit. Loves love and food and roundness. Loves struggle.*
Loves *the folk. Loves herself.* Regardless *(Walker
1983; quoted in Williams 2012: 58).*

Most importantly a womanist is "A Black feminist or feminist of
color" (Walker 1983; quoted in Williams 2012: 58). Though,
thanks to the doctrine of intersectionality, Black women
currently make up a large percentage of the feminist movement
in contemporary culture, which has caused womanism, as an
outlook designed for Black women and by Black women, to
currently be overlooked.

Notwithstanding, even in womanism there can be
distinguished a liberal-wing and a conservative-wing. Though
Walker's liberal stance represents the liberal-wing Hudson-
Weems has created a variation of womanism that is far closer to
conservative Black culture: "Africana womanism is not Black
feminism, African feminism, or Walker's womanism that some
Africana women have come to embrace. Africana womanism is
an ideology created and designed for all women of African
descent. It is grounded in African culture and, therefore, it
necessarily focuses on the unique experiences, struggles, needs,
and desires of Africana women" (Hudson-Weems 2003: 157).
And as sympathetic as I may be to Walker's views I must admit
to being closer to Hudson-Weems' more Afrocentric definition.
There is a cultural, aesthetic, and intellectual emphasis that she
exuded in her definition that must be appreciated, by both Black
and White women, and it is a crime that Clenora Hudson-Weems
is not more well-known within academia. Indeed, an Afrosensual
womanism inspired by her theoretics could have a huge potential
within the Black community.

Yet, just like the next step for a Black woman is from Black
feminism to Afrosensual womanism, so the step after that for the

Black woman is from Afrosensual womanism to godbodyism. With regard to men this would take the form of Godhood, with regard to women this would take the form of Earthhood, and while I personally may not agree with limiting the Black woman to the position of Earth, such is the actually existing situation among female godbodies. Nevertheless, at least in the 1990s, female godbodies were far more hypersexual and sensually liberated. Pre-"Hit 'Em Up" New York City Black women, as a result of the godbody prohibition of marriage, were able to have multiple sex partners while remaining in a committed relationship with one.

Some ask the question if art imitates life or life art, and Spike Lee's *She's Gotta Have It* (1986) about a New York City Black woman with three Black male lovers and a potential Black female one, was very much so a reflection of mechanisms put in place due to the godbody prohibition of marriage. New York City Black women therefore, at least in the 1990s, had a mentality aligned with the Earth mentality, street and sexually evolved beyond the need to settle down or be married. This was also the actually existing culture of 1990s Black sexuality in New York. These kinds of sexual liberalities encouraged womanist theologians like Douglas (1999) to say, "It is mandatory that the Black community initiate a comprehensive form of sexual discourse if it is to repel and disrupt the power of White culture in relation to Black bodies, sensuality, and spirituality" (Douglas 1999: 69).

Nevertheless, my saying that the godbodies prohibited marriage is a little inaccurate: the godbodies prohibited marriage according to the government, meaning the godbodies sought new ways to define marriage and sexuality. Goddesses had, in practice, several boyfriends but one main man, who she called both her King and her God, and her God had several girlfriends but one main girl, who he called his wife and his Queen. The terminology thus used back then was very reminiscent of the priestesses of Hethor, where they had several sexual partners but one Horu (the Pharaoh), and the Pharaoh had sexual access to all of them but had one Hethor (the Queen). While some Egyptologists try to downplay the sexuality and polyamory of the ancient Egyptian initiates in order to look smart and sophisticated, initiatory congregations like the *Shemsu Neteru* of ancient Egypt were just like the Christian Gnostics of classical Egypt: highly spiritual in writing but highly sexual in practice.

The Horu construction of the godbody male can thereby be conceived. However, it is here theorised that this construct exists even outside the godbody culture and within the universal Black soul. According to Freud, sexuality and sexualisation represents processes that transpire during the Oedipal phase of development. Such is the case in psychoanalysis, the child, if male, develops an incestuous lust for his mother and a murderous hatred for his father that Freud called the Oedipus complex (Freud 1997). Overtime, if navigated properly it develops into a castration complex and ultimately determines the child's sexuality and sexual mentality. Still, while this theory is somewhat universalistic and was even applied by Freud to non-human organisms, Adler's theories were very culture specific and applied purely to Eurocentric individuals. That is not to say they should be abandoned altogether by non-Europeans, just modified to suit non-European cultures.

As a Black man I speak for Black cultures, heterogeneous as they may be, to show forth the unity existing in the various mental topographies of the Black person. In Adler's own Victorian theories there was what he called a "masculine protest," which we are able to apply in a fundamentally different way. For Adler the masculine protest was based on an original psychic hermaphroditism within humanity – a theory that is in itself very questionable – which develops within the male gender a need to become proactive, strong, confident, brave, and aggressive to compensate for any so-called feminine attributes such as: passivity, weakness, shyness, frigidity, and submission.

Such a way of looking at the gender roles and traits is extremely Eurocentric, though somewhat outdated, and applies less frequently in most non-White social bodies. In place of Adler's feminine attributes and masculine protest the godbody perspective should adopt the Hethor construct and the Horu construct. Hethor being the ancient Egyptian Goddess concept and Horu the ancient Egyptian God of Kings concept. The goddess attributes of Hethor were far more in line with what she represented in ancient Egypt: she was the personification of love, music, dance, sensuality, aesthetics, culture, wisdom, hyper-intelligence, hypersexuality, hyperspirituality, et cetera. All attributes a woman can be proud of and even men can be proud of. Horu, on the other hand, was the personification of the self, the sun, royalty, courage, leadership, strategy, enlightenment, hyperintelligence, hypermartiality, hyperintegrity, et cetera., all great attributes for Black males to aspire towards. Further, the development of the Horu construct, far from coming about as a form of compensation for Hethor traits, comes about to compensate for certain social irregularities.

In ancient Egypt Horu was technically the surrogate son of Hethor but he was more so her husband and the maternal son of Auset. He was also fatherless due to the murder of Auset's husband Ausar by her brother Setekh. The injustice of his father's murder pushed him forward in life until he was old enough to confront Setekh. After defeating Setekh, with the help of Ausar in the Dwat and Hethor in Pet, Horu became king of Upper and Lower Egypt. Hethor, on the other hand, starts out as the wife of Ra, but takes pity on Horu in his struggle. For her assistance in helping him defeat Setekh Horu then married her and made her his main wife, while also becoming her main husband.

These two aspects: (i) a man determined to fight an injustice, and (ii) a woman who respects his struggle and marries him on that basis; signified the Horu and Hethor constructs. This defines the ideal Black family. Most real Black families, on the other hand, may also have a fatherless home but lack the struggle against injustice that signified the Hethor and Horu constructs. Instead there is working for a living wage and trying to either make ends-meet or to rise higher within whatever form of employment they are in. These women may have a form of the Hethor construct, being Black, but they repress it for the sake of social acceptance.

In the development of the Hethor/Horu constructions three traumas can also become distinguishable in all Black people: (i) Birth. This stage Freud identified in all infants, some call it postnatal traumata. This trauma is alleviated during the weaning and the post-weaning phases of infancy by a loving world. (ii) Racial inferiority. This trauma is initialised by a society that not only favours White people over all other races, but that considers Black people as the lowest racial strata in society. This trauma can only be alleviated by fighting against the injustice of White supremacy. (iii) Sexuality. This trauma is experienced differently for men and women. For the young man it starts at puberty and lasts till they either die or develop Ausar consciousness. For a young woman it starts when they realise that their gender is as unfavourable in society as their race and that they are doubly condemned. It too can last till they die or it can end when they develop Auset consciousness.

The trauma of sexuality is never really alleviated for either male or female only exacerbated by the loss of virginity. This loss does not add up to a new trauma but only heightens the already existing trauma of sexuality. While sexual energy was in the child from the beginning, it is only at puberty when it begins to be directed towards a sexual object for the purpose of having sexual relations. Still, the first two of these three traumas of Black psychological development can be either alleviated or exacerbated by circumstances in the personal lives of the person in question. At this time, the parent plays the key role in ameliorating any traumatic tensions that may arise in the child's life based on the phase they are at.

By the third phase neither parent nor anybody else will be able to alleviate the trauma of sexuality, or of the loss of virginity for that matter, the best a parent can do is prepare their child for both. As the child has always had a sexual drive but never properly understood it or used it to attain sexual gratification, the trauma of sexual experience, fear of sexual malfunctions, and inevitable virginal inabilities will be traumatic for the post-pubescent boy and girl. Though sex does get better for both, and the pleasures of sex increase with experience, sexuality, as inspired by the sexual drive, will haunt them ever afterward.

It is at this time that the Hethor/Horu constructs become a most effective means of explaining Black psychological development. Though the Electra/Oedipus phase is usually located among Freudians and neo-Freudians between ages 3 and 6 (Freud 1997), the Hethor/Horu constructions usually develop between ages 6 and 9 and can last deep into adulthood, and are not superseded until Auset/Ausar consciousness is developed, which can happen at any time in adult life; and though technically both male and female initiates were called Ausar in the *Prt m Hru*, and both male and female initiates were to proclaim, "*Nuk Auset*" (I am Auset) a few times in the *Prt m Hru*, Ausar and Auset consciousness is better understood here in their gendered roles.

For a boy, the Horu construct effectively begins at the second trauma or gets repressed at the second trauma. The boy either becomes more like Horu or becomes more Eurocentric. To explain this Eurocentrism a little more in-depth: Freud said that the White boy is brought to maturity by the Oedipus complex. He desires to marry his mother and murder his father. The father's task is therefore to internalise himself within the White boy thus becoming for him the superego, an internalised ideal. If the Horu construct is repressed within a Black boy then the Oedipal complex will rise, thus instead of the Black boy's sexual energy getting sublimated towards fighting injustice it gets directed at his mother, on the one hand, and the superego becomes a White man, on the other. The superego of a real Horu is either his father or his racial fathers (ancestors, national heroes, racial icons), these assist the Horu child in his psychological construction of self-identity.

What defines the girl developing a Hethor construct does not necessarily have to be her falling in love with a Horu, or a Black man who fights injustice. The Hethor construction for the Black girl actually begins, as with the Black boy, at the second traumata. However, there may be some confusion as for the girl this may occur either before or after the third traumata. Either way the discovering of racial inferiority begins the path of the Black girl's self-identity, who either constructs a Hethor identity or represses it. How one identifies a Black girl/woman who has developed the Hethor construct is she will be hypersexual, while yet remaining hyperspiritual. The spirituality may manifest as religiosity if that is the only outlet for her spirituality, or it may manifest acceptably through a mindful lifestyle, if her caregiver is able to guide her effectively.

A true Hethor, being inspired by a true Horu, will use her hypersexuality and hyperspirituality for the purpose of fighting racial injustice, regardless of which traumata she experienced first. Just as the Black male needs the hypereroticism of the Black female to strengthen his undeniable resolve in his fight against social injustice; so the Black female needs the hyperintegrity of the Black male to sublimate her vast sexual energy towards helping him fight against social injustice. For this cause, the Black girls and young women who repress their Hethor construct will very likely adopt as superego the White woman; and thereby direct their sexual energy toward White men. There will still be a kind of fight against injustice, but with the White woman taking the role of superego in her construction she will unfortunately stifle her sexuality and spirituality. A Hethor should therefore take her mother, or racial mothers (ancestors, national heroines, racial icons) as her superego.

V

The hypersexuality of the Hethor construct can even manifest itself in practicing a lifestyle of free love, therein having major points of agreement with the ideals of anarchist and feminist icon Emma Goldman, who believed that institutions like marriage should be abolished altogether. Moreover, the anarchist and anarcha-feminist advocacy of free love also comes masterfully close to the godbody's own prohibition of marriage; as Goldman stated, "Free love? As if love is anything but free!" "Love, the strongest and deepest element in all life, the harbinger of hope, of joy, of ecstasy; love, the defier of all laws, of all conventions; love, the freest, the most powerful moulder of human destiny; how can such an all-compelling force be synonymous with that poor little State and Church-begotten weed, marriage?" (Goldman 1911: 8). Freud also concurred, stating that, "Under today's cultural conditions marriage has long since ceased to be the panacea for women's nervous disorders; and even if we doctors continue to recommend it in such cases, we nevertheless know that a girl has to be fairly healthy in order to 'cope' with marriage" (Freud 2002: 97).

Effectively, the anarchist tradition of free love has more or less been based on the idea that issues of love such as marriage, divorce, sex, and adultery should not be left under the control of church or state. In fact, church and state should have no say in any of these affairs. Of course, such an idea may scare certain women today who fear *the threat* of rape or paedophilia. Here free love does not say that those who perpetrate such crimes should go unpunished, just that social bodies other than church or state should decide on these matters. According to French anarchist

Émile Armand, "It is not a matter of asking whether the practice of free love has rendered, when taken up by unprepared or inept natures, bad results. It is not a matter of posing amorous variability as a factor of the evolution of the sexual act. ... We will pose the question of sexual liberty just as we pose the question of intellectual or scientific liberty, or the question of the freedom to opine, gather, or associate" (Armand 2012: 77). The central demand of free love: that neither religion nor government have any say over issues of love, completely coincides with the godbody perspective. In fact, the tradition to not marry according to the government has its basis in free love, in that it frees both the male and the female to be as sexually opened up or closed off as they desire to be without the fear of any repercussions from the state.

If we thereby acknowledge that sexuality itself is able to be used as a weapon, we come to appreciate such a weapon can be used in either a good way or a bad way. A knife can be used murderously, threateningly, defensively, or surgically. Even so, sexuality can be used for good or bad depending on the person and situation. Hill said on the subject "overindulgence in sex expression may become a habit as destructive and as detrimental to creative effort as narcotics or alcohol" (Hill 2004: 221). It is herein that love becomes the perfect counterbalance to any hypersexual expressions as it increases those positive energies that build and heal instead of those that destroy. Hill continued the argument, saying, "Sex, alone, is a mighty urge to action, but its forces are like a cyclone – they are often uncontrollable. When the emotion of love begins to mix itself with the emotion of sex, the result is calmness of purpose, poise, accuracy of judgment and balance" (Hill 2004: 223). Ultimately, when hypersexuality is balanced out by love it is able to save from the extremities of free love should it be misused, and from all the violations of marriage according to the government.

Indeed, as Goldman expressed further in her theoretics, "the marriage institution is [the] only safety valve against the pernicious sex awakening of woman". "Oh, for the inconsistency of respectability, that needs the marriage vow to turn something which is filthy into the purest and most sacred arrangement that none dare question or criticize". "If, however, woman is free and big enough to learn the mystery of sex without the sanction of State or Church, she will stand condemned as utterly unfit to become the wife of a 'good' man ... Can there be anything more outrageous than the idea that a healthy, grown woman, full of life and passion, must deny nature's demand, must subdue her most intense craving, undermine her health and break her spirit, must stunt her vision, abstain from the depth and glory of sex experience until a 'good' man comes along to take her unto himself as a wife?" (Goldman 1911: 8, 5).

There could obviously be made at this point the objection that women in marriage relationships are happier and more complete, and that they feel none of what Goldman and Freud spoke of here. Yet, conversely, Goldman also stated of these more committed women that "a short period of married life, of complete surrender of all faculties, absolutely incapacitates the average woman for the outside world. She becomes reckless in appearance, clumsy in her movements, dependent in her decisions, cowardly in her judgment, a weight and a bore, which most men grow to hate and despise" (Goldman 1911: 7). Basically, if we looked deeper at the institution of marriage, we would find that it is incomparably different from any passionate and orgasmic love freed from the shackles of church and state.

As Goldman (1911: 4) further continued on the subject, "On rare occasions one does hear of a miraculous case of a married couple falling in love after marriage, but on close examination it will be found that it is a mere adjustment to the inevitable. Certainly the growing-used to each other is far away from the spontaneity, the intensity, and beauty of love, without which the intimacy of marriage must prove degrading to both the woman and the man." Marriage stifles love and makes both partners in the relationship a prisoner, such that as Freud explained, "The uninitiated find it quite incredible that, among couples subject to our civilized sexual morality, normal potency is found so rarely in the husband and frigidity so often in the wife, that marriage involves such a degree of renunciation, often for both partners, and that in married life, the happiness so fervently longed for, is reduced to so little" (Freud 2002: 102).

In all honesty the Black theologian and Black scholar, whether male or female, should seek to follow the example of the godbodies and not be tied down with such trivialities as marriage. Even the family itself should be deemed more than simply a man, a woman, and children. The entire community should be considered the family, and the freedom to love all those within the community should thereby be guaranteed by the community. Not only so, but, as Gladwell also pointed out, "Judith Harris has convincingly argued that peer influence and community influence are more important than family in determining how children turn out. [Effectively,] a child is better off in a good neighborhood and a troubled family than he or she is in a troubled neighborhood and a good family" (Gladwell 2013: 167). From all this, we can see that given a strong communal family a child will be far more likely to succeed than simply having a strong traditional family of two parents. Such is the kind of formation of Black family I advocate for; and free love leads inexorably to this kind of formation of the Black family.

Free love in effect is nothing more than the free association of a man and a woman in common relational accord with the possibility of sexual autonomy guaranteed, not by the religion or the government but by the community. It is neither men using law or faith to dominate women nor women using law or faith to dominate men. It is the abolition of dominion in sexual matters and the implementation of liberation to ameliorate both. Freud took the issue even further, saying, "Let us add that in general the restriction of sexual activity in a nation goes hand in hand with an increase in [its] anxiety about life and ... fear of death". "Especially obvious is the damage done to women's natures by the strict requirement of premarital abstinence. It is clear that education does not take lightly the task of suppressing a girl's sensuality until she marries, for it operates with the harshest means. Not only does it forbid sexual intercourse and put a high premium on the preservation of female innocence; it also shields the young woman from temptation as she matures, by keeping her in ignorance of any factual knowledge about the role she is destined for and by refusing to tolerate any amorous impulse that cannot lead to marriage" (Freud 2002: 104, 99).

I hope it is appropriate, at this time, to share with the reader a little of my own backstory: at the age of thirteen I had my very first sexual experience with a girl that was eleven. Though we only briefly had sex the event itself, the history and realities around the event, and the actual occurrence of the event, were all traumatic experiences for me at the time and for most of the time afterward. That said, whereas such occurrences would usually lead most males into becoming ultra-conservative, and into preaching against sex, sexual liberty, and sexual education for teens; I instead used it as a motivation to fuel my progression in the other direction, becoming more pro-sex, and preaching for more and better sexual education for teens. Indeed, I go so far as to say that while anyone older than eighteen should not have sex with anyone younger, those who are younger should actually be allowed and encouraged to go through their early sexual experiences with their fellow younger teens, without fear or condemnation.

This will hopefully remove from them the fear, pressure, awkwardness, uncomfortableness, weirdness, anxiety, angst, and inexperience many of them feel on their first time; the experience itself being handled with more care than my own personal experience. Further, their first few times should be in a safe, encouraging, and helpful environment, without the pressures that most of us experience on our first time. The truth is, sex is not just a thing, or a meaningless event detached from love. All sexual expressions – including the most solitary, as well as the most abusive or disgusting kinds, all sexual expressions – are for the most part already expressions of love. Now that does *not* give men or women the right to rape, violate, or molest anyone claiming that it was all done as an expression of love.

In the case of the abusive forms of sexual expression, let us be very clear, it is, first and foremost, still abuse and therefore *primarily* a form of dominance and control. However, if we honestly analyse with a more full and subtle understanding we can remember that the reason sadism, like so many other forms of sexual expression, turns people on at all, and works at all, is because of the interrelation between sexuality and aggression. During sadism, rape, molestation, or any form of sexualising children, what is being enacted is the dominance of their aggressive side over their sexual. The point is, in all that, the sexual is still there, and therefore love is also there, just a perverted, distorted, and corrupted love.

The situation is similar to, and can be compared to, the empathy of what is called the dark empath. They have discernible empathic feelings, but they are so overshadowed by toxic and narcissistic behaviours that they are even more dangerous than both sociopaths and psychopaths. That is not to say that every dark empath is a potential rapist, or that every rapist is a dark empath, but that even as empathy, an otherwise good and beautiful expression, can be corrupted into dark empathy, even so sexuality, another otherwise good and beautiful expression, can be corrupted into some form of sexual offense or violation.

That said, sexuality itself, for the most part, is still good; and as noted: all forms of sexual expression are pretty much performances of love. This word love is here defined as empathy and agape, however, so long as the empathy is not dark, and thereby able to be corrupted it is able to become something really special. These are things young people should learn in their teens, and not fear or dread over sex, sexual violence, or sexual misconduct. Of course, the young men will have to learn to be respectful of the young women they get the chance to have sex with, also understanding that, while it is true that the act of sex itself is unfortunately impossible without some form of sexual objectification and sexualisation, they must still appreciate that the *person* they are objectifying in the moment is so much more than a sex object, sexual fantasy, or that crush they are fond of over there. They are a real, living, thinking, feeling, engaging, hurting, worrying, crying, laughing, transgressing, artful, fearful, emotional, deep, flawed, scarred, and complex human being.

Ultimately, so long as both parties are able to learn and understand that sex and sexualisation are natural parts of the sex experience; and that when it comes to the female participant and any touching of her body, consent is fundamental. Moreover, any behaviours of aggression or dominance during the sexual experience, even if desired or demanded, shall and will be an automatic ending of the experience and denial of future contact *ever again*. Young people need to be taught, both from learning through our brutal honesty concerning our own earlier sexual experiences – despite the inevitable uncomfortableness on both our part and theirs – and through their own supervised and guided (though not watched, judged, or critiqued) early sexual experiences. I believe this will be safer and less traumatic for teens (rather than lying to ourselves about teenage innocence as though they cannot or will not find ways to do it without our adult input, which is the grossest of wilful self-deceptions).

Still, the main reason I endorse the hypereroticism of Black eroticism so fervently is that it may be used to generate within us libidinal love, thus thereby producing for us a Black sensual resurrection. To be clear, if the Bible intended for the first resurrection to be a mental resurrection then it would have said that the *nous* or the *noema* was to be resurrected. Instead, it said the psyche was to be resurrected. For those who do not know, however, the Greek word psyche, back in its day, actual meant something more along the lines of: the internal drives that produce our external behaviours/activities. In Freudian theory these drives are acknowledged as predominantly sensual drives inspired by the pleasure principle. Herein, we see why in the King James Bible they chose to translate the Greek word *psychikos* to the English word sensual, even if nowadays the word psychic has taken on a far more abstracted meaning. Based on the Freudian interpretation of a sensual, indeed, sexual psyche we can see how the first resurrection was always far more likely to have been considered to be a sensual resurrection.

Consequently, the godbody prohibition of marriage helps us to fulfil this *eschaton*, or last days' thing, by allowing us to practice a form of free love, or even plural love, in our communities. The truth is, we godbodies need to address this issue of Black eroticism in our philosophy as to not do so would make us hypocrites, using all this language of caring for children and educating the masses in our public discourse while, at the same time, practicing in secret sexual liberality. We either need to add sexual liberality to our public discourse, that is, add the discourse of Black eroticism, or abandon what Allah was trying to teach us and where he was trying to lead us. It should be clear to anyone who gives any serious thought as to why the Father taught us not to marry according to the government that his goal was to promote among us free love practices, thereby sexually liberating us. The fullest expression of this sexual liberation thereby leading us to become sexual objects to the rest of the Black community.

Through this the God would become the sexual object of Black women and the Goddess would become the sexual object of Black men – and though I recognise that the word object has acquired certain negative connotations since Martin Buber (1927) that relate it to the "dehumanising" of human beings, I use it here in the Freudian sense of the word – making us like selfobjects that can be conduits of their transferences. As the godbody male and godbody female thus become the sexual objects of Other they will thereby cause Other to discharge sexual energy in the sexual act. Again, if we do not address this issue of sexuality and sexual liberation we risk our word not being bond, claiming to only be about the family, while, at the same time, loving sex and behaving sexually without admitting that truth. At least if we publicly adopt a discourse of Black eroticism our word becomes bond to truth. Our word also stays *our* bond which others will be able to see in all our ways and actions toward the opposite sex.

That said, the sexual act must always be consensual between both: neither the male nor female godbody should ever rape anybody, nor allow anybody to rape them. The godbody must therefore practice the use of seduction in their hypererotic behaviour to break down all resisting or reactionary behaviour. In this, there ultimate aim should be to generate within the sexual subject the most powerful force in the universe: sexual energy. That sexual energy will then either be discharged in the sexual act or sublimated into progressive acts – obviously it could also get inhibited once generated if the godbody does not guide them to a fruitful outcome. Therefore the act of seduction must not be taken lightly. Though the key to Black eroticism must remain seduction, which can be both positive and progressive, as it can instigate the liberation of a Black person's sexuality from inhibition or prohibition.

To further clarify, when I use the word seduction it is not here spoken of in the Freudian sense of the word but in the commonsense of the word. Freudian seduction shall henceforth be referred to as perverse seduction in that it takes for granted the idea that an adult, older sibling, or trusted authority will molest a child (Schimek 2011). Seduction as I use it is still Freudian to a degree, in that it produces within the sexual subject a wish, but it is not *the* Freudian theory of seduction as it has nothing to do with sexual molestation or betrayal. In this version of seduction the sexual object becomes the sexual fantasy and thereby becomes fetishised – in the sense that they take on mystical attributes. The God becomes sex God to the Black woman thereby allowing her to recognise that the standards of society are and have always been artificial and illusory.

It is the central intent of this form of Black eroticism to liberate and empower Black minds, the methodology the God should use for achieving this objective thus remains seduction. Still, if one excuses the oversimplification, women will always be better seducers than men. Indeed, any woman can seduce any man she wants to simply by tempting his heart with constant and consistent exhibitions of her body or sexuality (Greene 2004). These exhibitions will be like sharp goads on the man's heart, especially when he tries to resist her. Eventually, the pain will become so unbearable that he will be completely in her power. Therefore a woman should never take anything a man says too seriously as she can easily break him with consistent sexual temptation whether through her words or her behaviour. Obviously, a woman should not have to expose the private areas of her body or her sexuality just to seduce a man, however, if she does, it is the most potent form of eroticism she could perform.

True, Feminist Jill Johnson did articulate back in the 1980s that, "Feminism at heart is a massive complaint, Lesbianism is the solution ... Until all women are lesbians there will be no true political revolution" (Johnson 1985; quoted in Kolawole 1997: 15); yet this was not as hopeless a call to action as it at first may seem. In my own experience women tend to prefer things like masturbation and lesbianism to male sexual relationships. Herein homosexuality may not be as genetic in the case of women as it is in the case of men. The truth is, women are generally better at sexual expression than men, knowing in many cases instinctively exactly how to sexually please both men and women. Add to that the emotional support, friendship, bonding, and compassion they are able to receive from other women, and the overall shittiness of men when they show or demonstrate the slightest bit of sexual independence or freedom and it makes it that much easier for them to leave the game entirely, either practicing lesbianism, or identifying as bisexual or pansexual. In certain cases, obviously, those women will continue to date or have relationships with men, however, in a lot of cases that will only be due to the stigma of self- or same-sex pleasure, or due to the wealth and power of men in the current world system.

Basically, while what Johnson was hoping for may at first have seemed somewhat impossible, especially considering how far a cry it is from the "you don't choose to be gay" rhetoric; choosing mainly instead the promotion of using love for political ends. Still, building on from her, a far more powerful war cry would be for *all* women to practice the lifestyle of free love and thus free themselves from the burden of marriage and the various other standards imposed on them by church and state. On the other hand, if we were to look deeper into the conception of Black eroticism, which is based fundamentally on Black love, free love, and plural love, it is definitely more than what marriage could ever be: it is a free expression of hypereroticism that possesses a high pneumatological potential.

We should also remember that according to Freud eroticism is the most powerful force in the universe. For this reason I have been fighting so hard to allow Black women to express their own eroticism or hypereroticism. Imagine if you will that all Black men were suddenly to possess a superpower: the ability to transmit their thoughts to other Black men. Imagine that only Black men possessed this superpower and that they could use it to uplift the Black community. Now imagine that society continued to stigmatise and demonise this superpower as evil and ignorant. Imagine they also labelled those who used this superpower as corrupt and backward. Would any of this stop

Black men from using their superpower to liberate Black people? Well, *all* women have a genuine superpower with eroticism, yet for some reason they despise their superpower unable to appreciate how great it is.

The truth is, men, even with all our political and social power, are unable to handle a very erotic woman, especially as women can stir in us all the aesthetic, spiritual, social, cultural, martial, political, economic, scientific, philosophic, and athletic genius we require in life through sublimation. Hill once briefly commented, "One of America's most able businessmen frankly admitted that his attractive secretary was responsible for most of the plans he created. He confessed that her presence lifted him to heights of creative imagination, such as he could experience under no other stimulus" (Hill 2004: 217). Yet rather than encouraging women, and particularly Black women, to use their superpower for their own liberation we condemn them whenever they do use it. They may think that eroticism is not that great a superpower but I disagree. It is an amazing, wonderful, and incredible superpower, and as stated before, by both me and Freud, it is *the* primary force of the universe. The only reason I can think of as to why so many women look down on such a force is because they have not yet learned to reject society's stigmatisation of it and use it to empower themselves.

Still, for a seductionist, *whether male or female*, their one overriding aim and desire is to give the greatest amount of erotic pleasure to the person(s) they are interacting with. Moreover, their seduction will always be revolutionary, though it should ultimately be a beneficial revolutionism used to liberate and not to oppress. Their seduction must also be an unoffendable, unapologetic, and unstoppable force; thereby not being discouraged by bad results but strengthened by them. Seduction by name means there is resistance. Indeed, with no resistance it is not seduction but arousal. They should therefore not feel too discouraged by these resistances though, as in their desire to

305

produce in that person the greatest amount of erotic pleasure they could possibly have, they will have effectively revealed to them the very essence of Allah, which is al-Ashiq (the Libidinal).

All seductionists could therein be called eroto-masochists, in that, each erotic act they perform represents a living, 100 percent demonstration and manifestation, not only of the erotic side of al-Ashiq; but also a powerful, unpretentious, unhypocritical, undeniable demonstration and manifestation of both the long-suffering and the kindness of the agapic side of al-Ashiq. Again, nobody is saying that any woman in her right mind must, or is being forced to, follow this path of seductionism. Just that women are a very complex phenomenon, and there are and will be those women that choose to walk this path, whether to seduce men or women or both; and these women deserve to have the right to exist and feel identified.

Yes, I am well aware of how controversial the idea of masochism can be for women, particularly Black women, due to their complex history with slavery, segregation, colonisation, and the sufferings and pains we as a people have endured, and still continue to endure. Such ideas even go beyond the already "problematic" notion of struggle love that many Black women in the upper classes outright reject (and many even in the lower classes are desperately seeking to escape from). However, at the risk of promoting concepts that are unacceptable to these types of Black people – many of whom themselves subscribing to the doctrines of Black Prosperity Theology – those who challenge and critique female suffering, masochism, or struggle love may, at the same time, be policing women's right to engage with and even get pleasure from such realities. Believe it or not there are plenty of women who actually like and respect the realities of suffering, masochism, and struggle love; obviously, within limits and with their caveats.

Even more troubling and problematic for some reason is the men, especially Black men like myself, who are masochists or

306

have masochistic tendencies. Our existence threatens the Black manosphere, and the image of hegemonic masculinity many Black males seek to display to the non-Black world. Herein the two dominant identifiers within the Black communities of the world, but particularly in America, are of Black excellence and of Black girl bosses. These highly idealised images of Black love and "Black Power," are promoted and encouraged to the Black communities of the world, not only as aspiration goals but as *Black* or Black authenticity.

Challenges to this model, such as consensual masochistic behaviour, can only be based on deception, weakness, confusion, trauma, or coercion. It seems there is such a determination to vocalise "the real" voice of those in such transgressive relationships that they fail to believe that we may actually like them. For example, I like behaving seductionistic, polyamorous, and masochistic in my relationships. To be clear, though, it is not that I enjoy suffering or pain, nor is it that I get large amounts of pleasure from pain (though I am able to); but that getting great amounts of pleasure filled with trace amounts of struggle and suffering, to me, can make life more worth living. Think of any novels, movies, or dramas that lack DRAMA. Such an epic failure would be such a boring, chessy, vanilla banality that its only entertainment value would either be as a cautionary tale of what not to do, or simply to read or watch the spectacles/ parade of awfulness for its sheer awfulness.

This is how I see those pristine, perfect, polished, couples on TV, and in magazines, shit, this is how I see most couples, period (though admittedly not all, whether celebrity or manosphere). These are definitely not "couples goals" to me: they are either a lie or an inhibition to me. Either way, leave me with my transgressive, slightly problematic relationships with the ghetto ass, ratchet, hood rats that I love. It seems that in seeking so hard to voice the miseries and difficulties/problems of suffering and struggle love a lot of commentators fail to articulate that there are also beauties in struggle love worth maintaining. That is not to down or vilify those who speak against struggle love, everybody has their thing, just to share another side to the story. There are Black men and women that actually like suffering, such men and women behave hypererotically, privately and publicly, not for validation, respect, or a round of applause, but for the pleasure of behaving hypererotically.

Moreover, if these eroto-masochists were to experience rejection, humiliation, or some other form of suffering for behaving hypererotically, they would not be weakened or destroyed but feed off of that suffering using it to go even further and behave even more transgressively, whether in their words (to seduce women) or their visuals (to seduce men). It must also be understood that any seduction, if practiced, works best when performed at times of peak emotion like anger, fear, anxiety, frustration, mourning, love, awe, wonder, or joy (although I would recommend being careful when it comes to anger as people may become violent at this time). In this, whenever the emotions, or even the circumstances that brought on the emotions, are triggered in the subject's life they will remember the seduction and thus be turned on again. Thereby the seductionist will become fetishised, and even deified, in the heart of the sexual subject. Though in all cases that person must be brought to the place of surrendering to these erotic actions before any real sexual activity can occur otherwise it will be rape, and a seductionist must be above all else anti-rape.

Effectively, by inspiring erotic ideas in the heart of the sexual subject during times of peak emotion the seductionist can free them from any traumatically produced superegos. Not only so, but they can also exorcise from them *all* previously possessed superegos allowing a Horu and a Hethor (that is the astral forces of hyperintelligence, hyperintegrity, and hypermartiality; and of hyperintelligence, hyperspirituality, and hypersexuality, respect-ively) to become their only superegos. In this, seduction can be

308

therapeutic and eroticism can be liberating, revealing to us the very face of Allah, and thereby becoming for us a form of psychotherapy where sexual object becomes like selfobject using sexuality as a means to inspire both pleasure and healing.

In order to finalise this point, however, I will now remind the reader that in the beginning of any new practice or lifestyle change the first thing to kick in will be the law of opposition. This will effectively produce both an equal and opposite reaction to the change, regardless of how instinctual that change is or should be, or how much unfair potential we have regarding it. For this cause, we must maintain the practice or lifestyle change for as long as possible, and with as much persistence as possible, with or without validation, until the law of repetition begins to kick in. Once the law of repetition kicks in then the practice or lifestyle will slowly start to become habitual, and what was once only a potential strength due to our innate ability and ancestral genetics, will become an actual strength through repetitious accomplishments and practical evidences. Soon, with these repetitious behaviours being maintained with time and consistency, the law of evolution will then begin to kick in and take over. From there, what was once simply a strength and capability will develop and multiply *exponentially*. At this point, our potential strengths move from being actual strengths to being unbeatable advantages. We will, from that point on, be the beneficiaries of the King Effect.

VI

For all the above reasons, the main add-on I provide to my version of Black eroticism is light exhibitionism. For those who have not read my first book, *Black Divinity*, I personally identify as a light exhibitionist, which is someone who permanently refuses to wear any underwear. This practice I also encourage for all godbodies, male and female, for two specific reasons: (i) to enflame White passions thereby weakening their discourse of superiority, to basically take the ground from under the feet of those White people who claim sexual superiority to Black people; and (ii) to make Black sexuality more spiritually refined, to basically reconnect Black sexuality to its spiritual centre.

Effectively, as we see from Barbara Watterson concerning the people of ancient Egypt, "Ancient Egyptian women wore their revealing dresses without much in the way of underwear" (Watterson 2013: 85). Or as Houston also confirmed, "Nude figures are seen as through a veil. Naked figures can be seen when the body is clothed" (Houston 1985: 90). The ancient Egyptians obviously valued the naked body as many of the common people were pictured naked. However, the nobles usually wore fine spun linen and cotton, practicing in their time the light exhibitionism of not wearing underwear. Indeed, the interesting thing about this hypersexual practice is that by normalising the naked body to their young people they stood a better chance of not being obsessed with the naked body by the time they reached puberty or adulthood. This is one of the main wisdoms (*hikam*) of light exhibitionism.

Accordingly, to resurrect the ancient Egyptian culture light exhibitionism will be essential, and as obsessed with hygiene and cleanliness as the ancient Egyptians were, it also makes White hygiene look ridiculous with their hiding of filth and soaking it into underwear. The truth is, there is actually no substantial hygienic value in wearing underwear that could not be found in keeping our lower regions completely clean. Therefore, though light exhibitionism may in itself appear to simply be an exhibition of Black bodies, it is in fact far deeper, far more sensual, and even, far more wise. It is nevertheless also a far greater exhibition of non-physical qualities than it is of merely the private areas of the body. Effectively, the private areas of the body may never get exposed at all. The point is not to walk around flashing everybody, the point is to stop wearing underwear for sensual reasons, to be a living manifestation of "adult situations." But in that case it must be adults, and only adults, who practice it. Youths under the age of eighteen should therefore be discouraged from practicing any form of light exhibitionism as they are not of the maturity to control their baser instincts.

Here light exhibitionism channels the fight and places it in three areas where White people have historically dominated Black people: the spiritual, the aesthetic, and the psychological. We gain spiritual liberation through light exhibitionism as it challenges sexual perceptions and conceptions: far from sex being considered weak and a form of weakness it assumes strength, it becomes power incarnate, even the expression of godhood. With regards to the aesthetic liberation it offers, that comes from the fact that the light exhibitionist practices within Black eroticism are excessively beautiful (as opposed to the skid marks on underwear) – so long as we keep them beautiful with a thorough maintenance of our lower regions through the soaping and rinsing of our genitals and anus at least four times in the shower immediately after we defecate; through the regular shaving and cleansing of our genitals and anus inside and outside the shower; and through the effective use of body lotions after we shower. It also means *measuring more accurately the gas in our stomach* – and makes White forms of beauty look very childish in comparison. Psychologically we find liberation as we have removed the safety net: as with diapers underwear hides filth; an actually clean person need not resort to such things but can display, even exhibit, their cleanliness for the world to see.

Nevertheless, the idea of opposing Black eroticism to White standards of beauty may at first sight seem like an unfair fight. What light exhibitionism does is it gives us an edge, and in more ways than one: it puts us in the position to define what we consider beautiful, sexy. Thus, White magazines and articles that seek to reinforce White standards of beauty will not have the levels of influence that they have enjoyed thus far. It also allows us to boycott four very powerful industries in the West: the panty industry, the lingerie industry, the boxers industry, and the briefs industry. While, at the same time, admittedly, strengthening the tampon industry, the cologne industry, and the perfume industry: as in maintaining the consistent, persistent, and permanent practice of light exhibitionism, we will have to be sure to both lotion, and to cologne or perfume our private areas regularly (as a warning though, putting cologne on your nuts is like a fire that cannot be quenched so breathe deeply).

The aftereffects of this one practice: on magazine and other media industries, on the various underwear industries, and on the sex industry, will also spill over into the marketing industries and bring them into a place where they will be forced to hire Black male and female models to advertise underwear. Such images will distract from the battle and make uninformed or unaffiliated Blacks feel no change; but something would have changed and the business community will know it, the White person at their job will know it, the White world as a whole will know it. There is even buried in the act of no longer wearing underwear a defiance of convention, of the rules, of religion, of morals, and of the state, that makes it progressive, positive, and very revolutionary (Armand 2012).

Nonetheless, the reason for this practice is not simply to inspire a Black revolution, it is to mainly inspire a hypereroticism in the Black community that boosts the morale of us godbodies, male and female, in our struggle against this White supremacist system. As we all know: sex is the best medicine and seduction is a river of life, yet we have not considered that the most potent form of seduction is in fact exhibitionism. At the same time, it is the *adult* individual and the *adult* social body that must ingest from this river of life: that is, the seduction must be for revolutionary reasons and not for perverse. If the godbody movement ever does choose to adopt light exhibitionism, they must reserve their seduction for adults only and never for pubescent youths or prepubescent children. As offended as some of the Gods and

Goddesses may be at my even suggesting that a godbody would try to seduce a child or teen, if I chose not to say anything and a godbody did seduce or molest a child or teen, the responsibility would fall on me and me alone. This way you have been informed.

Ultimately, light exhibitionism is hypersexual, it can also be seen as an act of anti-modern revolutionism; it is therefore not for every Black person to practice, only the strong and militaristic. Why I say the strong and militaristic are those who should practice light exhibitionism is: (i) If those who cannot resist the temptation of having sex with a White person practice it it defeats the purpose. We want White people to acknowledge the weakness of their discourse of White superiority without the victory of having taken one of our own. (ii) If a pacifist practices it and is confronted by a rapist it also defeats the purpose. This is one of the reasons why I am mainly encouraging this practice among us godbodies: Goddesses generally are not really that tempted by White men; and most Goddesses fear no rapists (having already been in the Square with a large number of godbody men one-on-one, and an even larger number of godbody women six-on-one, she definitely knows how to protect herself against any male rapist). Basically, even if a rapist was to have a weapon, as soon as he got close enough to touch her, she would automatically beat snot out his ass.

What I am trying to suggest is that if our godbody sisters are not wearing underwear, even if they were alone on the street at night, their universal flag should be repellent enough to protect them. They should effectively be seen as hypnotic sirens, good to look at but dangerous to touch. Any men, however, who do brave it will get the shock of their life as she literally breaks his face open. Nevertheless, her light exhibitionism will be a form of hypereroticism that makes a potent statement: her Black body is beyond the control of men. This statement, however, should only be made if she is willing and able to go without having sex with a White man. Remembering also that it is not only godbody women being encouraged here to give up their underwear, it is godbody men too.

Obviously, there will be those who wonder what eroticism itself has to do with Black theology and being a Black theologian. That, however, is only because they have been overfed the Victorian monogamous patriarchal standard of high religiosity for too long. There have, however, been other standards that we can learn from, for example, ancient Egypt. The ancient Egyptian people were most assuredly hypererotic. There is also the Native Americans before they began to take on the White man's morality. Then there is Tantric India, and pre-Wahhabi Islam. The point is that hypereroticism does have theological substance to it, just not in post-Victorian Christianity (Foucault 1998). Conversely, as we godbodies begin to practice Black eroticism (itself a type of hypereroticism) we can liberate ourselves from their standards of decency and religiosity and begin to develop and reacquire our own standards of sacred sexuality.

Some may now say at this point that what I have been saying the godbody should do only sexualises our godbody women. As I have already shared my opinions concerning anti-sex feminist corruptions I say the following only for Black feminists and womanists. Firstly, returning to sexualisation: if sexualisation is looked at as evil and dark then yes it will be problematic. Yet, as long as we live in a world where reproduction comes by sex alone then sex will be inevitable; and the social kinetic of any world where sex is inevitable is that sexual objectification and sexualisation will also be inevitable. It is impossible to have your cake and eat it too. If we live in a celibate society where sex is abolished and reproduction comes by artificial insemination, only then can and should sexualisation be condemned; but if a woman has a husband or a boyfriend and wants to have sex with him then he will need to sexualise her or someone else in order to get an erection.

As someone who loves and fights for Black women, I find it difficult to say but biologically men need to sexualise women to have sex with women, if not all you got is a limp biscuit. There is no way a man can have or maintain an erection without some form of sexualisation. Even the men who speak negatively about sexualisation in sympathy with women themselves also, must, sexualise a woman or women to have sex with women. This is non-negotiable: the social kinetic of sexual reproduction is that sexualisation will be inevitable. I really feel sorry for Black women in this regard as they spend so much time making themselves look beautiful, not for men, but for themselves; only to be told by White women that if a Black man desires her beautified Black body he is sexualising and objectifying her, which they hold as evil. While I understand that no woman is as objectified or as sexualised as the Black woman that is not to say it should carry as vile a connotation as it currently does. Indeed, McRobbie's (2008) fight against sexualisation is like King's fight against violence, respectable but unworkable.

The next argument then would be: even if men have to sexualise women to have sex why am I saying godbody females should hypersexualise and hypereroticise themselves through the practicing of light exhibitionism? To this I would say, Black cultures have always had an element of the hypersexual about them. From the communal cultures of Africa to the slave cultures of the Americas, hypersexuality has always been a prominent feature of Black cultures (Sheller 2012). All I am saying is, why should we sacrifice this authentic aspect of Black culture to fit in with White moral standards when we can in fact use our hypersexuality as a weapon against their systems of White supremacy and White privilege?

Indeed, the suggestion to practice light exhibitionism is not to disempower our godbody females but to show them how much power they already actually have. There is something about a light exhibitionist woman wearing a dress that reveals, in any way, that

315

she is not wearing underwear that releases something primal in the heart of a man. He cannot help but see it as the most beautiful thing he has ever seen, regardless of what the woman's face looks like. And if she does it repeatedly he will literally fall in love with her. Yet in spite of this, it is also understood in society that any man (or woman) who encourages women to behave hypersexually in any way will be said to be contributing to the pornification of that society and of the female body, therefore I will now challenge their definition of the pornographic.

Anything even remotely sexual or slightly related to sex is called pornographic by some conservative minds, and as Douglas said again, "[I]f one can establish that a people's sexual behavior is improper, then one can also suggest that that people is inferior" (Douglas 1999: 22). This is interesting as Hill pointed out that, "Millions of people, even in this age of enlightenment, have developed inferiority complexes because of this false belief that a highly sexed nature is a curse." Indeed, Hill believed, "The entire subject of sex is one of which the majority of people appear to be unpardonably ignorant. The urge of sex has been grossly misunderstood, slandered and burlesqued by the ignorant and the evil minded for so long that the very word sex is seldom used in polite society. Men and women who are known to be blessed – yes, *blessed* – with highly sexed natures are usually looked upon with suspicion" (Hill 2004: 220).

Conversely, in an over-moralistic world where the morals are based on Western monogamous marriage, sex or anything sexual is thereby considered pornographic. Pornography, coming from the Greek word *pornos* meaning sexually immoral, is a term used to criticise the showing of the naked body, male or female, in any public or semi-public spaces or media. Pornographic is a word particularly said of those who perform sex acts in public or semi-public media. However, the social static of pre- and post-monogamous societies is that public nudity is not considered immoral, for example, ancient and tribal societies. The problem is the post-Victorian definition of morality. Despite the vanities of feminism many of the women in tribal societies felt no levels of disempowerment or pornification for their public nudity until the White woman told them they should (Bakare-Yusuf 2011). The problem is not in the act of public nudity, but like with the serpent in the garden, the problem is doctrine, or as the Gods would say, the problem is trick knowledge.

Of course, it could also be said, to paraphrase a quote Douglas received at a lecture in New York, "For Blacks to behave sexually in public is like eating a watermelon in front of White people. All you do is confirm their images of you" (Douglas 1999: 68). But I am not here suggesting that we all walk around practicing public nudity – a practice which would anger most Gods and is most likely just as much a result of trick knowledge – I am merely suggesting that we godbodies, again, male and female, abandon the wearing of underwear altogether. There is nothing immoral about that, though it is definitely a type of public hypereroticism.

VII

Based on my early experiences in the street life I have come to appreciate that the only good thing a woman really gets from a monogamous marriage is the wedding day. Nevertheless, countless women are not so blessed as to even have this event ever occur in their lives. The modern standard of being a wife has been imposed on women for generations and those women who fail to live up to this standard usually get stigmatised by society or instructed by men as to why they are so unworthy. The only way to completely free all women from the standards of men is to free them from the institution of marriage.

It is a nice ideal to say that equality reigns as soon as a woman gets married but it can in fact be surmised that patriarchy usually reigns even after they get married, as Freud noted, "The cure for the nervous illness that arises from marriage would instead be marital infidelity; however, the more strictly a woman has been

317

brought up and the more seriously she has submitted to the requirements of civilization, the more afraid she is to take this way out" (Freud 2002: 97). Still, the answer to this is not in polyandry or in polygamy, but in polyamory. In the cases of polyandry and polygamy the institutionalisation of marriage still means that there is a level of imbalance when it comes to control, even if polyandry leans heavier toward the woman side. True, even polyamory or plural love can become phallocentric, as has happened in some polyamorous communities. However, polyamory has no patriarchy built into it like polygamy and monogamy do. Indeed, in the right hands polyamory can lead to matrilineality, which gives women a greater amount of control over the family (just like what a matriarchal – mother-led – household would produce).

In fact, polyamory proves to be a far better institution than marriage as it allows for a woman to have the freedom to love several men, sexually and/or non-sexually; and for those men to have the freedom to love her and several other women, sexually and/or non-sexually; without their being judged or considered immoral for it. Obviously, polyamory does have its flaws too, in that "the maintenance of the children will be the concern of the community, and their education will be the care and responsibility of everyone" (Malatesta 1922: 43); and not simply one mother and one father. But as noted earlier, communal child-raising can actually be better for the child than only having that one mother and one father (Gladwell 2008).

Though it appears that some people took issue with my book *Black Divinity* for promoting just that kind of lifestyle and for not calling all cases of running a train, gang rape, the classic case of this being Ayanna Jackson. As a teenager Ayanna Jackson was in love with Tupac Shakur and had sex with him a few times. Some would say this gave Tupac the right to have sex with her anytime and in any way he wished. The fact is, Jackson was *very likely* an obsessed fan, Jackson *very likely* did give him fellatio on the dancefloor of a nightclub, and as a Brooklyn girl Jackson *very likely* did have sex with most, if not all, the men in the room before that night. Those are not the issues at stake or in question. The issue in question is *that night*.

That night Tupac thought he was doing her a favour by sharing her. *That night* she did not *consent* to being shared out only wanting Tupac. A gesture that Tupac thought was an act of love was in fact a horrific act of violence: that was the problem. That was the issue. Jackson's being hypersexual was no excuse for Tupac to think that he could do with *her body* whatsoever *he wanted*. As an eighteen year old she was of consensual age, she therefore had the right and freedom to do with her own body whatsoever *she* chose. Some men are unable to handle or understand a hypersexual woman and therefore make mistakes, in his case to horrifying effect; but the second she said to Tupac that she was *not* with the situation he should have sent his boys away.

The truth is, there is a happy medium between a gang rape victim and a hoe that must be appreciated, even emulated. This medium was personified by Nola Darling in *She's Gotta Have It* (1986) and by Lil Kim in her street life days. It was also personified in many of the Goddesses (also called Moons) back in the 1990s before it became unpopular. Herein, revolutionary anarchist Malatesta (1922: 43) further solidified the argument, stating, "Assure everyone of the means to live properly and independently, give women the complete liberty to dispose of their own bodies, destroy the prejudices, religious and otherwise, that bind men and women to a mass of conventions that derive from slavery and which perpetuate it and sexual unions will be made of love, and will give rise to the happiness of individuals and the good of the species." He further still stated, again, "Do you think that enslaved love could really exist? Forced cohabitation exists, as does feigned and forced love, for reasons of interest or of social convenience; probably there will be men and women who will respect the bond of matrimony because of religious or moral convictions; but true love cannot exist, can not be conceived, if it is not perfectly free."

At the same time, as, back in the 1990s, the God did not have control over the Goddesses' sexual desires and sexual appetite he tried to control the one aspect of her bodily discourse that was available to him: her appearance. The whole: "a lady in the streets and a freak in the bedroom" discourse was defined in New York City women back in those days. Godbody men accepted that they could not stop the godbody women's sexual choices so they tried to control her public appearance. Yet in the same 1990s with the Black sexual revolution and the new discourse propagated by Biggie Smalls the New York City Goddess regained control of her physical appearance. Again, the Black sexual revolution of the 1990s had a lot more to do with hypereroticism than dress. The Black eroticism of the 1990s was far closer, back then, to plural love, not only for Black men but for Black women too. In fact, "Hit 'Em Up" may have been more Tupac's revenge against Jackson and the culture of Brooklyn women than it was against Biggie Smalls himself, but I digress.

As a further articulation of these practices which I witnessed in the godbody movement of 1990s New York I will add that polyamory is far more in line with the Black woman's current disposition. It means many loves or plural love, and says that, not only does a person have sex with other sex partners, but they also love *deeply* those sex partners. While this may not be as anarchistic as free love it is still respected within both anarchist and anarcha-feminist circles. Basically, what should a Black woman do when the man she loves is married to someone else? Monogamy says give up and find someone else. That is the standard and moral answer, to say otherwise would encourage cheating, adultery, and men having their cake. But it happens. The women who still sleep with the married man *genuinely* love them but their love is forbidden making it even stronger.

Black relationships like this are prevalent in the Black community mainly because we are unwilling to accept the ghetto mentality, where concepts like the train are actually considered a good thing. The act of running a sexual train, whether on a male or a female (growing up in Brooklyn I saw both), has been stigmatised so badly by White society that the Black community fails to appreciate any polyamorous proclivities within their own Black sexuality. Again, "It [seems] necessary for White society to control Black people's sexuality, meaning their bodies and reproductive capacities, so as to control them as a people. It is also necessary to impugn Black sexuality in order to suggest that Black people are inferior beings" (Douglas 1999: 23). Nevertheless, some White women may say at this time that the Black men seem here to be getting all the benefits. But in ghetto sexuality this is not true, Black women can run the train on Black men as much as Black men can run the train on them. They basically have far more sexual freedom than they would have in any other sexual reality.

Armand (2012: 104) also said on this subject, "Indeed, I want there to be 'unique' amorous temperaments. And, moreover, I will need to be convinced that the occasion for amorous plurality is not lacking for them – I mean by that an amorous plurality to their liking, which makes them vibrate." This kind of amorous plurality (polyamory) was practiced back in the 1990s by both Gods and Goddesses: and together with Black love, Afrosensuality, light exhibitionism, and seductionism complete my variation of Black eroticism. But amorous plurality leaves but little room for jealousy. It is only reached at a point when competition and jealousy have been completely overcome in both partners; and jealousy itself is only overcome when personal feelings are put aside for the sake of the other. When love of Other becomes stronger than any selfish feelings of possession or fears of personal humiliation.

To be sure, the only reason why jealousy has such a damning effect is that the person (usually the man) entertains those kinds of possessive thoughts over their partner's body and fears losing them to someone else. When that someone else enters the picture their worst fear is before them. Rather than talking it over with their partner they then allow their fears to dictate where they go from there. The truth is, their partner has not intentionally "humiliated" them, they have only succumbed to either emotion or seduction, in either case the main lover should not be threatened but should welcome the help with confidence that their relationship is strong enough for them to remain the main lover and never be pushed to the side. And even if they do get pushed to the side, they should still have the freedom in that case to choose a new wifey or husband while still holding on to their former main as a side.

Again, how all this works for practical purposes is, and let us use a woman as the example: suppose a woman has four boyfriends. Though she will love each of them equally she will love each of them in their own way. For instance, one of them may be someone she absolutely respects, he can be her main. One of them may be someone she has explosive sex with, he is extremely important for the relationship. One of them may be someone who allows them to have the type of lifestyle that makes her happy, she needs him for esteem reasons. Finally, one of them may be artistic in some way – whether poetry, painting, photography, novel writing, song writing, singing, or playing an instrument – she loves him for his talent.

It is fine for her to love each of these men, and have sexual and/or non-sexual relationships with them. She has not committed a crime having all these lovers, she has merely opened herself up to a more liberated lifestyle. The men should not feel threatened by this situation. If they love the woman and/or women who does/do this then they should be able to see that one man could never *honestly* satisfy any woman. There will always be something missing. Yet, though she loves several other men what he provides for her is unique and in a way that only he can provide. He is special to her and he is loved by her. Let him with that be satisfied.

Or take as another example all those countless women who embarrassed themselves on the Maury Povich show with the men they thought were the father of their child only to discover that they were not. This type of embarrassment could be avoided in future if it is understood that she is a polyamorous woman. Basically, polyamory, and running sexual trains, means more than simply having a bunch of threesomes, foursomes, tensomes, or fortysomes. It means loving sexually and/or non-sexually more than one person without the fear of embarrassment or being called or considered a cheater or any other negative for it. Therefore I say, those women who can should be polyamorous, but those women who cannot should not turn around and slut shame those who can by calling them pornographic.

It is my belief wholeheartedly that pro-sex views, especially concerning consenting – and not coerced or deceived – adults should not be demonised, criminalised, or stigmatised as though perverted or dangerous. Moreover, slut shaming those consenting women for consenting to pro-sex views makes the whole feminist project look very unhealthy and not very forward looking/thinking at all. However, I say none of this as an anti-feminist, I do not claim anti-feminism at all, in spite of my many criticisms of them. I say all this as one who believes firmly in their potential once they are freed from the louder more conservative voices that seem to dominate much of their movement. For this cause, I say that I stand in solidarity with any pro-sex feminists and womanists whatever race they may be.

There is, nonetheless, also a fear that any kind of sexualisation could ultimately lead to the disempowerment of women by giving men what they want, but such is a false fear. Men do want sex, but we actually desire it even more than we desire power. As sex is man's prime want, you give a man sex and he will forget his lust for power. Women could rule the world right now, very easily, and men would surrender their power in a heartbeat, simply if women started using their sexuality toward that end. If women only knew the power they had between their legs they would never be ashamed of their sexuality again. As Tee Noir said, "female sexuality is so powerful that we [women] can use it to advance ourselves in social spheres, and gain access to privilege, resources, even capital" (Noir 2019). This is not unique either. We men are able to sublimate or inhibit our desire for sex but we cannot escape it. Hence sexualisation, if used correctly, can lead to the empowerment of women, and us men sacrificing our power to give more power to women.

It could, therefore, be said at this point that women should just take the power themselves, and that is true, but as men currently hold high levels of power it is a difficult fight. The same with the godbody: those women that stay true and have stayed true since the beginning deserve some reward for their contribution to the cause; and if we are truly to be pillars of righteousness and equality then we need to stop denying our women the empowerment they deserve. Indeed, despite all our sufferings in the world as Black men … we have always had the Black woman, which has made it all worth it.

VIII

Having thus explained how the Wisdoms can represent a higher manifestation of godhood it is my view that we Gods should stop holding back from acknowledging such. To simply define the Black woman as a Wisdom or as a Moon instead of as a Goddess censors God and isolates the Black woman. The Black woman is among women not only a Queen but a Goddess. Her mahogany complexion, no different from ours; her melinated skin, the same as ours; her strong will, just like ours; her righteous nature, no lesser than ours; all this makes her just as much God as us, and on an equality with us. (And for those who now say that this is giving a partner to Allah, that is not so; it is simply saying that Allah is manifested (*zahir*) in women as much as he is manifested (*zahir*) in men). We have unfortunately allowed this overt inequality to flourish while, at the same time, claiming to be representatives of freedom, justice, and equality.

True indeed, the excuse could be made that Allah himself called us the Nation of Gods and Earths before he departed his physical form, and that Earth is therefore what the Black woman should be called. To this I would say: the Gods have changed other lessons before, like the 2nd degree of the 1-10 to take out "skunk of the planet earth" with regard to the Caucasian White man; or adding to the 1st degree of the 1-10 "father of civilization" with regard to the Asiatic Black man. We changed our lessons to make those adjustments, do we now find it so difficult to exalt our women, at least in our own minds, to the position of Goddess?

It appears, however, that I have had most of the opposition I have received over this from male godbodies. They assure each other that the Black woman cannot be a Goddess because Allah is male and there is no god besides him. Yet their refusal to appreciate the Black woman's divinity does more to make our Nation look bad than it does to strengthen it. The Elijah said, "Until we learn to love and protect our woman, we will never be a fit and recognized people on the earth" (Muhammad 1965: 58). But there are some who may now say that as Earth is the recognised means of glorifying Black women, that we display our love for them by calling these sisters Earth. True indeed, but it is also true that we display more love for them by calling them Goddess. At which point the answer could again be given, what is the point of fighting over semantics, they mean the same thing so just leave her with the name she has been given. That may also be true but as the Elijah said again, "[E]ven the name alone is sufficient to free you" (Muhammad 1965: 48). By actually calling her by the name Goddess we show how much we appreciate her as a person and as divine.

Consequently, as the Elijah was trying to show, this is actually important. "This is one of the reasons Almighty Allah has come among us, that is, to give us His Names, the Most Holy and Righteous Names of the Planet Earth" (Muhammad 1965: 55). Again, one of the ancient names of Allah was Pa Neter (the God) and as the first great truth of the ancient Egyptian religion stated: "*Pa Neter wa wa Neb-er-Tcher m Neteru*" – The God, only one Lord of all, manifests as gods and goddesses. Thus Allah manifests as Gods *and Goddesses*. Obviously, the studious godbody could object at this point, Neter has been mistranslated as God and Neteru has been mistranslated as gods and goddesses. Their real translation should be as principle or force. To which I would say, true indeed, the Neteru were supposed to be the forces of nature or natural forces.

However, in my personal interpretation all natural forces are just different variations of electromagnetism. Nevertheless, these natural forces can also be embodied by all, if not most, of the natural entities of existence. It may be true that we Original people are ourselves able to embody these natural forces, but only when we stop following the savagery of devilishment and, in our ways and actions, become righteous beings. It is, therefore, why the Neteru were usually embodied in anthropomorphised forms. Basically, saying something like Hethor – who symbolised the goddess principle – could not be embodied is to deny the whole ancient Egyptian system, in which the Neteru were psychological states, natural forces, and were also embodied in the form of *the initiates*.

On a more Quranic level, however, it could also be said how it is written in the Quran that: "He asks: When is the day of Resurrection?" and the answer given is to him, "when the sight is confused, And the moon becomes dark, And the sun and the moon are brought together" (Quran 75: 6-9). Obviously, on the one hand, this could just be predicting an eclipse or some natural phenomena in the sky. But, then again, sometimes Scriptures are best interpreted by further Scripture. In Solomon's Song of Songs it says, "Who is she that looketh forth as the morning, fair as the moon, clear as the sun, and terrible as an army with banners?" (Song of Songs 6: 10). Symbolic signs can be interpreted in concrete manifestations. In this case, the Queen of Sheba represented both sun and moon; yet in the case of the Quranic Scripture a godbody interpretation of the moon would be as the Asiatic Black woman. So when is the resurrection? When the Sun and the Moon are brought together – not only in body but in name also – then will come a sensual resurrection to coincide with the mental resurrection brought on by the Honorable Elijah Muhammad.

At the same time, one of the biggest bonuses that we Gods can receive from considering Black women as Goddesses is that we will have effectively begun the process of transfiguring them. Transfiguration itself is the Tantric art mentioned earlier that allows one to see their sexual partner as divine. Indeed, according to Tantric expert Dr. Ashby, "During Tantric training, each individual is instructed to regard the other as a divinity (which all humans are innately) and to worship each other as such and to alternate roles (each partner sees themselves as male or female) as they visualize the Life Force growing. During [any] 'physical' sexual intercourse between a man and a woman, it is the male who 'gives' and the female who 'receives'. Sexual intercourse [can accordingly, therefore, be] used to heighten the ecstatic feelings and to develop psychic energy for spiritual attainment" (Ashby 2003c: 86). Not only so, but transfiguring Black women also psychologically conditions us to give her more pleasure during the sexual encounter, which in turn gives us a better reason than thinking of death or sad dogs or something ugly to prolong the sexual experience.

Moreover, as mentioned earlier, as a result of these practices we Black men will literally be able to have multiple orgasms with the women we have thus transfigured. With these kinds of experiences we will undeniably come to discover that anyone who tells us that this or that thing is better than sex obviously, "Ain't having sex right." I can say myself, from my own experience: there actually comes a point in sexual congress when a man no longer wants, or even needs, to ejaculate due to the level and extent of non-delusional ecstasy and pure sexual pleasure he has reached through the simple process of transfiguring the Black woman into a Goddess.

In order to reach these states at will a man must, firstly, start practicing the art of letting the person he is having sex with enter *deep* into his heart through the process of transfiguration. Secondly, he must start practicing, for her sake, the self-discipline of non-ejaculating. Such a practice is based on fully understanding the Tantric drive to attain a unification with the deity through sexual intimacy. Dr. Ashby further explained how in Tantric sexual experiences, "[The] participants are not allowed to reach climax ... in order to channel all energies towards concentrating on the goal: development of their Life Force and its union with the Transcendental – Absolute ... through ever increasing ecstasy and devotion ... Through repeated stimulation and concentration of the energies to the higher energy centers, the sublimation of the primal sexual and mental energy is possible" (Ashby 2003c: 86).

From here it is also possible to understand the value and progress of what Tantric masters call: bindu sublimation. According to Swami Saraswati, a Tantric master in his own right, "Bindu means a point or a drop. ... The source of bindu is actually in the higher centres of the brain, but due to the development of emotions and passions, bindu falls down to the lower region where it is transformed into sperm and ova" (Saraswati 2012: 103). It is this concept of bindu that contains the secret as to why "edging" is currently acknowledged in the West as a form of transcendental meditation. It keeps sexual energy in a highly charged and explosive state.

Moreover, as Swami Saraswati continued on, "According to tantra, the preservation of the bindu is absolutely necessary for two reasons. Firstly, the process of regeneration can only be carried out with the help of bindu. Secondly, all the spiritual experiences take place when there is an explosion of bindu. This explosion can result in the creation of a thought or of anything. Therefore, in tantra, certain practices are recommended by which the male partner can stop ejaculation and retain the bindu." At the same time, this is mainly encouraged, "not so much to preserve the semen, but because [ejaculation] causes a depression in the level of energy" (Saraswati 2012: 103, 104).

Thereby we can see and understand that the practice of prolonging the sexual experience (edging), keeps the sexual energy at peak levels and ultimately allows for maximum pleasure to be experienced by us male figures. But the same is also true for the women, as Swami Saraswati further noted, "In the female body, the point of concentration is at mooladhara chakra, which is situated at the cervix, just behind the opening of the uterus. This is the point where space and time unite and explode in the form of an experience. In ordinary language of tantra it is called an awakening. In order to maintain the continuity of that experience, it is necessary for a build up of energy to take place at that particular bindu or point" (Saraswati 2012: 105).

Essentially, by allowing a love object to enter into the inner chambers of our heart and take deep root, that is, by transfiguring them, we effectively give ourselves access to receiving multiple orgasms. Conversely, I also recognise how difficult it can be for us men, particularly us Black men, to open our hearts to anybody, let alone a romantic interest. There is an unspoken fear that any displays of vulnerability will lead to emasculation and future pain or trauma. There is also the obvious humiliation of being called by our friends, or even by our love objects themselves, a simp, a bitch, or a chump who all up in their feelings, i.e. too emotional. "Never let anyone in your heart or they will either break it, abuse it, or take your kindness for weakness," so they say.

Though I am somewhat sympathetic to this advice, and I get the reasoning behind it, as someone who famously opens his heart regularly, and also gets disappointed regularly, I can say: I have no desire to ever stop opening my heart regardless of the name calling or mistreatment. First of all, I am confident enough in my own manhood to not care about name calling. Second, the rewards I get from opening my heart far exceed any pain I may have to endure as a result. To be sure, I never open my heart easily, and if someone breaks it I will never trust them again, even if we stay friends afterward. But that whole Stoic, cold, and closed off shit is dead. If such a person confronted me and called me a chump, I would very likely say, "You probably right," while deep in my heart I would be feeling sorry for them. I know far too well that such a person is not only missing out on the beauties, wonders, and joys of an emotionally intimate relationship, but they are also missing out on the orgasmic pleasures of sheer ecstasy that can only be reached by opening your heart to a love object and transfiguring them into a deity.

All that notwithstanding, it is only natural, after experiencing a few of these kinds of sexual encounters, especially when the amount of sexual orgasms reach into the double digits, for both parties to assume it will only ever improve from there. While I am not saying such is impossible, it is nonetheless definitely improbable. That means there *will* be days and moments that you orgasm back into the single digits, or even worse, ejaculate/discharge. Do not worry too much about that, it is just a matter of getting back to transfiguration. Further, so long as both the God and Goddess practice, both the transfiguration of their lover and the holding back of their own sexual discharge, they can open themselves up, in time, to storing enough sexual energy to possibly even gaining supersensory abilities, or what the Tantrics call *siddhis*. These abilities will, in turn, provide us with all the more reason to transfigure them and them with all the more reason to transfigure us, but in this I might be getting a bit ahead of myself.

All these are Tantric concepts that are taught within the Tantric arts. Conversely, Tantric training has three prominent schools of thought that share their basic disciplines: the dakshina marga, the vama marga, and the kaula marga. To further explain the traditions of these three schools Dr. Ashby expertly continued, saying, "The first path is the conservative mainline of Tantrism including mandala meditations and worship of the Divine in the form of the Mother Goddess. The second includes traditionally forbidden elements, especially sexual intercourse (with detachment and non-ejaculation). The third is practiced by the Kula sect and is equivalent to Kundalini Yoga (Serpent Power)" (Ashby 2003c: 66).

Furthermore, to provide a greater clarification of these three schools: First note, the dakshina marga is the right hand path. They teach a celibate, sensorial, devotional, and vegetarian lifestyle. Second, the vama marga is the left hand path. They teach polyamory, sorcery, sacrilegiousness, drunkenness, and eating various meats (including beef). (For the record, this path is not for the weak minded and is very dangerous for most people. It has even been related to mental illness when unstable minds tried to practice it). Finally, the kaula marga is the united path. They teach sexual, supersensorial, religious, pharmacological, and dietary union with the Creator and Creatrix (Shiva and Shakti). Having myself learned from the kaula school I will say: their lessons on transfiguring the Black woman have improved my sex life dramatically.

331

Moreover, I will add: one of the best ways for the Black woman to inspire Black men like us Gods to transfigure them is through the sacred practice of light exhibitionism, even as one of the best ways for us Gods to inspire Black women like the Goddesses to transfigure us is through the sacred practice of seductionism. Nevertheless, both God and Goddess should try to do both of these practices permanently. Even so, by us transfiguring them into Goddesses we also effectively destroy the White trick knowledge that is currently bringing about female vampyrism. Again, while I agree that it is important for the Black woman to practice the adoration and transfiguration of the Black man, I will also say, they should only do so as long as the Black man practices the adoration and transfiguration of Black women.

The purpose of this chapter has been to show where we godbody currently stand with regard to Black women and to show where we could go. Historically Black women have practiced a feminist ideology or a womanist ideology, they have not expanded beyond these two conceptions. What the godbody perspective inculcates is the possibility of adopting a Moon womanist ideology, or beyond that, a Goddess ideology. My question is, why be either a Black feminist or a Moon womanist when you can just as easily become a Black Goddess?

There are some who may now turn it around and say, "why not become a Black cyborg?" or something (Haraway 2000). Such an argument is moot, however, as to make the point for any of these displays an inherent weakness in the current feminist critique. Feminism still left women disempowered in relation to men and technology thereby creating cyborg culture. Feminism failed to notice or appreciate Black women and Black sexuality thereby creating pro-sex womanist culture. Womanism fails to appreciate Black women's interconnection to everything in the universe thereby now creating godbody culture and Black divinity. The Black woman is a Divine by nature, and though most of the Gods have failed to appreciate her divinity, she, as a Black woman, is beginning to acknowledge it despite his protests.

It finally appears as though the Black woman is becoming more aware of her potential and is advancing ever closer towards it. What will happen to Black female theologians now that we are entering the age of iGod is that they will either advance towards godhood thereby becoming Black Godbody Theologians, or they will forward the position of intersectional feminist theology thereby reinforcing White culture on Black women. Black female theologians will therefore have to choose to either fight for acceptance among White feminists in mainstream culture or fight for acceptance among the Black godbody theologians in godbody culture. The world is changing and I believe the feminist theology will not do for Black women; and while womanist theology may provide positive answers and support it does not look like womanism will survive beyond the twenty-first century with the rising popularity of intersectional feminism. The Black woman is a Goddess and therefore her theology must be a Goddess theology. Only this will do her any real justice.

Spooks and Holy Ghost

"5. Why did we take Jerusalem from the devil? And how long ago? Because one of our righteous brothers who was a prophet by the name of Jesus was buried there. They used his name to shield their dirty religion, which is called Christianity also to deceive the people and make them believe in him. The teachings of Jesus were not Christianity but freedom, justice, and equality. Jerusalem is in Palestine, which is in Asia Minor. The name Jerusalem was given by the Jews and means 'found in peace'. It was first built by the Original man who was called Jebus, Salem, and Ariel. We took the city from the devil about 750 years ago" (Lost Found Muslim Lesson No. 1).

The Charismatic movement has created in our time an entirely new, some would say otherworldly, perspective that has reached global proportions. Having its roots in the Holiness movement of mid-nineteenth century America (a movement which had largely contributed to both the Second Awakening and the American Civil War) the Charismatic movement drew from these "sanctified" fellowships the ideas of total salvation and baptism in the Holy Spirit. Where the Charismatic movement differed was that whereas the Holiness movement saw baptism in the Holy Spirit as evidenced by the removal of personal sin, the abolition of slavery, and the institution of an egalitarian society; the

Charismatic movement saw baptism in the Holy Spirit as "evidenced by glossolalia, charismatic (spiritual) gifts, healing, deliverance, prophecy, exuberant worship and a distinctive language of experiential spirituality" (Adogame 2011: xiii).

Nevertheless, the top gifts to the Charismatic movement were, and have always been, these three gifts: healing, exorcising (deliverance), and prophesying, and they guard over them zealously, claiming that, firstly, only God can perform them and, secondly, the fact that they can perform them shows their closeness to God. All three of these top gifts, however, are also closely related to their demonology: one which states that all bad things that happen: whether sin, imperfection, weakness, mental or physical illness, bad luck, poverty, curses, spells, witchcraft, idolatry, war, famine, natural disasters, infestation, desolation, or death are the result of the devil.

To the Charismatic, the devil is at work in every bad thing that happens and could ever happen. They basically personify any misfortune as the devil or as the works of the devil, therefore the top gifts of the Holy Spirit are tools for fighting the devil and his works. Evidently, Charismatic pneumatology is interrelated to its demonology. If devils are the cause of all bad things the Holy Spirit and the gifts of the Holy Spirit are the cure. Theoretically, the Charismatic social static could endure for as long as humanity has difficulty, that is, as long as bad things happens; but in the real world people get wise to an impossible system soon enough.

The problem with most faith-based systems is their overemphasis on God's mystique. He is a mystery God who works in mysterious ways. Such a conception is problematic in two ways: first, human curiosity forces and compels us to find the answers to the most challenging mysteries; second, any system with its foundation in the mysterious will inevitably crumble when the mystery is revealed or the secret exposed. Though not by any means perfect the Holiness movement was at least built upon a this-worldly foundation therefore it avoided all the mystiques of the Charismatic movement, even if it had its own mysticisms about it. As a social body the Charismatic Church's maintenance and progression are therefore dependent on keeping people deluded and steeped in mysticism or fighting against those who have already demystified God and the devil. If it ever rejects its demonology and pneumatology, however, then it will cease to be Charismatic altogether, even if it tries to maintain the veneer.

As an example of what I mean: if we were to take a demystified approach to the idea of pneumatology but still maintain a Charismatic demonology, first of all, as we have seen all essential motivating forces demystified are libidinal, that is, they derive from the combination of erotic, agapic, and empathic drives. Well, that is their most refined manifestation. A less refined manifestation is in electromagnetic waves. A less refined manifestation than that is in the Asiatic Black man and all the people of the Original nations. A less refined manifestation than that is in the physical universe. Finally, an even less refined manifestation than that can be seen in the *tawhid*.

Well, suppose someone in the Charismatic movement chose to adopt a demystified pneumatology while maintaining their Charismatic demonology, saying, the devil and the Holy Spirit are both seen in electromagnetic forces but that God is manifested (*zahir*) in all good people while the devil is manifested (*zahir*) in all the bad things that happen in a person's life or in the world. To a degree that would make the devil more powerful than God as he inflicts even the Gods and Goddesses with suffering and "bad things." They will thus ultimately need to return to a Charismatic pneumatology to confront and overcome the "powers of the devil."

But suppose we try again, this time with a Charismatic pneumatology and a demystified demonology. Again, demystified the devil is the White race, but, suppose someone in the Charismatic movement chose to say the devil is in all evil, unjust, and oppressive people, of what good then is the Charismatic Holy Spirit against that? Other than prophesying doom and gloom neither healing, nor exorcising, nor any other gift of the Holy Spirit is of any value. Still, suppose, however, that we said that an exorcism could cast the evil out of that person and make them good: as much evil people as have existed historically – from those that killed the prophets, and the Messiah, and the apostles, and the martyrs, and the slaves, and the Holocaust – if God could have just cast out the evil the whole time then what was the purpose.

Finally, by demystifying all these: God, the devil, and the essence of God, saying, the essence of God is in libido; the subtle body of God is in electromagnetic forces; the gross body of God is in the righteous people of the Original nations; the gross body of the devil is in the unrighteous people of the White race; the gross body of the vampyres is in the Original people corrupted by devilishment; and the fulness of God is in the universe as a whole; is one capable of remaining Charismatic? They can still claim to be Charismatic but they would know that what other Charismatics are doing and what they are worshipping are all falsehoods. Effectively, the spell would be broken.

Herein is seen my personal demonology, on the one hand, it is neither based on mysticism like the Charismatics nor biology like the Black Muslims, but is based on what Father Supreme said, "the devil is manufactured in the mind and the mind could be on G.O.D., good orderly direction, or devilishment" (The Five Percenter Vol 22.4; 2016: 4). The White people who buy into devilishment in this White supremacist world become devils, while the non-White people who buy into devilishment in this White supremacist world become vampyres. Herein, is seen my personal pneumatology, on the other hand, it is based on the idea that the central motivating force in the universe is the pleasure principle, and that this force has many manifestations such as strong, radioactive, bonding, astral, social, global, environmental, terrestrial, solar, globular, galactic, superclusteral, or cosmic.

As soon as one thus demystifies their demonology and pneumatology they cease to be Charismatic and effectively become godbody. Yet the Charismatic movement, and the Holy Ghost movement more generally, have a social kinetic ingredient that I have not mentioned so far that allows them to endure even in the age of iGod: the Last Days theory. Because Charismatics believe that all our problems are to be solved in the Last Days and that the devil will be banished in the Last Days, there is the possibility of the people maintaining their faith in the mysticism of the Charismatic movement indefinitely. For this cause it becomes necessary to take a more in-depth look at the social mechanics of Charismatic spirituality and compare it to that of the godbody movement.

I

To start with, the various Charismatic movements have been a response to modernity and rapid modernisation. The Charismatic movement began in industrialising and modernising America and its rapid spread into the so-called Third World is heavily influenced by modernisation in these so-called low income countries. The response in America to modernisation in the late nineteenth and early twentieth centuries was to increase conservatism. These Protestant conservatives in turn defined themselves as fundamentalists, thus beginning Christian fundamentalism.

Obviously, Adogame and Ukah (2011) took issue with Christians being defined as fundamentalists but it is clear to those who know the history of American Christianity that the first fundamentalists were, indeed, Christian. According to Heywood (2017), "The term 'fundamentalism' was first used in a religious context in debates within American Protestantism in the early twentieth century. Between 1910 and 1915, evangelical

Protestants published a series of pamphlets entitled *The Fundamentals*, upholding the inerrancy, or literal truth, of the Bible in the face of modern interpretations of Christianity" (Heywood 2017: 305). Christian fundamentalism, being related to the Holiness movement, evangelicalism, and Christian revivalism soon merged with the Charismatic movement turning it into a kind of neoconservative Protestant response to rapid modernisation. Consequently, the Charismatic Church, which came into being in the early twentieth century along with Christian fundamentalism, began to merge with same by the mid-twentieth century, becoming a neoconservative answer to the pressures of digitalisation by the late twentieth century and beginning of late modernity.

Conversely, if we look aetiologically at the Charismatic movement, it is really no more than a modern movement with a claim of returning to the Christianity of the first century during the days of the apostles. Yet such a religion and such a time are long past. It therefore becomes a question of, has the Charismatic Church really fulfilled its ambition? Or, has the Charismatic Church achieved the ends for which they have striven? Which brings to light another question: how do we go about answering these two questions? The most obvious answer to the latter is reading the Bible and seeing if the Charismatic movement is anything like the church presented in the Bible, particularly in the Book of Acts.

Two things must be acknowledged, however, before we give full credibility to the New Testament and to the Acts of the Apostles: firstly, the New Testament represents a small percentage of the letters and stories that were circulating about the Messiah and the early messianic movement (MacCulloch 2010). As an estimation, the most likely event within the different group meetings of the early messianic movement was that they each had at the most ten books and letters, and none of these would have been those we have in our Bible today.

The most popular early messianic writing was most likely the Gospel of Thomas (Meyer 1992), a book that never made it into the New Testament due to politics. The Gospel of Thomas was written by a disciple named Judas Thomas, whose surname meant Big Twin, which was a name he was given because he apparently looked just like the Messiah. The name Judas was a very popular name among the Judeans of the time, at least three of the Messiah's disciples had that name, including Iscariot, who betrayed him. The problem with Thomas' gospel was not in his name but in the way he wrote. The Messiah in Thomas' gospel appeared as a disembodied spirit speaking wise sayings. This style of writing was a favourite of the East, and as many believe that Thomas' mission was to the East (Foxe 2001) it is not surprising that he chose to write in their style.

Because Thomas' gospel was by far the most popular, and is believed by some today to have been the illustrious Q Gospel (Quelle gospel) that was a source for both Matthew and Luke (Meyer 1992); it is most likely that his book was the source for the majority of other written and oral traditions that passed about the Messiah during the early messianic movement too, even before the apostle Paul's writings became popular. Obviously, during the time of the early messianic movement there were literally thousands of written and oral traditions of the Messiah, and most of them are now lost to history. The three branches of the messianic movement to stem from these were James and Peter's followers, who were called the Judaizers, practicing a Pharisaic tradition with their messianism; Simon Magus' followers, who were called the Simonians, practicing a more Gnostic, that is, a more liberal, sexual, and violent tradition with their messianism; and Paul's followers, who walked the tight balance between the two.

One has to also remember at this time that the real messianic movement was, first and foremost, a revolutionary movement against Roman imperialism of the similitude to the Maccabean movement. The early messianic movement was based largely on the idea of a government of Allah on earth; and in the first century this had serious political implications. Again, the apostles asked the Messiah, "Lord, wilt thou at this time restore again the kingdom to Israel?" (Acts 1: 6). This question was a political question about a political kingdom on earth and not a mystical one in the great beyond. Even the Apostle's Creed was more than simply a statement of faith, it was a statement of a kind of historicist, anti-imperialist, and spiritualist defiance. In practical terms, they not only declared that their only King was the Messiah, they also declared, whether implicitly or explicitly, that Caesar was a usurper they had no need or desire for.

It is herein that a central idea and theme of early messianism becomes clear: their devotion to the concept of agape. Still, if we genuinely wish to understand what agape is and how the early messianic movement saw it we must first turn to the apostle Paul's first letter to the messianic community in Corinth. It is in this letter that he wrote the famous, "Charity suffereth long, and is kind" (1Corinthians 13: 4). Again, the Greek word translated here as charity was not the actual word charity, though charity is itself a Greek word, but the word agape. In fact, every mention in the New Testament of the word charity actually derived from the original Greek word agape.

At the same time, the word translated as grace came from the original Greek word *charis*, from where we get the word charity. Indeed, the word charity itself is a Greek word meaning beneficence or acceptance. These two are especially interesting as the word translated as kind in the apostle Paul's statement above is the word *chresteuomai*, which actually translated to: beneficent acts. This is because *chresteuomai* was rooted from the word *chrestos*, which meant benefited or graced; and was itself rooted in the word *charis*, which meant grace and graciousness. Moreover, *chresteuomai* may have had a lot more in common with the word *charizomai*, which meant to favour, forgive, or accept, than it did with the word *chrestos*.

Essentially, we find here the clue to understanding agape: agape suffers long and is *accepting*. Indeed, though agape is usually translated as a love that is unconditional, it actually contains a very noticeable condition to it: there must be a commitment to accepting, enduring, and maintaining relations for the long haul. That means no easy exits or quick escapes, only devotion and a determination to work through any conflicts or problems; while, at the same time, enjoying the beauties of the interconnection and its subtleties. This also means there should be no judging, envying, accusing, denigrating, belittling, blaming, hurting, hating, or bullying. Therein is perceived the kindness aspect of agape. Not actual kindness *per se*, but acceptance, unconditional acceptance, acceptance that is palpable, an acceptance that you can physically feel.

This acceptance that is worth suffering for, even suffering long for. This acceptance is worth suffering the rejection of heaven and the tortures of hell for. This acceptance ensures psychological safety and feelings of trust that no judgment or condemnation will ever be used to condemn any failures, faults, or weaknesses. Herein can also be felt a deep comfort in spite of failing in front of others, knowing also that no faults will be used to condemn. This level of trust is therefore deep seated, not rationally experienced. It shows that value, respect, and care have been and will be given throughout the fellowship. Thereby is also created a commitment culture based on deep empathic brotherhood.

Now, however, a word on long-suffering. Many Black theologians and womanist theologians deny redemptive suffering and all suffering as sin or fault or as not desired by God. While it may be true that Allah dislikes suffering and feels all the pain of it, even James Cone acknowledged, "The life of Jesus also discloses that freedom is bound up with suffering" (Cone 2020a:

107). Moreover, life itself would be boring without suffering. I think this is important because many in the New Thought movement claim to interact with angelic beings, and they experience all the wonderful acceptance but have no thought of suffering. How can it be true acceptance if there is no suffering? How can you value what you have not suffered for? Love suffers long, maybe even eternally long, but love never fails. Effectively, when you value something or someone you suffer for it or for them. This is a secret even the angels do not know or appreciate, if New Thought is to be believed.

Still, the willingness and drive to suffer and to suffer long does not, at the same time, mean becoming a pushover. The clearest and most definitive definition of this pushover philosophy being in the oft-misinterpreted and oft-misunderstood words of the very Messiah himself, "Ye have heard that it hath been said, An eye for an eye, and a tooth for a tooth: But I say unto you, That ye resist not evil: but whosoever shall smite thee on thy right cheek, turn to him the other also. And if any man will sue thee at the law, and take away thy coat, let him have thy cloke also. And whosoever shall compel thee to go a mile, go with him twain" (Matthew 5: 38-41). These, however, were clearly not to be taken as hard and fast laws for all the followers of the Messiah. His use of exaggeration and hyperbole here were not so as to promote the idea of non-violence. Indeed, the Messiah himself used violence when he overthrew the merchants in the Temple (John 2: 14-16).

Essentially, they were highly unlikely to have ever been considered hard and fast practices for any of the early believers as demonstrated by the apostle Paul, "And Paul, earnestly beholding the council, said, Men and brethren, I have lived in all good conscience before God until this day. And the high priest Ananias commanded them that stood by him to smite him on the mouth. Then said Paul unto him, God shall smite thee, thou whited wall: for sittest thou to judge me after the law, and commandest me to be smitten contrary to the law?" (Acts 23: 1-3). Although it is definitely true the apostle Paul repented afterward, it was heavily implied that the only reason for his repentance was due to the station of the high priest, and were he not at that station the apostle Paul would have maintained the curse. Even in the early Roman historical records the early messianic movement was most definitely not a non-violent movement, but in fact believed by many to be seditious, or at least violently revolutionary.

True, we in our day believe and consider the early messianic movement to have been non-violent and so therefore perceive the apostle Paul's reaction to have been simply one of the few responses a non-violent practitioner could make. However, in reality our perceptions of the early messianic movement are highly distorted and idealised. The apostle James had this to say about the early believers of those days, "From whence come wars and fightings among you? come they not hence, even of your lusts that war in your members? Ye lust, and have not: ye kill, and desire to have, and cannot obtain: ye fight and war, yet ye have not, because ye ask not" (James 4: 1, 2).

Obviously, many modern day Christians, especially among the Charismatics, will say that he was clearly being figurative and metaphorical. This they will consider metaphorical and not the bombast of the one who said things like, "Ye blind guides, which strain at a gnat, and swallow a camel." Or "Wherefore if thy hand or thy foot offend thee, cut them off, and cast them from thee" (?) (Matthew 23: 24; 18: 8). The Messiah was more the one known for exaggeration and hyperbole, the apostle James, on the other hand, was known for being very legalistic, just, and formal.

That said, let us now take a deeper dive into the actual Greek words used by the apostle James to see if we can fit them better into the social and historical context of the early movement, in particular the historical records and documents about it, without corrupting or diluting the apostle's attempted purpose, "Where do your *polemeo* (meaning riots) and *mache* (meaning struggles, but in the violent sense of the word) come from? Do they not come from *epithymia* (meaning frustration, literally: post-anger) and *strateuomai* (meaning stratagems) among your members? You have frustration and *phoneus* (meaning homicidal crime: specifically banditry, terrorism, or sedition). You have *zeloo* (meaning to be zealous, which is where we get the term zealot from) and *apeirastos* (meaning are unmoveable, literally: untemptable). You struggle and riot and yet gain nothing because you fail to demand anything."

This quotation paints a far more historically correct and accurate picture of the early messianic movement. Not some goody-two-shoes pushoverism created to keep slaves and royal subjects in line, and from the potential of actually rioting or revolting against King James' Crown. In essence, the early messianic movement, just like its Maccabean predecessor, was a revolutionary movement; and its revolution was against Roman imperialism. Essentially, we can see here how the words of the Messiah now could ring truer than ever, "For from the days of John the Baptist until now he kingdom of heaven has been coming with violence, and violent people have been trying to bring it about" (Matthew 11: 12; my rewording).

But as we noted earlier, the kingdoms of heaven and hell are within, in other words, perception is the key to heaven or hell. The Messiah said, "Notwithstanding in this rejoice not, that the spirits are subject unto you; but rather rejoice, because your names are written in heaven." "For verily I say unto you, That many prophets and righteous men have desired to see those things which ye see, and have not seen them; and to hear those things which ye hear, and have not heard them" (Luke 10: 20; Matthew 13: 17). Indeed, one can be in the midst of a ghetto hell and still be in heaven, especially if they subscribe to the words of Dr. Ben, "Heaven is between the legs of an African woman" (Ben-Jochannan; quoted in Kwesi & Kwesi 2014).

Basically, the intention of the Messiah's more hyperbolic statements, specifically those to turn the other cheek and to go the extra mile, were never to promote non-violence or pushoverism. They were instead spoken to cause a stronger degree of unity and brotherhood among the children of Israel. Indeed, the language the Messiah used, and that the early messianic movement continued, was a clear sign of this insight: brothers, sons of man, children of Abraham, seed of Abraham, Hebrews, Israel of God, and church of God. Moreover, the Greek word used throughout the Bible for church, being the word *ekklesia*, was a word that actually translated to either assembly or council, but always originally in the political sense of the words.

Effectively, the original purpose of the *ekklesia* was to be a political institution for those faithful to the Messiah that was of the similitude to the ancient Roman council. From this we see that the messianic movement was always supposed to represent a revolutionary entity, and therefore that the truth about the Gnostics actually suits this view far better. See, most of the Gnostics were outlaws, bandits, and slaves from the lower classes well known for their seditious, violent, and radically disrespectful manners. They were also known for having wild orgy parties and celebrating their sexuality. Yet the Gnostic claim of having the secret to salvation – which to them was knowledge, a secret knowledge which was that sin was a lie and that the body was a prison for the soul, which when liberated was freed from the ability to sin – was a fundamental view of the vast majority of the early messianic communities.

These messianic communities, however, were mostly hated by decent Roman society for their having both disreputable members and disreputable practices. They were called cannibals because certain Roman spies spoke of their agape feasts in which they would apparently eat flesh and drink blood. They were called incestuous because those Roman spies also said that at their agape feasts they would have sexual orgies with their "sisters" and "brothers." They were called atheists because they refused to worship any of the deities of the Romans, and sacrilegious because of their lack of respect for things Rome deemed sacred. They were called rebels because they refused to appear when called on to serve in the Romans legions, and lunatic because when threatened with punishment they welcomed it with laughter and pleasure, even to the point of death. Still, in spite of all this, and the numerous persecutions and lynchings they received on a regular basis, these messianic communities just seemed to get stronger and grow faster.

It is by this logic that we can understand the behaviour of the early Gnostic communities. Their aim and struggle was not simply for a spatial decolonisation, but more so for a mental and bodily decolonisation. Though they did use violence, and believed in using violence, it was based on their own understanding of this truer meaning of agape. Indeed, true agape, to them, also included wrath, anger, and violence. It is said that perfect love casts out all fear, but that can only happen where violence and strength are present to protect. The West, in its thirst to build prisons to protect people from violence has instead created a world where fear and violence, dangerous and threatening violence, rule the day. To erase this dangerous and threatening violence we need to respect again defensive violence. We need to see again that not all violence is evil. Violence, wrath, criticism, vitriol, and aggression can be good. We currently trust so much in police violence to protect us, but yet we fail to use violence to defend ourselves: which was a concept very much so believed and taught within the various Gnostic communities.

MacCulloch further articulated concerning these beliefs of the Gnostic communities that they were, essentially that, "Mortal flesh must be mortified because it is despicable – or, on the contrary, the soul might be regarded as so independent of the body that the most wildly earthly excesses would not imperil its salvation" (MacCulloch 2010: 124). Now this mortification of the flesh is perhaps the most obvious unifying detail one discovers after reading the various books of the Nag Hammadi Library. This collection of the non-canonical books, letters, and Scriptures read in the various early messianic communities, does "not generally support many anti-Gnostic accusations, particularly as far as condemnations of sexual libertinism are concerned. We just don't seem to find libidinous Gnostics in the Nag Hammadi codices. Indeed, many authentic documents veer toward antisexual 'Encratism' in orientation or influence, holding theological positions favourable to celibate monks attempting to live in closed communities" (Churton 2015: 9). Yet to one who knows more fully the Gnostic doctrines and the invaluable place given to secretive knowledge and hidden meanings by their teachers it becomes abundantly clear that the collection in the Nag Hammadi Library must not be read with surface and superficial interpretations.

The evidence that the Gnostics were extremely sexual, violent, and revolutionary far outweighs the austerity of the Scriptures they used. Conversely, "Immoral indifference to the body was certainly an accusation leveled at [these] heretics: they didn't care what they did with their bodies, their enemies insisted, since the bodily life was held to be fundamentally unreal of itself ('dust to dust') from the spiritual perspective" (Churton 2015: 10). Churton went even further, saying of the Gnostics how "groups described by their enemies as 'Barbelo Gnostics,' 'Sethians,' 'Ophites,' 'Borborites,' 'Valentinians,' 'Marcosians,' 'Naasseni,' 'Simonians,' 'Carpocratians,' among other names derived from their teachers or from derogatory nicknames, were accused of disgraceful – that is, 'filthy' – practices, where sex and sexual fluids were allegedly used by adults within ostensibly religious ceremonies, along with magical rites, secret signs of recognition, and an undefined palette of pharmacological products conducive to dream states" (Churton 2015: 3).

These kinds of Gnostic circles were not the exception either. According to Christopher Rowland, "It is clear that by the middle of the second century AD, Gnosticism was a series of major religious systems, and was probably the dominant form of Christianity espoused by several religious communities" (Rowland 1985: 295). Basically, gnosticism would effectively have been considered interchangeable with Christianity in most early messianic communities. Indeed, "After the destruction of Jerusalem as a viable center for the Jesus messianic assembly in and after 70 CE, the grip of Jewish Christianity (championed until 62 CE by Jesus's brother James) had weakened considerably as the Gentile churches of Asia Minor, North Africa, Rome, Gaul, Spain, and Britain grew. Gnostic communities' outspoken practice of ... sin does suggest that Paul's more nuanced teaching on this subject, and his whole scandalous stance against applying the Torah to Gentiles ... had taken deep root in Gnostic circles and may even have been a first point and means of differentiating themselves" (Churton 2015: 48). Notwithstanding this, what happened to end it all? The doctrine of Irenaeus of Lyon became popular nearing the end of the third century.

Irenaeus, like all other leaders of the messianic movement, only possessed a handful of apostolic letters. These were mainly from the apostles Paul and John, which he understood literally and not contextually. Remember, this was before Rome converted to Christianity, before Catholicism was truly invented at Nicaea, and before the New Testament books and letters were chosen and collected. Irenaeus suggested which books and letters to collect and which books and letters were important. Then all other books and letters he condemned as heretical, all traditions and practices he could not relate back to the apostle Paul he condemned as heretical, and allegiance to any traditions other than those of the apostles Peter and Paul, or the four evangelists (Matthew, Mark, Luke, and John) he condemned as heretical. He even despised James, the brother of the Messiah, who was the original leader of all the early messianic communities; and refused to allow any of the many writings attributed to him to be collected into his canon but one.

Secondly, Luke, the author of the Book of Acts, wrote the Acts of the Apostles mainly as a propaganda tool. Luke was somewhat of a spin-doctor and he sought to vindicate his friend Paul in the eyes of this, possibly important man, Theophilus. What is written in Acts is powerful, moving, and triumphal but what is not written speaks even louder volumes. He mentions nothing of the debate between Peter and Paul – a debate that was the biggest issue in the early messianic movement. He mentions nothing of the Gnostics, although based on tradition they began with Simon the Samaritan, who he did speak of in the Book of Acts (Acts 8: 9-24) as being a former Magus (magician). True, he mentions how having converted to messianism, Simon sought to purchase with money the ability to pass on the Holy Spirit, and that for such ignorant and materialistic behaviour he was forthwith chastised by the apostle Peter. Further, he from that point on paints no strong picture of the true and definitive enmity the two had thereafter, though several historical documents go into detail about it. It is due to these clear gaps and absences why Luke's account, though useful and informative, is completely incapable of providing us with the full story of the early messianic movement.

Moreover, an even more "noticeable and possibly telling absence from the Acts account … is any note of the presence of Simon's feminine consort. All other accounts of Simon are consistent in naming her as Helen or Helena, and all accounts make it clear that this woman was not only his constant traveling companion but was a central figure and symbol of his personal cult" (Churton 2015: 63). This Helena was apparently a brothel prostitute he liberated from Tyre, in what is now Lebanon. To the Simonians, the first real Gnostics, she represented the Prostitute (*Porne*) in the oracles of Hosea, the Wisdom (Sophia) in the proverbs of Solomon, the Idea in the philosophy of Plato, and the Forethought (*Pronoia*) in the metaphysics of Hermes Trismegistos. Moreover, Simon was even able to develop a highly complicated mythological schema around her, the angels, the archangels, the Messiah, the God of the Messiah (who, lo and behold, was none other than, himself), and the God of the Judeans (the Old Testament God); in which the God of the Old Testament was called Saklas, Samael, or Azazel. Based on this tradition, Saklas, being a malevolent demiurge, created the world with imperfection based on a vision he saw of the perfect world created by him and his Sophia.

Considering that the Judeans and the Samaritans each had very different canonical Scriptures (and thereby had completely different versions of what we call the Old Testament), and considering that two of the most popular Samaritan Scriptures were the two books of Enoch: Book 1 telling the story of the fall of the angels and archangels from heaven and Book 2 telling the story of Enoch's *miraj* (rapture) through the ten heavens. The popularity of these non-canonical books throughout Samaria during the first century; and Simon's own development of his complicated series of angels, archangels, concepts, structures, and systems all show that Simon designed the abstract internal structures that he believed would liberate the soul based on the Enochian tradition. Yet the Simonian universe, while definitely dualistic, was also familiarly Tantric too. As in some versions of Tantrism and Buddhism *moksha* (liberation/salvation) from *samsara* (mundanity/the endless cycles of life) is to exit this existence (nirvana) and enter a higher existence (*samadhi*). Even so, Simon claimed to be the source and creator of the otherworld with the help and inspiration of his Helena.

This philosophy, theology, and mythology developed by Simon and Helena was predominantly based on abstraction and conceptualisation, however, to them the destiny of the human soul (or human sensuality) was to escape this evil and dark world created by Saklas and his fallen angels and archangels (each of them representing a Greek conception in their own right) and to enter into the paradise the Messiah sought to bring to humanity. Though this message may seem positive enough, the Egyptian Neoplatonist, Plotinus, many years later, felt that the Simonian view that this universe is evil and dark – a fundamental Christian doctrine too – and was governed by malevolent spirits (whether angels or *jinni*), was based largely on their ignorance of the inherent good and unity of all things. Indeed, "To the hard-core [Simonian] Gnostics, the world was a fraud; it could be laughed at from the heights of exalted realization. Once this was recognized, things taught to be taboo could be revealed, au contraire, as gateways to knowledge, as symbols denied and forbidden by the repressive pseudo-deity. [Thus] Gnostics penetrated into disturbed territory of the psyche" (Churton 2015: 30).

Simon himself apparently attracted a large following from the start, yet while he may have also been a follower of the messianic tradition, his variation of it clearly instigated the disapproval of certain very senior members of that same tradition. The apostle Peter obviously considering Simon to be his enemy from the start. The problem, however, was more than simply his mythological system, it was also his being blasphemous, non-Kosher, and sexually excessive. Although it may be true that "the issue of sex reappears consistently in a Gnostic and anti-Gnostic context. Simon's intuition may have revealed to him that the authentic sexual impulse [was] the impulse of divine creation – the First Thought – a magical power that has become enslaved and perverted by men terrified of false gods" (Churton 2015: 71).

Herein we can remember, the first and original, Edenic, commandment Allah gave to humanity was, "Be fruitful, and multiply, and replenish the earth" (Genesis 1: 28); and it is hereby that we can see the true genius of Simeon's sexualising of God, indeed, his becoming *the* sexualised God himself, which thereby allowed his message to grow and spread throughout the messianic communities of the Greco-Roman world. This was all the more reason for the apostle Peter to fear him, "God is not to be regarded as 'sexy' in any respect among proponents of the predominantly male, but apparently sexless, God. The idea of linking sex with worship [seemed] utterly anathema to mainstream religion – a veritable nightmare for those encouraged to be suspicious of female sexuality" (Churton 2015: 5).

Hence, though the popularity of the early messianic movement may, in a technical sense, by attributed to Simon's sexual innovations (and my personal beliefs concerning the identity of Simon himself are that he was in fact the Niger spoken of in Act 13: 1) and though its growth internationally can also be sought for in these Simonian innovations; Simon himself was looked on by most of the early leaders with contempt. When most people think of the spread of early messianism they usually think of the apostle Paul travelling the world and preaching the gospel. The truth, however, may be a little more complex.

Even so, there is one more, somewhat surprising, element missing from this puzzle before we go any further: it may in fact be highly likely, even almost certain, that the apostle Paul was himself a ringleader of the early Gnostic movement. This can be detected throughout the apostle Paul's first letter to Corinth, the apostle Paul himself, saying, "Awake to righteousness, and sin not; for some have not the knowledge of God: I speak this to your shame." "But the manifestation of the Spirit is given to every man to profit withal. For to one is given by the Spirit the word of wisdom; to another the word of knowledge by the same Spirit" (1Corinthians 15: 34; 12: 8). Again, both these uses of the word knowledge in their original Greek were the word *gnosis*. If anyone really created the Gnostic movement and led it after Simeon's own early death, and maybe even especially during his life, it would have been none other than the apostle Paul.

In order to present a little more evidence of this rather questionable assumption I need go no further than 1Corinthians itself, where the apostle Paul said, "Now I beseech you, brethren, by the name of our Lord Jesus Christ, that ye all speak the same thing, and that there be no divisions among you; but that ye be perfectly joined together in the same mind and in the same judgment. For it hath been declared unto me of you, my brethren, by them which are of the house of Chloe, that there are contentions among you. Now this I say, that every one of you saith, I am of Paul; and I of Apollos; and I of Cephas; and I of Christ" (1Corinthians 1: 10-12). Two things can be detected in the subtext immediately: first, the apostle Paul wanted and believed in the unity of all the messianic communities; second, he makes no mention of Simon's faction, even though it would have definitely existed at the time. Where were the Gnostics in the apostle Paul's definition of contentions?

There are, effectively, two answers to this: either the apostle Paul did not believe they were real messianic believers, or he saw himself as the real leader of the Gnostic movement. Hereby we come to the real issue of contention: the Gnostic existence is an historical fact; the apostle Peter's enmity with Simon is also an historical certainty; and Simon's identity as an early Gnostic, if not as the first Gnostic, is also definitive. Based on these historically determined facts, that cannot be changed, why the silence in all of Paul's letters. Indeed, even in 1Timothy we can get a glimpse of the apostle Paul's awareness that they existed, but even here we get only the very cryptic, "vain babblings, and oppositions of science falsely so called" (1Timothy 6: 20). The word science, again, being the English translation of the Greek word *gnosis*. So was the apostle Paul here speaking against the entire Gnostic movement or just false Gnostics?

Based on what we know so far we can see that this is very confusing territory. What adds to the confusion is that the Gnostics main claim to fame was in having the mysteries of

God; yet even that can be traced back to the apostle Paul when he made clear to his Corinthian followers, "But we speak the wisdom of God [theosophy] in a mystery, even the hidden wisdom, which God ordained before the world unto our glory:" "Let a man so account of us, as of the ministers of Christ, and stewards of the mysteries of God" (1 Corinthians 2: 7; 4: 1). What we can say then is that the most likely occurrence was that the names of the various early messianic traditions: Simonian, Pauline, Petrine, Nicolaitan, and Judaizer, were actually most likely derogatories created by their opponents to challenge the validity of their claim to represent the Messiah. Basically, the apostle Paul may have thereby actually been the real leader of the Gnostic movement.

But if, then, the case is that the Book of Acts was written not with the intent of telling the true story of the days of the apostles but an idealised account, does that make it any more or less trustworthy? One could obviously say it makes it more as it is telling us only the events that God wanted us to hear about and only the information that God wanted us to know about. Gnostic liberality was kept from us because God did not agree with or demand it. God demanded Catholic style Christianity and so at Nicaea Catholicism won the day. But if we were to use that kind of logic we could just as easily say God did not agree with Catholicism (which was officially created at Nicaea) as both Trinity and conservatism eventually fell in the East to Islam, and Islam itself was a global superpower far greater than Catholic Rome ever was, up until they themselves abandoned their liberality and became conservative in the nineteenth century and neofundamentalist in the twentieth with Wahhabism.

II

We now come to the ultimate question: is the Charismatic movement a true representative of the first century messianic movement? The answer is no. Are they a representative of the ideal of the leaders of the first century messianic movement? Again, the answer is no. This truth is actually evidenced in the letters of the apostle Paul. But before we consider these more in-depth we must first appreciate one of the Messiah's statements during his famous Sermon on the Mount: "Ye have heard that it was said by them of old times, Thou shalt not commit adultery: But I say unto you, That whosoever looketh on a woman to lust after her hath committed adultery with her in his heart" (Matthew 5: 27, 28). This, again, was an obvious exaggeration and hyperbole spoken for rhetorical effect. But to what end? According to the apostle Paul, "that every mouth may be stopped, and all world may become guilty before God" (Romans 3: 19).

Effectively, the three branches of the early messianic movement: Judaizer, Pauline, and Simonian all held to their own version of this idea, interpreting it in different ways while maintaining its basic premise. For the record, various historical accounts expose that both Peter and James were married so the Judaizers obviously took a hardline on it. Indeed, the apostle James wrote, "For whosoever shall keep the whole law, and yet offend in one point, he is guilty of all" (James 2: 10). The Encratites, a species of the Judaizers, took that even further shunning all intimate relations and contact entirely. It is even believed that both the apostle Peter's disabled daughter and the apostle Philips' seven daughters were members within this tradition.

For the record, it is also very likely that these Encratites migrated into Egypt and Ethiopia during the early days of the messianic movement, and became particularly pronounced in the Ogaden region of what was then known as a part of Axum but is now in modern day Somalia. If this is so, then these Encratites, over time, would have become those who later adopted the name al-Hur al-Oyum (the Black eyed-virgins). All the girls chosen to be in this elite grouping have usually been those considered the most beautiful of the Ethiopian/Somalian territory. For this cause, even the Prophet himself took note of them in the Quran stating that very paradise (Eden) was filled with many from al-Hur al-Oyum, themselves dressed in fine spun or coarse spun clothing, and were most likely light exhibitionists (that is, they permanently did not wear underwear). On the other hand, the Simonians clearly rejected the idea, not only of virginity, but also of the entire institution of marriage, practicing instead, as we read earlier, an early form of polyamory in which orgies and other excesses were continued.

This leads to a very interesting point: if the largest version of the early messianic movement during its first four centuries was most likely Gnostic (MacCulloch 2010) and the Gnostics were excessively more liberal when it came to their sexuality, how was that seen by the apostle Paul? To answer this questions we shall now consider the social dynamics of the actually existing first century messianic movement and measure it against what the apostle Paul wrote. First, let us consider what was written at the Jerusalem Council, "For it seemed good to the Holy Ghost, and to us, to lay upon you no greater burden than these *necessary* things; *That ye abstain from meats offered to idols, and from blood, and from things strangled, and from fornication*" (Acts 15: 28, 29; emphasis mine). At first sight, all these not may seem that necessary at all but instead to be rather trivial issues. What does eating Kosher meats have to do with one's salvation: which is a subject that should have been far more necessary for the Gentile converts to understand? Also, what relation does Kosher meats have to do with fornication?

This all becomes clear when we understand the early messianic tradition of the agape feasts or feasts of love. These feasts, heavily influenced by the Simonians, were where the messianic communities, being extremely diverse back then, would remember the Messiah's sacrifice with a meal at house one of their members. The interesting part, however, was after the meal was eaten because it was at that time that they would all begin making love with each other, that is, they all had a group orgy. As the word used by the Jerusalem Council for fornication was the word *porneia*, which can translate as: sexual immorality (but actually meant any form of sexual excess), what the Jerusalem Council was likely trying to do was either control the excesses of these orgies, or eliminate the orgies altogether. The fact that, not only was it not eliminated, but was continued on in virtually every messianic community, and that it had fierce defenders such as the likes of none other than the apostle Paul promoting it shows the problem was never the sexual orgies it was the sexual excess. Again, these were the only traditions the Jerusalem Council spoke of for the new converts – not baptism, or preaching, or praying, or the laying on of hands – so, ultimately, they must have held the agape feasts to be a fundamental aspect of the messianic movement.

Now as we have already seen, the Gnostics practiced sexual excess, and the records show that they were also blasphemous during their orgy parties. The records also show that they participated in what the Greeks called *theothyta* (eating food offered in sacrifice to deities) and what the rest of the early messianic movement called *eidolothyta* (eating food offered in sacrifice to idols). In other words, they did not buy Kosher meats for their agape feasts. Thus in a technical sense it could be said that the Gnostics contradicted every respectable aspect of the agape feast that was trying to be promoted by the Jerusalem Council.

We can already guess how the apostle Peter perceived this? "But these, as natural brute beasts, made to be taken and destroyed, speak evil of the things that they understand not; and shall utterly perish in their own corruption; And shall receive the reward of unrighteousness, as they that count it pleasure to riot in the day time. Spots they are and blemishes, sporting themselves with their own deceivings while they feast with you;

Having eyes full of adultery and that cannot cease from sin; beguiling unstable souls" (2Peter 2: 12-14). He spoke here not of the apostle Paul *per se*, but of the Gnostic movement, which as we know, began with the Simonians.

But this debate also clearly contributed to an argument he had with the apostle Paul: "But when Peter was come to Antioch, I withstood him to the face, because he was to be blamed. For before that certain came from James, he did eat with the Gentiles: but when they were come, he withdrew and separated himself, fearing them which were of the circumcision. And the other Jews dissembled likewise with him; insomuch that Barnabas also was carried away with their dissimulation" (Galatians 2: 11-13). It is clear from this that the apostle Paul was more liberal than Peter and James, however, his letter makes it look like the issue was over nothing more than circumcision when by the apostle Peter's standard it was actually about the *blasphemia, porneia*, and *eidolothyta* of the Gentiles of the time.

As stated, this debate was not even mentioned in Acts but as a side note, and unless one has studied the Scriptures and other early messianic writings deeply one could miss it. Luke said in the Acts of the Apostles: "And some days after Paul said unto Barnabas, Let us go again and visit our brethren in every city where we have preached the word of the Lord, and see how they do. And Barnabas determined to take with them John, whose surname was Mark. But Paul thought not good to take him with them, who departed from them from Pamphylia, and went not with them to the work. And the contention was so sharp between them, that they departed asunder one from the other" (Acts 15: 36-39). The issue of contention was clearly not Mark, the issue was the apostle Paul's liberality. To go deeper: the apostle Peter and the rest refused to eat with the Gentiles, not because they were uncircumcised but because of that *blasphemia, porneia*, and *eidolothyta*. The apostle Paul was never despised by the apostle Peter but the Gnostics were. Why? Because of their excess. But this particular excess was still being practiced at the time in the vast majority of the early messianic communities.

Conversely, due to the Messiah's early association with so-called prostitutes (*porne*) and his apparent prohibition of marriage (Matthew 22: 30), the early messianic movement was filled with an influx of the sexually excessive. But this created a problem to the conservative minded apostles Peter and James. Even Paul with his slightly greater tolerance of sexual liberality, had his own limits, as he said to the Corinthian believers, "It is reported commonly that there is fornication among you, and such fornication as is not so much as named among the Gentiles, that one should have his father's wife. And ye are puffed up" (1Corinthians 5: 1, 2). What, however, was also subtly implied in this statement was that fornication, or (in the case of the written record) orgy parties, were originally considered such honourable and respectable practices within the early messianic movement that the Corinthian believers were puffed up because of their excesses with regard to it. But here even the somewhat libertine Paul felt that they may have taken this early tradition a little too far.

Herein, though it could be argued that the apostle Paul said, "Now concerning the things whereof ye wrote unto me: It is good for a man not to touch a woman" (1Corinthians 7: 1); most readings of this misunderstand the apostle Paul, imposing on the early messianic movement our own modern worldview. The word used for "touch" in its Greek original was the word *haptomai*, which actually meant: attach (yourself to); which gave further credence to what he said immediately afterward, "Nevertheless, to avoid fornication, let every man have his own wife, and let every woman have her own husband" (1Corinthians 7: 2). The apostle Paul was basically saying that a man need not attach himself to one woman as his main, however, so as to avoid fornication it is alright if he does choose to have a main, and if women also choose to have a main.

Now the word the apostle Paul used there and throughout for fornication was, in its original Greek, the word *porneia*, which again brings us right back to the declaration of the Jerusalem Council and the question of sexual excess. When does sex become excessive? This question is all the more complicated when the apostle Paul said, "A bishop then must be blameless, *the husband of one wife*, vigilant, sober, of good behaviour, given to hospitality, apt to teach" (1Timothy 3: 2; emphasis mine). Though the bishop is here encouraged to have only one wife the implication here, again, being based on the historical records of Roman spies that infiltrated the early messianic movement (both Gnostic and non-Gnostic), is that the non-bishops actually tended to not have main lovers, or at least one main lover, that is, they had polyamorous orgies.

Moreover, as the apostle Paul continued, "if they cannot contain, let them marry: for it is better to marry than to burn" (1Corinthians 7: 9). Consequently, the word used here for burn was *pyro*, which meant burn with fire, but was also able to mean burn with passion, anger, or zeal. Interestingly, the apostle Paul was not the first person in the Scriptures to consider passion to be a fire: in Solomon's Song of Songs it says, "Set me as a seal upon thine heart, as a seal upon thine arm; for love is strong as death; jealousy is cruel as the grave: the coals thereof are coals of fire, which hath a most vehement flame" (Song of Songs 8: 6). Furthermore, the word translated as "jealousy" in its original Hebrew was the word *qinah*, which, again, meant zeal or passion.

So what was the definition of *porneia* to the apostle Paul? The apostle Paul wrote to the Corinthian *ekklesia*, "All things are lawful unto me, but all things are not expedient: all things are lawful for me, [and] I will not be brought under the power of any. Meats for the belly, and the belly for meats: but God shall destroy both it and them. Now the body is not for fornication, but for the Lord; and the Lord for the body. And God hath both raised up the Lord, and will also raise up us by his own power. Know ye not that your bodies are the members of Christ? shall I then take the members of Christ, and make them the members of a harlot? God forbid. What? know ye not that he which is joined to a harlot is one body? for two, saith he, shall be one flesh" (1Corinthians 6: 12-16). And again, the word used here for fornication was the word *porneia* while the word used here for harlot was the word *porne*.

Basically, given its correct interpretation the apostle Paul was saying that the early messianic movement should avoid sexual excess by not having sex with the sexually excessive, that is, with those with no sexual boundaries. But again, what took sexuality from *gamos* to *pornos*? Moreover, if the Messiah said that those accounted worthy of the resurrection "neither marry, nor are given in marriage" (Matthew 22: 30) then can even marriage ever become sacred? One has to now remember, at this time, that sexual excess by today's standards did not exist in the first century. Further, the apostle Paul and most of the other leaders of the early messianic movement, very likely had no problem with the orgiastic tradition of the movement, just so long as there were structured boundaries such as no rape, paedophilia, necrophilia, incest, bestiality, et cetera.

Remember also that this sexual side to the agape feasts was a very fundamental aspect of the early messianic tradition – not like today with only bread and wine. Back then they were actually whole big feasts at somebody's house: with Kosher meats, greens, unleavened bread, and red wine; and only after they had all eaten would they then have these sexual orgies. The tradition itself was very likely even started by the Messiah himself – minus the sexual element – who would often go to the houses of notable people in Galilee and feast with them. He even encouraged the practice among his disciples, as was said later, "And as they were eating, Jesus took bread, and blessed it, and brake it, and gave to the disciples, and said, Take, eat; this is my body. And he took the cup, and gave thanks, and gave it to them, saying, Drink ye all of it; For this is my blood of the new testament, which is shed for many for the remission of sins" (Matthew 26: 26-28).

If we move on from here we can now consider two other traditions of the early messianic movement before we begin evaluating whether modern Christian ecclesiology actual matches up with first century messianic ecclesiology. These traditions are: The court of the saints and the communal confession of faults. The first tradition, the court of the saints, was also started by the Messiah himself, even as he said to his disciples, "Moreover if thy brother shall trespass against thee, go and tell him his fault between thee and him alone: if he shall hear thee, thou hast gained thy brother. But if he will not hear thee, then take with thee one or two more, that in the mouth of two or three witnesses every word may be established. And if he shall neglect to hear them, tell it unto the church: but if he neglect to hear the church, let him be unto thee as an heathen man and a publican" (Matthew 18: 15-17). It is clear that when the Messiah said "tell it unto the church" his intention was for the *ekklesia* to judge the matter and punish the one who broke their rules.

The apostle Paul took this idea to the next level claiming that the court of the *ekklesia* should be considered a higher authority than the court of the state, saying, "Dare any of you, having a matter against another, go to law before the unjust, and not before the saints? Do ye not know that the saints shall judge the world? and if the world shall be judged by you, are ye unworthy to judge the smallest matters? Know ye not that we shall judge angels? how much more things that pertain to this life?" (1Corinthians 6: 1-3). Now, while neither the Messiah nor the apostle Paul ever said explicitly what these courts of the early *ekklesia* were to look like, we can assume that they were very similar to the training element of our own Square within the godbody movement, that is, that they had violence.

Finally, the next tradition to be discussed is the communal confession of faults. This tradition was started by the apostle

James, as he wrote in his only canonised letter: "Confess your faults one to another, and pray one for another, that ye may be healed. The effectual fervent prayer of a righteous man availeth much" (James 5: 16). We can see here that the early Gnostics took this idea to the extreme in actively blaspheming the Hebrew God and the Hebrew traditions at their own agape feasts. But in a genuine *ekklesia*, at the time of the confession of faults the entire *ekklesia* would hear what was said, the bishop would then pray for the pardon of their sins, and the entire *ekklesia* would then forgive them.

If the fellowship was all, at that time, gathered together in someone's house, then these confessions very likely took place before the actual agape feast: as the apostle Paul said concerning the even earlier agape feasts, "But let a man examine himself, and so let him eat of that bread, and drink of that cup. For he that eateth and drinketh unworthily, eateth and drinketh damnation to himself, not discerning the Lord's body" (1Corinthians 11: 28, 29). While it is clear that before this time the agape feasts may have actually been quite random, it is also very likely that over time in the early messianic movement confession became structured to be practiced before the actual meal was eaten.

Conversely, my estimation, based on sound critical deduction and logical historical reasoning, is that the central ritual body of the early messianic movement was the *ekklesia*. Within the *ekklesia* were then several ritual practices. Again, based on sound critical deduction it can be estimated that within the structure of the *ekklesia* were: First, the court of the saints, then the reading and interpreting of Scriptures (the Old Testament) or the sharing of lessons, then the confession of faults, then the actual agape feast, then the sexual orgies, and then, finally, to end it all, it is very likely that they entered into ecstasies of songs and prophecies (hymnology). Moreover, based on all these truths, six suggestions could be made concerning our own godbody rituals.

The first suggestion is that we introduce into our social movement and social enterprise the adoption of ten notable principles that, firstly, define and demarcate us, and, secondly, should be enforced with strict disciple for future godbodies: (1) No God but Allah (the Force of all interactions); (2) No power imbalances; (3) No non-authors; (4) No non-fighters; (5) No Divine fights alone; (6) No problems handled in the Square should ever leave the Square; (7) No marriage or marriages; (8) No denying another Divine; (9) No underwear ever; and (10) No harassment or rape of any kind ever. Any breaking of the rape prohibition should lead to permanent expulsion; stripping of titles, ranks, names, and honours; and beat down from any Gods who hear about what was done, as a final "fuck you!" (Obviously, violation and breaking of any other principle should or could lead to the Square, including the harassment clause; leaving only rape itself to lead to all the punishments mentioned above).

The second suggestion is that the structure of our weekly parliaments moving forward should be that we: First, provide training in the fundamentals of MMA (that is, in form, method, and technique), for all members willing or desiring to learn. Second, hold the fighting ring of the Square, to ensure all godbodies keep and maintain genuine love for each other, not secretly harbouring animosity, bitterness, or resentment towards each other. Third, hold the court of the Square, to ensure the enforcement of strict discipline concerning godbody rules and doctrines. Fourth, have the eating of Halal foods together aspect of the Square; being sure also to pour out a small libation, of whatever drinks we then have, in memory of the fallen Black souls that were enslaved, lynched, segregated, colonised, and that are even now being incarcerated by this White supremacist system. Fifth, have the actual building section of the parliament; where a captain or lieutenant shares a general message with the parliament based on either the Bible, Quran, 120 lessons, history, or sciences, that the rest of the Gods and Goddesses can then add-on to, sharing how they understand it. Finally, have the parliament close with the captain or lieutenant leading the parliament in reciting the Divine Army Chant.

The third suggestion concerns the structure of our ghetto parliaments, essentially, we would be of far greater value to the Black community if we added-on to our parliament system monthly parliaments for godbody workplaces, neighbourhoods, and universities where there is a godbody presence, that we call workers' parliaments, consumers' parliaments, and students' parliaments, respectively (Albert 2003). Effectively, by organising workers' parliaments for all godbody workers in any godbody or majority Black business, corporation, or organisation; by organising consumers' parliaments in any godbody neighbourhood; and organising students' parliaments in any university where there is a godbodies presence. The instituting of this kind of participatory system is what I have given the name Black syndicalism.

The fourth suggestion for the godbody movement is that we make sure that we set the initiation age for all adolescents into the weekly parliaments at 18 years old. The main reason behind this is the exhibitionist elements encouraged throughout my former books, as well as the violent realities already existing within our movement. Not to mention that we are a kind of Army Nation, and as most armies have their initiation prerequisite the reaching of the age of 18, such should only be seen as fitting for our own army as well. Moreover, once they have completed the initiation process they should then immediately get full access to everything: the universal flag, the light exhibitionism, the weapons, the weekly parliaments, and monthly workers', consumers', and students' parliaments, and the status of Knowledge 120. Granted, as an adolescent they would already have access to the teachings, the ciphers, the Square, the unarmed training, the protection, the sexual train, the title of God or Goddess, and the entire community of fellow

Gods and Goddesses, but we want initiation to mean something, therefore we should make it count.

The fifth suggestion is based on my being somewhat of an amateur anthropologist. Because of this, I have been able to see the cultural potential within our own godbody movement; and even its relation to the ancient cultures of Africa. Indeed, in many of the various African cultures the various transitions that occur in the human experience are themselves celebrated and highlighted with ritual significance. This, nonetheless, was not due to any ignorance or superstition on the part of these tribal communities, but to their wisdom and understanding that we sometimes need to mark important events in our own and other people's lives, especially in relation to the culture. These also cement our place within the culture; give us a clear sense of belonging to the culture and community; raise our level of devotion and commitment to the culture; and also raise the value of the culture and community these rituals are performed for in the minds and hearts of each person in the culture.

Hereby, as in many tribes of Africa there is a ritual of dedication to celebrate a child's birth and dedication to the culture. Then there is a ritual of probation to celebrate a child's transition to becoming an adolescent. Then there is a ritual of induction to celebrate an adolescent's transition to becoming an adult. Then there is a further ritual of ordination or officiation to mark an adult's transition to higher levels within the community. Further there is a ritual of initiation to mark those same adult's transition to becoming an elder. Then, finally, there is a final ritual to celebrate an elder's transition to becoming one of the ancestors, and entering forever into the astral plane to dwell among the other ancestors.

Well, from this life structure we godbodies can draw clues: From age 6-9 a child should be brought to the parliament to make a vow of dedication to the godbody teachings and community. From age 12-13 a child should be inducted into the Square to mark their transition to adolescence. From age 18 an adolescent should stand before the parliament for examination to mark their transition of adulthood. From age 18 and up they will have the opportunity at any time to transition from adulthood to Ausarhood/Ausethood as soon as they prove worthy. At that point, they will be an *ordained* enlightener and able to spread the message. Then, from age 55 an adult should stand again before the parliament to be initiated into the cipher of the elders (Older Gods and Goddesses). Finally, at any God or Goddess' death there should be a celebration for their transition to the company of the ancestors. All this should and can be done within the context of the godbody.

Finally, my sixth suggestion is that we begin adjusting our Allah Schools to become boarding schools exclusively for children. All parental raising of godbody children should be until they turn 6-9 when they should officially be dedicated to an Allah School, from that point on becoming a Horu or a Hethor. From there they should be sent off to their 360 day annual, co-education Allah School boarding school. It should be there that they will be introduced to languages (preferably Arabic), to the supreme alphabets, to the supreme mathematics, to Black history, and to basic biophysics, quantum physics, molecular physics, geophysics, astrophysics, and digital physics.

From the day the child becomes a Horu or Hethor they should be dedicated to their Allah School boarding school and should from that time on no longer be *simply* the responsibility of their two parents but of the entire godbody community *internationally*, and that should be for life. Finally, after they graduate the Allah School boarding school at age 12 or 13 (whichever age they reach puberty), they should be initiated into another boarding school that I call the Allah College. Here they should learn the 120 lessons, What We Teach, mechanical analysis, more supreme mathematics, and get access to the ciphers, the Square, unarmed training, sex education, and the sexual train (when they consent to it).

True, as all these customs and practices having thus been mentioned and underscored, one may now ask the pertinent question: why do we have to eat Halal meats at all when the Messiah said, "There is nothing from without a man, that entering into him can defile him: but that things which come out of him, those are they that defile the man." Moreover, "And the voice spake unto him again the second time, What God hath cleansed, that call not thou common" (Mark 7: 15; Acts 10: 15). The same could also be asked as to why I encourage the cultural practices of the godbody wearing the universal flag, the godbody wearing no underwear, the male godbody wearing the *kufi*, the female godbody wearing the *hijab* (head-covering) or short hair if they do not wish to wear the *hijab*, and the cultural practices of the Build Allah Square with strict discipline? The answer is not to be annoying, aggressive, rude, intrusive, or problematic, but to encourage the decolonisation of Black minds and bodies from this modernised "civilisation," back to more Black forms of civilisation.

The relation of all these practices to the rituals of the early messianic movement should still be somewhat evident, yet within both movements there was, and can still be, an initiation process that is very valuable to remember and maintain. Within the early messianic movement it was adult baptism in water and the Holy Spirit. With us a newborn goes through the process of writing, at the Allah School, in front of all the Gods and Goddesses, all of the 120 lessons: verbatim and from memory with no written prompts to help them. Though in a technical sense that newborn was already a God or Goddess, and may even have been called a God or Goddess from birth, they would not, however, have had the full status of God or Goddess until initiation. Once initiated they would get full status as a God or Goddess and of having gained Knowledge 120. That said, all I say is that these examinations should take place at Allah Colleges instead of at Allah Schools.

III

As we move on to the social aetiology of the Charismatic movement it can be shown to in fact have been borne of a dilemma within Christianity: How can God love the world and yet predestine some to hell. Those in the "God loves the world" camp usually have an anti-essentialist mentality, while those in the predestination camp tend to be more essentialist. Nevertheless, contrary to the age old aphorism, we were not all created equal (in the literal, biological, psychological, political, societal, or sociological senses). If there really were no essential differences between the races, then even if we transmit some of the blame to institutions and institutional racism for the problems within the Black community it still does not account for the obvious – almost everywhere and in all places Blacks are the bottom rung of all social ladders: in relationships, in family cohesion, in education, in employment, in finances, in role models, in representation, and in legality. Though it could be said that all these are by definition examples of institutions, and that such can be racist, that is exactly my point.

On the one hand, the question could be asked why the same institutions are not set against, say, the Indians or the Chinese or the Ashkenazi; but, on the other hand, the old aphorism: "There is no smoke without fire," also applies. The old existentialist argument that human beings stand in a relationship with existence absolutely free, and that the choices we make are generally our own may carry the same level of political correctness as "all men are created equal," but it does not carry any scientific correctness.

While it is true that science is subjective and has been for centuries, the general premise of science to find the truth (*al-haqiqa*) has at least inspired some forms of ingenuity. What I am

370

trying to say is that though the essentialisms of the past may have been emphatically wrong that does not exclude essentialism entirely. Take the social institutions mentioned earlier: though the Indians, the Chinese, and the Japanese may have integrated into the Western way of participating in them, we Blacks have not been fully integrated. The reasons behind that, while predominantly based on the racism of the institutions, also have the socio-ethical and socio-cultural mechanisms internal within the Black individual and the Black community in them. The Black community may not be filled with *only* criminals but there is a high percentage of criminals in it; the Black community may not have *only* high school and college drop-outs but it does have a high percentage of drop-outs in it; the Black community may not be filled with *only* dysfunctional families but it does have a high percentage of dysfunctional families in it. If looked at from a logical perspective the truth appears to be quite obvious: we do not fit in with Western civilisation.

Though, again, this can all be attributed to racist institutions there must also be something different in us as a race as all other races have come up against the same racist institutions and still seem to thrive within the system. While some may simply attribute it to these institutions being more racist towards us than they have been towards other races that is a bit of a cop-out. Others may attribute it to Black culture so as to keep from essentialising Black non-integration but this also does no justice to either Blacks or the truth, and only creates a pseudonoir among those who desire to represent Black culture.

For Whites to blame institutions alone for the Black predicament is paternalistic and creates for this generation of White people the same spirit that inspired their fathers to colonise Africa in the hopes of "civilising" those poor Negroes, only this time it would be of somehow "saving" those poor Africans and slum-dwellers. Then again, to say the Black situation is the fault of Black people alone is to be overtly racist in that it starts from the dodgy premise that Western civilisation is in itself perfect, from a universal basis, therefore if Black people are unintegrated into it that must be because something is inherently wrong with us Blacks: we Blacks must therefore be biologically inferior.

The complex debate that goes on between both the essentialist and the existentialist is relatively outlandish if one considers that it is based on judging things from a false perspective. Historically, the essentialists were generally equated with racists as the two held and maintained the same idea – that Blacks were inherently inferior. The existentialists nowadays are more popular because they ascribe more freedom to the individual, thus allowing them to escape any biological and sociological constraints to be whatever they want to be. Such existentialist arguments are true, in an ideal world, maybe; in the real world it is harder to escape our biology any more than we can escape our personal history.

Indeed, according to No et alia., "Race itself may take on different meanings, as some believe that race is biologically rooted, reflects abilities and traits, and is unchangeable, [and] others believe that race is socially constructed, arbitrary, and fluid across time and contexts" (No et alia. 2011: 218). This fact of perspective, however, can be racist from either angle. If one perceives race to be unchangeable and yet believes that certain races are superior to others and that certain other races are worthless or incapable, et cetera. that is racist. If one perceives race to be changeable and arbitrary that can also be racist: a colourblind racism that undervalues a person's racial identity, on the one hand; and negates the self-differentiation necessary to develop a people psychologically, on the other. Many Black people during Jim Crow were also the victims of this colourblind racism, believing, and even hoping, that God would not see their Blackness. That their Blackness would be washed away when they died. That they would somehow become whiter than snow, not only metaphorically, but even physiologically.

Effectively, by saying something like, "I don't see colour," most White people are actually denying their own and other racial groups' racial validity and silencing the voice of the very racial groups they believe they are uplifting. Not only so, but they are also undermining that group's racial identity, their racial existence, their racial history, and their racial humanity. Another problematic with the phrase, "I don't see colour," is that it is an obvious lie. We cannot avoid seeing someone's race, so by saying their colour does not exist that person is actually making their race invisible and their racial struggles invisible. It is almost like saying their racial history of subjugation and racial current of persecution means nothing.

Conveniently, this is something White people are able to avoid with their White privilege. They can afford to say things like not seeing race, even though they obviously and undeniably do, as their race is not being persecuted and held back by societal institutions and superstructures that have their foundation in a discourse of White superiority. Even Erdman also stated, "We can study values, or things that are important to the collective, in order to describe national cultures because they are replicated and reinforced over time through social organizations and institutions such as families and educational systems" (Erdman 2017: 22). Therein, if we now consider that the discourse of White superiority has allowed among the White people of their various national cultures the instituting and organising of structures that perpetuate White supremacy then, indeed, we can see how the foundations of this White supremacist structure, have beginnings that are undeniably based on a pseudoscience, that is, the trick knowledge of White superiority.

Yet, in taking the signs and symbols of the actual realities of the godbody culture as practiced in 1990s New York City, it could also be interpreted that the godbody lifestyle itself adopted mechanisms that reinforced the trick knowledge of White superiority culturally. Nevertheless, as has already been articulated, the psychology of the actual individuals who currently live the lifestyle are far from dehumanised, in fact, they are ultra-humanised to the point of deification. Moreover, for them this deification has led to the adopting of what in society is held to be a high cultural standard. Nothing could be further from the truth than to presume that the socio-cultural aesthetic of the godbody is a result of the discourse of White superiority we condemn so flagrantly in our brothers and sisters of the 10 percent. We simply believe that as poor, righteous, teachers it is our duty to provide therapeutic assistance to our brothers and sisters in the ghetto.

With this objective of providing therapy to the ghetto *for free* we godbodies may be compelled into social relations that many of us will not understand. Yet if we considered deeply the superstructural mechanisms of human subjectivity we would in fact discover that they are all based on a merging of several social factors: the socio-sexual, the socio-ethical, the socio-cultural, the socio-religious, the socio-economic, the socio-legal, the socio-political, the socio-historical, the socio-linguistic, and the socio-symbolic; and all these factors are intersubjective in orientation. They further represent relations that developed through social dynamics with astral and social bodies that, like selfobjects, are as much a part of the self as one's own subjectivity.

IV

Intersubjectivity – being based in large part on an empathic interconnection to various self-identities – holds the key to understanding the mechanisms that operate within the infrastructure of social relations. Though an individual is more likely to be empathic towards self and selfobject, and it is unlikely that they will display any serious intersubjective links with Other until Other enters their libidinal sphere, even here there is no guarantee that connections will be created between their astral or social bodies.

This is where a term called introjection provides a most useful assistance. According to Ferenczi, the man who apparently coined the term, "introjection [is] *an extension to the external world of the original autoerotic interests, by including its objects in the ego* ... I put the emphasis on this 'including' and [desire] to show thereby that I [consider] every sort of object-love (or transference) both in normal and in neurotic people (and of course also in paranoiacs as far as they are capable of loving) as an extension of the ego, that is as introjection" (Ferenczi 1980; quoted in Torok 1994: 112; emphasis Torok's).

Introjection thereby is an act of selfobject transference, an act-specie that allows Other, that is, alterego, to become intersubjective ego. Therein, it becomes a reconnection to the memory of those considered selfobject through the exchange of empathic, agapic, and erotic love. Freud further said on the subject: "the ego itself is occupied by libido, ... it is in fact the libido's original home and remains to some extent its headquarters. This narcissistic libido turns towards objects, thus becoming object-libido, and can change back again into narcissistic libido" (Freud 2002: 55). Or said another way, "In principle, man can love only himself; if he loves an object he takes it into his ego. ... I used the term 'introjection' for all such growing onto, all such including of the loved object in, the ego" (Ferenczi 1980; quoted in Torok 1994: 112); and such only occurs through a reconnection to selfobject.

What Freud and Ferenczi were basically saying was that originally object-love starts out as self-love (as narcissistic love), but then evolves into object-love as objects become selfobjects. Such is only accomplished through the process of selfobject transference, and the simplest form of selfobject transference is introjection. As a form of selfobject transference introjection thereby carries many similarities to its more technical predecessor, "Like transference … introjection is defined as the process of including the Unconscious in the ego through objectal contacts. The loss of the object will [therefore] halt this process" (Torok 1994: 113). Accordingly, the central means of losing object contact is with the death of the object.

Things can go terribly wrong with the introjection process if the object dies, be that object an individual or a social body, "According to Freud, the trauma of objectal loss leads to a response: incorporation of the object [into] the ego [as a *tyrannical* superego]. The incorporated object, with which the ego would identify partially, makes it possible both to wait while readjusting the internal economy and to redistribute one's investment [of libido]. Given that it is not possible to liquidate the dead and decree definitively: 'they are no more,' the bereaved become the dead for themselves and take their time to work through, gradually and step by step, the effects of the separation." "Incorporation … is invariably distinct from introjection (a gradual process) because it is instantaneous and magical. The object of pleasure being absent, incorporation obeys the pleasure principle and functions by way of processes similar to hallucinatory fulfillments" (Torok 1994; 111, 113; emphasis mine). Incorporation denies the truth of the object's separation and keeps them alive internally and illegally. It must, in that sense, be *phantasmic*, as is the incorporated object: "Secrecy is imperative for survival" (Torok 1994: 114).

Moreover, "In Abraham and Torok's sense, the secret is a trauma whose very occurrence and devastating emotional consequences are entombed and thereby consigned to internal silence, albeit unwittingly, by the sufferers themselves. The secret here is intrapsychic. It designates an internal psychic splitting; as a result two distinct 'people' live side by side, one behaving as if s/he were part of the world and the other as if s/he had no contact with it whatsoever" (Rand 1994; quoted in Abraham & Torok 1994: 100). What happens when the selfobject or love object is lost is introjection is prohibited as they were the object that mediated the libido during the process of introjection. Once the introjection process is prohibited bereavement sets in, yet in some cases, where bereavement is denied a phantasm gets incorporated creating an *endocryptic identification* to calm the now chaotic ego, or astral body, made incomplete by the disappearance of the object (Abraham & Torok 1994). Such is what Torok (1994: 117) called the illness of mourning, the heightened level of libido one experiences after the loss of a loved one (love object). "The increase in libido is a desperate and final attempt at introjection, a sudden amorous fulfillment with the object."

The incorporated alterego is a *phantasmic* spook that haunts the primordial ego becoming a new superego or master to primordial ego. Indeed, "Incorporation denotes a [phantasy], introjection a process." "Thus, it is not at all a matter of 'introjecting' the object, as is all too commonly stated, but of introjecting the sum total of the [libidinal] drives, and their vicissitudes as occasioned and mediated by the object" (Abraham & Torok 1994: 125; Torok 1994: 113). Or said another way, one introjects not the love object but the libidinal energy they inspire and mediate.

At the same time, phantasies of the love object get revived using the memories taken from the relationship, and, transferring them alive, with their own topography, to be incorporated into the mourning individual. The phantasy world thereby created by this incorporation must be concealed from the subject. The dead, now revived, becomes a spook that stands guard at the crypt he or she now haunts, producing strange behaviours and words that emanate from the subject at inappropriate moments. Phantasy is, again, an indication that introjection has been refused and a gap created; and the incorporated phantasm is a phantasy that may cause neuroses, hallucinations, paranoia, or psychosomatic behaviours in individuals depending on the circumstances.

Effectively, the incorporated spook becomes an inhibitive agent in our psychic infrastructures. Yet Freud traced this kind of inhibition, from what he called the death drive, all the way back to our childhood, "A considerable measure of aggressivity must have developed in [a] child against the authority that deprives him of his first … satisfactions, no matter what kind of deprivations were required. The child is obliged to forgo the satisfaction of this vengeful aggression. He helps himself out of this difficult economic situation by recourse to familiar mechanisms. By means of identification he *incorporates* this unassailable authority into himself; it now becomes the super-ego and takes over all the aggression that, as a child, one would have liked to exercise against it" (Freud 2002: 65; emphasis mine). Incorporation is thus not only manifested in *endocryptic identification*, but, like in the case of the mob, the superego of the authority can also be incorporated whenever traumatic pain is caused by them. The secret is the secret. Once a trauma has blocked the introjection process mediated by a love object they will instantly be incorporated into primordial ego as a kind of tyrannical superego. Remember, incorporation is not a process, like introjection is, incorporation is instant and illegal.

Basically, we are able to see that what in contemporary psychoanalysis is called "developmental systems of pathological accommodation" was simply called by Freud "incorporation of the authority." What is meant when contemporary analysts say developmental systems of accommodation is the accommodating systems a child forms during the process of their development and socialisation. If their accommodative systems are suitable then they effectively assist the child in self-other differentiation thereby allowing the child to introject the libidinal energy they feel towards their caregivers, and turn them into selfobjects. But when there is repeated traumata, due to the presence of an ineffectual caregiver in the child's development, then their systems of accommodation will become pathological (dysfunctional) causing them to inadequately develop self-boundaries and self-differentiation processes.

Indeed, "what is entailed in 'accommodation' in Brandchaft's terms is scarcely limited to being 'accommodating' in the ordinary sense" (Doctors & Sorter 2010: 258). Herein we can see the potential of pathological accommodation manifesting itself not only in submissive and depressive behaviours but also in rebellious and anti-social behaviours; both developing as defence mechanisms for dealing with "incompetent caregivers" (Sander 2002). "For example, self-doubt might regularly follow self-assertion – a pattern memorializing the psychological accommodation to a parent when the parent is unable to acknowledge or validate [the] child's perception or affect. The temporal sequence of the interaction characteristic of the developmental system is conserved, and the pattern becomes part of the child's repertoire ... As a defense, [this] pathologically accommodative system is [then] geared to preserve the self [thus] forestalling annihilating experiences of self- and object loss" (Doctors & Sorter 2010: 257). Effectively, during the process of pathological accommodation the ineffectual caregiver gets incorporated into the child's superego through the child's fear of self- and object loss and their unrequited need for external validation.

Furthermore, as in the case of the individual so we must also remember that cultural and social bodies have superegos too. "The super-ego of a cultural epoch has an origin not unlike that of the individual; it rests upon the impression left behind by the personalities of great leaders, people who were endowed with immense spiritual or intellectual power or in whom some human striving found its strongest and purest, and hence often most one-sided, expression" (Freud 2002: 78). This social superego we discussed in brief in Chapter 3; however, what we can add here is that the social superego could either be an incorporation or an internalisation.

Accordingly, "both the cultural and the individual super-ego make stern ideal demands, and ... failure to meet these demands is punished by 'fear of conscience'." (Freud 2002: 78). Indeed, the social body haunted by a spook is also tortured by the trauma caused by the spook by way of the secret, even to the point that they cannot identify their own neuroses or psychoses. When a social superego has placed the individuals in the social body under any kind of sexual inhibition, and not simply a sexual sublimation, then it is a spook.

Yet there is another kind of spook that can inhibit an astral, social, or global body: what Abraham (1994) called "the phantom." The phantom can be the individual or collective phantasm of the love object that, though an invention of the mind, disrupts the activities of the astral or social body. In this case, however, the sexual object or love object that haunts is not a result of introjective disruption, but of familial or ancestral incorporation. The spook that haunted one individual or several now haunts the family and descendants of those individuals. Though one inhibited by a phantom may be disconnected from direct contact with the secret, "what comes back to haunt are the tombs of others" (Abraham 1994: 172). Again, these *phantasmic* spooks can inhibit astral bodies, social bodies, or global bodies in accordance with how many people incorporated the original object. Either way, they are transgenerational spooks, thereby moving from astral forces to social and global forces.

Ultimately, while neurotic, hallucinatory, paranoid, delusional, or psychosomatic behaviour in an astral or social body may be traced to any number of reasons including incorporation, these symptoms in a racial group can usually be traced back to a phantom. "The phantom is a formation of the unconscious that has never been conscious – for good reason.

It passes [effectively] from the parent's unconscious into the child's. Clearly, the phantom has a function different from dynamic repression. The phantom's periodic and compulsive return lies beyond the scope of symptom-formation in the sense of a return of the repressed; it works like a ventriloquist, like a stranger within the subject's own mental topography" (Abraham 1994: 173).

With greater scientific research we have come to find that these phantom-like behaviours should be considered the result of epigenetics. The trauma of one generation getting passed down to the next generation via this process. Here the existence of the phantom must be accepted for it to be exorcise from an unconscious. There is inherently something dark, hidden, and secretive about the *phantomatic* that causes it to elude detection, whether in the astral, the social, or in the global body of the haunted. Nonetheless, inhibition from the spook will continue on so long as it haunts the unconscious of any astral, social, or global body.

Astral forces and social forces thereby transmute into global forces through the transforming of the incorporated spook into the *phantomatic* spook. Herein, the problem is not in the transmission of culture or practices from one generation to the next, the problem is in the incorporation of what was once a selfobject or love object, and has now, due to the secret/trauma, become a phantasm. Again, this only transpires when the object carries a secret, be it libidinal or traumatic (Rand 1994), otherwise it is merely an internalisation based on introjection. Original incorporation thus becomes transgenerational haunting as children carry the *phantasmic* spooks of their parents.

Pathologically speaking these collective secrets must be discovered and uncovered for the therapeutic freedom of the racial or transgenerational grouping. Rand (1994: 167) further pointed out that "the psychoanalytic idea of the phantom concurs [ingeniously] with Roman, Old-Norse, Germanic, and other lore, according to which only certain categories of the dead return to torment the living: those who were denied the rite of burial or died an unnatural, abnormal death, were criminals or outcasts, or suffered injustice in their lifetime." If we consider that the roles of most godbodies are to live with hypermartiality, hypersexuality, and hyperintelligence we could thereby conclude that in these sorts of situations we godbodies have a duty, in spreading the message of the thearchy, of warring with, and so exorcising these spooks.

V

As all phantoms are by nature transgenerational spooks they must be carried from a parent to a child, all "the words used by the phantom to carry out its return ... do not refer to a source of speech in the parent. Instead, they point to a gap, they refer to the unspeakable. ... The presence of the phantom indicates the effects, on the descendants, of something that had inflicted narcissistic injury or even catastrophe on the parents." "Yes, the shameful and therefore concealed secret always does return to haunt. To exorcise it one must *express it in words*. But how are we to accomplish this when the phantoms inhabiting our minds do so without our knowledge, embodying the unspeakable secret of ... *an other*? This other, of course, is a love object" (Abraham 1994: 174, 188).

The answer to this question for Abraham was abundantly clear, send the patient into astral crisis by speaking the unspeakable and exposing the secret that inflicted these catastrophes. "The aim, in other words, is to cancel the secret buried in the unconscious and to display it *in its initial openness*. But how can the secret be exposed if the guilt and shame attached to it persist? Their exorcism leads necessarily not to the punishment, real or imagined, of the other, but to a higher wisdom about oneself and the world of humans at large" (Abraham 1994: 189). The aim therefore of any exorcism must not simply be to cause this kind of crisis, though crisis will occur, or be to condemn or judge the subject, as they will do enough of that to themselves; but to understand, to search out, and to identify truth (*haqiqa*).

During these processes of therapy (be they psychotherapy or sociotherapy) the God or Goddess may encounter either an incorporated spook or a *phantomatic* spook; in both cases what they have in common is the secret, the unspoken, and unspeakable. Where they differ is that the incorporated spook can be exorcised simply by the godbody sending the *jinn* that currently haunts them into astral crisis through speaking the unspeakable during the process of an introjective seduction; doing so in such a way that the truth of the unspeakable is essentially inescapable (Greene 2004).

Basically, what they will be doing is hurting them, hurting them hard, during the process of their introjective seduction; but they will be hurting them to heal them (Greene 2004). As with operatic conditioning, what will have happened in the subject's mind is that, from that point on, every time they think of the unspeakable it will now trigger neither pain nor shame but desire (Greene 2004). They would have effectively linked the unspeakable with the seduction. And though in the immediate they may get angry, perhaps even very angry, at the godbody for doing it, it will nevertheless create such a release from the pain of the unspeakable that they will never be held prisoner to it again. I have to say, however, that I myself am not a doctor nor a professionally trained or licensed psychoanalyst, therefore the advice I have just given here is not orthodox psychoanalysis, it is only recommended here due to the effectiveness of what Robert Greene taught in his masterpiece *The Art of Seduction*.

On the other hand, the *phantomatic* spook, being completely heterogeneous to the host, is a little harder to exorcise as the secret is not theirs directly but their parent's or their ancestors'. Here the secret should be exorcised using other forms of selfobject countertransference instead of simply with a seductive form of introjection. With the godbody thereby performing these therapies for the lost they must also keep in mind that they mainly maintain their credibility, being trained, licensed, or untrained by making the decision, internally as well as openly, to not charge for any therapy they do provide to the people. Moreover, they will have to appreciate that in any of these actual therapies they will "always [remain], background or fore-ground, a part of the field. When a patient is silent or when he is at his most demanding or complaining, in short whatever the content of what is apparently occupying his attention, he is affected by the analyst according to his experience and his anticipation" (Brandchaft 2010: 34).

Whenever dealing with either kind of *phantasmic jinn* during a therapeutic encounter, the godbody will have to be very observant and also careful not to expose their own prejudices. The intersubjective interaction must thereby be based on the bond built up throughout the process of their person-to-person interaction. Accordingly, the astral, social, or global body's topography can be separated from that of the *phantasmic* spook. It will effectively be their unconscious desire to be free from the *jinn* that will make them susceptible to the godbody's charms. However, the pain and horror of exposing the parent's or ancestors' guarded secret will no doubt prevent any full exposures; or said another way, the spook that they embody will lie: "A ghost returns to haunt with the intent of lying: its would-be 'revelations' [will thereby be] false by nature" (Abraham 1994: 188).

It will essentially be important for the godbody to empathise with any astral or social body they are attempting to help, but also to watch out for any symptoms of neurosis or psychosis: for example, symptoms of compulsion, during the process of their interaction. Should these appear the godbody must then consider whether the symptoms are neurotic or psychotic. If they are neurotic then the godbody can probe a little deeper before diagnosis to see how these behaviours or states came about and why. Should there be no satisfactory answer then their astral or social body may be haunted by a spook or by spooks. From here they must diagnose whether these spooks are incorporated or *phantomatic*.

If the spooks are incorporated then a God or Goddess should be able to seduce either the person (if it is an astral body) or two or three of the leading members (if it is a social body). But they must be sure to do so while exposing the secret; thereby exorcising the spooks and opening the astral or social body up to internalising a Horu/Hethor construct after experiencing the astral crisis of the exposure of their secret. For a Goddess the act of seduction itself can be something as simple as wearing a dress that reveals that they are not wearing underwear during the therapeutic process. For a God it will require a little bit more subtly, using sexual language and behaviours that are both enticing and flirtatious during the therapeutic process. Nevertheless, if the godbody is still unable to exorcise the spook (being untrained), or if the symptoms they manifested were psychotic, then the godbody should encourage them to seek professional help.

Furthermore, if the diagnosis is that the spook is a phantom then exorcism may prove a lot harder still as the secret will not be obvious to that person if an astral force, or to any person if a social force. Secondly, the phantom haunts because it fears being exposed, therefore, "Reducing the 'phantom' [will entail] reducing the sin attached to someone else's secret and stating it in acceptable terms so as to defy, circumvent, or domesticate the phantom's (and our) resistances, its (and our) refusals, gaining acceptance for a higher degree of 'truth.'" (Abraham 1994: 189.) While it is possible to do this by speaking the unspeakable during the process of seducing, it is better by far, *in the case of a phantom*, to sublimate all sexuality by practicing communicational (*kalim*) forms of selfobject countertransference.

By using more communicational forms of selfobject counter-transference in the case of a phantom the godbody ensures that the astral forces of the one receiving the therapy or the social forces and the leading members receiving the therapy do not take the exposure of the secret as a complete disrespect of themselves and/or their ancestors. While exposing a secret will be perceived as disrespectful with or without the sexual connotations and allurements, it is not safe to challenge one's ancestral beliefs and hint at sexuality at the same time. Even if the sexuality is not meant to imply disrespect it may be perceived to do so. The God or Goddess during the process of these ghetto therapies must therefore be empathic and decentre themselves from their own primordial ego to see the crisis that could be inflicted on those they are hoping to free. Such a crisis could breakdown trust and responsiveness, and thus alienate those being healed or it could cause systems of pathological accommodation to be built up in their mind thereby creating a new spook to prohibit them.

Ultimately, there are four possibilities that can transpire with regard to a *phantasmic* spook (*jinn*): (i) they can become incorporated through the hiding of a secret, (ii) they can become *phantomatic* through the transgenerational migration of the secret, (iii) they can be exorcised through the acceptance of the secret, or (iv) they can be resurrected through the re-enactment of the secret. There are also two causes for its incorporation: *endocryptic* identification (Abraham & Torok 1994) and pathological accommodation (Brandchaft, Doctors & Sorter 2010). In both cases, however, we find there is actually only one real cause of its incorporation: a traumatic experience caused by the incorporated. This traumatic experience is the secret: the pain that haunts the astral, social, or global body.

Whether a *jinn* becomes an *endocryptic* incorporation or an accommodative incorporation, if it is not exorcised in the first generation it will become a phantom for all succeeding generations until it is. In this instance the godbody must try to avoid, verbally and non-verbally, using ideas like "you should do this" or "you should stop that" in the definitive sense of the words. This is because such terminology is not based on the self-demarcation of their own astral or social body but on the imposed demarcations of the godbody, and such demarcations, being provided by the godbody, may end up only reinforcing instances of pathological accommodation.

VI

This all effectively bringing us to the crux of the situation: based on an in-depth hauntology (Derrida 2006) of the Black Charismatic movement it is my diagnosis that there is a spook that currently haunts the Black Charismatic movement, creating in those that practice it psychotic symptoms that they are unable to recognise. Why are the Black Charismatics in this state? What is the spook currently haunting them collectively? Firstly, the spook currently haunting them is a "lying spirit in the mouth of all [their] prophets" (1 Kings 22: 22) that they call the "Holy Spirit." Secondly, it has a secret that is known unconsciously by the devout Black Charismatics but hidden for fear of the consequence of its exposure. What is this secret? That we people of the Black diaspora are the real and original Hebrews and that the Bible was written by our Black ancestors for us and about us.

This secret becomes evident when one reads concerning the Children of Israel a foreshadowing of Black suffering:

> *If thou wilt not observe to do all the words of this law that are written in this book, that thou mayest fear this glorious and fearful name, THE LORD THY GOD; Then the*

Lord will make thy plagues wonderful, and the plagues of thy seed, even great plagues, and of long continuance, and sore sicknesses, and of long continuance. Moreover he will bring upon thee all the diseases of Egypt, which thou wast afraid of; and they shall cleave unto thee. Also every sickness, and every plague, which is not written in the book of this law, them will the Lord bring upon thee until thou be destroyed. And ye shall be left few in number, whereas ye were as the stars of heaven for multitude; because thou wouldest not obey the voice of the Lord thy God.

And it shall come to pass, that as the Lord rejoiced over you to do you good, and to multiply you; so the Lord will rejoice over you to destroy you, and to bring you to nought; and ye shall be plucked from off the land whither thou goest to possess it. And the Lord shall scatter thee among all people, from the one end of the earth even unto the other; and there thou shalt serve other gods, which neither thou nor thy fathers have known, even wood and stone.

And among these nations shalt thou find no ease, neither shall the sole of thy foot have rest: but the Lord shall give thee there a trembling heart, and failing of eyes, and sorrow of mind: And thy life shall hang in doubt before thee; and thou shalt fear day and night, and shalt have none assurance of thy life: In the morning thou shalt say, Would God it were even! and at even thou shalt say, Would God it were morning! for the fear of thine heart wherewith thou shalt fear, and for the sight of thine eyes which thou shalt see. And the Lord shall bring thee into Egypt again with ships, by the way whereof I spake unto thee, Thou shalt see it no more again: and there ye shall be sold onto your enemies for bondmen and bondwomen, and no man shall buy you (Deuteronomy 28: 58-68).

It could easily be asked: Why is it that death seems to haunt Black communities? Disease ravishes Black communities far worse than all other communities, including high blood pressure, HIV/AIDS, and COVID-19. Black-on-Black murder partners with White-on-Black Negricide to produce an almost genocidal reality in Black communities. Unhealthy attitudes towards food, alcohol, and narcotics plague our communities far worse than most other communities. And, finally, we Blacks have in our history the horror of being brought by ships into slavery, and thus share among ourselves the self-identity of former slaves.

All these realities exist only for Black people and not for any other race, including the Ashkenazi, therefore it is very likely that the Israel prophesied about in this Scripture, and in all other Scriptures, was Black and has always been Black. The exposure of this secret can bring astral crisis to the spooks oppressing the Black Charismatics for four reasons: (i) It is too hard to validate the truth behind it. (ii) It means that *our* ancestors betrayed and murdered their own Messiah; and to cover over it we have been projecting the betrayal onto the Ashkenazi saying that their ancestors were the perpetrators. (iii) It means that Israel has a lot more in common with Ham than has been appreciated historically. (iv) It means that White people are not the real Israel and never were, therefore everything we have believed about the White Jesus has been based on a lie.

Concerning the first fear, "Mendelssohn points out that 'Egypt may be regarded as the cradle of the Jewish race, and in all probability it has never been without a Hebrew or Jewish population since the days when Joseph and his brethren laid the foundation of the nation. In all the other countries of Northern Africa, the Jewish population has resulted from a later immigration'" (Williams 1928: 258). Margolis and Marx continued the argument, stating: "It was the poorest sort of Jews that took up their abode in the Delta. The Jewish settlement in Egypt was destined to become a center rivalling Babylonia, but the Jews had commenced to drift into the land of the Pharaohs at a much earlier period. The constant relations with Egypt since the rise of the Libyan dynasty in the times of Solomon, especially the trade in horses, led to many a Jew settling in that country" (Margolis & Marx 1927; quoted in Williams 1928: 262).

What we see therefore is that there was most likely as many Jews in Egypt as there was in Babylonia during its ancient history. Again, this Jewish population in Egypt grew substantially during the days of the Neo-Babylonian Empire, whereby Jeremiah prophesied to the Jews of that time, saying:

> *Therefore thus saith the Lord of hosts, the God of Israel; Behold, I will set my face against you for evil, and to cut off all Judah. And I will take the remnant of Judah, that have set their faces to go into the land of Egypt to sojourn there, and they shall all be consumed, and fall in the land of Egypt; they shall even be consumed by the sword and by the famine: they shall die, from the least even unto the greatest, by the sword and by the famine: and they shall be an execration, and an astonishment, and a curse, and a reproach. For I will punish them that dwell in the land of Egypt, as I have punished Jerusalem, by the sword, by the famine, and by the pestilence (Jeremiah 44: 11-13).*

Moreover, as the Jewish historian Philo stated during the days of the Roman Empire about this Jewish community in Egypt: "the city [of Alexandria in Egypt] had two classes of inhabitants, our own [Jewish] nation and the people of the country [Egypt], and … the whole of Egypt was inhabited in the same manner, and [the] Jews who inhabited Alexandria and the rest of the country from the Catabathmos on the side of Libya to the boundaries of Ethiopia were not less than a million of men" (Philo 2016: 728). Effectively noting that the Jews who fled to Egypt during the days of Jeremiah and the Neo-Babylonian Empire had grown to over a million people by the time of the early Roman Empire.

Williams further continued the story, explaining, "If then, we might be allowed a conjecture as to the ultimate fate of the Judaeans who took refuge in Egypt in 586 B.C. we would suggest that possibly, after a series of migrations of their own, they eventually lost their identity in the Jewish settlements of Egypt, and that these in turn, at least in part, migrated further and further inland, ever carrying with them their perverted and divided worship of Yahweh, and gradually through intermarriage with the natives came to exercise a widespread influence in many parts of Africa, as for example possibly among the Songhois" (Williams 1928: 291). C. K. Meek also said on the subject, "It is quite probable that [these] Songhai did find their way from Egypt to the western Sudan about the time of the first Arab invasions of North Africa" (Meek 1925; quoted in Williams 1928: 302) and of these Songhai Williams (1928: 291) also stated how, "P. Amaury Talbot ... added his testimony: 'The mass of the Songhai,' he says, 'are certainly negroes, though there is little doubt that their ruling families had a strain of Hamitic or even Semitic blood.'"

One can even trace the steps of the Songhai as they travelled from East to West Africa. According to Comte René le More, "One traces back the foundation of Gao to the year 640. It is thought that it was built by the Songhois emigrants come from the banks of the Nile and fleeing from the Arab invasion which at this period had laid waste its borders" (le More 1913; quoted in Williams 1928: 302). As Williams continued on, "[Felix] Dubois has further reconstructed for us the probable line of march of the Songhois, as follows: 'The route taken by the emigrants, keeping south of the Libyan desert, passing by Agades and north of Lake Chad, would meet the Niger somewhere near Gao. They would naturally follow the outskirts of the desert, as the line of less dense population would be the least likely to impede progress. In this manner they would reach the Niger, in spite of the enormous tract of land to be covered, in a comparatively short time'" (Williams 1928: 301).

So now, if we consider that, of the conservatively speaking still one million Jews living in Egypt in the 7th century CE, most of them fled the Arab invasions and went deeper into the heart of the African continent, then the story becomes clear. What we learn from this is that the "continuous influx of Jewish colonists, trekking up the Nile ... [and spreading] ... clear across Africa to the Niger, and thence over pretty much the whole of West Africa" (Williams 1928: 36) began around about the time of the early Arab invasion of Egypt.

So the question now becomes: if the Songhai were Judean why did they worship the God N'debi and not the God Djahwe? The answer becomes apparent when one considers, first of all, that languages are a very fluid substance. They morph and change with time and location. Etymologically, for example, many Hebrew words came from Egypt. The Egyptians, however, did not have the letter L in their alphabet, therefore the Egyptian R became the Hebrew L sometimes. So words like *harel*, which translates as both altar and mountain of God, clearly came from the Egyptian *harara*, which also meant mountain of God. Or, as *mala* in Hebrew means fill, accomplish, and satisfy so *mara-t* in Egyptian meant fill and satisfy. Indeed, the Hebrew name Jonah went through a great etymological transformation, whereby to the Greeks he was called Ionas and to the Arabs he is called Yunus.

Names can change based on geography and generation. Even so with the Judeans. As they mingled with the so-called Negroes of West Africa their race and culture became creolised and produced the Songhai people, language, and culture. The name N'debi therefore very likely came from the word *dabar*, which is Hebrew for *word*, as in, "the Word of the Lord"; and as Williams also stated, "the prefix N, ... would imply that it is a collective noun" (Williams 1928: 76), an etymology practiced throughout

West Africa. Thus, we see that the Songhai worshipped a God with the plural form of the name Word.

Furthermore, "Edrisi, speaking of Lamlam, [from] whence slaves were dragged into captivity by the inhabitants of Ghana, Tacour, [and elsewhere:] states that there were only two towns in this district which he places to the south of the kingdom of Ghana, and adds: 'According to what the people of this country report, the inhabitants are Jews, but for the most part they are plunged in impiety and ignorance. When they have reached the age of puberty they brand the countenance or at least the temples with fire. This is with marks that serve to identify them." "This Jewish Kingdom of Ghana, asserting as it did the mastery over the greater part of Negro Land, must have had a widespread influence on Negro customs and manners almost to the Coast of Guinea" (Williams 1928: 234, 327). Of which location, John Ogilby also stated, "Many Jews also are scattered over this region; some Natives, boasting themselves of Abraham's seed, inhabiting both sides of the River Niger" (Ogilby 1679; quoted in Williams 1928: 292).

Again, this Jewish Kingdom of Ghana spoken of here is not the Republic of Ghana founded in 1957 but the empire of Ghana founded long before the Arab invasion of Egypt. Not to mention the Fulani, who were believed (by the mostly White) International African Institute (1959) to have definitively been Judean. And as most Nigerians know of the Ebos – so called because the Europeans who met them believed (correctly) that they were Hebrews (Bruder 2012). Not to mention the Bayajidda legend of the Hausa which gives a Judean origin to them (Lange 2012). All these reports go far in showing that the migration of the Judeans out of Canaan land led many of them, first into Egypt, and then from Egypt into the interior of Africa, even as far as West Africa.

But such a migration of the Judeans should not be surprising to anyone who has read the Bible with an open mind, for we read in Zephaniah how, "From beyond the rivers of Ethiopia my suppliants, even the daughter of my dispersed, shall bring mine offering. In that day shalt thou not be ashamed for all thy doings, wherein thou hast transgressed against me" (Zephaniah 3: 10, 11). If it was predicted that Israel would be dispersed beyond the rivers of Ethiopia, what is beyond the rivers of Ethiopia but the interior of Africa? Moreover, these Judeans in the interior of Africa would, again, most likely be Black people.

As to the second fear, it could now possibly be said that our current humiliation as Black people is a result of our ancestors' rejection of one of the most revolutionary teachers of the message of *tawhid*. Indeed, the very Messiah they had been hoping and praying for. Therefore, it could be said, both we and they are now currently under the curse of God. But what does the Bible say, "Christ hath redeemed us from the curse of the law, being made a curse for us: for it is written, Cursed is every one that hangeth on a tree" (Galatians 3: 13). To be fair, Israel's curse of a return to slavery should have all been abolished at the Messiah's sacrifice, who – "having forgiven you all trespasses; Blotting out the handwriting of ordinances that was against us, which was contrary to us, and took it out of the way, nailing it to his cross" (Colossians 2: 13, 14) – had set us free. But, how was the curse of the law really taken away at the cross?

It is written in the Scriptures, "And if a man have committed a sin worthy of death, and he be to be put to death, and thou hang him on a tree: His body shall not remain all night upon the tree, but thou shalt in any wise bury him that day; (for he that is hanged is accursed of God;) that thy land be not defiled, which the Lord thy God giveth thee for an inheritance" (Deuteronomy 21: 22, 23). Basically, as Allah looked into the future he could invariably foresee that this would be the main way that Black people would be lynched, so in solidarity with the Black brothers and sisters to be lynched in the future by White people, chose to have our Messiah die this form of death.

He was beaten just like the Black slaves were beaten, he was spit on just like the Black slaves were spit on, he was stripped naked just like the Black slaves were stripped naked, he was humiliated just like the Black slaves were humiliated, he wore chains just like the Black slaves wore chains, he was hung on a tree just like the Black lynched were usually hung on trees, and though he was not castrated like the Black lynched were usually castrated, they did mutilate in his hands and his feet (Cone 2020b). Basically, *he* was one of *us*. Thereby making it understandable for someone to believe at this point that the whole drama of the Black experience with Whites was all really just a somatisation, a concrete re-enactment, of what our ancestors allowed to happen to their Messiah.

Accordingly, it could very well be asked why Allah would choose to have our Messiah go through this form of death at all. He could have easily been beheaded: and so shown solidarity with the numerous Europeans who would fall by the guillotine. He could have easily been fed to wild beasts: and so shown solidarity with most of the martyrs of early Christendom. He could have easily died by the sword: and so shown solidarity with the countless Muslims who died as martyrs by the sword. He could have easily died by being burned to death: and so shown solidarity with the countless bomb and Holocaust victims; and with the torched martyrs of early Protestantism. He could have easily died by the bow: and so shown solidarity with the countless Asian and gun crime victims who died from being shot to death. Allah, in his infinite wisdom and foresight, chose to let our Messiah die as the Black lynched would die, being hung on a tree so as to show and prove that the Messiah was very much so a Black man.

Allah executed this not so as to completely take away the curse of Moses. Indeed, our ancestors of that time said, "His blood be on us, and on our children" (Matthew 27: 25). But he executed this to take away the sting of the curse of Moses. In fact, the most common means of executing religious or political rebels and revolutionaries in the land of Israel during those times was by stoning, yet had the Messiah actually died by stoning, true, it would have connected him to the countless Blacks who die a violent death, but it would have been an indictment against other Blacks and not against a White power structure that takes pleasure in the destruction Black bodies.

Still, this now opens up the obvious question of surrogacy in the Black struggle (Williams 2013). The fact that Allah chose for the Messiah to die this way, and that the Messiah accepted it, could be translated to mean Allah intends for all Black people, and particularly Black women, to be surrogates for White people in their suffering. That Black people must suffer for, and endure the persecution of, White people because such is "Christlike." This is an argument many womanists will definitely have a problem with. So what is the answer? This is where godbodyism becomes very helpful. In godbody theory the Messiah is no more God than any other Original man, therefore it is not necessary for us to imitate our Messiah in order for us to become God, or even Godlike. We can and should honour our Messiah and what he sacrificed and went through, but we do not have to repeat it, or the slavery, or the lynching. Instead we must seek to avoid them at all costs.

Moreover, it could now be asked: if our suffering was a result of Moses' curse, was there ever any injustice in slavery? Did we just deserve what White people put us through? The answer and solution to this is that the purpose of our suffering was twofold: it was, firstly, to get us to appreciate the genuine affinity we have with our Messiah, and, secondly, like with any somatisation, to get us to acknowledge a secret. That secret is that our distant ancestors participated in the murder of their own Messiah. It is not enough for us to believe in a White Jesus and project his murder onto the Ashkenazi and the Romans; we need to acknowledge our ancestors' own part in his murder. Remember, they said to Pontius Pilate, "His blood be on us, and on our children" (Matthew 27: 25). This is thereby a black mark that we all need to acknowledge and repent of.

But an even more troubling question at this point is: based on what we have considered so far, is it ever right, or, indeed, theological, for Black people to oppose Black oppression, especially considering that it was clearly ordained by Allah as a punishment for our ancestors' betrayal? To this I would say, in the history of the Hebrews there were numerous occurrences of their betrayals and backslidings, yet Allah would still raise some to be judges and some to be prophets from among the people. Their oppression was ordained in that they participated in an act of disobedience to Allah, but whenever they acknowledged their betrayal Allah would always raise up a deliverer.

Black people must therefore fight and oppose oppression (*zulm*) at every turn, but as Cone (1997) also said we must still remember that oppression can come from disobedience, and therefore examine our hearts and minds. Herein lies the difficulty: we must now collectively acknowledge what our ancestors did in murdering their Messiah, feeling a genuine sense of remorse for it, and stop projecting his murder onto White people, believing it was all a part of their history. Indeed, Allah even said through his prophet Hosea, "I will go and return to my place, till they acknowledge their offence, and seek my face" (Hosea 5: 15). We *must* therefore acknowledge that because of our failure to do this we have historically been completely cut off.

It is also written in the Scriptures: "If they shall confess their iniquity, and the iniquity of their fathers, with their trespass which they trespassed against me, and that also they have walked contrary unto me; And that I also have walked contrary unto them, and have brought them into the land of their enemies; if then their uncircumcised hearts be humbled, and they then accept of the punishment of their iniquity: Then will I remember my covenant with Jacob, and also my covenant with Isaac, and also my covenant with Abraham will I remember" (Leviticus 26: 40-42). Our recovery from our historical traumas cannot come about until we do this. We must acknowledge our own betrayal and our ancestors' betrayal, only then will we be free.

Of course there are many within the Black community who may take offence at my claim that Black suffering has come about as a punishment for past betrayals, and ultimately to make us a more perfected people till we become the Divines we were always destined to become. This has been a hot button in Black theology ever since James Cone (1970) first challenged the White establishment with his own version of liberation theology. God, to Cone, must always be on the side of the oppressed, and the proof of this for him was in the Exodus narrative. The fact that God saved slaves was a clue, to Cone, that the God of the Hebrews is a God of liberation. This, however, is a myopic view of the Hebrew God.

Far more common among the people of the Scriptures was them falling into ungodliness, Allah punishing them, and them repenting, *then* Allah would send them a deliverer. Cone focused on the deliverance part as though that was liberation, or as though Allah has to be a God of liberation because he would always deliver the people of Israel, but such was never so. There always had to be an acknowledgment of guilt first, a nationwide acknowledgment of guilt, for the heart of Allah to be turned. Until we acknowledge that our ancestors murdered their Messiah, and acknowledge that the guilt of his blood is, even today, on all of our heads as their descendants, we will continue to be out of favour with Allah.

VII

Let us now move on and consider the third painful fear, as it is an interesting one. Sigmund Freud presented the argument in his book *Moses and Monotheism* "that the man Moses, the liberator and law-giver of the Jewish people, was not a Jew, but an Egyptian. That his name derived from the Egyptian vocabulary had long been observed, though not duly appreciated. [Freud also] added to this consideration the further one that the interpretation of the exposure myth attaching to Moses necessitated the conclusion that he was an Egyptian whom a people needed to make into a Jew. ... [Finally,] important and far-reaching conclusions could be drawn from the suggestion that Moses was an Egyptian" (Freud 2010: 29). These conclusions shall be considered following, however, let us start by saying that it is not problematic that the prophet Moses should be considered an Egyptian, or even that the Hebrew people should be considered Black, as we have known for centuries which section of the world they happen to be found in. Moreover, based on this interpretation, the prophet Moses being an Egyptian that liberated the Hebrews should be considered no more troublesome than an Afro-Brazilian of our time rising up to liberate the Black people of America.

Consequently, the first conclusion that Freud drew from the idea that the prophet Moses was an Egyptian was through understanding the fact that, "The Jewish people in Egypt were certainly not without some kind of religion, and if Moses, who gave them a new religion, was an Egyptian, then the surmise cannot be rejected that this other new religion was the Egyptian one" (Freud 2010: 31). But now the question could be asked: which Egyptian religion was it, as the ancient Egyptians had several religions? To find it we can, firstly, speak of the God Amen as the historical Moses was a *Sebi* in the Order of Amun; and Amen is also, to this day, a recognised word in the Hebrew language – though obviously distorted from its original Egyptian meaning. Another is the tradition of the Aton or Adjon, as this was also a God worshipped during the time of the prophet Moses, and is also recognised as a God to the Jewish people, though without the symbolic iconography, as Adon or Adonai.

All that said, here is where it becomes quite interesting: the Egyptian religion the prophet Moses most likely introduced the Hebrew people to has only one real potential candidate: that of the God Djehwti. Djehuti or Djehwti, if we take out the t, becomes Djehwi very easily; and this was an obvious way the Hebrew people expressed their God. Djehwti also definitely makes a great God figure for the Hebrew people as he was the God of wisdom, law, writing, mathematics, the crescent moon, and the spoken word. Furthermore, *Dj* in the ancient Egyptian Medu Neteru translated to word or speech, and when it combined with *heh* it would have produced Djeh or Djah meaning the eternal word. Also the ancient Egyptian word *wa* meant one, only, and alone; thereby Djahwe could translate from the Medu Neteru to produce "The Word of the Eternal One."

So the Hebrew people most likely started out as a sect in ancient Egypt that followed the Shetaut Djehwti, who, as we have noted, was the grandmaster of all the ancient sciences. Here are some further proofs of this matter: Firstly, in the Hebrew tradition their cosmogony is very similar to that of Net Djehwti, as it says in their Scriptures, "In the beginning God created the heaven and the earth. And the earth was without form, and void; and darkness was upon the face of the deep. And the Spirit of God moved upon the face of the waters" (Genesis 1:1, 2). As should be obvious to most people by now: these four principles of formlessness, void, darkness, and spirit are the same four principles that existed in the cosmogony of Net Djehwti. The prophet Moses would have therefore learned this tradition from nowhere else but the *Sebis* of Net Djehwti.

Secondly, when "Moses gave the Jews … a new religion; it is equally certain that he introduced the custom of circumcision" to them (Freud 2010: 43). The custom of circumcision was practiced by the priesthoods of Kemet many centuries before the time of Moses, as Freud continued, "The fact remains that the question concerning the origin of circumcision has only one answer: it comes from Egypt. Herodotus, 'the Father of History,' tells us that the custom of circumcision had long been practised in Egypt, and his statement has been confirmed by the examination of mummies and even by drawings on the walls of graves. No other people of the Eastern Mediterranean has – as far as we know – followed this custom; we can assume with certainty that the Semites, Babylonians and Sumerians were not circumcised" (Freud 2010: 44). The fact is, the priests of Kemet had been practicing circumcision for thousands of years before Abram introduced it to his people, therefore he most likely also learned it from the *Sebis* of Kemet while he was in Kemet during his many travels.

Still, before we go any further down this rabbit hole we must also remember: the Hebrew Bible is a collection of works written by several different authors. First, Genesis, and possibly Leviticus, were most likely written by the prophet Moses himself. Then Exodus, Numbers, Joshua, and Ruth were most likely written and added to the Bible during the days of King David and King Solomon along with various Psalms, Songs, Proverbs, and teachings. Then it was rewritten again during the days of King Hezekiah and the Neo-Assyrian Empire, as well as the adding of certain other books including some by various prophets. Then it was rewritten again during the days of the prophet Jeremiah and the Neo-Babylonian Empire, as well as the adding of Deuteronomy, the four books of Kings, the two books of Chronicles, and a few more prophets. Then, during the days of the prophet Ezra and the Neo-Persian Empire, it was rewritten again with the addition of the last few prophets and a little more history. Finally, all these books were Hellenised during the days of the Maccabean revolt and the Hasmonean Dynasty. Therefore, "The Mosaic religion we know [today] only in its final form as it was fixed by Jewish priests in the time after the Exile" (Freud 2010: 41).

The Hebraic movement itself started out as the philosophy of the prophet Abram, a Chaldean prophet of around about the sixteenth or seventeenth century BCE. The prophet Abram, to perfect his own philosophy, ventured into Kemet where he would have learned of the custom of circumcision from the *Sebis* of Kemet. The prophet Abram would have also learned several Egyptian Yoga practices, such as, the *sesh* (yogic stretchings) and *khentu* (tai chi) techniques, to stay young in old age while he was in Kemet. Sema Tawi, Egyptian Yoga proper, had various other facets too, such as: *sesenti* (meditation), *hekau* (magic words), *baau* (kundalini training), *usert* (physical training), and *montu-kha* (martial training) that the prophet Abram very likely also learned while he was in Kemet, and that he incorporated into his original Hebraic vision. The knowledge of all this must have shamed the prophet Ezra who saw gods like Djehtwi as false gods and so removed the t from all instances of his name in the Masoretic text he compiled.

Yet there is a slight problematic with the idea that Djahwe is in fact Djehwti: in Exodus we read how, "Pharaoh said, Who is the Lord, that I should obey his voice to let Israel go? I know not the Lord, neither will I let Israel go" (Exodus 5: 2). Surely, if the prophet Moses said Israel sought to follow Djehwti then the Pharaoh would have known exactly who he was and would have granted them leave? Here we can see that the words written in Exodus as having come from the Pharaoh were most likely edited in by a future writer who himself knew nothing of the Egyptian God Djehwti. Basically, the moment the prophet Moses said the God guiding the Hebrews was the God Djehwti the Pharaoh should have instantly known who he was but refused to believe that Djehwti would really be on the side of slaves. Again, the editing and rewriting that took place in the Masoretic text means that many truths have been lost to us, however, the real Pharaoh most definitely did not utter that particular sentence from Exodus 5: 2 for he would have known exactly who Djehwti was.

That said, Djehwti, like Hermes, was actually a secondary figure in the ancient Kemetic pantheon; so the prophet Moses very unlikely ever really taught the ancient Hebrew people that Djehwti was the Most High God. Yet, was not Djehwti, or the Angel of Djehwti, what appeared to him in the burning bush? Hereby we have a deeper understanding of the actual meaning of the Angel of the Lord. Just as the Prince Angel Gabriel (Jibril) appeared to several prophets to help guide them towards the truth, so the Prince Angel Djahwe (the Angel of the Lord) appeared to the prophet Moses as a guide for him towards the truth. So if the prophet Moses always saw Djahwe as only an astral being (whether angelic or *jinni*) and not as the true and living God; who did he really see as the true and living God? And what was his true message to the Hebrew people?

The clue to this can be found in the unifying and universal religion of ancient Kemet, the religion of Pa Neter. As mentioned, within this religion was the fundamental tenet *Pa Neter wa wa Neb-er-Tcher m Neteru* (the God, only one Lord of all, manifests as gods and goddesses). This principle and tenet is similar to, though not the same as, *La ilaha il al-wahad Rabbi alamin* (there is no god but the one Lord of all worlds). Basically, the prophet Moses was bought up and raised in a culture that was originally very *tawhidi* but had ultimately lost its way. Conversely, Moses' call to prophethood was initially to bring the Pharaoh back to the authentic religion of his ancestors; and to guide the Hebrew people toward the concept and person of Pa Neter, which was the ancient Egyptian equivalent of the concept and person of Allah.

Essentially, the Hebraic movement the prophet Moses led and instigated was a noble movement, inspired by Allah, with the central intent of restoring that authentic culture of monism to the world. True indeed, anyone who actually, genuinely does their research will find that the proper Semitic/Falashic name for God given by Abraham at the very beginning was actually the very familiar name Allah. Moreover, the proper Hebrew name for God given in the Masoretic Bible – the supposedly most authentic Bible – was never properly Elohim. Elohim in the Hebrew language being a plural for God, as in, gods. Yet even if we now say, alright, maybe a correct translation or transliteration should probably be Elah; again, clearly even in this compromise we can still find a distortion. The truth is, the proper name for God in the Hebrew Bible has always been, and will always be, Allah.

Furthermore, during the days of the New Testament: when the Baptist and the Messiah spoke to the people in the common language, which was neither Hebrew nor Greek, the actual common language of the Israeli and Judean states of the time was Aramaic, which is itself a completely different Semitic language. Here, Aramaic is a language still spoken in Palestine even to this day by various Palestinian/Arab Christians; and again, what is the name they use in Aramaic for God? It must be accepted today as Allah. Effectively, the original and enduring message of the *Nebi* (prophet) Moses was the same message as that of all the prophets: the message of *tawhid*. Therefore, the historical Moses was most likely to have been both an Egyptian *Sebi* and a Hebrew *Nebi* who taught theocentric-monism to the Hebrew people in the name of the Angel (god) of Djehwti. From this beginning, all succeeding Hebrew prophets (*nebis*) would also speak in the name of Djehwti, but the concept and person they all spoke of and led people to, was always, even in the original Hebrew, the concept and person of Allah.

Consequently, even when the Angel of Djehwti walked before the prophet Moses he revealed the truth to him: "And the Lord passed by before him, and proclaimed, The Lord, The Lord God, merciful and gracious, long-suffering, and abundant in goodness and truth, Keeping mercy for thousands, forgiving iniquity and transgression and sin, and that will by no means clear the guilty; visiting the iniquity of the fathers upon the children, and upon the children's children, unto the third and to the fourth generation" (Exodus 34: 6, 7). This theme would even continue with most of the other early Hebrew prophets, as the prophet David also said, "The Lord is merciful and gracious, slow to anger, and plenteous in mercy. He will not always chide: neither will he keep his anger for ever." Even so, the prophet Jonah continued, "Therefore I fled before unto Tarshish: for I knew that thou art a gracious God, and merciful, slow to anger, and of great kindness, and repentest thee of the evil" (Psalms 103: 8, 9; Jonah 4: 2). The concept in these Scriptures used for God was again the word Allah.

So, by the time we got to the prophet Ezra translation of the Bible (the Masoretic text), he very likely removed the t from the name Djehwti, seeing Djehwti as an Egyptian god – thus officially changing the name of Djehwti to Djahwe in all post-exilic texts. But even in spite of the name change the concept and person of Allah remained the same. The Levites during the post-exilic times continued the legacy, saying, "but thou art a God ready to pardon, gracious and merciful, slow to anger, and of great kindness, and forsookest them not" (Nehemiah 9: 17). Moreover, the theme and revelation of God was even able to continue into the days of the early messianic movement, where the evangelist Timothy said to the believers of his time, "Let us therefore come boldly unto the throne of grace, that we may obtain mercy, and find grace to help in time of need" (Hebrews 4: 16). In this Scripture he was clearly speaking of the same basic concept. Thus the same God who revealed himself through the Hebrew prophets was thus still at work in the early messianic movement.

Then, finally, by the time we reached the days of the Prophet Muhammad God's final revelation was ready to be given, "In the name of Allah, the Beneficent, the Merciful. Whatever is in

405

the heavens and the earth declares the glory of Allah, and He is the Mighty, the Wise. His is the kingdom of the heavens and the earth. He gives life and causes death; and He is Possessor of power over all things. He is the First and the Last and the Manifest and the Hidden, and He is Knower of all things" (Quran 57: 1-3). Basically, there has always been a continuity occurring historically: from the ancient Egyptian concept of Pa Neter, to the ancient Hebrew concept of Allah, to the early messianic concept of the *Theos*, back to the modern Islamic concept of Allah. Herein the Lord God of the holy prophets has been without change in spite of a few name changes. Indeed, the same Pa Neter who revealed himself to the prophet Moses through the Prince Angel Djehwti is the same Allah who revealed himself to the Prophet Muhammad through the Prince Angel Gabriel.

Now with regard to the fourth fear of the Black Charismatic: those Black Charismatics that currently cry injustice to the Whites and those that in contradistinction identify with the aggressor are both in many cases haunted by either the *jinni* of their ancestors, or by the *jinn* of a White Jesus. Indeed, the Christ most often seen on the walls of churches all over the world is derived from an artist's rendition of Cesare Borgia, the son of Pope Alexander VI of Rome, during the Renaissance. Prior to that time the paintings of the Messiah were always Black, bronze, or darkened to some extent. Since the Renaissance the Messiah's future paintings have been of a White man and all his previous paintings have been remastered and repainted White so as to keep up the illusion. Here the *jinn* of the White Jesus, Cesare Borgia, haunts White people just as much as it haunts us Blacks.

Of course, a lot of us Blacks, and particularly the Black Charismatics, tend to be so respectful of all that the Ashkenazi suffered at the hands of the Nazis and various other anti-Ashkenazi groups that we fear them misunderstanding or even despising us for making this suggestion. We do not think that perhaps the Ashkenazi are themselves also haunted by the secret, a secret that their ancestors may have feared being exposed because it would make their love objects – their own ancestors – out to be liars. The secret of the spook is so unspeakable that it haunts both races. To be sure, Deuteronomy is a part of the Torah, therefore it is read by both devout Black Christians and devout Ashkenazi Jews. It either pains both groups like a splinter that the secret might be exposed or they ignore and overlook it being blinded to its meaning by the spook. Either way, the Ashkenazi are just as inhibited by the lie as we are, but, at the same time, they want it hidden just as much as we want it hidden.

This secret is the root of the collective Black Charismatic psychosis and the collective Ashkenazi Jewish neurosis. Though it is true that Professor Poliak (1941), who was the one that published the evidence proving that Ashkenazi Jewishness was the result of the conversion of the tribe of the Khazars in the 8th century, has been discredited post-Holocaust due to the use of his works by those of the White supremacist crowd, that is not to say that his theories were incorrect, just that the misuse of them was. Again, the conversion of the Khazars to the religion of Judaism is not a crime, and the Ashkenazi definitely do not deserve to be persecuted by either Black people or White people for it. They have the right to practice and follow one of our ancient Black cultures should they choose to, the spook is in the detail: they must acknowledge that they are in fact gentile converts that have appropriated one of our cultures in order to be set free.

Nevertheless, because the histories of both the Blacks and the Ashkenazi have been so pernicious it could at this time be said that the Hebrew God proves himself to be either an anti-Semite or an anti-Black racist. Either way it does not look too good for the Hebrew God historically speaking. There is even an

407

unspoken competition between we Blacks and the Ashkenazi over which group has suffered more: the Ashkenazi for being the victims of the exiling, persecuting, pogroming, and the attempted genocide of their people; or the Blacks for being the victims of the enslaving, lynching, segregating, and the colonising of our people.

There is moreover, obviously, one major problem with the Black God/Black Hebrews narrative that glares in our faces every time we try to build any kind of hope in it: the Ashkenazi Holocaust. This one event shook the world and still shakes it to this day. The Blacks who try to reconcile the Black Hebrew theory with the Holocaust either have to deny the Holocaust, and so become horrifically anti-Ashkenazi, or abandon the theory altogether, and so become shamefully over-identified with White people. This creates a paradox: how do we justify the Black Hebrew theory in the face of the Holocaust without resorting to racism and anti-Ashkenazism? Again, what does the Black person say in the presence of the Holocaust? How does a Black person reconcile a Black God with Ashkenazi suffering?

The Holocaust is an historic event that has troubled the mind of many an Ashkenazi, causing them to ultimately reject the religion of Judaism. Indeed, how could they stay faithful to a God who was so deafeningly silent at such an horrific event? Emil Fackenheim had this to say on the subject of the Holocaust:

> *As we have seen, even the ancient rabbis were forced to suspend the biblical 'for our sins we were punished,' perhaps not in response to the destruction of the temple by Titus, but in response to the paganization of Jerusalem by Hadrian. We too may at most only suspend the biblical doctrine, if only because we, no more than the rabbis, dare either to deny our own sinfulness or to disconnect it from history. Yet, suspend it we must. For however we twist and turn this doctrine in response to Auschwitz, it becomes a*

religious absurdity and even a sacrilege. Are 'sin' and 'retribution' to be given an individual connotation? What a sacrilegious thought when among the Nazi's victims were more than one million children! Are we to give them a collective connotation? What an appalling idea when it was not our western, agnostic, faithless, and rich but rather the poorest, most pious and most faithful Jewish communities which were most grievously stricken! As in our torment we turn, as an ultimate resort, to the traditional doctrine that all Israelites of all generations are responsible for each other, we are still totally aghast, for not a single one of the six million died because they failed to keep the divine-Jewish covenant: they all died because their great-grand-parents had kept it, if only to the minimum extent of raising Jewish children. Here is the point where we reach radical religious absurdity. Here is the rock on which the 'for our sins are we punished' suffers total shipwreck" (Fackenheim 1970; quoted in Katz 2008: 27).

There is a temptation to view the suffering of the Ashkenazi as proof of their calling and election from Allah and not as divine chastisement, however, Katz (2008) was not deceived by this in any ways. Knowing the history of the Jews from Scripture Katz could see that the Hebrew God would always chastise those he wanted to teach. So what was Allah trying to teach the Ashkenazi that merited such a loud and tragic occurrence as the Holocaust? Indeed, the arguments of William R. Jones and Anthony B. Pinn are that God reveals himself as racist no matter how you look at it, therefore the best thing we can do is just abandon the God-concept altogether and adopt a more anthropocentric, and, indeed, humanist, approach to seeing life.

While I agree that the histories of the Blacks and the Ashkenazi have both been horrific and grotesque I do not believe that is to be blamed on the Hebrew God, let alone on some "divine racism" (Jones 1998) as such. This is only "divine racism" if we prioritise Allah's omnipotence like most Sunni schools of theology do. However, if we take his omnipotence to be based on supersensory interactivity then we can see that he had no part in any of our sufferings but, in fact, identifies with all our sufferings. This kind of non-coercive omnipotence can be seen in his dealings with the Hebrew people throughout the Scriptures. He encourages, questions, challenges, and demands but never forces. The sufferings of the Ashkenazi can thus be explained not as desired by Allah but as planned and foreseen by Allah to chastise them.

But now we come to the question of: for what reason were they chastised so harshly? And again, why was it the religious and pious Ashkenazi that were the victims of the Holocaust, and so many other tragic events in Jewish history? The answer here is found in the secret. Allah has no problem with them being Jews, but he does have a problem with them believing they are the original and authentic Jews, the Hebrews of old. This deception has caused White people to believe the Messiah is White and the apostles were White and that it is okay to commit great atrocities around the world for the sake of their Whiteness. This deception has also caused Black people to worship two White men believing them to be Gods and to despise their own kind believing themselves to be inferior. The deception has furthermore blinded the whole world to the truth about Allah, and the Messiah, and the real Hebrew people.

At the same time, I repeat, Allah was not the cause of the Holocaust but felt the pain of the Holocaust, having "no part in any of our sufferings but, in fact, [identifying] with all our sufferings" (Islam 2024: 409). Still, a large amount of White people may now fear these ideas because they mean that their ancestors held in slavery the very people they have admired and studied for over fifteen hundred years. They also mean that vengeance is coming for them for putting the real Hebrew people through a historical slavery. As is written in the oracle of the prophet Obadiah, "For the day of the Lord is near upon all the heathen: as thou hast done, it shall be done unto thee; thy reward shall return upon thine own head" and in Deuteronomy, "Rejoice, O ye nations, with his people: for he will avenge the blood of his servants, and will render vengeance to his adversaries, and will be merciful unto his land, and to his people" (Obadiah 1: 15; Deuteronomy 32: 43). White people fear vengeance awaiting them, therefore in the hopes of preventing it they tell themselves that the blood of their White Jesus will save them from any bad karma and will free them from all unrighteousness.

But remember, the White Jesus they exalted from the time of the Renaissance, in order to justify their conquering and dominating various indigenous peoples: whether in Africa, Asia, Australia, or the Americas, was most likely a *jinn*. From that time to this good Christian people have committed all of the greatest atrocities in human history believing that they are his servants. No one empire or people have committed the amount or gravity of criminal actions that faithful Christians have committed from the time of the Renaissance in service to their White Jesus. From the terror and inhumanity of the slave trade; to the death and brutality of slavery; to the conquering and genocide of the Native and Meso-Americans; to the torture and murder of Protestants during the Reformation; to the torture and murder of Catholics during the Counter-Reformation; to the blood spilled during the revolutionary wars of Europe and America; to the colonial conquests of Africa, Asia, and Australia; to the barbarity and racism of the European empires; to the deaths and tragedies of World War I; to the deaths and tragedies of World War II and the Holocaust; to the segregating and lynching of the African diaspora; to the legality and corruption of apartheid South Africa; to the mercilessness and madness of Christians killing Christians in Latin America, Ghetto America, and all over the African continent; all the way to the raping and humiliating of indigenous women and children all over the world. All these crimes were committed in service to and with the historical appreciation of the White Jesus.

Effectively, whether the White Jesus actively inspired these historical crimes or simply passively observed them, he still benefited from them substantially. Today, all over the world people of all races, creeds, and ethnicities worship, fear, and adore a White man that they believe to be sinless, blameless, and completely innocent of all the crimes committed for his sake and with his blessing. Indeed, the fact of the matter, for all us non-White people, is: not only is the White Jesus actively fighting against us, but in all actuality he most definitely hates us, has always hated us, and will never stop hating us. He only uses and manipulates us so that we will worship and serve his cause; but in reality we non-White people are most likely a joke to him considering all his crimes against us historically and to this day.

Indeed, the problem, the great tragedy of history, is that if all those crimes and atrocities committed since the Renaissance by good Christian people were actually motivated by a living, thinking, and intelligent force; then that would make that force the biggest monster and criminal in the history of the world, which uses the cloak of sinlessness, blamelessness, and godhood to hide all his evils. Not only so, but he would also, most likely be, the very arch-nemesis of the actual historical Messiah. There will therefore be no man coming (Anti-Christ) who could possibly commit any atrocities worse than those already committed by this White Jesus *jinn*, if we appreciate that this *jinn* is a thinking, feeling, and intelligent force.

Moreover, it says in the Scriptures concerning the actual Anti-Christ, "And he opened his mouth in blasphemy against God, to blaspheme his name, and his tabernacle, and them that dwell in heaven. And it was give unto him to make war with the saints, and to overcome them: and power was given him over all kindreds, and tongues, and nations. And all that dwell upon the earth shall worship him, whose names are not written in the book of life of the Lamb slain from the foundation of the world" (Revelation 13: 6-8). Yet while no true Charismatic would ever believe that the White Jesus was in fact the Beast of Revelation, or that him calling himself God or the son of God was blasphemy, if the White Jesus was in fact a *jinn* and not the historical Jesus that died on the cross, then even the Charismatics cannot deny that when it says "all that dwell upon the earth shall worship him," such is fulfilled, and will likely only be fulfilled, by none other.

No doubt, it is unlikely that any Charismatic would be convinced simply by the fact that billions of people all over the world worship a White Jesus that that makes the White Jesus the Anti-Christ, nor by the fact that all the greatest atrocities committed from the time of the Renaissance to this very day were committed for his sake by people who believed themselves to be obeying his will. Indeed, to them Jesus is God, he is on the throne now, and he was on the throne then, patiently waiting for humanity to stop rebelling. However, it is also written concerning the Anti-Christ, "Let no man deceive you by any means: for that day shall not come, except there come a falling away first, and that man of sin be revealed, the son of perdition; Who opposeth and exalteth himself above all that is called God, or that is worshipped; so that he as God sitteth in the temple of God, shewing himself that he is God" (2Thessalonians 2: 3, 4). And again, "Know ye not that ye are the temple of God, and that the Spirit of God dwelleth in you" (1Corinthians 3: 16). If the historical Messiah was really a White man then it makes no difference that at a certain moment in history the Catholic Church began painting him White instead of the standard bronze, because the temple of God would have effectively been cleansed. But if the historical Messiah was in fact, both physically and biologically, a Black man, then the White Jesus is in fact a *jinn* that not only currently sits in the temple of God, mocking the true and living God, but he exalts himself, and has historically exalted himself, above all gods, making him the most likely Anti-Christ.

At the same time, if the White Jesus *jinn* is in actual fact the Anti-Christ then what of the Holy Spirit, all the glory felt in the presence of the Christian God, and all the miracles worked in so many Christian's lives to help them get through life's struggles. As they say, that Jesus may be a devil but my Jesus is a friend in the times of trouble. "All other ground is sinking sand." The truth is, if the historical Messiah was actually a Black man then *every single White Jesus* is a devil, no matter how many miracles and signs occur at his hand. It is written: "And then shall that Wicked be revealed, whom the Lord shall consume with the spirit of his mouth, and shall destroy with brightness of his coming: Even him, whose coming is after the working of Satan with all power and signs and lying wonders, and with all deceivableness of unrighteousness in them that perish, because they received not the love of the truth, that they might be saved. And for this cause God shall send them strong delusion, that they should believe a lie: That they all might be damned who believed not the truth, but had pleasure in unrighteousness" (2Thessalonians 2: 8-12).

What was effectively being said there was that the deception of the false messiah would be strong, so much so that all the earth would see him as genuinely worthy of being worshipped; genuinely worthy of being called, treated like, and believed to be God; and genuinely worthy of being beloved, admired, and adored; though he is in fact history's greatest monster. What was being said there was also that not only would the false messiah gaslight billions of people all over the world, he would even leave them in a state of delusion, *strong delusion.*

What we should hopefully now realise is that no human being coming in the future can ever fulfil these ideas better than the White Jesus has already fulfilled them. Furthermore, if the White Jesus is, in fact, a *jinn* then that high most modern Charismatics feel when worshipping him – a force that is guilty of such vast horrific acts around the world – could never be based on the actual Holy Spirit but must in fact be based on an ecstatic state reached through chemicals in the brain. In other words, they are literally getting high, only the drug they receive from the White Jesus *jinn* and from worshipping him, does not ruin their brain it ruins their astral body.

They have been sung a lullaby that this *jinn* is God, that he loves them, and that he is the one who died for them; and the thought of such a one, such a God, takes them to ecstasies. But it is not real. None of it is real. Though some may be so addicted to the high of this lying spirit, this strong delusion, that they still believe that there is nothing wrong in God's sight with them worshipping a White Jesus, and in fact that worshipping any Jesus is doing the will of God. Ultimately, because they are unwilling to give up the love they believe he has for them (a love that laid down its life), they would rather go to hell for him to defend him from those who accuse him of such hateful crimes, let alone of actually hating them. Yet, indeed, his hatred of us is of long standing. Not only so, but even his rebellion against the historical Messiah and his future defeat at his hands have also been of long standing.

Long before his rebellion actually took place, long before the historical Messiah was even born, the prophet Isaiah had this to prophesy: "How art thou fallen from heaven, O Lucifer, son of the morning! how art thou cut down to the ground, which didst weaken the nations! For thou hast said in thine heart, I will ascend into heaven, I will exalt my throne above the stars of God: I will sit upon the mount of the congregation, in the sides of the north: I will be like the most High. Yet thou shalt be brought down to hell, to the sides of the pit" (Isaiah 14: 12-15). Most Charismatics currently believe that this rebellion took place in the beginning, before the creation of the world, but if the historical Messiah was in fact a Black man then this Scripture

415

is far better and far more accurately to have been a prophecy fulfilled in the historical rebellion that exalted the *jinn* of the White Jesus to the throne of heaven, thus proving that *jinn* to have been Lucifer all along.

Conversely, many Charismatics may be willing to accept that a false Jesus, of any kind, comes from Lucifer; and that Lucifer hates us, has always hated us, and will never stop hating us; but they may question the racial element to all this. Why is the colour of Jesus' skin so important? Surely, God has never valued such things? That may be true, and there may even still be a last *dajjal* (Anti-Christ figure) who comes in the future to launch an Armageddon Battle of some sort; but such a *dajjal* would most likely only be a false prophet of the Great *Dajjal*, who, as we can see, is in fact Lucifer. Consequently, as the Scriptures explain, "every spirit that confesseth not that Jesus Christ is come in the flesh is not of God: and this is that spirit of antichrist, whereof ye have heard that it should come; and even now already it is in the world" (1John 4: 3). Though, indeed, this Scripture refers mainly to the humanity of the historical Messiah; it cannot be denied that all flesh has a colour, and all flesh has a race. Therefore by giving the historical Messiah the wrong flesh they have thereby denied the *true* flesh of living Messiah and have identified themselves with the Anti-Christ.

True, our generation of White people try not to believe that race really matters to God because such would make God out to be a racist; but they promote this idea while, at the same time, following a White Jesus, who, again, is currently, to this day, still being worshipped around the world by all true Christians as God, son of God, sinless, blameless, innocent in all his ways, lover of humanity, who gave his life for us. So all I have done throughout this chapter is throw this White Jesus *jinn* into astral crisis; for if what has been said so far is in fact true then that means that this spook Jesus is in fact Lucifer, the Anti-Christ, who was the driving force behind all the racist atrocities committed by good Christian people against all non-White people. What this also shows is that since the time of the Renaissance we have all been in the midst of the Great *Fitnah* (Great Tribulation) of the Great *Dajjal*, who in his one-eyed determination to rule over humanity, now does so with the help of a lying spirit. What lying spirit? The spirit of White supremacy.

Of course this theory only stands if the historical Messiah was non-White, if the historical Messiah really was a White man then all that really happened was that at certain moments in history certain White people have used the name and the glory of Jesus to justify their crimes against humanity. Nevertheless, as James Cone said, "If Jesus Christ [was] white and not black, he is an oppressor, and we must kill him" (Cone 2020a: 117). However, if the historical Messiah was in fact non-White in any way, be it Black, Near Eastern, North African, or Asian, then *every* White Jesus is and has always been the Anti-Christ, who hates us, has always hated us, and will never stop hating us no matter how nice he sounds when he comes to us or how many miracles he works on behalf of us. He and his angels would also effectively be the same ones who actively encouraged, whether through visions or dreams, all the crimes committed today and historically against non-White people since the time of the Renaissance.

Not only so, but even the Holy Spirit he has given us for worshipping him induces in us a high more powerful than any drug, that blinds us to the reality of all his crimes, all his hatred, and all his blasphemies. Again, the actual historical Messiah was far more likely to have been a Black Dread from Galilee who taught holism and monism to the people of Israel through an Injil that has now been lost to history. He would have been then rejected by the people, crucified at their request, for which cause Allah then destroyed the Jerusalem of that time scattering the Judeans of that generation.

417

What we have seen throughout this chapter is a brief social kinetic of the Holy Ghost movement. We have also seen that it may take a Black astralism for the Black Charismatics to understand that true holiness is in the internalisation of refinement, and not in the babbling of nonsense, rolling on the floor, screaming, spontaneous crying, foaming at the mouth, manic hallucinations, identification with the aggressor, inappropriate empathy, weak self-other differentiation, induced ecstasies, or strong delusions. Obviously, it could also be said at this time, "The biblical Hebrews attempted to discredit their more embarrassing prophets by calling them insane, and the social [scientist] who talks of the 'authentic schizoid component' of the religion he is studying is hardly a potential recruit" (Littlewood 2006: 14); but I am not completely adverse to the Black Charismatics, and believe we Gods and Goddesses have failed in our duty to reach out to them as our brothers and sisters. We must always remember as God Allah Shah confirmed, "Nothing is greater [to a Black person] than the knowledge of the Blackman is God" (The Five Percenter Vol 22.7; 2017: 4).

Though I may have admittedly caused a few astral crises in the Black Charismatics it has not been out of viciousness but out of love. Consequently, the most likely reason why most Black Charismatics wander right passed Deuteronomy and several other "Black Scriptures" without ever considering that perhaps the original Hebrews were Black, even though they may have read them several times over, is because a strong delusion has blinded them. They want so hard to avoid the truth that they deny it and say that the Ashkenazi suffer because they are the chosen ones and we Blacks suffer because we are cursed with Ham. Yet if they applied a true hauntology (Derrida 2006) of the Holy Spirit to their history, whether understood pneumato-logically or existentially, they would see that he is in fact a lying *jinn* that is currently haunting them, not as an internalisation of the true Messiah but as the incorporation of a spook messiah given power by the secret.

All that notwithstanding, as we enter the age of iGod a revolution is coming. Not a revolution in politics but a revolution in our minds. The Black theologian must now show their Charismatic brothers and sisters that there are no real demons haunting them only unnatural forces that we call *jinni*. These *jinni* are neither good nor evil, they are merely incorporated superegos that motivate or inhibit behaviours. So we can see clearly from all this that a truly demystified demonology is that White people are the only real devils in the world, and that the White Jesus is in fact Lucifer. Whether we say White people only became devils after the time of the Renaissance, when they began following Lucifer; or we say White people have always been devils – their history pre-Renaissance is not that sparkling either – the fact remains that White people today are the main *jinni* haunting the minds of the Black Charismatics.

Indeed, the day may come when a Black theologian can ask their Christian brethren, "Do you have knowledge of self?" and from there know whether they have been influenced by the godbody movement or not. If not, the Black theologian must take the same stance with the Black Christian that the intersubjective psychoanalysts take with their patients, "When one is able to become reasonably comfortable in continuing to wonder and pursue the investigation of what is happening, then in the place of the analyst's discomfort in comparisons with what 'should be' and is not taking place, change will frequently emerge. Evidence of such change is for the most part silent, slow, precarious, emergent, and incremental, and it is more likely to occur when it 'just happens' and is not being looked for" (Brandchaft, Doctors & Sorter 2010: 190). Effectively, while there is no problem with someone being Christian and being godbody, or being Muslim and being godbody, such a one must still accept responsibility for their Black brethren and sistren and reveal to them the God that is in their own mirror.

It is herein that they will find a new type of thearchy, one in which all we Black people, being genuine Gods and Goddesses, can actually rule. Not as oppressors of the world to destroy the world; but as caretakers of the world and of the ecology of the world. This will ultimately bring about a truly religionless, pollutionless, stateless, classless, moneyless, marriageless, and pantyless society even as existed in ancient Ta Neteru (the land of the gods and goddesses). Indeed, as Ta Neteru was the only place in history in which there was no oppression on the basis of religion, race, class, gender, sexuality, or ecology, Ta Neteru is thereby the original blueprint for a this Black thearchy.

Conclusion

"37. Tell us why the devil teaches the 85 percent that God is a righteous unseen being that exists everywhere? Allah is God in the earth and the heavens and is just and true and there is no unrighteousness in him. But he is not unseen, for he is seen and heard everywhere, for he is the All-Eye Seeing" (Lost Found Muslim Lesson No. 2).

One may find it strange that a book that has in its subtitle "the Age of iGod" has no serious mention of information technology or the digital revolution (started from the mid-twentieth century onward) within. The author made this decision due to the importance of explaining the consequences of the shift society has been making as a result of the digital revolution. While it may seem that we have very little time now, here at the beginning of the 21st century, to actually redefine any theology, let alone a Black theology; because more young people are beginning to internalise God, the godbody perspective is becoming more and more pertinent. This tendency towards internalising God is the basis of the age of iGod, thereby opening up the door to godbody interpretations and further sophistication.

The godbody theology I teach ultimately presents eight theses of the theophany that I have tried to articulate throughout this book: (i) that Black people are a divine people, (ii) that Black people are civilised by nature, (iii) that Black people are the fathers and mothers of civilisation, (iv) that White people are devils, (v) that it is tricknology that makes White people devils, (vi) that the Black people who use and teach tricknology are vampyres, (vii) that religions and governments are tools of trick knowledge, and (viii) that knowledge of self and of the physical and social sciences are the path to Black Divinity.

There is no doubt in my mind that for this book I will be called bigot, racist, misogynist, and anti-Semite. Nevertheless, I have written it and hope it progresses society and the world towards true empowerment and towards accepting godbodyism as a ghetto theology and ideology. Effectively, there are six core concepts within our godbody ideology: Black divinity, Black revolutionism, Black eroticism, Black astralism, Black demodernisation, and Black syndicalism. Recognising, moreover, that though James Cone (1997) did say that ideology was just the objectification of a view point: we also know that ideology can actually be subjective, indeed, intersubjective through empathic interrelations. Therefore, as I envision it: just as neo-Labourism was basically a liberalised socialist ideology; even so, neo-Islamism should be seen as a radicalised thearchic ideology, though in fact it is actually far more than that due to the definition of neo-Islamism being anarcho-Islamism.

I have therefore also tried throughout this book to demonstrate the closeness of the godbody tradition to the that of the anarchist tradition; and though I am also able to say with Bey (2020), "I care little ... about bringing people into the institutional fold of anarchism" (Bey 2020: 51), I do care about anarchic themes that demonstrate themselves through godbody interpretations and illustrations. We godbodies, as believers and practitioners of righteousness, and as refusing to be corrupted by pressures from the United

States government to submit to their authority; already have striking similarities to anarchism that we definitely need to appreciate.

Hereby, due to the current illegalism of some of our members, and our own aggressive hatred of the police, most of us are already anti-state seeing the state as a means of oppression against the people that corrupts nations. While some of us may be willing to work with the government to fight for social change, for the most part the government is deemed just as corrupted as the state it directs. Ultimately, we godbodies seek the overthrow of the state and its replacement with ghetto parliaments and ciphers. This is the second area where the godbodies agree with anarchism: we have a syndicalist structure. Our parliaments operate similar to labour councils and would be very effective as labour councils if put into practice as such. A third area where the godbodies are similar to anarchists is with the use of social revolutionism, predominantly illegalism. Though most anarchists are ideologically social revolutionaries we godbodies have thus far had no ideological training. But our righteousness is an even higher righteousness than that of the state, whose laws we do not recognise, therefore there is some serious significance to our illegalism. Finally, our prohibition of marriage according to the government means that we also advocate for free love, and some even go so far as practicing plural love. In these ways we have much in common with anarchism, so it is my hope that through introducing these truths to us godbody I may help us to achieve the goal of becoming a world class Black ideology.

The third purpose of this book has been to articulate the relevance of the godbody theory delineated throughout, which had been designed to be a kind of Black ideology that uses various ideas, language, and expressions from chaos theory, deconstruction theory, decolonising theory, postcolonial theory, critical race theory, pro-Black anarchist theory, and pro-sex womanist theory into the outlook and world vision of the Five Percent Nation. It has also allowed me to apply the methodologies of supreme mathematics, mechanical analysis, and *observant participation* (Wacquant 2008) to various correspondences I had with my enlightener God Born Supreme Allah for the spreading of his GBSA-ideology.

See, it has been the main aim of the godbody movement to create a collective continuum of over 28,000 years of history and science. This continuum starts from the historical *Shemsu Hor*, on through to the priesthood of Ta Neteru, to the chiefs/priests of pre-Dynastic Kemet, to the *Sebis* of Dynastic Kemet, to the *Nebis* of the Hebrew tradition, to the apostles of the messianic tradition, to the *ulamaa* of the Islamic tradition, all the way to the Fruit of the Nation of Islam tradition. We consider ourselves to be the heirs of all these traditions, and it is this richness that has made and has been making us so appealing to young people. If you yourself wish to be a part of this movement or set up a parliament in your own community, just write to:

The Allah School in Mecca
2122 7th Avenue
New York, NY 10027
USA

Also be sure to let them know that it was this book that inspired you to join. Once they have been informed as to your intentions they should be willing to give you everything you need to be a part of this movement. Still, while it may also be true that the best place to get a universal flag bandana made and sent to you is currently Etsy, I would highly recommend not making that purchase until you have learned the science behind the universal flag, out of respect for our traditions. It is a godbody's most precious item: we guard and protect it with our very lives.

Finally, this has been a very joyful project to write about and I am so glad the reader made it all the way to the end. If you are willing I have one final request: if you have gained or learned anything you feel to be of value please remember to leave a review on the platform that you purchased this book from. It is little things like that that allow authors like myself to gain wider readership and validation for our efforts. I would also love to hear some of the stories from those who have been touched by this work. Thank you so much for your love and support, and to you my people: all the love in the world. Peace.

Attention African American Theologians!!!

In an Age of American Empire What Real Hope is There for Black People?

On Cultural Islam is Shahidi Islam's third instalment in his Shahidi Collection series.
With the world becoming more plutocratic our freedom is becoming less and less certain. To learn how to resist shop now.

On Cultural Islam

Glossary

All words names and definitions in this glossary are provided by Merriam Webster's Dictionary and Thesaurus and The Encyclopaedia Britannica Standard Edition unless the word is accompanied by an *.

Absolutize: to make absolute: convert into an absolute.
Accelerate: 1: to bring about at an earlier time ‹~ their departure›; 2: to cause to move faster ‹accelerated his steps›; also: to cause to undergo acceleration; 3 a: to hasten the progress or development of ‹~ our efforts› b: increase ‹~ food production›
4 a: to enable (a student) to complete a course in less than usual time b: to speed up (as a course of study)
Accelerate: 1 a: to move faster: gain speed ‹the car slowly accelerated› b: grow increase ‹inflation was accelerating›; 2: to follow an accelerated educational program.
Accentuate: (ca. 1731): accent emphasize; also: intensify ‹~s the feeling of despair›.
Actuality: 1: the quality or state of being actual, 2: something that is actual: fact reality.
Adept: (1709): a highly skilled or well-trained individual: expert ‹an ~ at chess›.
Adept: (ca. 1691): thoroughly proficient: expert ‹~ at fixing cars› proficient.

Aetiology: etiology.

Agrarian: (1600) 1: of or relating to fields or lands or their tenure; 2 a: of, relating to, or characteristic of farmers or their way of life ‹~ values› b: organized or designed to promote agricultural interests ‹an ~ political party› ‹~ reforms›.

Agrarian (1818): a member of an agrarian party or movement.

Ahistorical: (1945): not concerned with or related to history, historical development, or tradition ‹an ~ attitude›; also: historically inaccurate or ignorant ‹an ~ version of events›.

Alignment: (1790) 1: the act of aligning or state of being aligned; esp: the proper positioning or state of adjustment of parts (as of a mechanical or electronic device) in relation to each other; 2 a: a forming in line b: the line thus formed; 3: the ground plan (as of a railroad or highway) in distinction from the profile; 4: an arrangement of groups or forces in relation to one another ‹new ~s within the political party›.

Allusion: 1: an implied or indirect reference esp. in literature; also: the use of such references; 2: the act of alluding to or hinting at something.

Alterego: *any ego other to primordial ego.

Amalgamation: (1612) 1 a: the action or process of amalgamating: uniting b: the state of being amalgamated; 2: the result of amalgamating: amalgam; 3: merger ‹~ of two corporations›.

Ameliorate: (1767): to make better or more tolerable.

Amoral: (1779) 1 a: being neither moral nor immoral; specif: lying outside the sphere to which moral judgments apply ‹science as such is completely ~ —W. S. Thompson› b: lacking moral sensibility ‹infants are ~›; 2: being outside or beyond the moral order or a particular code of morals ‹~ customs›.

Amplitudes: 1: extent of dignity, excellence, or splendour, 2: the quality or state of being ample: fullness abundance, 3: the extent or range of a quality, property, process, or phenomenon: as a: the extent of a vibratory movement (as of a pendulum) measured from the mean position to an extreme b: the maximum departure of the value of an alternating current or wave from the average value, 4: the angle assigned to a complex number when it is plotted in a complex plane using polar coordinates called also argument compare absolute value 2.

Anti-Modernism: *opposed to the values of modernism or modernity.

Antinomian: 1: one who holds that under the gospel dispensation of grace the moral law is of no use or obligation because faith alone is necessary to salvation, 2: one who rejects a socially established morality.

Aphorism: (1528) 1: a concise statement of a principle; 2: a terse formulation of a truth or sentiment: adage.

Appendage: (1647) 1: an adjunct to something larger or more important: appurtenance; 2: a usu. projecting part of an animal or plant body that is typically smaller and of less functional importance than the main part to which it is attached; esp: a limb or analogous part (as a seta); 3 [appendant]: a dependent or subordinate person.

Apperception: (1753) 1: introspective self-consciousness; 2: mental perception; esp: the process of understanding something perceived in terms of previous experience.

Archaic: (1832) 1: having the characteristics of the language of the past and surviving chiefly in specialized uses ‹an ~ word›; 2: of, relating to, or characteristic of an earlier or more primitive time: antiquated ‹~ legal traditions›; 3 cap: of or belonging to the early or formative phases of a culture or a period of artistic development; esp: of or belonging to the period leading up to the classical period of Greek culture; 4: surviving from an earlier period; specif: typical of a previously dominant evolutionary stage; 5 cap: of or relating to the period from about 8000 b.c. to 1000 b.c. and the North American cultures of that time old.

Artificial Insemination: *is the introducing of sperm into a female uterus or cervix in order to impregnate them without the need for sexual intercourse.

Ashkenazi: (1839): a member of one of the two great divisions of Jews comprising the eastern European Yiddish-speaking Jews compare Sephardi.

Askesis: *extreme self-discipline, particularly for religious reasons.

Astral: (1605) 1: of, relating to, or coming from the stars ‹~ influences› ‹unusual ~ occurrences›; 2: of or relating to a mitotic or meiotic aster; 3: of or consisting of a supersensible substance held in theosophy to be next above the tangible world in refinement; 4 a: visionary b: elevated in station or position: exalted.

Authenticate: (1652): to prove or serve to prove the authenticity of ‹~ a document› confirm.

Axiom: 1: a maxim widely accepted on its intrinsic merit; 2: a statement accepted as true as the basis for argument or inference: postulate; 3: an established rule or principle or a self-evident truth.

Bourgeois: 1: of, relating to, or characteristic of the townsman or of the social middle class, 2: marked by a concern for material interests and respectability and a tendency toward mediocrity, 3: dominated by commercial and industrial interests: capitalistic.

Bourgeois: 1 a: burgher b: a middle-class person, 2: a person with social behavior and political views held to be influenced by private-property interest: capitalist, 3 pl: bourgeoisie.

Bureaucracy: 1 a: a body of nonelective government officials b: an administrative policy-making group; 2: government characterized by specialization of functions, adherence to fixed rules, and a hierarchy of authority; 3: a system of administration marked by officialism, red tape, and proliferation.

Carbon Chauvinism: *a term used to deride those who believe that extraterrestrial life must primarily be constructed from carbon.

Castrate: (1554) 1: to render impotent or deprive of vitality esp. by psychological means; 2 a: to deprive of the testes: geld b: to deprive of the ovaries: spay.

Centripetal: (1709) 1: proceeding or acting in a direction toward a center or axis; 2: afferent; 3: tending toward centralization: unifying.

Clairalience: *extrasensory Perception through scent, clear smelling.

Clairaudience: *extrasensory Perception through hearing, clear hearing.

Clairgustance: *extrasensory Perception through taste, clear tasting.

Clairsentience: *extrasensory Perception through touch, clear touching or clear feeling.

Clairvoyance: *extrasensory Perception through sight, clear vision. Cohesion:

Congenial: (ca. 1625) 1: having the same nature, disposition, or tastes: kindred ‹~ companions›; 2 a: existing or associated together harmoniously b: pleasant; esp: agreeably suited to one's nature, tastes, or outlook ‹a ~ atmosphere› c: sociable genial ‹a ~ host›.

Cognitive: 1: of, relating to, being, or involving conscious intellectual activity (as thinking, reasoning, or remembering) ‹~ impairment›; 2: based on or capable of being reduced to empirical factual knowledge.

Contradiction: 1: act or an instance of contradicting; 2 a: a proposition, statement, or phrase that asserts or implies both the truth and falsity of something b: a statement or phrase whose parts contradict each other ‹a round square is a ~ in terms›; 3 a: logical incongruity b: a situation in which inherent factors, actions, or propositions are inconsistent or contrary to one another.

Conspicuous: 1: obvious to the eye or mind ‹~ changes›, 2: attracting attention: striking ‹a ~ success›, 3: marked by a noticeable violation of good taste noticeable. Corpuscles: (1660) 1: a minute particle; 2 a: a living cell; esp: one (as a red or White blood cell or a cell in cartilage or bone) not aggregated into continuous tissues b: any of various small circumscribed multicellular bodies.

Correlate: (1643) 1: either of two things so related that one directly implies or is complementary to the other (as husband and wife); 2: a phenomenon that accompanies another phenomenon, is usu. parallel to it, and is related in some way to it ‹precise electrical ~s of conscious thinking in the human brain —Bayard Webster›.

Correlate: 1 a: to establish a mutual or reciprocal relation between ‹~ activities in the lab and the field› b: to show correlation or a causal relationship between; 2: to present or set forth so as to show relationship ‹he ~s the findings of the scientists, the psychologists, and the mystics.

Cybernetic: (1948): the science of communication and control theory that is concerned esp. with the comparative study of automatic control systems (as the nervous system and brain and mechanical-electrical communication systems).

Decelerate: (1899) 1: to reduce the speed of: slow down ‹~ a car›; 2: to decrease the rate of progress of ‹~ growth› ‹~ soil erosion›.
Degenerate: 1 a: having declined or become less specialized (as in nature, character, structure, or function) from an ancestral or former state b: having sunk to a condition below that which is normal to a type; esp: having sunk to a lower and usu. corrupt and vicious state c: degraded; 2: being mathematically simpler (as by having a factor or constant equal to zero) than the typical case ‹a ~ hyperbola›; 3: characterized by atoms stripped of their electrons and by very great density ‹~ matter›; also: consisting of degenerate matter ‹a ~ star›; 4: having two or more states or subdivisions ‹~ energy level›; 5: having more than one codon representing an amino acid ; also: being such a codon vicious.

Degenerate: (1545) 1: to pass from a higher to a lower type or condition: deteriorate; 2: to sink into a low intellectual or moral state; 3: to decline in quality ‹the poetry gradually ~s into jingles›; 4: to decline from a condition or from the standards of a species, race, or breed; 5: to evolve or develop into a less autonomous or less functionally active form ‹degenerated into dependent parasites›.

Degenerate: (1555): one that is degenerate: as a: one degraded from the normal moral standard b: a sexual pervert c: one showing signs of reversion to an earlier culture stage.

Dehumanize: (1818): to deprive of human qualities, personality, or spirit.

Delimit: (1852): to fix or define the limits of.

Demarcate: (1816) 1: delimit; 2: to set apart: distinguish.

Demonology: (1597) 1: the study of demons or evil spirits; 2: belief in demons: a doctrine of evil spirits; 3: a catalog of enemies.

Depersonalize: 1: to deprive of the sense of personal identity ‹schools that ~ students›, 2: to make impersonal ‹depersonalizing medical care›.

Detract: 1 archaic: to speak ill of; 2 archaic: to take away; 3: divert ‹~ attention›.

Diagnosis: (1655) 1 a: the art or act of identifying a disease from its signs and symptoms b: the decision reached by diagnosis; 2: a concise technical description of a taxon; 3 a: investigation or analysis of the cause or nature of a condition, situation, or problem ‹~ of engine trouble› b: a statement or conclusion from such an analysis.

Dialectic: 1: logic; 2 a: discussion and reasoning by dialogue as a method of intellectual investigation; specif: the Socratic techniques of exposing false beliefs and eliciting truth b: the Platonic investigation of the eternal ideas; 3: the logic of fallacy; 4 a: the Hegelian process of change in which a concept or its realization passes over into and is preserved and fulfilled by its opposite; also: the critical investigation of this process b (1)usu pl but sing or pl in constr: development through the stages of thesis, antithesis, and synthesis in accordance with the laws of dialectical materialism (2): the investigation of this process (3): the theoretical application of this process esp. in the social sciences; 5 usu pl but sing or pl in constra: any systematic reasoning, exposition, or argument that juxtaposes opposed or contradictory ideas and usu. seeks to resolve their conflict b: an intellectual exchange of ideas; 6: the dialectical tension or opposition between two interacting forces or elements.

Diametric: (1553) 1: of, relating to, or constituting a diameter: located at the diameter; 2: completely opposed: being at opposite extremes ‹in ~ contradiction to his claims›.

Diatribe: (1581) 1 archaic: a prolonged discourse; 2: a bitter and abusive speech or writing; 3: ironic or satirical criticism.

Differentiate: (1816) 1: to obtain the mathematical derivative of; 2: to mark or show a difference in: constitute a difference that distinguishes; 3: to develop differential characteristics in; 4: to cause differentiation of in the course of development; 5: to express the specific distinguishing quality of: discriminate.

Disclosure: (1567) 1: the act or an instance of disclosing: exposure; 2: something disclosed: revelation.

Discourse: 1: the capacity of orderly thought or procedure: rationality; 2: verbal interchange of ideas; esp: conversation; 3 a: formal and orderly and usu. extended expression of thought on a subject b: connected speech or writing c: a linguistic unit (as a conversation or a story) larger than a sentence; 4 obs: social familiarity; 5: a mode of organizing knowledge, ideas, or experience that is rooted in language and its concrete contexts (as history or institutions) ‹critical ~›.

Discourse: (1559) 1: to express oneself esp. in oral discourse, 2: talk converse: to give forth: utter.

Discrepancy: (ca. 1623) 1: the quality or state of being discrepant; 2: an instance of being discrepant.

Discursive: (1598) 1 a: moving from topic to topic without order: rambling b: proceeding coherently from topic to topic; 2: marked by analytical reasoning; 3: of or relating to discourse ‹~ practices›.

Disillusion: condition of being disenchanted.

Disillusion: (1855): to free from illusion; also: to cause to lose naive faith and trust

Disingenuous: (1655): lacking in candor; giving a false appearance of simple frankness: calculating.

Disposition: 1: the act or the power of disposing or the state of being disposed: as a: administration control b: final arrangement: settlement ‹the ~ of the case› c (1): transfer to the care or possession of another (2): the power of such transferal d : orderly arrangement; 2 a: prevailing tendency, mood, or inclination b: temperamental makeup c: the tendency of something to act in a certain manner under given circumstances.

Double-Slit Test: *first performed by Thomas Young in 1801, to show how light can behave as a wave the double-slit experiment basically takes a coherent source of light, like a laser beam, which passes through a plate with two parallel slits. As the light has wave properties when it passes through the two slits it causes an interference, which makes dark spots appear on a screen behind the two slits in a counterintuitive way.

Durkheim, Emile: French social scientist who developed a vigorous methodology combining empirical research with sociological theory. He is widely regarded as the founder of the French school of sociology.

Effectuate: effect.

Efficacious: (1528): having the power to produce a desired effect ‹an ~ remedy› effective.

Egalitarian: (1885): asserting, promoting, or marked by egalitarianism.

Egalitarianism: (1905) 1: a belief in human equality esp. with respect to social, political, and economic rights and privileges; 2:

a social philosophy advocating the removal of inequalities among people.

Electrotheism: *the belief that God is electromagnetic energy.

Eliminate: (1568) 1 a: to put an end to or get rid of: remove eradicate ‹the need to ~ poverty› ‹~ errors› b: to remove from consideration ‹cannot yet ~ him as a suspect› c: to remove from further competition by defeating ‹the team was eliminated in the first round of the playoffs›; 2: to expel (as waste) from the living body; 3: to cause (as an unknown) to disappear by combining two or more mathematical equations.

Ellipse: (ca. 1753) 1 a: oval b: a closed plane curve generated by a point moving in such a way that the sums of its distances from two fixed points is a constant: a plane section of a right circular cone that is a closed curve; 2: ellipsis.

Elucidate: (ca. 1568): to make lucid esp. by explanation or analysis ‹~ a text›.

Emanate: (1756): to come out from a source ‹a sweet scent emanating from the blossoms›.

Embody: (ca. 1548) 1: to give a body to (a spirit): incarnate; 2 a: to deprive of spirituality b: to make concrete and perceptible; 3: to cause to become a body or part of a body: incorporate; 4: to represent in human or animal form: personify

Entity: (1596) 1 a: being existence; esp: independent, separate, or self-contained existence b: the existence of a thing as contrasted with its attributes; 2: something that has separate and distinct existence and objective or conceptual reality; 3: an organization (as a business or governmental unit) that has an identity separate from those of its members.

Ephemeral: (1576) 1: lasting one day only ‹an ~ fever›; 2: lasting a very short time ‹~ pleasures› transient.

Epigenetic: (1883) 1 a: of, relating to, or produced by the chain of developmental processes in epigenesis that lead from genotype to phenotype after the initial action of the genes b: relating to, being, or involving changes in gene function that do not involve changes in DNA sequence; 2 of a deposit or structure: formed after the laying down of the enclosing rock.

Epignosis: *1: after-knowledge; 2: knowledge of the history of an entity from just a little information; 3: the science of intuition.

Erotogenic: erogenous.

Erogenous: 1: producing sexual excitement or libidinal gratification when stimulated: sexually sensitive; 2: of, relating to, or arousing sexual feelings.

Eschatology: (1844) 1: a branch of theology concerned with the final events in the history of the world or of humankind; 2: a belief concerning death, the end of the world, or the ultimate destiny of humankind; specif: any of various Christian doctrines concerning the Second Coming, the resurrection of the dead, or the Last Judgment.

Ethnocentric: (1900): characterized by or based on the attitude that one's own group is superior.

Etiquette: (1750): the conduct or procedure required by good breeding or prescribed by authority to be observed in social or official life.

Etiology: (ca. 1555) 1: cause origin; specif: the cause of a disease or abnormal condition; 2: a branch of knowledge concerned with causes; specif: a branch of medical science concerned with the causes and origins of diseases.

Exacerbate: (1660): to make more violent, bitter, or severe ‹the proposed shutdown…would ~ unemployment problems — Science›.

Exhibitionism: 1 a: a perversion in which sexual gratification is obtained from the indecent exposure of one's genitals (as to a stranger) b: an act of such exposure, 2: the act or practice of behaving so as to attract attention to oneself.

Existentialism: (1941): a chiefly 20th century philosophical movement embracing diverse doctrines but centering on analysis of individual existence in an unfathomable universe and the plight of the individual who must assume ultimate responsibility for acts of free will without any certain knowledge of what is right or wrong or good or bad.

Expedition: 1 a: a journey or excursion undertaken for a specific purpose b: the group of persons making such a journey; 2: efficient promptness: speed; 3: a sending or setting forth haste.

Explicate: (1531) 1: to give a detailed explanation of; 2: to develop the implications of: analyze logically explain.

Fictive: (1612) 1: not genuine: feigned; 2: of, relating to, or capable of imaginative creation; 3: of, relating to, or having the characteristics of fiction: fictional.

Frequency: 1: the fact or condition of occurring frequently; 2 a: the number of times that a periodic function repeats the same sequence of values during a unit variation of the independent variable b: the number, proportion, or percentage of items in a particular category in a set of data; 3: the number of repetitions of a periodic process in a unit of time: as a: the number of complete alternations per second of an alternating current b: the number of complete oscillations per second of energy (as sound or electromagnetic radiation) in the form of waves.

Glossolalia: (1879): tongue.

Godbody: *the militant, street section of the 5 Percent Nation.

Grand Narratives: *any religious, institutional or ideological knowledge system.

Gynaecocracy: gynecocracy.

Gynecocracy: (1612): political supremacy of women.

Hegel, Georg Wilhelm Friedrich: German philosopher who developed a dialectical scheme that emphasized the progress of history and of ideas from thesis to antithesis and thence to a synthesis.

Hegelian: (1838): of, relating to, or characteristic of Hegel, his philosophy, or his dialectic method.

Hegelian: (1843): a follower of Hegel: an adherent of Hegelianism.

Heterogeneous: (1630): consisting of dissimilar or diverse ingredients or constituents: mixed.

Homogeneous: (1641) 1: of the same or a similar kind or nature; 2: of uniform structure or composition throughout ‹a culturally ~ neighborhood›; 3: having the property that if each variable is replaced by a constant times that variable the constant can be factored out: having each term of the same degree if all variables are considered ‹a ~ equation›.

Hypothalamus: (1896): a basal part of the diencephalon that lies beneath the thalamus on each side, forms the floor of the third ventricle, and includes vital autonomic regulatory centers.

Idiom: (1588) 1 a: the language peculiar to a people or to a district, community, or class: dialect b: the syntactical, grammatical, or structural form peculiar to a language; 2: an expression in the usage of a language that is peculiar to itself either grammatically (as no, it wasn't me) or in having a meaning that cannot be derived from the conjoined meanings of its elements (as Monday week for "the Monday a week after next Monday"); 3: a style or form of artistic expression that is characteristic of an individual, a period or movement, or a medium or instrument ‹the modern jazz ~› ; broadly: manner style ‹a new culinary ~›.

Imminent: (1528): ready to take place; esp: hanging threateningly over one's head ‹was in ~ danger of being run over›.

Imperative: 1 a: of, relating to, or constituting the grammatical mood that expresses the will to influence the behavior of another b: expressive of a command, entreaty, or exhortation c: having power to restrain, control, and direct; 2: not to be avoided or evaded: necessary ‹an ~ duty› masterful.

Imperative: (1530) 1: the imperative mood or a verb form or verbal phrase expressing it; 2: something that is imperative: as a:

command order b: rule guide c: an obligatory act or duty d: an imperative judgment or proposition.

Implicate: 1: to involve as a consequence, corollary, or natural inference: imply; 2 archaic: to fold or twist together: entwine; 3 a: to bring into intimate or incriminating connection ‹evidence that ~s him in the bombing› b: to involve in the nature or operation of something.

Improprietous: *improper or indecent.

Inanimate: 1: not animate: a: not endowed with life or spirit ‹an ~ object› b: lacking consciousness or power of motion ‹an ~ body›; 2: not animated or lively: dull.

Inconsistent: (1620): lacking consistency: as a: not compatible with another fact or claim ‹~ statements› b: containing incompatible elements ‹an ~ argument› c: incoherent or illogical in thought or actions: changeable d: not satisfiable by the same set of values for the unknowns ‹~ equations› ‹~ inequalities›.

Inculcate: (1539): to teach and impress by frequent repetitions or admonitions implant.

Inerrant: (1837): free from error.

Inertia: (1713) 1 a: a property of matter by which it remains at rest or in uniform motion in the same straight line unless acted upon by some external force b: an analogous property of other physical quantities (as electricity); 2: indisposition to motion, exertion, or change: inertness.

Inexorable: (1542): not to be persuaded, moved, or stopped: relentless ‹~ progress›.

Inhibition: 1 a: the act of inhibiting: the state of being inhibited b: something that forbids, debars, or restricts; 2: an inner impediment to free activity, expression, or functioning: as a: a mental process imposing restraint upon behavior or another mental process (as a desire) b: a restraining of the function of a bodily organ or an agent (as an enzyme).

Initiate: (1533) 1: to cause or facilitate the beginning of: set going ‹~ a program of reform› ‹enzymes that ~ fermentation›; 2: to induct into membership by or as if by special rites; 3: to instruct in the rudiments or principles of something: introduce begin.

Initiate: (1537) 1 a: initiated or properly admitted (as to membership or an office) b: instructed in some secret knowledge; 2: relating to an initiate.

Initiate: (1811) 1: a person who is undergoing or has undergone an initiation; 2: a person who is instructed or adept in some special field.

Instigate: (1542): to goad or urge forward: provoke incite.

Institution: 1: an act of instituting: establishment; 2 a: a significant practice, relationship, or organization in a society or culture ‹the ~ of marriage›; also: something or someone firmly associated with a place or thing ‹she has become an ~ in the theater› b: an established organization or corporation (as a bank or university) esp. of a public character; also: asylum.

Institutionalize: (1865) 1: to make into an institution: give character of an institution to ‹institutionalized housing›; esp: to incorporate into a structured and often highly formalized system ‹institutionalized values›; 2: to put in the care of an institution ‹~ alcoholics›.

Internalize: (1884): to give a subjective character to; specif: to incorporate (as values or patterns of culture) within the self as conscious or subconscious guiding principles through learning or socialization.

Interpolate: (1612) 1 a: to alter or corrupt (as a text) by inserting new or foreign matter b: to insert (words) into a text or into a conversation; 2: to insert between other things or parts: intercalate; 3: to estimate values of (data or a function) between two known values.

Intersubjective: 1: involving or occurring between separate conscious minds ‹~ communication›, 2: accessible to or capable of being established for two or more subjects: objective ‹~ reality of the physical world›.

Intolerable: 1: not tolerable: unbearable ‹~ pain›; 2: excessive.

Invocate: (1526) archaic: invoke.

Juxtapose: (1851): to place side by side.

Kropotkin, Peter: Russian revolutionary and geographer, the foremost theorist of the anarchist movement. Although he achieved renown in a number of different fields, ranging from geography and zoology to sociology and history, he shunned material success for the life of a revolutionist.

Legitimate: (1531): to make legitimate: a (1): to give legal status or authorization to (2): to show or affirm to be justified (3): to lend authority or respectability to b : to put (a bastard) in the state of a legitimate child before the law by legal means.

Libido: (1909) 1: instinctual psychic energy that in psychoanalytic theory is derived from primitive biological urges (as for sexual pleasure or self-preservation) and that is expressed in conscious activity, 2: sexual drive.

Libidinal: (1922): of or relating to the libido ‹~ impulses›.

Linear: (ca. 1656) 1 a (1): of, relating to, resembling, or having a graph that is a line and esp. a straight line: straight (2): involving a single dimension b (1): of the first degree with respect to one or more variables (2): of, relating to, based on, or being linear equations, linear differential equations, linear functions, linear transformations, or linear algebra c (1): characterized by an emphasis on line ‹~ art› (2): composed of simply drawn lines with little attempt at pictorial representation ‹~ script› d: consisting of a straight chain of atoms; 2: elongated with nearly parallel sides ‹~ leaf› see leaf illustration; 3: having or being a response or output that is directly proportional to the input; 4: of, relating to, or based or depending on sequential development ‹~ thinking› ‹a ~ narrative›.

Lucid: (1591) 1 a: suffused with light: luminous b: translucent ‹snorkeling in the ~ sea›; 2: having full use of one's faculties: sane; 3: clear to the understanding : intelligible clear.

Malcolm X: *original name Malcolm Little, Muslim name el-Hajj Malik el-Shabazz* Black militant leader who articulated concepts of race pride and Black nationalism in the early 1960s. After his assassination, the widespread distribution of his life story—*The Autobiography of Malcolm X* (1965)—made him an ideological hero, especially among Black youth.

Masochism: (1892) 1: a sexual perversion characterized by pleasure in being subjected to pain or humiliation esp. by a love object compare sadism; 2: pleasure in being abused or dominated: a taste for suffering.

Mathematization: (1908): reduction to mathematical form.

Matriarch: (1606): a woman who rules or dominates a family, group, or state; specif: a mother who is head and ruler of her family and descendants.

Methodology: (1800) 1: a body of methods, rules, and postulates employed by a discipline: a particular procedure or set of procedures; 2: the analysis of the principles or procedures of inquiry in a particular field.

Milieu: (1854): the physical or social setting in which something occurs or develops: environment background.

Misclassify: *to classify incorrectly.

Misgiving: (1582): a feeling of doubt or suspicion esp. concerning a future event.

Monism: (1862) 1 a: a view that there is only one kind of ultimate substance b: the view that reality is one unitary organic whole with no independent parts; 2: monogenesis; 3: a viewpoint or theory that reduces all phenomena to one principle.

Monogenesis: (ca. 1859): origin of diverse individuals or kinds (as of language) by descent from a single ancestral individual or kind.
Monogenism: *theory of monogenesis.
Mortify: 1: to destroy the strength, vitality, or functioning of; 2: to subdue or deaden (as the body or bodily appetites) esp. by abstinence or self-inflicted pain or discomfort; 3: to subject to severe and vexing embarrassment: shame.
Muhammad, Elijah: *original name Elijah Poole* leader of the Black separatist religious movement known as the Nation of Islam (sometimes called Black Muslims) in the United States.

Narrative: (1567) 1: something that is narrated: story account; 2: the art or practice of narration; 3: the representation in art of an event or story ; also: an example of such a representation.
Negrotheism: *the theory that Black people are a divine people.
Neoconservative: (1952) 1: a former liberal espousing political conservatism; 2: a conservative who advocates the assertive promotion of democracy and U.S. national interest in international affairs including through military means.
Neoliberalism: (1945): a liberal who de-emphasizes traditional liberal doctrines in order to seek progress by more pragmatic methods.
Neurosis: (ca. 1784): a mental and emotional disorder that affects only part of the personality, is accompanied by a less distorted perception of reality than in a psychosis, does not result in disturbance of the use of language, and is accompanied by various physical, physiological, and mental disturbances (as visceral symptoms, anxieties, or phobias).
Neurotic: (1873): of, relating to, constituting, or affected with neurosis.
Neurotic (1896) 1: one affected with a neurosis; 2: an emotionally unstable individual.
New Right: *a sociological and ideological perspective begun in the 1970s based on radical conservative views and ideas.

444

Nihilism: (ca. 1817) 1 a: a viewpoint that traditional values and beliefs are unfounded and that existence is senseless and useless b: a doctrine that denies any objective ground of truth and esp. of moral truths; 2 a: a doctrine or belief that conditions in the social organization are so bad as to make destruction desirable for its own sake independent of any constructive program or possibility b cap: the program of a 19th century Russian party advocating revolutionary reform and using terrorism and assassination.

Non-Linear: *when there is no straight line or direct relationship between variable.

Objective: 1 a: relating to or existing as an object of thought without consideration of independent existence — used chiefly in medieval philosophy b: of, relating to, or being an object, phenomenon, or condition in the realm of sensible experience independent of individual thought and perceptible by all observers: having reality independent of the mind ‹~ reality› ... compare subjective 3a c of a symptom of disease: perceptible to persons other than the affected individual compare subjective 4c d: involving or deriving from sense perception or experience with actual objects, conditions, or phenomena ‹~ awareness› ‹~ data›; 2: relating to, characteristic of, or constituting the case of words that follow prepositions or transitive verbs; 3 a: expressing or dealing with facts or conditions as perceived without distortion by personal feelings, prejudices, or interpretations ‹~ art› ‹an ~ history of the war› ‹an ~ judgment› b of a test: limited to choices of fixed alternatives and reducing subjective factors to a minimum material, fair.

Obsolete: 1 a: no longer in use or no longer useful ‹an ~ word› b: of a kind or style no longer current: old-fashioned ‹an ~ technology›, 2: of a plant or animal part: indistinct or imperfect as compared with a corresponding part in related organisms: vestigial old.

Obsolescence: (ca. 1828): the process of becoming obsolete or the condition of being nearly obsolete ‹the gradual ~ of machinery› ‹reduced to ~›.

Oedipus: (1557): the son of Laius and Jocasta who in fulfillment of an oracle unknowingly kills his father and marries his mother.

Oedipal: (1939): of, relating to, or resulting from the Oedipus complex.

Oedipus Complex: (1910): the positive libidinal feelings of a child toward the parent of the opposite sex and hostile or jealous feelings toward the parent of the same sex that may be a source of adult personality disorder when unresolved.

Omnibenevolence: *unlimited or infinite in goodness usu. regarded as unconditional love.

Omnipresent: (1609): present in all places at all times.

Omniscient: *all-knowledge; prognostic, diagnostic, and epignostic abilities.

Omnivision: *all-sight; foresight, hindsight, and insight.

Opine: to express opinions.

Operatic Conditioning: *a form a behavioural science whereby a stimulus is made to produce a response in the mind and body.

Organic: (1517) 1 archaic: instrumental; 2 a: of, relating to, or arising in a bodily organ b: affecting the structure of the organism; 3 a (1): of, relating to, or derived from living organisms ‹~ evolution› (2): of, relating to, yielding, or involving the use of food produced with the use of feed or fertilizer of plant or animal origin without employment of chemically formulated fertilizers, growth stimulants, antibiotics, or pesticides ‹~ farming› ‹~ produce› b (1): of, relating to, or containing carbon compounds (2): relating to, being, or dealt with by a branch of chemistry concerned with the carbon compounds of living beings and most other carbon compounds; 4 a: forming an integral element of a whole: fundamental ... b: having systematic coordination of parts : organized ‹an ~ whole› c: having the characteristics of an organism: developing in the manner of a living plant or animal ‹society is ~›; 5: of, relating to, or constituting the law by which a government or organization exists.

Paedophilia: pedophilia.

Palpable: 1: capable of being touched or felt: tangible; 2: easily perceptible: noticeable ‹a ~ difference›; 3: easily perceptible by the mind: manifest perceptible.

Parapsychology: (1925): a field of study concerned with the investigation of evidence for paranormal psychological phenomena (as telepathy, clairvoyance, and psychokinesis).

Pathogenesis: (1876): the origination and development of a disease.

Pathology: (1611) 1: the study of the essential nature of diseases and esp. of the structural and functional changes produced by them; 2: something abnormal: a: the structural and functional deviations from the normal that constitute disease or characterize a particular disease b: deviation from propriety or from an assumed normal state of something nonliving or nonmaterial c: deviation giving rise to social ills.

Patriarchy: (1632) 1: social organization marked by the supremacy of the father in the clan or family, the legal dependence of wives and children, and the reckoning of descent and inheritance in the male line; broadly: control by men of a disproportionately large share of power; 2: a society or institution organized according to the principles or practices of patriarchy.

Paul the Apostle: *original name Saul of Tarsus* 1st-century Jew who, after first being a bitter enemy of Christianity, later became an important figure in its history.

Pauperism: (1516) 1: a person destitute of means except such as are derived from charity; specif: one who receives aid from funds designated for the poor; 2: a very poor person.

Pedophilia: (1906): sexual perversion in which children are the preferred sexual object.

Perls, Fritz: *German-born psychiatrist and psychoanalyst who invented Gestalt therapy.

Permutation: 1: often major or fundamental change (as in character or condition) based primarily on rearrangement of existent elements ‹the system has gone through several ~s›; also: a form or variety resulting from such change ‹technology available in various ~s›; 2 a: the act or process of changing the lineal order of an ordered set of objects b: an ordered arrangement of a set of objects.

Pernicious: 1: highly injurious or destructive: deadly, 2: wicked.

Personification: (ca. 1755) 1: attribution of personal qualities; esp: representation of a thing or abstraction as a person or by the human form; 2: a divinity or imaginary being representing a thing or abstraction; 3: embodiment incarnation.

Pertinent: having a clear decisive relevance to the matter in hand relevant.

Phantasm: 1: a product of fantasy: as a: delusive appearance: illusion b: ghost specter c: a figment of the imagination; 2: a mental representation of a real object.

Phenomenology: (ca. 1797) 1: the study of the development of human consciousness and self-awareness as a preface to or a part of philosophy; 2 a (1): a philosophical movement that describes the formal structure of the objects of awareness and of awareness itself in abstraction from any claims concerning existence (2): the typological classification of a class of phenomena ‹the ~ of religion› b: an analysis produced by phenomenological investigation.

Phoenix: a legendary bird which according to one account lived 500 years, burned itself to ashes on a pyre, and rose alive from the ashes to live another period ; also: a person or thing likened to the phoenix.

Plutocracy: (1652) 1: government by the wealthy; 2: a controlling class of the wealthy.

Pneumatology: * the study of forces.

Polyamory: *having intimate, loving, sexual relationships with more than one person.

Polyandry: (1780): the state or practice of having more than one husband or male mate at one time compare polygamy polygyny.

Polygenesis: (ca. 1882): development from more than one source.

Polygenism: *theory of polygenesis.

Post-Colonialism: *historical epoch that transpired after the fall of European colonies in Africa and Asia.

Posterity: 1: the offspring of one progenitor to the furthest generation; 2: all future generations.

Postmodern: 1: of, relating to, or being an era after a modern one ‹~ times› ‹a ~ metropolis›; 2 a: of, relating to, or being any of various movements in reaction to modernism that are typically characterized by a return to traditional materials and forms (as in architecture) or by ironic self-reference and absurdity (as in literature) b: of, relating to, or being a theory that involves a radical reappraisal of modern assumptions about culture, identity, history, or language ‹~ feminism›.

Potentiality: 1: the ability to develop or come into existence, 2: potential.

Post-Structuralism: (1977): a movement or theory (as deconstruction) that views the descriptive premise of structuralism as contradicted by reliance on borrowed concepts or differential terms and categories and sees inquiry as inevitably shaped by discursive and interpretive practices.

Precarious: (1646) 1: depending on the will or pleasure of another; 2: dependent on uncertain premises: dubious ‹~ generalizations›; 3 a: dependent on chance circumstances, unknown conditions, or uncertain developments b: characterized by a lack of security or stability that threatens with danger dangerous.

Precaution: (1603) 1: care taken in advance : foresight ‹warned of the need for ~›; 2: a measure taken beforehand to prevent harm or secure good : safeguard ‹take the necessary ~s›.

Precognition: (ca. 1611): clairvoyance relating to an event or state not yet experienced.

Predelineated: *an occurrence before delineation.

Predicament: 1: the character, status, or classification assigned by a predication; specif: category; 2: condition state; esp: a difficult, perplexing, or trying situation.

Predispose: (1646) 1: to dispose in advance ‹a good teacher ~s children to learn›; 2: to make susceptible ‹malnutrition ~s one to disease›.

Prerogative: 1 a: an exclusive or special right, power, or privilege: as (1): one belonging to an office or an official body (2): one belonging to a person, group, or class of individuals (3): one possessed by a nation as an attribute of sovereignty b: the discretionary power inhering in the British Crown; 2: a distinctive excellence.

Prescription: 1 a: the establishment of a claim of title to something under common law usu. by use and enjoyment for a period fixed by statute b: the right or title acquired under common law by such possession; 2: the process of making claim to something by long use and enjoyment; 3: the action of laying down authoritative rules or directions; 4 a: a written direction for a therapeutic or corrective agent ; specif: one for the preparation and use of a medicine b: a prescribed medicine c: something (as a recommendation) resembling a doctor's prescription ‹~s for economic recovery›; 5 a: ancient or long continued custom b: a claim founded upon ancient custom or long continued use; 6 : something prescribed as a rule.

Presuppose: 1: to suppose beforehand; 2: to require as an antecedent in logic or fact.

Primordial: 1 a: first created or developed: primeval 1 b: existing in or persisting from the beginning (as of a solar system or universe) ‹a ~ gas cloud› c: earliest formed in the growth of an individual or organ: primitive ‹~ cells›; 2: fundamental primary.

Principium Primus: *lit. first principle.

Prognosis: *1: foreknowledge; 2: knowledge of the destiny of an entity from just a little information; 3: the ability to predict future events or diseases based on a limited number of causes or symptoms.

Proletariat: 1: the laboring class; esp: the class of industrial workers who lack their own means of production and hence sell their labor to live; 2: the lowest social or economic class of a community.

Promiscuous: (1601) 1: composed of all sorts of persons or things; 2: not restricted to one class, sort, or person: indiscriminate …; 3: not restricted to one sexual partner; 4: casual irregular ‹~ eating habits›.

Propaganda: 1 cap: a congregation of the Roman curia having jurisdiction over missionary territories and related institutions; 2: the spreading of ideas, information, or rumor for the purpose of helping or injuring an institution, a cause, or a person; 3: ideas, facts, or allegations spread deliberately to further one's cause or to damage an opposing cause; also: a public action having such an effect.

Propagation: the act or action of propagating: as a: increase (as of a kind of organism) in numbers b: the spreading of something (as a belief) abroad or into new regions c: enlargement or extension (as of a crack) in a solid body.

Propitiation: 1: the act of propitiating; 2: something that propitiates; specif: an atoning sacrifice.

Proscription: 1: the act of proscribing: the state of being proscribed; 2: an imposed restraint or restriction: prohibition.

Protestant: (1539) 1 capa: any of a group of German princes and cities presenting a defense of freedom of conscience against an edict of the Diet of Spires in 1529 intended to suppress the Lutheran movement b: a member of any of several church denominations denying the universal authority of the Pope and affirming the Reformation principles of justification by faith alone, the priesthood of all believers, and the primacy of the Bible as the only source of revealed truth; broadly: a Christian not of a Catholic or Eastern church; 2: one who makes or enters a protest.

Protestant (1539) 1 cap: of or relating to Protestants, their churches, or their religion; 2: making or sounding a protest.

Pseudoscience: (1844): a system of theories, assumptions, and methods erroneously regarded as scientific.

Psychogenesis: (1838) 1: the origin and development of mental functions, traits, or states; 2: development from mental as distinguished from physical origins

Psychopathology: (1847): the study of psychological and behavioral dysfunction occurring in mental disorder or in social disorganization; also: such dysfunction

Psychosis: (1847): fundamental derangement of the mind (as in schizophrenia) characterized by defective or lost contact with reality esp. as evidenced by delusions, hallucinations, and disorganized speech and behaviour.

Psychotic: (ca. 1890): of, relating to, marked by, or affected with psychosis ‹a ~ patient› ‹~ behavior›.

Regurgitate: (1653): to become thrown or poured back.

Reich, Wilhelm: Viennese psychologist who developed a system of psychoanalysis that concentrated on overall character structure, rather than on individual neurotic symptoms. His early work on psychoanalytic technique was overshadowed by his involvement in the sexual-politics movement and by "orgonomy," a pseudoscientific system he developed.

Reinforce: (1567) 1: to strengthen by additional assistance, material, or support: make stronger or more pronounced ‹~ levees› ‹~ the elbows of a jacket› ‹~ ideas›; 2: to strengthen or increase by fresh additions ‹~ our troops› ‹were reinforcing their pitching staff›; 3: to stimulate (as an experimental animal or a student) with a reinforcer; also: to encourage (a response) with a reinforce.

Repellent: (1643) 1: serving or tending to drive away or ward off
— often used in combination ‹a mosquito-repellent spray›; 2:
arousing aversion or disgust: repulsive

Repellent: (1661): something that repels; esp: a substance that
repels insects

Retrocognition: *extrasensory knowledge of the past.

Retrograde: 1 a (1): having or being motion in a direction contrary
to that of the general motion of similar bodies and esp. east to
west among the stars ‹Saturn is ~ for another week› ‹the ~ motion
of Mercury› (2): having or being a direction of rotation or
revolution that is clockwise as viewed from the north pole of the
sky or a planet ‹a ~ orbit› b (1): moving, occurring, or performed
in a backward direction ‹a ~ step› (2): occurring or performed in
a direction opposite to the normal or forward direction of
conduction or flow ‹~ ejaculation› compare anterograde 1 c:
contrary to the normal order: inverse; 2: tending toward or
resulting in a worse or previous state
3 archaic: contradictory opposed; 4: characterized by
retrogression; 5: affecting memories of a period prior to a shock
or seizure ‹~ amnesia›; 6: retro ‹~ fashion›.

Sadism: (1888) 1: a sexual perversion in which gratification is
obtained by the infliction of physical or mental pain on others (as
on a love object) compare masochism; 2 a: delight in cruelty b:
excessive cruelty.

Schizophrenia: (1912) 1: a psychotic disorder characterized by
loss of contact with the environment, by noticeable deterioration
in the level of functioning in everyday life, and by disintegration
of personality expressed as disorder of feeling, thought (as
delusions), perception (as hallucinations), and behavior called
also dementia praecox compare paranoid schizophrenia; 2:
contradictory or antagonistic qualities or attitudes.

Seductionist: *anyone who receives pleasure from the suffering of trying to give others the greatest amount of pleasure they could possibly have in the moment.

Self-Disclosure: *the process of revealing the full details of one-self.

Selfobject: *any childhood object that helps establish a sense of self.

Semblance: 1 a: outward and often specious appearance or show: form ... b: modicum ...; 2: aspect countenance; 3 a: a phantasmal form: apparition b: image likeness; 4: actual or apparent resemblance ‹her story bears some ~ to the truth›.

Socialize: (1810) 1: to make social; esp: to fit or train for a social environment; 2 a: to constitute on a socialistic basis ‹~ industry› b: to adapt to social needs or uses; 3: to organize group participation in ‹~ a recitation›.

Socio-elastic: *theory that social groups and social movements when bent do not break but can return to their original position.

Spookism: *a term used to express the non-existent nature of a being or object.

Stasis: (1745) 1: a slowing or stoppage of the normal flow of a bodily fluid or semifluid: as a: slowing of the current of circulating blood b: reduced motility of the intestines with retention of feces; 2 a: a state of static balance or equilibrium: stagnation b: a state or period of stability during which little or no evolutionary change in a lineage occurs.

Sublimate: 1 a: sublime 1 b archaic: to improve or refine as if by subliming; 2: to divert the expression of (an instinctual desire or impulse) from its unacceptable form to one that is considered more socially or culturally acceptable.

Sublimate (ca. 1626): a chemical product obtained by sublimation.

Substratum: (1631): an underlying support: foundation: as a: substance that is a permanent subject of qualities or phenomena b: the material of which something is made and from which it derives its special qualities c: a layer beneath the surface soil; specif: subsoil d: substrate.

Systemic: (1803): of, relating to, or common to a system: as a: affecting the body generally b: supplying those parts of the body that receive blood through the aorta rather than through the pulmonary artery c: of, relating to, or being a pesticide that as used is harmless to the plant or higher animal but when absorbed into its sap or bloodstream makes the entire organism toxic to pests (as an insect or fungus).

Telekinesis: (1890): the production of motion in objects (as by a spiritualistic medium) without contact or other physical means.

Teleology: (1740) 1 a: the study of evidences of design in nature b: a doctrine (as in vitalism) that ends are immanent in nature c: a doctrine explaining phenomena by final causes; 2: the fact or character attributed to nature or natural processes of being directed toward an end or shaped by a purpose; 3: the use of design or purpose as an explanation of natural phenomena.

Thatcher, Margaret: *in full Margaret Hilda Thatcher, Baroness Thatcher of Kesteven , née Margaret Hilda Roberts* British Conservative Party politician and prime minister (1979–90), Europe's first woman prime minister. The only British prime minister in the 20th century to win three consecutive terms and, at the time of her resignation, Britain's longest continuously serving prime minister since 1827, she accelerated the evolution of the British economy from statism to liberalism and became, by personality as much as achievement, the most renowned British political leader since Winston Churchill.

The Enlightenment: *French Siècle De Lumières ("Age of the Enlightened"), German Aufklärung,* a European intellectual movement of the 17th and 18th centuries in which ideas concerning God, reason, nature, and man were synthesized into a worldview that gained wide assent and that instigated revolutionary developments in art, philosophy, and politics.

Central to Enlightenment thought were the use and the celebration of reason, the power by which man understands the universe and improves his own condition. The goals of rational man were considered to be knowledge, freedom, and happiness.
The Great Awakening: A series of religious revivals known collectively as the Great Awakening swept over the colonies in the 1730s and '40s. Its impact was first felt in the middle colonies, where Theodore J. Frelinghuysen, a minister of the Dutch Reformed church, began preaching in the 1720s. In New England, in the early 1730s men such as Jonathan Edwards, perhaps the most learned theologian of the 18th century, were responsible for a reawakening of religious fervour.
The Reformation: the religious revolution that took place in the Western church in the 16th century; its greatest leaders undoubtedly were Martin Luther and John Calvin. Having far-reaching political, economic, and social effects, the Reformation became the basis for the founding of Protestantism, one of the three major branches of Christianity.
The Renaissance: literally "rebirth," the period in European civilization immediately following the Middle Ages, conventionally held to have been characterized by a surge of interest in classical learning and values. The Renaissance also witnessed the discovery and exploration of new continents, the substitution of the Copernican for the Ptolemaic system of astronomy, the decline of the feudal system and the growth of commerce, and the invention or application of such potentially powerful innovations as paper, printing, the mariner's compass, and gunpowder. To the scholars and thinkers of the day, however, it was primarily a time of the revival of classical learning and wisdom after a long period of cultural decline and stagnation.
Theocentric: (1886): having God as the central interest and ultimate concern ‹a ~ culture›.
Topography: 1 a: the art or practice of graphic delineation in detail usu. on maps or charts of natural and man-made features

of a place or region esp. in a way to show their relative positions and elevations b: topographical surveying; 2 a: the configuration of a surface including its relief and the position of its natural and man-made features b: the physical or natural features of an object or entity and their structural relationships ‹the ~ of human chromosomes› ‹the political ~ of our time›.

Turbulence: (1595): the quality or state of being turbulent: as a: great commotion or agitation ‹emotional ~› b: irregular atmospheric motion esp. when characterized by up-and-down currents c: departure in a fluid from a smooth flow.

Ubiquity: (1579): presence everywhere or in many places esp. simultaneously: omnipresence.

Unequivocal: (1784) 1: leaving no doubt: clear unambiguous; 2: unquestionable.

Uninhibited: (1880): free from inhibition ‹~ exuberance›; also: boisterously informal ‹a festive ~ party›.

Univocal: (1599) 1: having one meaning only, 2: unambiguous ‹in search of a morally ~ answer›.

Velocity: 1 a: quickness of motion: speed ‹the ~ of sound› b: rapidity of movement ‹[my horse's] strong suit is grace & personal comeliness, rather than ~ —Mark Twain› c: speed imparted to something ‹the power pitcher relies on ~ —Tony Scherman›; 2: the rate of change of position along a straight line with respect to time : the derivative of position with respect to time; 3 a: rate of occurrence or action: rapidity.

Vicissitude: (ca. 1576) 1 a: the quality or state of being changeable: mutability b: natural change or mutation visible in nature or in human affairs; 2 a: a favorable or unfavorable event or situation that occurs by chance: a fluctuation of state or condition ‹the ~s of daily life› b: a difficulty or hardship attendant on a way of life, a career, or a course of action and usu. beyond one's control c: alternating change: succession.

Wavelength: (1850) 1: the distance in the line of advance of a wave from any one point to the next point of corresponding phase; 2: a particular course or line of thought esp. as related to mutual understanding ‹two people on different ~s›.

Bibliography

The Five Percenter Vol 20.8 (2015).
The Five Percenter Vol 20.9 (2015).
The Five Percenter Vol 20.10 (2015).
The Five Percenter Vol 20.12 (2015).
The Five Percenter Vol 22.2 (2016).
The Five Percenter Vol 22.4 (2016).
The Five Percenter Vol 22.7 (2017).
The Five Percenter Vol 22.10 (2017).
The Five Percenter Vol 22.11 (2017).
The Holy Bible Authorized King James Version with Apocrypha; Oxford University Press (2008).
The Holy Qur'an: Maulana Muhammad Ali Translation (2002); Ahmadiyya Anjuman Isha'at Islam Lahore Inc.

Abraham, N (1994); "Notes on the Phantom a Complement to Freud's Metapsychology." In N. T. Rand (Ed), *The Shell and the Kernel*; University of Chicago Press.
Abraham, N (1994); "The Phantom of Hamlet or The Sixth Act preceded by The Intermission of 'Truth'." In N. T. Rand (Ed), *The Shell and the Kernel*; University of Chicago Press.
Abraham, N & Torok, M (1994); "Mourning or Melancholia: Introjection Versus Incorporation." In N. T. Rand (Ed), *The Shell and the Kernel*; University of Chicago Press.

Adler, A (1964); *The Individual Psychology of Alfred Adler A Systematic Presentation in Selections From His Writings*; Harper & Row, Publishing, Inc.

Adogame, A (2011); "Introduction." In A. Adogame (Ed), *Who is Afraid of the Holy Ghost? Pentecostalism and Globalization in Africa and Beyond*; Africa World Press.

Adogame, A & Ukah, A (2011); "Viewing a Masquerade from Different Spots? Conceptual Reflections on the 'Globalization' and 'Pentecostalism' Discourses." In A. Adogame (Ed), *Who is Afraid of the Holy Ghost? Pentecostalism and Globalization in Africa and Beyond*; Africa World Press.

Afrika, L (2013); Dr Llaila Afrika We Are Different; http://m.youtube.com/watch?v=r6aaP6Ynoj4, accessed in May 2014.

Albert, M (2004); *Parecon: Life After Capitalism*; Verso

Alexander, M (2011); *The New Jim Crow: Mass Incarceration in the Age of Colorblindness*; The New Press.

Apicella, I (1990); *Spain and France Influence in Europe and in the New World*. [ONLINE] Available at: https://teachersinstitute.yale.edu/curriculum/units/1990/1/90.0108.x.html. [Accessed 19/04/2018].

Armand, É (2012); *Individualist Anarchism: Revolutionary Sexualism*; Pallaksch Press.

Asante, M. K (2003); "The Afrocentric Idea." In A. Mazama (Ed), *The Afrocentric Paradigm*; Africa World Press, Inc.

Asante, M. K (2013); "Afrocentricity Imagination and Action." In V. Lal (Ed), *Afrocentricity Imagination and Action*; Multiversity & Citizens International.

Ashby, M (2003a); *African Religion Vol. 3 Memphite Theology*; Cruzian Mystic Books.

Ashby, M (2003b); *The Serpent Power & The Lost Book of Djehuti and the Wisdom of The Caduceus Fifth Edition Expanded*; Sema Institute.

Ashby, M (2003c); *Sacred Sexuality: Ancient Egyptian Tantric Yoga*; Sema Institute of Yoga/C.M. Books.

Ashby, M (2005a); *Egyptian Yoga African Religion Vol. 2*; Cruzian Mystic Books.

Ashby, M (2005b); *The Egyptian Book of the Dead: The Book of Coming Forth by Day "Book of Enlightenment" Pert m Hru*; Cruzian Mystic Books.

Atwood, G. E & Stolorow, R. D (2014); *Structures of Subjectivity*; Routledge.

Ayegboyin, D (2011); "New Pentecostal Churches and Prosperity Theology in Nigeria." In A. Adogame (Ed), *Who is Afraid of the Holy Ghost? Pentecostalism and Globalization in Africa and Beyond*; Africa World Press.

Bakare-Yusuf, B (2011); "Nudity and Morality: Legislating Women's Bodies and Dress in Nigeria." In S. Tamale (Ed), African Sexualities; Pambazuka Press.

Baldwin, J. D (1874); *Pre-Historic Nations: or, Inquiries Concerning Some of the Great Peoples and Civilizations of Antiquity, Their Probable Relation to a Still Older Civilization of the Ethiopians or Cushites of Arabia*; Harper & Brothers, Publishers.

Bey, M (2020); *Anarcho-Blackness: Notes Toward a Black Anarchism*; AK Press.

Biggie Smalls (1994); "Everyday Struggle." In: *Ready to Die* [CD]; Bad Boy Records/Arista.

Biggie Smalls (1994); "Juicy" In: *Ready to Die* [CD]; Bad Boy Records/Arista.

Biggie Smalls (1994); "Me & My B*tch." In: *Ready to Die* [CD]; Bad Boy Records/Arista.

Biggie Smalls (1994); "Things Done Changed." In: *Ready to Die* [CD]; Bad Boy Records/Arista.

Brandchaft, B, Doctors, S, and Sorter, D (2010); *Toward an Emancipatory Psychoanalysis: Brandchaft's Intersubjective Vision*; Routledge.

Brown, F, Driver, S and Briggs, C (2014); *The Brown-Driver-Briggs Hebrew and English Lexicon*; Hendrickson Publishers.

Brown, T (1990); *Syndicalism*; Phoenix Press.

Bruder, E (2012); "The Proto-History of Igbo Jewish Identity from the Colonial Period to the Biafra War, 1890-1970." In E. Bruder & T. Parfitt (Eds), *African Zion: Studies in Black Judaism*; Cambridge Scholars Publishing.

Buber, M (2008); *I and Thou*; Simon & Schuster.

Chiu, C-Y, Leung, A. K-Y. & Hong, Y-Y (2011); "Cultural Processes: An Overview." In A. K-Y. Leung, C-Y Chiu & Y-Y Hong (Eds), *Cultural Processes A Social Psychological Perspective*; Cambridge University Press.

Churton, T (2015); *Gnostic Mysteries of Sex: Sophia the Wild One and Erotic Christianity*; Inner Traditions.

Collins, J (2006); *Good to Great and the Social Sectors: A Monograph to Accompany Good to Great*; Random House Business.

Collins, J (2011); *Great By Choice:* [Kindle App Edition]; The Perfect Library. [ONLINE] Available at: https://www.amazon.co.uk. [Accessed 18/1/20224].

Collins, J & Porras, J. I (2005); *Built to Last: Successful Habits of Visionary Companies*; Random House Business Books.

Comte, A (1986); *The Positive Philosophy*; Bell & Sons.

Cone, J. H (1997); *God of the Oppressed*; Orbis Books.

Cone, J. H (2020a); *A Black Theology of Liberation Fiftieth Anniversary Edition* Orbis Books.

Cone, J. H (2020b) *The Cross and the Lynching Tree*; Orbis Books.

Cone, J. H (2021); *Black Theology and Black Power Fiftieth Anniversary Edition*; Orbis Books.

Covey, S. R (2004); *The 7 Habits of Highly Effective People*; Simon & Schuster.

Dach-Gruschow, K, Au, E. W. M., Liao, H-Y (2011); "Culture as Lay Personal Beliefs." In A. K-Y. Leung, C-Y Chiu & Y-Y Hong (Eds), *Cultural Processes A Social Psychological Perspective*; Cambridge University Press.

Dalal, F (2010); *Race, Colour and the Processes of Racialization: New Perspectives From Group Analysis, Psychoanalysis and Sociology*; Routledge.

De Beauvoir, S (2009); *The Second Sex*; Vintage Classics.

Derrida, J (2006); *Specters of Marx*; Routledge Classics.

Douglas, K. B (1999); *Sexuality and the Black Church: A Womanist Perspective*; Orbis Books.

Durkheim, E (2014); *The Rules of Sociological Method*; Free Press.

Elias, N (2014); *The Civilizing Process*; Blackwell Publishing.

Entrekin, R (2016); *God vs. Chance: Which Is The Most Probable Explanation For Our Existence?*; Marshall Entrekin.

Erdman, K. M (2017); *A Macat Analysis of Geert Hostede's Culture's Consequences: Comparing Values, Behaviors, Institutions and Organizations across Nations*; Macat International Ltd.

Ethiopia: From the Ancient Kushites to the Black Lions (2009); A. Kwesi and M. Kwesi; Available at: Kemet Nu Productions. [Accessed 17/10/2021]

Fanon, F (1965); *A Dying Colonialism*; Grove Press.

Fanon, F (1969); *The Wretched of the Earth*; Penguin Books.

Fanon, F (2008); *Black Skin, White Masks*; Pluto Press.

Faruq, E. W. (1986); "The Power of the Spiritual Dimension in Ancient Egyptian City Life." In M. Karenga & J. H. Carruthers (Eds), *Kemet and the African Worldview: Research, Rescue and Restoration*; University of Sankore Press.

Foucault, M (1998); *The History of Sexuality Vol. 1: The Will to Knowledge*; Penguin Books.

Foucault, M (2001); *Madness and Civilization*; Routledge.

Foxe, J (2001); *Foxe's Book of Martyrs*; Bridge-Logos Publishing.

Foxy Brown (1996); "Ain't No Nigga." In: *Reasonable Doubt* [CD]; Roc-A-Fella/Priority.

Fractal (2022); Encyclopædia Britannica. *Standard Edition*; Chicago: Encyclopædia Britannica.

Freeden, M (2013); "The Morphological Analysis of Ideology." In M. Freeden, L. T. Sargent, and M. Stears (Eds), *The Oxford Handbook of Political Ideologies*; Oxford University Press.

Freud, S (1997); *The Interpretation of Dreams*; Wordsworth Editions Limited.

Freud, S (2001) *The Standard Edition of the Complete Psychological Works of Sigmund Freud Vol 13: Totem and Taboo* and *Other Works*; Vintage Books.

Freud, S (2002) *Civilization and its Discontents*; Penguin Books Limited.

Freud, S (2010); *Moses and Monotheism*; Martino Publishing.

Fryer, P (2018); *Staying Power: The History of Black People in Britain*; Pluto Press.

Galatariotou, C (2005); "The Defences." In S. Budd & R. Rusbridger (Eds), *Introducing Psychoanalysis*; Routledge.

Gaughran, D (2020); *Let's Get Digital: How to Self-Publish, and Why You Should Fourth Edition*; Amazon Kindle Direct Publishing.

Gentles-Peart, K (2016); *Romance with Voluptuousness: Caribbean Women and Thick Bodies in the US*; University of Nebraska Press.

Gilroy, P (1999); *The Black Atlantic: Modernity and Double Consciousness*; Verso.

Gladwell, M (2008); *Outliers: The Story of Success*; Penguin Boos.

Gladwell, M (2013); *The Tipping Point: How Little Things Can Make a Big Difference New Edition*; Abacus.

Gleick, J (1998); *Chaos: The Amazing Science of the Unpredictable*; Vintage Books.

Goldman, E (1911); *Marriage and Love*; Mother Earth Publishing Association.

Graves-Brown, C (2010); *Dancing for Hathor: Women in Ancient Egypt*; Continuum Books.

Greene, R (2004); *The Art of Seduction*; Profile Books.

The Gza (1996); "Swordsman." In: *Liquid Swords* [CD]; Geffen/MCA.

Hardt, M & Negri, A (2000); *Empire*; Harvard University Press.

Haraway, D. J (2000); *The Cyborg Manifesto*; Routledge.

Hedges, L. E (2011); *Sex in Psychotherapy: Sexuality, Passion, Love, and Desire in the Therapeutic Encounter*; Routledge.

Herring, G (2006); *Christianity: From the Early Church to the Enlightenment*; Continuum International Publishing Group.

Heywood, A (2017); *Political Ideologies: An Introduction*; Palgrave.

Hill, N (2004); *Think and Grow Rich Revised and Expanded by Dr Arthur R. Pell*; Vermillion London.

Home Team History (2020); *History of Judaism in Africa: Are the Black Hebrews Right?* [ONLINE] Available at: https://www.youtube.com/watch?v=2HGDsgJrBCk&t=699s [Accessed 08/08/2020].

Houston, D. D (1985); *Wonderful Ethiopians of the Ancient Cushite Empire*; Black Classic Press.

Hudson, M (2021) *Super Imperialism: The Economic Strategy of American Empire Third Edition*. Dresden: ISLET-Verlag.

Hudson-Weems, C (2003); "Africana Womanism." In A. Mazama (Ed), *The Afrocentric Paradigm*; African World Press.

Intelexual Media (2023); *A Short History of Masturbation*; [ONLINE] Available at:
https://www.youtube.com/watch?v=0aoY6Ihjips. [Accessed 29/01/2024].

Ibn Katheer Dimashqi, H (2006); *Book of the End: Great Trials and Tribulations*; Maktaba Dar-us-Salam.

Islam, S (2019); *Black Divinity: Institutes of the Black Theocracy, Shahidi Collection Vol I*; Global Summit House LLC.

Islam, S (2023); *Demystifying God: Redefining Black Theology in the Age of iGod Shahidi Collection Vol 2*; Divine Black People Ltd.

Jackson, S. A (2009); *Islam and the Problem of Black Suffering*; Oxford University Press.

Jakes, T. D (2008); *Life Overflowing: 6 Pillars for Abundant Living*; Bethany House Publishers.

Jones, W. R (1998); *Is God a White Racist? A Preamble to Black Theology*; Beacon Press.

Karenga, M (1989); *Introduction to Black Studies*; University of Sankore Press.

Katz, A (2008); *The Holocaust: Where Was God? An Inquiry into the Biblical Roots of Tragedy*; Burning Bush Press.

Kolawole, M. E. M (1997); *Womanism and African Consciousness*; African World Press.

Koestler, A (1976); *The Thirteenth Tribe*; Random House, Inc.

Kropotkin, P (2006); *Mutual Aid: A Factor of Evolution*; Dover Publications Inc.

Lange, D (2012); "The Bayajidda Legend and Hausa History." In E. Bruder & T. Parfitt (Eds), *African Zion: Studies in Black Judaism*; Cambridge Scholars Publishing.

Lenin, V (2010); *Imperialism: The Highest Stage of Capitalism*; Penguin Books.

Lenin, V (2014); *State and Revolution*; Haymarket Books. Square Press, Inc.

Lenin, V (2020); *What Is to Be Done? Burning Questions of Our Movement*; Science Marxiste.

lil' bill (2023); *How Black Elites LIE to Us*; [ONLINE] Available at: https://www.youtube.com/watch?v=Uu-X_E8cwaA. [Accessed 29/01/2024].

Littlewood, R (2006); *Pathology and Identity: The Work of Mother Earth in Trinidad*; Cambridge University Press.

Lizokin-Eyzenberg, E & Shir, P (2021); *Hebrew Insights From Revelation*. Israel: Jewish Studies for Christians.

Lonergan, G, Lewis, H, Tomalin, E & Waite, L (2021); "Distinctive or Professionalised? Understanding the Postsecular in Faith-Based Responses to Trafficking, Forced Labour and Slavery in the UK." In S. Fadaee & H. Holmes (Eds), *Sociology: A Journal of the British Sociological Association Vol 55, Number 3, June 2021*; Sage Publishing.

MacCulloch, D (2010); *A History of Christianity*; Penguin Random House.

Malatesta, E (1922); *At the Café: Conversations on Anarchism*; KDP Amazon Publishing.

Malcioln, J. V (1996); *The African Origins of Modern Judaism: From Hebrews to Jews*; Africa World Press.

Marshall, P (2013); *80/20 Sales and Marketing: The Definitive Guide to Working Less and Making More*; Entrepreneur Media, Inc.

Maxwell, J. C (2013); *A Dynamical Theory of the Electromagnetic Field*; Rough Draft Printing.

McRobbie, A (2008); *Pornographic Permutations*; Routledge.

McTaggart, J. M. E (1908); *The Unreality of Time* [Kindle App Edition]; The Perfect Library. [ONLINE] Available at: https://www.amazon.co.uk. [Accessed 4/4/2021].

Means, S, M (1945); *Ethiopia And the Missing Link in African History*; Lushena Books.

Meiu, G. P (2011); "'Mombasa morans': embodiment, sexuality and Samburu men in Kenya." In S. Tamale (Ed), *African Sexualities: A Reader*; Pambazuka Press.

Meyer, M, W (1992); *The Gospel of Thomas: The Hidden Saying of Jesus*; Harper.

Moltmann, J (1993); *Theology of Hope: On the Ground and Implications of a Christian Eschatology*. Minnesota: Fortress Press.

Muhammad, E (1965); *Message to the Blackman in America*; Muhammad's Temple No. 2, The Final Call Inc.

Muhammad, E (1973); *The Fall of America*; Muhammad's Temple No. 2, The Final Call Inc.

Newton, H (2002); *The Huey P. Newton Reader*; Seven Stories Press.

Newton, I (1999); *The Principia: Mathematical Principles of Natural Philosophy*; University of California Press.

No, S, Wan, C, Chao, M, M, Rosner, J, L & Hong, Y-Y (2011); "Bicultural Identity Negotiation." In A. K-Y. Leung, C-Y Chiu & Y-Y Hong (Eds), *Cultural Processes A Social Psychological Perspective*; Cambridge University Press.

Noir, T (2019); *Hypersexual Female Rap is Misleading*. [ONLINE] Available at: https://www.youtube.com/watch?v=AeFMzviBT3o. [Accessed 10 March 2021].

Nkrumah, K (2006) *Class Struggle in Africa*. London: Panaf Books.

Nkrumah, K (2009) *Consciencism: Philosophy and Ideology for De-Colonization*. New York: Monthly Review Press.

Nkrumah, K (2022) *Neo-Colonialism: The Last Stage of Imperialism*. Great Britain: African People's Conference.

Nye, J S, Jr. (2004) *Soft Power: The Means to Success in World Politics*. New York: Public Affairs Books.

Nzegwu, N (2011); "'Osunality' (or African eroticism)." In S. Tamale (Ed), *African Sexualities: A Reader*; Pambazuka Press.

Poliak, A. N. (1941); "The Khazars' Conversion to Judaism." In M. Toch and N. Na'aman (Eds); *Zion - Israel History Quarterly*; Published by the Israeli Company for History and Ethnography.

Poliak, A. N. (1951); *Khazaria: History of a Jewish Kingdom in Europe*; Bialik Institute by Masada.

Rabaka, R (2015); *The Negritude Movement: W.E.B. Du Bois, Leon Damas, Aime Cesaire, Leopold Senghor, Frantz Fanon, and the Evolution of an Insurgent Idea*; Lexington Books.

Rand, N. T (1994); "New Perspectives in Metapsychology: Cryptic Mourning and Secret Love." In N. T. Rand (Ed), *The Shell and the Kernel*; University of Chicago Press.

Rand, N. T (1994); "Secrets and Posterity: The Theory of the Transgenerational Phantom." In N. T. Rand (Ed), *The Shell and the Kernel*; University of Chicago Press.

Roberts, A (2011); *Evolution: The Human Story*; Dorling Kindersley Limited.

Roberts, J. D (2012); "Dignity and destiny: black reflections on eschatology." In *The Cambridge Companion to Black Theology*, eds. Dwight N. Hopkins and Edward P. Antonio. Cambridge: Cambridge University Press.

Rodney, W (2018); *How Europe Underdeveloped Africa* [Kindle App Edition]; Verso. [ONLINE] Available at: https://www.amazon.co.uk. [Accessed 26/02/2021].

Rowland, C (1985); *Christian Origins: An Account of the Setting and Character of the most Important Messianic Sect of Judaism*; SPCK.

Said, E (2003); *Orientalism*; Penguin Books.

Saraswati, S (2012); *Kundalini Tantra*; Yoga Publications Trust.

Schimek, J-G (2011); *Memory, Myth, and Seduction: Unconscious Fantasy and the Interpretive Process*; Routledge.

Seleem, R (2004); *The Egyptian Book of Life*; Watkins Publishing.

Seligman, C. G (1966); *Races of Africa*; Oxford University Press.

Shakur, T (1996); "Heaven Ain't Hard to Find." In: *All Eyez on Me* [CD]; Death Row Records.

Shakur, T & Nas (2002); "Thugz Mansion." In: *Better Dayz* [CD]; Amaru Records.

Sheller, M (2012); *Citizenship From Below Erotic Agency and Caribbean Freedom*; Duke University Press.

She's Gotta Have It; film produced by Forty Acres and a Mule Filmworks, Inc.; New York, NY; (distributed by Island Pictures, 79 Wardour St, Soho, London W1D 6QB 1986) DVD, 81mins.

Shu, F (2023); Cosmos: Encyclopædia Britannica; *Standard Edition*; Encyclopædia Britannica.

Skousen, M (2017); *The Big Three in Economics: Adam Smith, Karl Marx and John Maynard Keynes*; Routledge.

Stelling, D. J (1959) *Savannah Nomads: A Study of the Wadaabe Pastoral Fulani of Western Bornu Province Northern Region, Nigeria*; Oxford University Press.

Strong, J (1990); *The New Strong's Exhaustive Concordance of the Bible*; Thomas Nelson Publishers.

Strachey, J (1936); *The Theory and Practice of Socialism*; Victor Gúllancz Ltd.

Torok, M (1994); "The Illness of Mourning and the Fantasy of the Exquisite Corpse." In N. T. Rand (Ed), *The Shell and the Kernel*; University of Chicago Press.

Turman, E. M (2018); "Heaven and Hell in African American Theology." In *The Oxford Handbook of African American Theology*, eds. Katie G. Cannon and Anthony B. Pinn; Oxford University Press.

Tyldesley, J (2011); *The Penguin Book of Myths & Legends of Ancient Egypt*; Penguin Books.

Von Neumann, J & Morgenstern, O (2004); *Theory of Games and Economic Behavior*; Princeton University Press.

Watterson, B (2013); *Women in Ancient Egypt*; Amberley Publishing.

Wikipedia: The Free Encyclopedia. Wikimedia Foundation Inc. Updated 24 March 2018, at 21:21. UTC. Encyclopedia [ONLINE] Available at:
https://en.wikipedia.org/wiki/Der_Judenstaat [Accessed 11 May 2018].

Wikipedia: The Free Encyclopedia. Wikimedia Foundation Inc. Updated 14 May 2018, at 15:24. UTC. Encyclopedia [ONLINE] Available at https://en.wikipedia.org/wiki/Free_love [Accessed 11 May 2018].

Williams, D. S (1993); *Sisters in the Wilderness: The Challenge of Womanist God-Talk*; Orbis Books.

Williams, D. S (2011); "Black Theology and Womanist Theology." In D. N. Hopkins & E. P. Antonio (Eds), *The Cambridge Companion to Black Theology*; Cambridge University Press.

Williams, J (1928); *Hebrewisms of West Africa From the Nile to the Niger with the*

Wolfe, L (1981); *The Cosmo Report: An In-depth Landmark Work Revealing the Sexual Behavior of 106,000 "Cosmopolitan" Readers – the Largest Number Ever Polled About Human Female Sexuality*; Arbor House Pub Co.

Yaki Kadifi (1999); "Black Jesuz." In: *Still I Rise* [CD]; Interscope Records.

Milton Keynes UK
Ingram Content Group UK Ltd.
UKHW010812220424
441551UK00001B/183